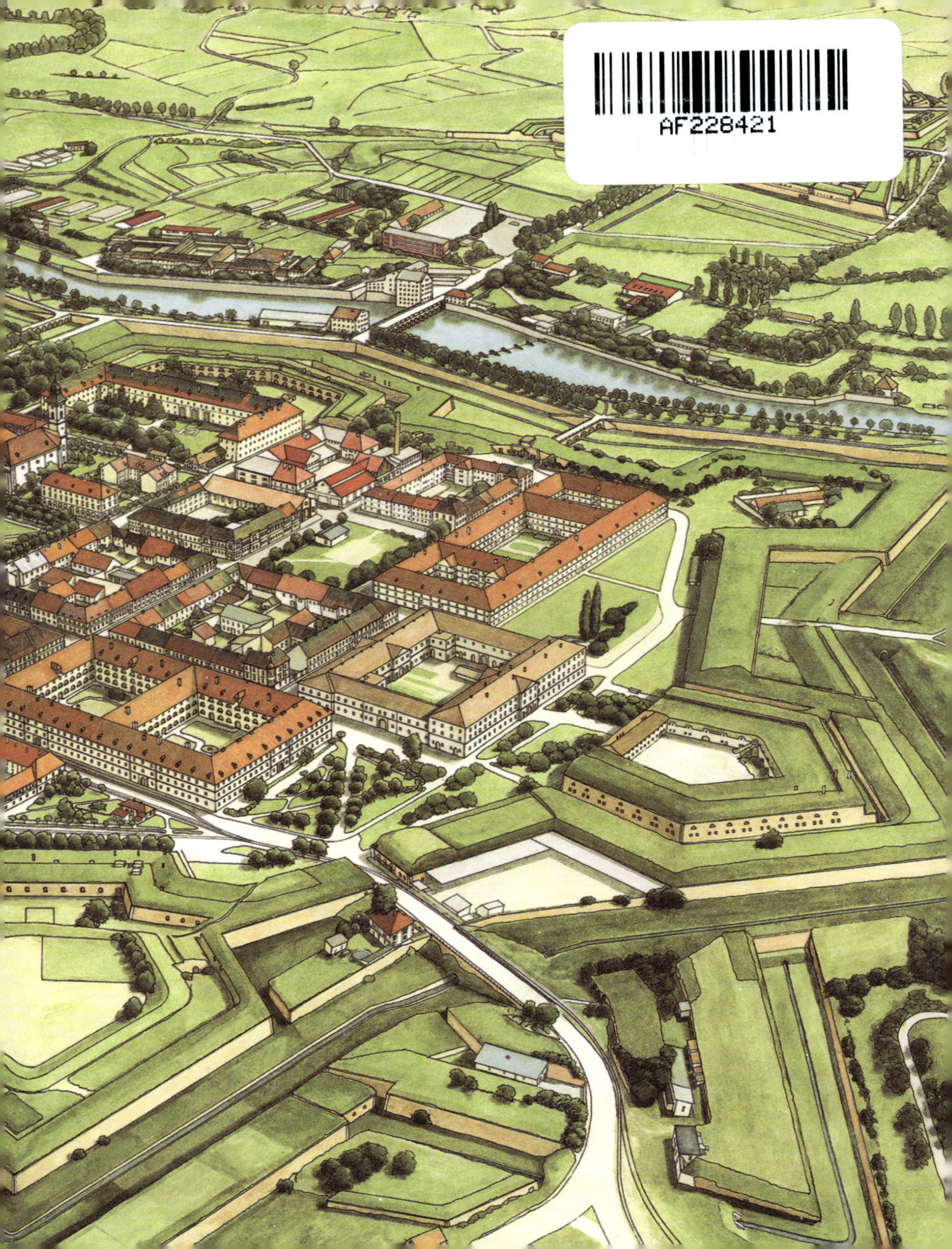
AF228421

In Performance

EDITED BY
CAROL MARTIN

In Performance is a book series devoted to national and global theater of the twenty-first century. Scholarly essays providing the theatrical, cultural, and political contexts for the plays and performance texts introduce each volume. The texts are written both by established and emerging writers, translated by accomplished translators and aimed at people who want to put new works on stage, read diverse dramatic and performance literature, and study diverse theater practices, contexts, and histories in light of globalization.

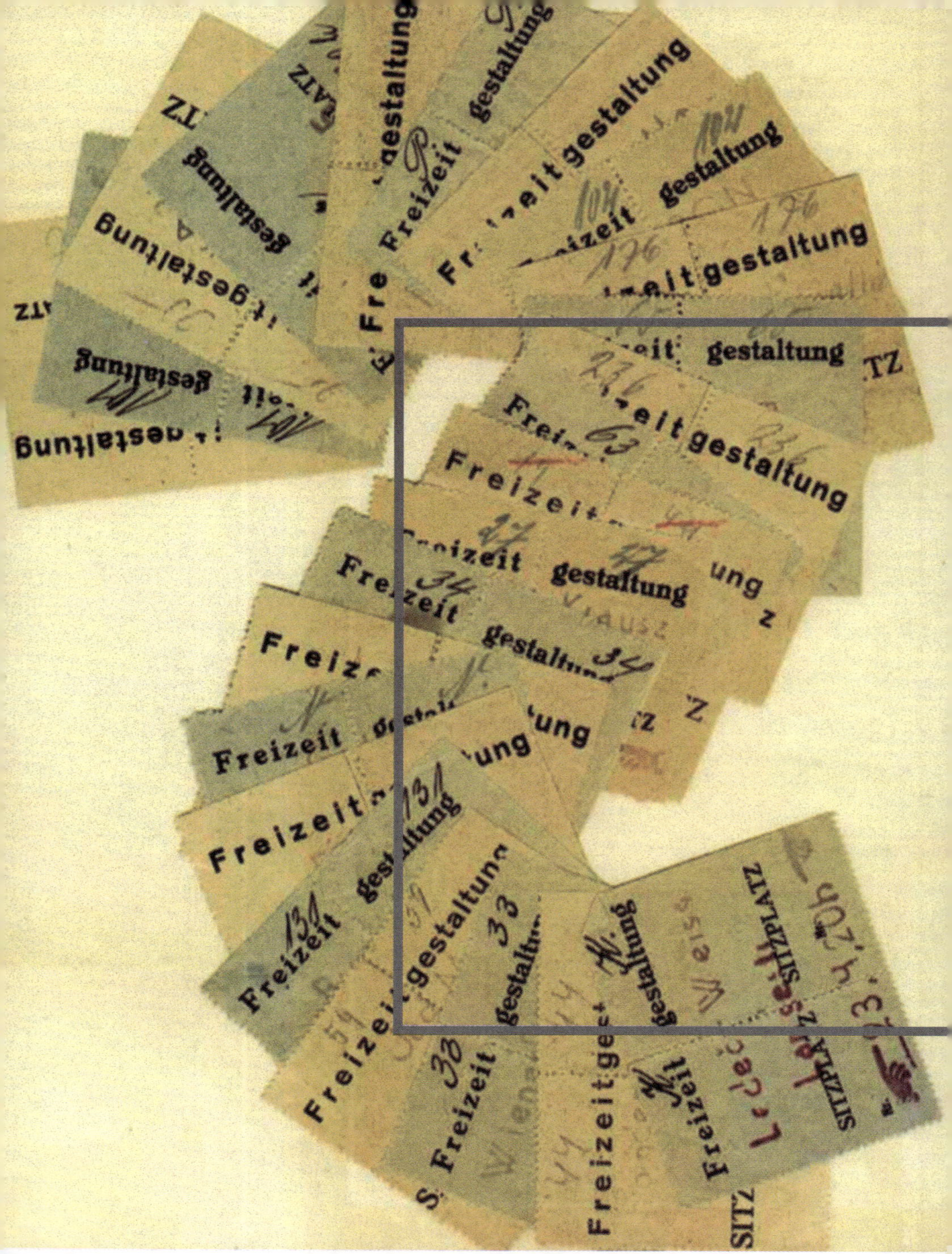

Freizeitgestaltung

SITZPLATZ

PERFORMING CAPTIVITY, PERFORMING ESCAPE

CABARETS AND PLAYS FROM THE TEREZÍN/THERESIENSTADT GHETTO

Edited by **Lisa Peschel**

LONDON NEW YORK CALCUTTA

Seagull Books, 2023

This anthology is a revised and expanded version of the Czech–German edition *Divadelní texty z terezínského ghetta / Theatertexte aus dem Ghetto Theresienstadt, 1941–1945* (Prague: Akropolis, 2008).

Commentary and English translations © Lisa Peschel, 2014
English translation of *The Smoke of Home* © Dorothy Elias, 2008
Prologue © Ivan Klíma, 2008
This compilation © Seagull Books, 2014
Book Design © Seagull Books, 2014

The preparation of this edition was made possible through support from the Memorial Fund for Jewish Culture, the Adalbert Stifter Association, the United States Holocaust Memorial Museum, and the Harvard University Center for Jewish Studies.

The statements made and views expressed are solely the responsibility of the editor and authors.

The editor thanks the following individuals and institutions for permission to publish the works in this anthology:
Dorothy Elias, Kate Elias, Eva Hirschová, Karen Jackman, Marie Rút Křížková, Zdeněk Prokeš, Winfried Radeke, Pavel Stránský, Philip Warden, Lisa Zeckendorf-Kutzinski, Raja Žádníkova, Beit Terezín, the Jewish Museum in Prague, the Terezín Memorial, and Yad Vashem.

Images and music were published with the permission of the following individuals and institutions:
Dorothy Elias, Kate Elias, Eva Hirschová, Jan, Miroslav and Zdeněk Prokeš, Winfried Radeke, Pavel Stránský, Margaret Warden, Raja Žádníková, the Jewish Museum in Prague, M'PLAN s.r.o., the National Archive of the Czech Republic, the Terezín Memorial, Yad Vashem, and the United States Holocaust Memorial Museum.

The rights for all works are reserved and permission must be obtained from the above-mentioned individuals and institutions. For *The Smoke of Home*, apply to Dorothy Elias (eliasd@shaw.ca) and Kate Elias (k.s.elias@comcast.net). For all other works, apply to Lisa Peschel (lisa_peschel@yahoo.com).

ISBN 978 1 80309 2 027

British Library Cataloging-in-Publication Data
A catalog record for this book is available from the British Library

Typeset in Galliard BT and Franklin Gothic Book/Medium
Book designed by Bishan Samaddar, Seagull Books, Calcutta, India
Printed and bound by WordsWorth India, New Delhi, India

To the survivors

and

to those who did not survive

CONTENTS

Illustrations   **viii**

Acknowledgements   **xv**

Pronunciation Guide   **xxi**

Edition Notes and Conventions   **xxiv**

INTRODUCTION   Lisa Peschel   **1**

Prologue: **TEREZÍN THEATER**   Ivan Klíma   **36**

Part 1: CZECH-LANGUAGE TEXTS

RADIO SHOW   Felix Prokeš, Vítězslav "Pidla" Horpatzky, Pavel Stránský, and Kurt Egerer   **46**

LOOKING FOR A SPECTER   Hanuš Hachenburg   **96**

Songs from the Revue PRINCE BETTLIEGEND   František Kowanitz   **114**

THE SMOKE OF HOME   Zdeněk Eliáš and Jiří Stein   **140**

LAUGH WITH US **The Second Czech Cabaret**   Felix Prokeš, Vítězslav "Pidla" Horpatzky, Pavel Weisskopf, and Pavel Stránský   **166**

Part 2: GERMAN-LANGUAGE TEXTS

From the STRAUSS CABARETS — Leo Strauss and Myra Strauss-Gruhenberg — **224**

THE TREASURE
A Puppet Play in Ten Acts — Arthur Engländer — **250**

PURIMSPIEL — Walter Freud — **281**

THE DEATH OF ORPHEUS — Georg Kafka — **332**

THE INSULT—BUT UNINTENDED;
or, THE MAN WITH THE DEFECTIVE MEMORY
A Theresienstadt Courtroom Scene — Author Unknown — **361**

From the HOFER CABARETS — Hans Hofer — **370**

Epilogue: NEW YEAR'S EVE
IN THE OEDERAN SLAVE-LABOR CAMP — Lisa Zeckendorf-Kutzinski — **398**

Glossary — **403**

Bibliography — **409**

ILLUSTRATIONS

INSIDE FRONT COVER A panoramic view of the site of the ghetto: the Terezín/Theresienstadt Large Fortress. The Small Fortress is visible in the upper right corner. Courtesy of M'PLAN s.r.o.

INSIDE BACK COVER A color-coded plan of the Terezín/Theresienstadt Ghetto, probably drawn in early 1944. Archive of the Terezín Memorial, A 10544.

1.1 An organizational chart of the *Freizeitgestaltung* after June 1943. Divisions K/31–5 are German theater, Czech theater, cabaret, and the *Blockveranstaltungen*. Terezín Memorial, Heřman Collection, PT 3863.

1.2 The census on November 11, 1943. By F. Bloch. Yad Vashem, 2147_a_64.

2.1 A souvenir poster for *Brundibár*, Hans Krása's opera for children, April 1944. By Walter Heimann. Terezín Memorial, Heřman Collection, PT 4010.

2.2 Women's quarters. By F. Bloch. Jewish Museum in Prague, H1995-0119.

2.3 Kurt Gerron's cabaret Carousel. By F. Bloch. Terezín Memorial, Heřman Collection, PT 3958.

3.1 The ghetto as a set design, probably for the operetta *Girl of the Ghetto*. By Adolf Aussenberg. Terezín Memorial, Heřman Collection, PT 3855.

3.2 Interior courtyard of Block A IV, where the ghetto bakery and central provisions storehouses were located. By A. Berlinger. Yad Vashem, 77.

3.3 Military ID of Felix Prokeš (né Porges), April 1938. Private collection of Jan, Miroslav, and Zdeněk Prokeš.

3.4 Vítězslav Horpatzky in the late 1930s. National Archives of the Czech Republic.

3.5   Pavel Stránský in the 1930s. Private collection of Pavel Stránský.

3.6   Pavel Stránský's wedding, 1945. Private collection of Pavel Stránský.

3.7   Building the railroad spur into the ghetto, May 1943. By L. Haas. Terezín Memorial, PT 1744.

3.8   Funeral wagons in the ghetto, 1943. By F. M. Nágl. Jewish Museum in Prague, H157143.

3.9   Interior courtyard of the Hamburg barracks. The prisoners used such courtyards for cabaret performances, soccer games and other events. Terezín Memorial, Heřman Collection, PT 4228.

3.10   A player for the ghetto soccer team Hollandia. By W. Thalheimer. Terezín Memorial, Heřman Collection, PT 4250.

3.11   Original sheet music for "Song of Prague" ("Píseň o Praze"). Music and lyrics by Felix Prokeš. Private collection of Jan, Miroslav, and Zdeněk Prokeš.

3.12   Original sheet music for "March of the Young" ("Pochod mládi"). Music by Felix Prokeš, lyrics by Pavel Stránský. Private collection of Jan, Miroslav, and Zdeněk Prokeš.

4.1   The first page of the manuscript *Looking for a Specter*. Archive of the Terezín Memorial, 1a.

4.2   A doll made in the ghetto representing a *Ghettowachmann* (member of the Ghetto Guard). Terezín Memorial, PT GW.

4.3   A souvenir poster for a marionette theater performance. Terezín Memorial, Heřman Collection, PT 3857.

5.1   A souvenir poster for the revue *Prince Bettliegend*. Terezín Memorial, Heřman Collection, PT 4305.

5.2   A souvenir poster for a cabaret by Karel Švenk marking the six-month anniversary of the arrival of the AK I transport. Terezín Memorial, Heřman Collection, PT4308.

5.3 Spectators standing on a funeral wagon to watch an outdoor performance. The columns of the wagon have been removed. By A. Aussenberg. Yad Vashem, 3074_07.

5.4–5 Illustrations for *Ben Akiba Lied*. Terezín Memorial, Heřman Collection, PT 3896 and PT 3897.

6.1 A set design, probably by Bedřich Fritta for J. L. Perez's *The Golden Chain*. Terezín Memorial, Heřman Collection, PT 4051.

6.2 Zdeněk Eliáš' pre-war university identification card, showing his post-war name change. Private collection of Kate Elias.

6.3 Zdeněk Eliáš (left) with Kate Elias, 1999. Private collection of Kate Elias.

6.4 Jiří Stein. From the estate of Věra Elias. Private collection of Dorothy Elias.

6.5 A bunk built by Lev Willinger, 1943. By F. M. Nágl. Jewish Museum in Prague, H104353.

7.1 A souvenir poster for *Laugh with Us*: *The Second Czech Cabaret*. Terezín Memorial, Heřman Collection, PT 3826.

7.2 Felix Prokeš and Elly Bernsteinová's wedding, 1945. Private collection of Jan, Miroslav, and Zdeněk Prokeš.

7.3 Vítězslav Horpatzky with his wife Anna, 1930s. Private collection of Eva Hirschová.

7.4 Vítězslav Horpatzky's transport card, showing the second transport to Osvětím (Auschwitz). United States Holocaust Memorial Museum, Kartei Theresienstadt, International Tracing Service Collection, 1.1.42.2, document no. 5050031.

7.5 A folk dancer in the ghetto wearing the Czech national colors. By C. Burešová. Yad Vashem, 2147_b_4.

7.6   One of the ghetto *Verschleißstellen*: the "grocery store." The jars in the foreground are labeled *Senf* (mustard). By F. Bloch. Yad Vashem, 2147_a_38.

7.7   The coffeehouse in the ghetto. By L. Haas. Terezín Memorial, Heřman Collection, PT 3961.

7.8   A poster for the opera *The Bartered Bride* (*Prodaná nevěsta*) featuring F. Weissenstein and K. Berman, with an image of Kecal the marriage broker. Terezín Memorial, Heřman Collection, PT 4295.

7.9   Original sheet music for "Long Live Cabaret" ("Ať žije kabaret"). Music by Felix Prokeš, lyrics by Pavel Stránský and Felix Prokeš. Private collection of Jan, Miroslav, and Zdeněk Prokeš.

7.10   Original sheet music for "Andalusian Nights" ("Andaluzské noci"). Music by Felix Prokeš, lyrics by Pavel Stránský (version 1). Private collection of Jan, Miroslav, and Zdeněk Prokeš.

7.11   Original sheet music for "Andalusian Nights" ("Andaluzské noci"). Music by Felix Prokeš, lyrics by Pavel Stránský (version 2, using their pen names Jaroslav Felix and Pavel Jeník). Private collection of Jan, Miroslav, and Zdeněk Prokeš.

7.12   Original sheet music for "Abandoned" ("Opuštěný"). Music by Felix Prokeš, lyrics by Felix Prokeš and Pavel Stránský (version 1). Private collection of Jan, Miroslav, and Zdeněk Prokeš.

7.13   Original sheet music for "Abandoned" ("Opuštěný"). Music by Felix Prokeš, lyrics by Felix Prokeš and Pavel Stránský (version 2, using their pen names Jaroslav Felix and Pavel Jeník). Private collection of Jan, Miroslav, and Zdeněk Prokeš.

7.14   Original sheet music for "Couplet" ("Kuplet"). Music and lyrics by Felix Prokeš. Private collection of Jan, Miroslav, and Zdeněk Prokeš.

8.1 The ghetto as a set design, probably for the operetta *Girl of the Ghetto*. By Adolf Aussenberg. Terezín Memorial, Heřman Collection, PT 3856.

8.2 A souvenir poster for the *Literary Strauss Cabaret*. Terezín Memorial, Heřman Collection, PT 4079.

8.3 A caricature of Leo Strauss from 1944. By Aloe Durra. Terezín Memorial, Heřman Collection, PT 4177.

8.4 A drawing of Myra Strauss-Gruhenberg by an unknown artist, labeled "Myra in 1935." Terezín Memorial, Heřman Collection, PT 4081.

8.5 Signatures of the members of the Strauss Ensemble. Terezín Memorial, Heřman Collection, PT 4080.

8.6 A hospital in the ghetto, 1943. By J. Ullmann. Terezín Memorial, PT 12108/7.

8.7 A performance in one of the interior courtyards. By L. Haas. Terezín Memorial, PT 1884.

9.1 Designs for marionettes. Terezín Memorial, Heřman Collection, PT 3858.

9.2 Arthur Engländer in the 1930s. Private collection of Raja Žádníková.

9.3 A souvenir poster for the marionette theater performance *Circus*. Arthur Engländer is listed as responsible for technical aspects of staging. Terezín Memorial, Heřman Collection, PT 3885.

10.1 The synagogue in the Cavalier barracks. By E. Neugebauer. Terezín Memorial, PT 5237.

10.2 A souvenir poster for the *Purimstück* by Walter Freud (the title in the script is *Purimspiel*), performed in March 1943. Terezín Memorial, Heřman Collection, PT 4041.

10.3 A souvenir poster for a Hanukkah celebration in December 1943, organized and hosted by Walter Freud. Terezín Memorial, Heřman Collection, PT 3917.

10.4 A souvenir poster for *Menorah*, a Hanukkah play by Walter Freud performed in December 1942. Terezín Memorial, Heřman Collection, PT 4050.

10.5 A souvenir poster for *The Pied Piper of Hamelin*, adapted by Walter Freud. Terezín Memorial, Heřman Collection, PT 4310.

10.6–17 Sheet music for the medley from Act VII of the *Purimspiel*. Reconstructed and arranged by Winfried Radeke, graphics by Andreas Jocksch.

11.1 Souvenir poster for the performance of Georg Kafka's *Orpheus*. United States Holocaust Memorial Museum, Morris and Hildegard Henschel Collection, inv. no. RG-24.021.

13.1 Tickets for various performances, including Hofer's cabaret and the Strauss Ensemble. Terezín Memorial, Heřman Collection, PT 3867.

13.2 Lisl Steinitz in the 1930s. Private collection of Margaret Warden.

13.3 Lisl and Hans Hofer in the late 1930s. Private collection of Margaret Warden.

13.4 Hans Hofer immediately after his return from the concentration camps, 1945. Private collection of Margaret Warden.

13.5 Hans Hofer in a post-war theatrical role. Private collection of Margaret Warden.

13.6 Hans and Lisl Hofer in the 1950s. Private collection of Margaret Warden.

13.7 A souvenir poster for Hans Hofer's revue *Laugh Yourself Well*. Terezín Memorial, Heřman Collection, PT 4074.

13.8 A souvenir poster for Hans Hofer's revue *Everything with Music*. Terezín Memorial, Heřman Collection, PT 4073.

13.9 A souvenir poster for Hans Hofer's cabaret. Terezín Memorial, Heřman Collection, PT 4072.

13.10 A souvenir poster for *Die Fledermaus*, directed by Hans Hofer and featuring Lisl Hofer as Prince Orlovsky. Terezín Memorial, Heřman Collection, PT 4045.

13.11 A souvenir poster for Puccini's opera *Tosca*, mentioned in Hofer's song "The Theater Ticket." Terezín Memorial, Heřman Collection, PT 3925.

13.12 A souvenir poster for Bedřich Smetana's opera *The Kiss* (*Hubička*), mentioned in Hofer's song "The Theater Ticket." Terezín Memorial, Heřman Collection, PT 4294.

13.13 A *Wagenkolonne* of Jewish laborers pulling elderly prisoners in a traditional funeral wagon. By F. Bloch. Terezín Memorial, PT 8183.

13.14 The main square of the ghetto before the *Stadtverschönerung*. By L. Haas. Terezín Memorial, PT 1616.

13.15 The main square of the ghetto after the *Stadtverschönerung*. By J. Spier. Terezín Memorial, PT 2696-2.

14.1 A performance in the ghetto. By P. Kien. Terezín Memorial, PT 4311.

14.2 A souvenir poster for the performance *What Was Mordechai Like?* This original work, written and directed in the ghetto by Walter Freud, featured Lisa (Liese) Zeckendorf as one of the actors. Terezín Memorial, Heřman Collection, PT 3852.

While editing *Performing Captivity, Performing Escape: Cabarets and Plays from the Terezín/Theresienstadt Ghetto* I have had the privilege of working with many outstanding individuals and institutions. I would like to express my thanks to those who have helped to make this English-language edition a reality and acknowledge once more those who played key roles in the Czech–German edition *Divadelní texty z terezínského ghetta/Theatertexte aus dem Ghetto Theresienstadt, 1941–1945* (2008).

First and foremost I would like to thank the survivors of the Terezín/Theresienstadt ghetto and their contemporaries who agreed to be interviewed during the course of my research. Some of them I have also quoted in the introductions and footnotes to the individual plays. Each and every one of them has shaped my view of these texts: Edna and Arie Amit, Hilda Arnsteinová, Zvi Bachrach, Věra Bednářová, Michal Beer (née Maud Stecklmacherová), Kitty Berger, Karel Berka, Jiří Shmuel Bloch, Ruth Bobek, Gavriel Dagan (né Paťa Fischl), Miloslava Dohnalová, Michal Efrat, Zdenka Ehrlich-Fantlová, Ruth Elias, Luděk Eliáš and Eva Eliášová, Walter Fantl-Brumlík, Jan Fischer, Marianna Foltýnová, Jiří Franěk, Rudi Gelbard, Helena Glancová, Martin Glas, Eva Gross, Doris Grozdanovičová, Anna Hanusová-Flachová, Petr Herrmann, Eva Herrmannová, Jarmila Horálková, Margarethe Horowitz-Trentini, Helga Hošková, Anna Hyndráková, Zuzana Justman, Helga Kinsky, Ivan Klíma, Greta Klingsberg, Kurt Jiří Kotouč, Dita Kraus, Grete Lendvay, Dagmar Lieblová, Hana Lojínová, Anna Lorencová, Eva Lukash, Leo Luster, Max Mannheimer, Evelyna Merová, Miriam Merzbacher-Blumenthal, František Miška, Bernhard Morgenstern, Marianna Müllerová, Alena Munková, Eva Musilová, Bohumil Porges, Hana Pravdová, Irena Ravelová, Hana Reinerová, Eva and Jan Roček, Eva Roubíčková, Zuzana Růžičková, Marietta Ryba, Alisa Scheck,

Alisah Schiller, Margit Silberfeld, Alice Sommer-Herz, Ruth Stein, Věra Steinerová, Edith Stern, Alena Sternová, Pavel Stránský, Lilka Trojanová, Věra Vrbová, Suzie and Freddie Weiss, Ela Weissberger, Lisa Zeckendorf-Kutzinski, and Raja Žádníková.

I am grateful to Czech novelist and survivor Ivan Klíma for the sensitive and insightful prologue, and to survivor Lisa Zeckendorf-Kutzinski for the fitting epilogue.

I would like to thank the survivors and their family members who have graciously granted me permission to publish these texts and have worked with me extensively on the introduction and footnotes: Pavel Stránský, as the last surviving author represented in this volume; Jan, Miroslav, and Zdeněk Prokeš; Eva Hirschová; Marie Rút Křížková; Kate and Dorothy Elias; Raja Žádníková and her cousins Shulamit Amir, Rahel Ardon, and Deborah Vietor-Engländer; and Margaret and Michael Warden, Philip Warden and Karen Jackman. Hana Lojínová and her sister and brother-in-law Lilka and Jindřich Trojan, Gisele Pfeiffer and Karin Schroeder, Kate Rys, and Hana Drozdová played key roles in bringing texts to my attention and putting me in touch with surviving family members. Several institutions granted me permission to publish works from their archival collections: the Jewish Museum in Prague and the Terezín Memorial in the Czech Republic, and Beit Terezín and Yad Vashem in Israel.

I am grateful to series editor Carol Martin and publisher Naveen Kishore for the opportunity to publish this revised and expanded English edition; it has been a pleasure to work with both of them as well as everyone at Seagull Books. I would also like to thank Filip Tomaš, publisher of the Czech–German edition, designer Jaroslav Vlček, and translators Dalibor Dobiáš and Michael Wögerbauer for their excellent work and their help in initiating the project.

An earlier, abridged translation of *Laugh with Us: The Second Czech Cabaret* was published in my article "Nonsurvivor Testimony: Terezín Ghetto Theatre in the Archive and the *Second Czech Cabaret*" in *Theatre Survey* 48(1) (May 2007). I would like to thank Cambridge University Press for permission to publish a revised version of the cabaret in this edition.

Financial support for the volume was provided by the Memorial Foundation for Jewish Culture in New York and the Adalbert Stifter Association in Munich. The Czech–German edition was funded by the Austrian Fund for the Future, the Institute for Czech Literature, the Ministry of Culture of the Czech Republic, Shulamit Amir, Kateřina Reinerová and Michaela Schleifová, and The Rabbi's Good Works Fund of Temple Sholom of West Essex, Cedar Grove, New Jersey.

Several organizations in the US, Israel, and the Czech Republic played key roles in the project.

The survivor organization in Prague, the Terezín Initiative, has assisted me with this project in innumerable ways. I am grateful to president Dagmar Lieblová for her long friendship and her advice since we first met in the summer of 2000, and to all the members of that organization who have enriched this project in various ways. I am also greatly indebted to her husband, Petr Liebl, for his assistance with the translation of the plays.

A Charles H. Revson Foundation Fellowship at the Center for Advanced Holocaust Studies, United States Holocaust Memorial Museum, and an Alan M. Stroock Fellowship for Advanced Research in Judaica at the Center for Jewish Studies, Harvard University, provided me with financial support and access to outstanding archival collections and libraries. I am grateful to the scholars and staff of both institutions for their help.

The J. W. Fulbright Commission provided the grant for my first research year in the Czech Republic. I would like to thank Hana Ripková and the whole staff of the Fulbright office in Prague for their support and friendship and my host at Charles University in Prague, Josef Herman.

A fellowship from the Institute for Czech Literature of the Academy of Sciences of the Czech Republic and South Bohemian University enabled me to conduct additional research in the Czech Republic and also provided me with a network of congenial colleagues with whom I look forward to working for years to come. I am grateful to the former director and former deputy director of the Institute, Pavel Janoušek and Alice Jedličková, and, at the university, Vladimír Papoušek, Dean of the Faculty of Philosophy.

At the Arts and Theatre Institute in Prague Eva Šormová, former head of the Czech Theater Studies Department, has been unfailingly generous with advice and rare archival materials from her own pioneering work on Terezín/Theresienstadt theater, and served as a meticulous reviewer of the Czech–German edition. I am grateful to Mirka Potůčková of the International Cooperation and External Relations Department for her advice and friendship since my first research trip in 2000.

At Masaryk University and the theater department of the Janáček Academy of Musical Arts in Brno/Brünn, Bořivoj Srba, David Drozd, Hana Drozdová, Andrea Jochmannová, and Pavel Drábek have provided me with invaluable advice and opportunities to present my work. I am grateful to Andrea Jochmannová and Katharina Wessely for their assistance with the section on Czech and Austrian theater in my introduction.

At the Institute of the Terezín Initiative I would like to thank director Jaroslava Milotová for her detailed commentary on the Czech–German edition and our many conversations about Czech and US views of the history of Terezín/Theresienstadt.

At the Terezín Memorial I am grateful to director Jan Munk and deputy director Vojtěch Blodig for their support of this project and to the entire staff for their help over the last 10 years. I would like to thank Alice Beránková, Tomáš Fedorovič, Iva Gaudesová, Ludmila Chládková, Pavla Jelínková, Eva Němcová and especially Martina Šiknerová for their quick replies to my many requests.

The opportunity to draw on the resources of the Jewish Museum in Prague has greatly enriched this work. I would like to thank director Leo Pavlát and the entire staff, including present and former directors of the Educational and Cultural Center, Miroslava Ludvíková, Miloš Pojar, and Vladimír Hanzel; head of the Department for the History of the Shoah, Michal Frankl; curators Jana Šplíchalová and Pavla Neuner; head of external relations, Noemi Holeková; curator of the visual art collection, Michaela Sidenberg; and curator of the photo collection, Martin Jelínek.

In Israel I would like to thank the staff of Yad Vashem, especially Leah Teichthal, Niv Goldberg, and Sandrine Rebibo, and at the Beit Terezín/Theresienstadt Martyrs Remembrance Association, former director Anita Tarsi, Sima Shachar, and Anat Elazar for their warm welcome and assistance during my research.

Gary Cohen, Wilma Iggers, and Jindřich Toman graciously consented to review the translations and made many helpful suggestions for the introduction and footnotes. Marsha L. Rozenblit and Hillel J. Kieval provided invaluable commentary on the historical introduction. I would also like to acknowledge once more the reviewers of the Czech–German edition: Eva Herrmanová, Roy Kift, Ulrike Migdal, Jaroslava Milotová, and Eva Šormová.

Several colleagues and friends assisted me with the music in the cabarets. I would like to thank Blanka Hemelíková, Vladimír Just, Hana Kazatelová, Ondřej Pivoda, Přemysl Rut, and Jiří Weinberger for their help in tracking down song titles, Zuzana Lejčarová and Daniel Dobiáš for performing the songs for me, and Winfried Radeke, for identifying all the songs in the *Purimspiel* medley and for his delightful arrangement, skillfully transcribed by Andreas Jocksch.

My thanks to the friends and colleagues who have provided me with information, advice and support during my work on this anthology: Marie Bernardová, Daniela and Dennis Beck and Ladislava Jilková, Kateřina Bláhová, Hannelore Brenner-Wonschick, John Crane and Luboš Šťastný, Lucie Černohousová, Verena Dolle and Jörg Klinger, Dalibor and Milena Dostal, Peter and Tanja Düsing, Gideon Eckhaus, Oliver Engelhardt, Herbert Exenberger, Melissa Feinberg, Gaby Flatow, Ben Frommer, Arnošt Goldflam, Anna Hájková, Bill Henry, Vicki, Kevin, and Chris

Kalnins, Stefan Benedik Karner, Jaromír Kazda, T. Mills Kelly, Blanka Kynclová and her family, Arnošt Lustig, Lena Makarova and her family, Beate Meyer, Bonnie and Johanna Naradzay, Martin Niklas, Thomas Öllermann, Sofia Pantouvaki, Naomi and Norman Patz, Richard Pinard, Karel Piorecký, Jennifer Ranglová and her family, Tomáš and Milena Rangl, Rebecca Rovit, Wolfgang Schellenbacher, Frank Schroeder, Susanne and Markus Spröer-Hugo, František Steiner, Eva Strusková, Olga Strusková, Hana and Zdeněk Škvor, Petr Štědron, Marianna Štěpitová-Klaučová, David Vaughan, and Anke Zimmermann.

Special thanks to Petr Brod for supplying me with an unending stream of hard-to-find resources, and to David Faux of the Dramatists Guild for his excellent and timely advice.

I would like to thank the actors who have read through these scripts with me to help create stageworthy translations. I have appreciated their patience, insight and suggestions as well as the sheer fun of working with them. In Seattle: Travis Michael Anderson, Michael Clarke, Julia Leichman, Will Ransom, and Diana Smith. In the Czech Republic: CESTA, the cultural exchange station in Tábor, and Hilary Binder, John Brent, George Cremaschi, Melissa Ramos, Christopher N. Rankin and Jessica Serran. In Washington DC: Krista Hegburg, Alan S. Hegburg, Martin Holler, Olivier Pairault, Dirk Rupnow, Steven F. Sage, Vincent E. Slatt, and Leah Wolfson.

Finally, I would like to thank my family for all their help.

In the cabarets and plays in this volume, many German and Czech words, proper names, and words from the Czech- and German-based slang that developed in the Terezín/Theresienstadt ghetto have been left in their original spellings. This guide provides a quick summary of Czech and German pronunciation, focusing on the features that are most different from American English.[1]

CZECH PRONUNCIATION

The stress is always on the first syllable of the word. A diacritic over a vowel (á, é, í, ě, etc.) lengthens the syllable or modifies the sound of the vowel but does not shift the stress away from the first syllable.

Short and long vowels

a like the o in pop
á as in father
e as in bet
é as in pair
ě like the ye in yes
i or y as in pit
í or ý as in seat
o as in noble
ó as in door
u like the oo in toot
ů or ú like the oo in fool

Vowel combinations

au like the ou in foul
ie like the ye in yes
ia like the ya in yak

---

1 The pronunciation guidelines published here have been adapted from several travel guides.

iu like the u in (British) flute
ou like the oe in foe

Consonants

Consonants not listed here are pronounced like their American English equivalents. If there is no vowel in a syllable, *r* and *l* function as vowels. For example, the city of Brno is pronounced "BER-no."

c like ts in boats (Václav Havel's name is pronounced "VAHT-slav")
č like ch in chicken
ch like ch in loch
ď like d in (British) duped
j like y in yes
kd like gd
mě like mnye
ň like n in lasagne
r as in Spanish, lightly rolled
ř like r and ž combined
š like sh in shop
ť like t in (British) tutor
ž like s in pleasure

GERMAN PRONUNCIATION

The stress is usually on the first syllable of the word, but there are many exceptions. For best results, consult a native speaker.

Vowels

a as in father
e as in day or as in wet
i as in pit
o as in bottom or as in rose
u as in boot
ä is a combination of a and e, sometimes like e in bet and some-
        times like ai in paid

ö is a combination of o and e, like the French eu
ü is a combination of u and e, like true, only sharper in sound

Vowel combinations

ai as in lie
au as in house
äu as in oil
ie as in free
ei as in height
eu as in oil

Consonants

Consonants not listed here are pronounced like their American English equivalents.

ch like the ch in loch
j like the y in yes
r similar to French r
s, at the beginning of a word, like z, otherwise like s
sch like sh
sp, at beginning of word, like shp
ss and ß like s
st, at beginning of word, like sht
v between f and v
w like v
z like ts in boats (Mozart is pronounced "MOAT-sart")

Many of the places mentioned in this volume have both Czech and German names. In my own texts I have used a dual form (e.g. Terezín/Theresienstadt, Plzeň/Pilsen). In the translated texts I have used the form that the author used. In cases where there is a commonly used English-language name (e.g. Prague, Vienna) I have used that throughout the volume.

In the case of women's names, conventions of each language have been followed. In Part I (Czech-language Texts), all women's names end with the suffix -(ov)á, (e.g. Hirschová, Černá) except for the names of women who do not use the -(ov)á suffix themselves. In Part II (German-language Texts), -(ov)á is only used in the case of interviews from the post-war period with Czech-Jewish survivors who use -(ov)á in their surnames.

Many survivors who remained in Czechoslovakia after the war changed their surnames. Men often selected more Czech-sounding surnames (e.g. changing Eckstein to Eliáš). Women most often changed their names through marriage. In my introductions and footnotes I have used the post-war surname but have provided the pre-war surname (indicated by né or née). In the translated theatrical texts I have retained pre-war surnames.

Some of the formatting features of the original scripts have been retained. Elements such as character lists, the way scene and act breaks are indicated, etc., may vary from script to script. In some scripts, scene numbers, stage directions, etc., have been added for consistency and clarity.

LISA PESCHEL

This volume presents theatrical works that speak to us from the very heart of the Holocaust: they were written by Czechoslovak and Austrian Jews imprisoned during the Second World War in the Terezín/Theresienstadt ghetto. Before engaging with the plays themselves, however, let us engage with a question that has vexed scholars for decades: What to call this place where such a thriving cultural life sprung up and where so many lost their lives? The right to grant a name is a particular form of power. In this volume I use the names chosen by those who have the greatest right to that power: the prisoners themselves.

Should the Czech "Terezín" or the German "Theresienstadt" be used? When the Nazis chose this fortress town as the site of the ghetto, both names had been in use for over 150 years. It was built in the 1780s in a bilingual region about 60 km northwest of Prague, near the present-day Czech–German border. The Czech- and German-speaking authors of the plays in this volume used the name more familiar to them. Therefore, in the translations of the authors' texts I use the name they used; in my own texts, except for proper names of organizations, etc., I use the dual form "Terezín/Theresienstadt."

Should Terezín/Theresienstadt be called a "ghetto"? [1] A concentration camp? Or was it, as Czech historian and survivor Miroslav Kárný argued, *unikum sui generis*, a site unlike any other in the Nazi system of ghettos and camps? The prisoners themselves, as their texts reveal, called it the "ghetto;" the survivors in their testimony often alternate between "ghetto" and "camp." I will call it, as the prisoners did, the ghetto. However, more important than the name is an understanding of the conditions the

---

1 Some scholars today find the term "ghetto" too euphemistic. It was not euphemistic enough for the Nazis. As of May 1, 1943, the term was forbidden and the term *Jüdisches Siedlungsgebiet* (Jewish settlement area) was used in all official documents. See Martin Niklas, " . . . *die schönste Stadt der Welt*": Österreichische Jüdinnen und Juden in Theresienstadt (Vienna: DÖW, 2009), p. 51.

prisoners actually faced. The historical overview later in this introduction describes daily life in Terezín/Theresienstadt and the setting in which these plays were written and performed.

Finally, what should the phenomenon of theatrical performance in the ghetto be called? The word used most often today to describe the cultural life of Terezín/Theresienstadt is "resistance." If resistance is defined too narrowly, however, as defiance against the Nazis, it may limit our understanding of the many reasons why the prisoners performed.

THEATRICAL TEXTS FROM TEREZÍN/THERESIENSTADT AND RESISTANCE

Terezín/Theresienstadt played a prominent role in Nazi propaganda as a "model ghetto," displayed to representatives of the Red Cross in June 1944 to deceive the world about the true nature of the Final Solution. Although it is well known that performances took place during this inspection—for example, the commission watched the children's opera *Brundibár*—the cultural life of the ghetto did not emerge on Nazi orders. In fact, the vast majority of the cultural events in the ghetto were initiated by the prisoners, for the prisoners. The first documented event, a "variety evening" in the prisoners' barracks, took place on December 5 or 6, 1941, just two weeks after the first transport arrived.[2] By the spring of 1944, performances and lectures were taking place on more than a dozen stages in the ghetto.[3]

Although the Nazis attempted to portray Terezín/Theresienstadt as an independent "Jewish settlement area," the reality of the ghetto was much grimmer. It was the final stop for more than 30,000 Central and Western European Jews, most from

2 See Erich Weiner, "*Freizeitgestaltung* in Theresienstadt," in Rebecca Rovit and Alvin Goldfarb (eds.), *Theatrical Performance during the Holocaust: Texts, Documents, Memoirs* (Baltimore: Johns Hopkins University Press, 1999), pp. 209–30, see p. 217; and the Terezín Memorial, inv. no. PT 3878.

3 For a list of the performance spaces see the Terezín Memorial, inv. no. PT 3765.

Czechoslovakia, Austria, and Germany, who perished within its walls. For thousands more, it was only a way station on the journey to the slave-labor and death camps. Yet it was also a place where many prisoners became intensely aware of the meaning and power of art.[4] Among those who spent months, or even years, in Terezín/Theresienstadt, a vigorous cultural life emerged: adults and children drew and painted, composed, played and sang musical works, wrote poems, essays, and plays. Not all the prisoners participated in the cultural life, and only a small fraction of the works produced has survived. Nevertheless, the testimony of those who were involved, and the drawings, texts, and sheet music that have been preserved reveal a world where art, as one survivor wrote, "transcend[ed] itself and acquir[ed] a dimension of sheer survival."[5]

During my research in Europe and Israel on theatrical performance in the ghetto, the works in this volume—cabarets, puppet plays, historical and verse dramas, short sketches, poems and songs, a radio program, and a *Purimspiel*—came to light in private collections and small archives. Although short texts from Terezín/Theresienstadt had been published in previous anthologies, these newly discovered works included complete, full-length scripts, some including original sheet music.[6] Most of the authors were unknown; for those whose works had been published, significant new material had come to light.[7] With the help of survivors who explained to me the meaning of many disguised jokes and veiled references, a bilingual Czech–German annotated volume of the texts was published in 2008.[8]

---

4 See the prologue in this volume.

5 Mirko Tůma, "Memories of Theresienstadt," in Rovit and Goldfarb, *Theatrical Performance during the Holocaust*, pp. 265–73; see p. 271.

6 See the bibliography for a list of previously published collections of theatrical texts from the ghetto.

7 For previously published authors Leo Strauss and Hans Hofer, new songs and poems were found. For František Kowanitz's song lyrics for the musical revue *Prince Bettliegend*, an outline of the plot was reconstructed on the basis of several survivor testimonies. Significant new information on Hanuš Hachenburg's puppet play *Looking for a Specter* was provided by his friend and fellow survivor Kurt Jiří Kotouč.

8 See the acknowledgements in this volume and www.akropolis.info/terezin for information in Czech, German, and English.

For this revised and expanded English-language edition, all translations were prepared with performance in mind. The brief introductions to each play are based on survivor testimony, archival materials, a wealth of published diaries and secondary sources on the ghetto, and, above all, a network of living memory. Very few of these scripts are abandoned artifacts. Surviving relatives and friends were able to provide much insight into the influences that shaped the scripts and their authors' lives. In addition, within the texts themselves, extensive footnotes explain references to life before the war and in Terezín/Theresienstadt.

Insight into these texts, however, requires more than footnotes. We must also consider the prisoners' own relationship to theatrical performance. As testimony reveals, the survivors have long been concerned about misinterpretations of the cultural life of the ghetto. In an essay written in Prague in 1961, Terezín/Theresienstadt actress Jana Šedová warned against "two dangerous and incorrect views:" underestimating the prisoners' suffering (that is, assuming that conditions must not have been so bad if cultural activities could take place), and overestimating the heroism of the performers.[9]

In the historical section of the essay that follows I attempt to address Šedová's first concern and dispel any suspicion that the cultural activities took place because life in the ghetto was easy. Instead, readers are presented with a paradox: deprivation itself spurred the prisoners to perform. As one survivor wrote, "In spite of all the harassment, dirt, ugliness, and horror, or rather, exactly because of them, we all sought stimulus through which it would be possible to live and draw hope. It was in the cabaret [. . .] that we forgot about the powerlessness of our daily lives."[10]

Šedová's second concern becomes clearer when we consider its context. Various groups in post-war and subsequently communist Czechoslovakia tried to use the prisoners as symbols—of suffering,

---

9 Jana Šedová, program notes to *Poslední cyklista*, Divadlo Rokoko, Prague, 1961. Šedová (née Truda Popperová) performed in one of the works in this volume, *Prince Bettliegend*.

10 Ib, "Svědectví 'posledního cyklisty,'" *Hlas revoluce*, June 22, 1961.

of resistance, of victimization—to serve ends that were sometimes in conflict with those of survivors.[11] Šedová's warning is still valid. Works from Terezín/Theresienstadt are now performed and exhibited all over the world, and one rarely finds a set of program notes that does not include the phrase "spiritual resistance." Musical works from the ghetto that have received the most recognition tend to be those that contain an element of defiance: *Brundibár*, where children defeat the black-mustached villain, and *The Emperor of Atlantis* (*Der Kaiser von Atlantis*), where the tyrannical Emperor is forced to surrender to Death. But as the works in this volume reveal, the prisoners sometimes had other goals: to indulge in nostalgia for their homes, to satirize their own behavior and that of their leaders, to enjoy a moment of aesthetic pleasure and escape. A narrow definition of resistance that includes only acts of defiance leaves no room to acknowledge how important these aspects of theater were to the prisoners themselves. If resistance is more than defiance, how can we widen our view of this concept without defining the term so broadly that it becomes meaningless?

We can craft a more compelling definition by asking the question: Resistance against what? In addition to resistance against the Nazis, the prisoners had to fight a more general and insidious enemy, one mentioned by the survivor quoted above: resistance against powerlessness. This is not an abstract problem, for it is intimately tied with an issue that directly affected the prisoners' survival: they had to find ways to manage the feelings of fear, helplessness, and loss of control that are the symptoms of psychological trauma. According to Judith Herman, Professor of Clinical Psychiatry at Harvard University Medical School, "Traumatic events are extraordinary [. . .] because they overwhelm the ordinary

---

11 For example, in the immediate post-war period, communists used narratives of Nazi brutality in the ghetto to support their program of expelling all "Germans" from Czechoslovakia, even though some of those labeled "Germans" were actually German-speaking Czechoslovak Jews. See Lisa Peschel, "The Prosthetic Life: Theatrical Performance, Survivor Testimony and the Terezín Ghetto, 1941–1963" (Ph.D. diss., University of Minnesota, Minneapolis and St. Paul, 2009), pp. 97–8.

human adaptations to life."[12] In the ghetto, quick adaptation to the new conditions was a matter of life and death. Theatrical performance could not change these conditions, but it could help the prisoners counteract the intense feelings of fear and helplessness in a way that kept them from becoming paralyzed by despair and enabled them to go on with the daily fight for life.

How might this have functioned? As Herman argues, since helplessness is the essential insult of trauma, the guiding principle of recovery is to restore a sense of power and control.[13] In Terezín/Theresienstadt, where the prisoners' ability to control any aspect of their environment was greatly limited, the cultural life became a sphere where they could actually exercise some agency— that is, where they could exert some degree of control over their experience. In some performances, they exercised this agency by confronting the ghetto, experiencing it in a more psychologically manageable way by bringing it onto the stage and forcing it to behave according to their rules. In others, the prisoners shut out the ghetto, escaping into a world of their own creation.

Escapism in Terezín/Theresienstadt theater often meant escape into the past, which was also an engagement with their imagined future. Few of the prisoners were able to acknowledge that, even if they survived, the post-war world would be a radically different place. Instead, most of them firmly believed they would return to a life just like the one they remembered.[14] Therefore, the theater artists brought the world of their past onto the stage, not to mourn its loss, but to anticipate its return. Perhaps the most vivid example is *Laugh with Us: The Second Czech Cabaret*. Written and performed in the spring of 1944, the cabaret is set in a post-war Prague that is identical with the Prague of the authors' past. As the main characters, Porges and Horpatzky, stroll around the city, "reminiscing" about their time in Terezín, they visit well-known

---

12 Judith Herman, *Trauma and Recovery: The Aftermath of Violence from Domestic Abuse to Political Terror* (New York: Basic Books, 1992), p. 33.

13 Ibid., pp. 41, 159.

14 Emil Utitz, *Psychologie života v terezínském koncentračním táboře* (Prague: Dělnické nakladatelství, 1947), p. 24.

pre-war bars and clubs, listen to music from the 1930s, and avoid one of their favorite restaurants—Horpatzky still owes the head-waiter money from the pre-war days.

Authors who confronted the ghetto in their works often created comic allegories. In one scene of *Radio Show*, co-author Kurt Egerer placed Terezín in a harmless, familiar framework by reinterpreting it as the setting for a fairy tale based on *Snow White and the Seven Dwarfs*. In his story for children, hardships in the ghetto are transformed into advantages for the "dwarfs." For example, the bedbugs that plagued the prisoners are described as little pets that watch over them at night as they sleep. Even the meager food supply is explained in a fairy tale-appropriate way: dwarfs have little tiny stomachs, so tiny rations are enough for them.

As the plays in this volume reveal, defiance toward their captors was just one element in a whole range of strategies the authors used to confront the unprecedented crisis they faced. If we widen our definition of resistance to encompass all the forms of opposition to powerlessness that they exercised within the symbolic space of performance, we become true witnesses to these authors and to all the Terezín/Theresienstadt prisoners who engaged so intensely with theatrical performance in the ghetto.

THE JEWS OF VIENNA, BOHEMIA, AND MORAVIA, AND THEATER BEFORE THE SECOND WORLD WAR

The scripts written in Terezín/Theresienstadt bear the marks of their authors' experiences in the ghetto, but they reflect just as vividly the cultural influences that shaped them before the war. All the plays in the collection were written by Czech- and German-speaking Jews from Bohemia and Moravia (the western provinces of Czechoslovakia) and the Austrian city of Vienna.[15] To appreciate the diversity of the prisoners' theatrical responses to

---

15 Surprisingly, during my research for this collection, no new theatrical texts by German-Jewish authors came to light.

Terezín/Theresienstadt, we must first look at the diversity of the Central European Jews.

Until 1918, Jews from these regions had all been citizens of a vast empire ruled by the Habsburg dynasty. They had shared the historical process of emancipation that began in the late eighteenth century, when emperor Joseph II lifted certain legal restrictions on Jews, and were fully emancipated in 1867—the year that the Habsburg Empire became the Dual Monarchy of Austria-Hungary—when parliaments of both Austria and Hungary granted them equality before the law. During the processes of modernization and secularization, regional differences created different forms of Jewish identity and different kinds of relationships with non-Jews.

The Jews of Austria-Hungary lived in a monarchy where people of different languages, cultures, and ethnicities considered themselves different nations. Unlike German Jews, who lived in a country where language, nation, and state were the same (German language, German *Volk*, German state), Jews under Habsburg rule had to reconcile various claims to their loyalty. Historian Marsha L. Rozenblit suggests that, as a result, Jews developed a tripartite identity. They were loyal to their Habsburg rulers, identified with the languages and cultures of their own region, and still felt they belonged to the Jewish people. Jewish identity could range from the traditional position that Jews were a nation in exile awaiting redemption, to a liberal perspective that saw Jewish identity as simply a religious one, to a Zionist or diasporic nationalist stance with its insistence that Jews should form a modern secular nation.[16]

The influence of Reform or Liberal Judaism was also different in Germany and Austria-Hungary. In Germany, Liberal Jews rejected the traditional notion that Jews still formed a separate nation hoping to return to Israel and professed their full loyalty to the

---

16 Marsha L. Rozenblit, *Reconstructing a National Identity: The Jews of Habsburg Austria during World War I* (Oxford and New York: Oxford University Press, 2001), p. 162.

German state and people.[17] In Vienna, because of differences in the way that the Reform movement was introduced and waves of Jewish migration in the late nineteenth century, modern Jews adopted the form of Liberal Judaism but the content of worship remained traditional. On the one hand, there was pressure from more traditional Jews from other parts of Austria-Hungary to retain prayers for a return to Zion; on the other, because Austria-Hungary was composed of so many different nations, the idea of a separate Jewish nation was not such an anomaly.[18] Ultra-orthodox tradition was represented in Vienna as well, due to the migration of Yiddish-speaking Jews from Galicia, the Bukovina, and the Pressburg area of Hungary (now Bratislava in Slovakia). They quickly adopted the German language; some modernized, but others retained their own traditional religious practices.

Jews in Bohemia and Moravia adopted a similar style of worship that combined Liberal form with traditional content, but ultra-orthodoxy gained little foothold in this region. Bohemian and Moravian Jews spoke the languages of their non-Jewish neighbors, German and Czech, and, especially in small towns, continued to lead a traditional Jewish lifestyle.[19]

In the late nineteenth century, anti-Semitism affected both groups in different ways. In Vienna, largely due to the influence of powerful mayor Karl Lueger and his Christian-Social Party (which controlled the Vienna City Council from 1895 to 1919), anti-Semitism became a political instrument, and was considered "respectable" even for the middle classes.[20] Austrian anti-Semitism was different from Nazi anti-Semitism in that, at least until the late 1930s, it was not based on "racial" hatred but rather on

---

17 Marsha L. Rozenblit, "The Jews of Germany and Austria: A Comparative Perspective," in Robert S. Wistrich (ed.), *Austrians and Jews in the Twentieth Century: From Franz Joseph to Waldheim* (New York: St. Martin's Press, 1992), pp. 1–18, see p. 3.

18 Ibid., pp. 11–12.

19 Ibid., p. 2.

20 Robert S. Wistrich, *The Jews of Vienna in the Age of Franz Joseph* (New York: Oxford University Press, 1989), p. 236.

Catholic teachings and economic resentment, especially by the lower middle classes who blamed Jews for their economic problems. However, Lueger's own recognition that Vienna needed its Jewish economic elites led to an uneasy but functioning coexistence. As historian Robert S. Wistrich succinctly puts it, "In spite of its vulgarity, Christian-Social anti-Semitism did not generate any pogroms in Vienna."[21] In fact, during this period, Jews made tremendous contributions to what we know as Viennese culture: Sigmund Freud, Arthur Schnitzler, Hugo von Hofmannsthal, Arnold Schoenberg, and Gustav Mahler were all Jewish or of Jewish descent.[22]

In response to increasing anti-Semitism, Liberal Jews founded the Austria-Israelite Union. Its members emphasized their dedication to German-language Austrian culture, but they also helped to define a positive Jewish group identity that exceeded the bounds of religion to include a sense of ethnic consciousness.[23] The rise of the Zionist movement, whether focused on actual emigration to a Jewish homeland or on a sense of Jewish nationhood in the diaspora, also offered new positive models of Jewish identity.

In Bohemia and Moravia, a different factor emerged as a central element in anti-Semitism: Jews were caught in the middle of the nationality conflict. During the nineteenth century, Czech and German speakers in the region began increasingly to consider themselves not just separate language communities but separate nations. During the process of emancipation, many Jews had assimilated to the elite language and culture of the empire, that is, German. Now they found themselves alternately pressured to join the Czech national movement, rejected by both sides as a group that could never belong to either nation, and criticized for taking sides out of opportunism. Nevertheless, even though the dominant

---

21 Ibid., p. 237.

22 For a more detailed description of Jewish contributions to Viennese *fin de siècle* culture see Steven Beller, *Vienna and the Jews, 1867–1938* (New York: Cambridge University Press, 1989).

23 Rozenblit, "The Jews of Germany and Austria," p. 7.

political party, the Young Czechs, began to use anti-Semitism as a political weapon in the late eighteenth century, the influence of the Czech national movement increased among Jews.[24] Many Czech-assimilated Jews shifted their support to the Realist party, led by the future president of Czechoslovakia, Thomas Garrigue Masaryk.[25] The Zionist movement also gained ground, especially because the idea of a separate Jewish nationality offered a way out of the increasingly tense Czech–German nationality conflict.

By the early twentieth century, the patterns of Jewish identification that would persist in Bohemia and Moravia until the Second World War had been established. As Hillel Kieval writes,

> [Modern Czech Jewry] grew out of the transformation of "Bohemian" Jewry: the Czech national Jew, the discoverers of Jewish nationality, the bilingual, but nationally indifferent, mass of rural and small-town Jews, the bridge-builders between German and Czech culture, and the ever-dwindling number of defenders of the German cultural ideal. All of these tendencies are present in the modern Czech-Jewish community.[26]

After the First World War, when Austria-Hungary was divided into several successor states, the Jews of Vienna, Bohemia, and Moravia found themselves in different countries, under different governments, and in fundamentally different situations.

After 1918, all that remained of once-great "Austria" was a small republic, initially named "German Austria" (Deutschösterreich),

---

24 In the census of 1890, 66 percent of Bohemian Jews indicated German as their language; by 1900, 54 percent declared it to be Czech. See Hillel J. Kieval, "Jews, Czechs and Germans in Bohemia before 1914," in Robert S. Wistrich (ed.), *Austrians and Jews in the Twentieth Century: From Franz Joseph to Waldheim* (New York: St. Martin's Press, 1992), pp. 19–37, see p. 26. However, many of those who assimilated to Czech-language culture continued to value a German cultural affiliation. Even in 1910, almost 90 percent of Jewish children in Prague were enrolled in German-language schools. See Gary B. Cohen, *The Politics of Ethnic Survival: Germans in Prague, 1861–1914* (Princeton: Princeton University Press, 1981), p. 224.

25 Ibid., pp. 21, 28.

26 Hillel J. Kieval, *The Making of Czech Jewry: National Conflict and Jewish Society in Bohemia, 1870–1918* (Oxford: Oxford University Press, 1988), p. 4.

plagued by post-war shortages, economic crises, and political instability.[27] The Christian-Social Party continued to play a dominant role in Austrian politics, and the peculiarly Austrian form of religious and economic anti-Semitism remained firmly woven into the social fabric of the Republic. Although the government refused the Zionists' repeated attempts to gain formal recognition for Jews as a separate nationality, Austrian anti-Semitism did not translate into official discrimination and anti-Jewish laws. In the Social Democratic Party, the only party that accepted Jewish members, many held positions of leadership. However, their role in public life ended in 1934, when the Austrian Civil War led to a form of authoritarian rule called "Austrofascism." The new regime identified itself as pro-Austria and anti-National Socialism; unlike Hitler's rise to power in Germany, Austrofascism did not translate into state persecution of Austrian Jews. Many Jewish leaders in the Social Democratic Party were arrested after the social democratic movement was outlawed, but conditions did not substantially worsen for the Jewish population in general.

Many Jews in Austria continued to try to balance political loyalty to the Austrian state with dedication to German-language culture and their own sense of Jewish identity, whether that identity was Zionist/nationalist or religious with a sense of ethnic belonging. However, as the influence of Nazi Germany increased, more and more non-Jewish Austrians began to adopt a sense of belonging to a German *Volk* or nation rather than simply to German-language culture—a *Volk* to which Jews could not hope to belong. In response, Jewish communities became more insular and they asserted their Jewish identity more forcefully.[28]

---

27 On September 10, 1919, the name of the republic was changed from "German Austria" to "Austria."

28 Marsha L. Rozenblit, "Jewish Ethnicity in a New Nation-State: The Crisis of Identity in the Austrian Republic," in Michael Brenner and Derek Jonathan Penslar (eds.), *In Search of Jewish Community: Jewish Identities in Germany and Austria, 1918–1933* (Bloomington: Indiana University Press, 1998), pp. 134–53, see p. 145.

The situation in the new state of Czechoslovakia was more hospitable for many reasons.[29] Newly won independence created a mood of optimism rather than defeat.[30] The territories within its borders included much of the former empire's industrial base, placing the new state on a firm economic footing. Perhaps most importantly, the new government refused to condone anti-Semitism. Although incidents of anti-Jewish violence erupted after the war, the Jews had faith that President Thomas Masaryk would bring the situation under control and create a tolerant and just society.[31]

Jewish attitudes toward the new state were mostly positive. Those who identified with the Czech national struggle supported the new order enthusiastically.[32] Others were encouraged when Czechoslovakia granted wide-ranging rights to the "national minorities" within its borders, which included Germans, Hungarians, Ruthenes, Poles, and Jews, recognized as a nationality in the country's first constitution of February 29, 1920.[33] Thus, in Bohemia and Moravia, Jews were able to maintain a tripartite identity if they so desired: politically Czechoslovak, culturally Czech or German, and religiously, ethnically, or nationally Jewish.[34]

---

29 Czechoslovakia was formed from the provinces of Bohemia and Moravia, the Hungarian territory of Slovakia, and parts of Silesia and Subcarpathian Ruthenia.

30 Not all groups wanted to be citizens of the new state: German-speaking regions unsuccessfully sought independence or union with Austria. See Derek Sayer, *The Coasts of Bohemia: A Czech History* (Princeton, NJ: Princeton University Press, 1998), pp. 168–69.

31 Marsha L. Rozenblit, "Sustaining Austrian 'National' Identity in Crisis: The Dilemma of the Jews in Habsburg Austria, 1914–1919," in Pieter M. Judson and Marsha L. Rozenblit (eds.), *Constructing Nationalities in East Central Europe* (Oxford: Berghahn Books, 2005), pp. 178–91, see p. 186.

32 Kieval, *The Making of Czech Jewry*, pp. 183–86, 192.

33 Tatjana Lichtenstein, "Making Jews at Home: Jewish Nationalism in the Bohemian Lands, 1918–1938" (Ph.D. diss., University of Toronto, 2009), p. 68. Debates raged as to whether "nationality" on the Czechoslovak census should mean the individual's subjective choice of nationality or whether it should be based on more objective criteria. The Statistical Bureau ultimately decided that nationality was to be understood as ethnic belonging, with mother tongue as the main criterion; however, Jews were allowed to choose Jewish nationality regardless of language spoken. See ibid., pp. 80–1.

34 Rozenblit, "Sustaining Austrian 'National' Identity," p. 186.

However, because the government rejected anti-Semitism, and because Czech anti-Semitism was often associated with resentment of Jews' perceived preference for German-language culture, other options were open to them. Some Jews who embraced Czech language and culture encountered little anti-Semitism and assimilated thoroughly into the Czech cultural sphere—their Jewishness became simply a religion or, for those who were completely secular, only a vague sense of family origin.

The situation was more complex for those who were assimilated to German-language culture. In Prague, as the proportion of Czech speakers increased, the German-speaking Jews—a group that included noted authors Franz Kafka and Max Brod—saw their world as "a game preserve whose ground was always shrinking . . . an iceberg that the surrounding waters slowly eroded."[35] As Hitler's power grew, those who lived in the largely German-speaking border regions (called the Sudetenland) saw their non-Jewish neighbors' sense of belonging to a racially defined German nation increase. The Zionists of Czechoslovakia, encouraged by the government's recognition of Jewish nationality, continued to try and persuade their fellow Jews to consider themselves a separate Jewish nation, removed from the Czech–German nationality conflict.[36] Others saw no conflict in belonging simultaneously to both Zionist and Czech or German organizations.[37] In the 1930 census in Bohemia, Moravia, and Silesia, of those who indicated Judaism as their religion, 36 percent chose Czechoslovak nationality, 31 percent chose Jewish, and 30 percent chose German,[38] with Jews in

---

35 Emil Utitz, quoted in Scott Spector, *Prague Territories: National Conflict and Cultural Innovation in Franz Kafka's Fin De Siècle* (Berkeley: University of California Press, 2000), p. 3.

36 Lichtenstein, "Making Jews at Home," p. 7.

37 See the example of Karel Fleischmann in Kateřina Čapková, "Tschechisch, Deutsch, Jüdisch—wo ist der Unterschied? Zur Komplexität von nationalen Identitäten der böhmischen Juden 1918–1938," in Marek Nekula and Walter Koschmal (eds.), *Juden zwischen Deutschen und Tschechen: sprachliche und kulturelle Identitäten in Böhmen 1800–1945* (Munich: Oldenbourg Wissenschaftsverlag, 2006), pp. 73–84, see p. 73.

38 Livia Rothkirchen, "The Jews of Bohemia and Moravia: 1938–1945," in Avigdor Dagan, Gertrude Hirschler, and Lewis Weiner (eds.), *The Jews of*

Moravia much more likely to claim Jewish nationality than those in Bohemia.[39]

Religious practice among the Bohemian and Moravian Jews varied widely. Although some continued in orthodox observance of Jewish law, many observed only selected holidays, while thousands left Judaism completely, or converted to other faiths.[40] Instances of intermarriage also increased; of Jews who married between 1928 and 1933, 43 percent in Bohemia and 30 percent in Moravia married non-Jews.[41] Geographically, they were also much more integrated with their non-Jewish neighbors than their Austrian counterparts. In 1934, the vast majority (92 percent) of Austria's 191,000 Jews lived in Vienna.[42] In Bohemia, according to the 1930 census, approximately 50 percent of the province's 76,000 Jews lived in Prague; in Moravia, less than 30 percent of the province's 41,000 Jews lived in the capital city of Brno/Brünn.

Furthermore, most political organizations had Jewish members.[43] They participated actively in the public life of the state, where a democratic government remained in power right until the eve of the Second World War.

Czechoslovakia: Historical Studies and Surveys, VOL. 3 (Philadelphia: Jewish Publication Society of America, 1984), pp. 3–74, see p. 12.

39 In Bohemia, 46 percent chose Czechoslovak, 31 percent German, and 20 percent Jewish nationality. In Moravia-Silesia, 52 percent chose Jewish, 29 percent German, and 18 percent Czechoslovak nationality. See Ezra Mendelsohn, *The Jews of East Central Europe* (Bloomington: Indiana University Press, 1983), p. 159.

40 In March 1941, of the 74,417 Jews "by race" still in Bohemia and Moravia, 12,168 were not of Jewish faith. Of those, 46 percent were unaffiliated with any church. The next largest group, comprising 40 percent, were baptized Catholics. See Livia Rothkirchen, *The Jews of Bohemia and Moravia: Facing the Holocaust* (Lincoln and Jerusalem: University of Nebraska Press; Jerusalem: Yad Vashem, 2005), pp. 341, 92ff.

41 Kateřina Čapková, *Češi, Němci, Židé? Národní identita Židů v Čechách, 1918–1938* (Prague: Paseka, 2005), p. 21.

42 Gerhard Botz, "The Dynamics of Persecution in Austria, 1938–45," in Wistrich, *Austrians and Jews in the Twentieth Century*, pp. 199–219, see p. 201.

43 Exceptions included specifically Christian parties such as the Catholic People's Party and pro-Hitler parties, including the Sudeten German Party and Czech fascist parties, such as the Flag (Vlajka).

In both Austria and Czechoslovakia, Jews took part in the vibrant cultural life of the inter-war years that generated the theatrical influences we see in the Terezín/Theresienstadt scripts. In Bohemia and Moravia, they had every opportunity to participate in the cultural boom that followed the establishment of the new state. Austrian Jews' investment in cultural pursuits may have increased, as Michael Pollak suggests, during this period "when all political pursuits appeared to be in vain."[44]

In Austrian theater of the period immediately following the First World War, social and political critique did not play a prominent role.[45] Unlike the Berlin cabarets, which were marked by biting satire, Viennese cabarets indulged primarily in harmless humor and *Austattungsrevues*—comic and musical acts linked by a common theme with extravagant sets and costumes. Comic duo Karl Farkas and Fritz Grünbaum created a tremendously popular new form of musical revue that combined the visual spectacle of the *Austattungsrevue* with the verbal humor of the literary cabaret.

With the rise of Nazi Germany and Austrofascism, cabarets and revues became more pointed. Stella Kadmon's literary cabaret Dear Augustin (Der liebe Augustin) began to address the political situation with texts by anti-fascist writers, including Kurt Tucholsky and Erich Kästner. Rudolf Spitz's The Gooseberry (Die Stachelbeere) presented politically aggressive one-act plays and playlets. ABC, politically the sharpest among the cabarets, featured the works of authors like Jura Soyfer, who satirized the National Socialists and the Austrofascists. Unlike in Nazi Germany, where all criticism was repressed, censorship in Austria was neither as extreme nor as effective.[46] Theater artists developed great skill in

---

44 Michael Pollak, "Cultural Innovation and Social Identity in *fin-de-siècle* Vienna," in Ivar Oxaal, Michael Pollak, and Gerhard Botz (eds.), *Jews, Anti-Semitism, and Culture in Vienna* (New York: Routledge and Kegan Paul, 1987), pp. 59–74, see p. 71.

45 Jürgen Doll, *Theater im roten Wien. Vom sozialdemokratischen Agitprop zum dialektischen Theater Jura Soyfers* (Vienna, Cologne and Weimar: Böhlau, 1997).

46 Horst Jarka, "Einleitung," in Horst Jarka (ed.), *Jura Soyfer. Das Gesamtwerk* (Vienna, Munich and Zurich: Europaverlag, 1980), pp. 13–27, see p. 18.

hiding their critical views between the lines to avoid drawing the attention of the censor while still reaching their intended audience.

Specifically Jewish theater and cabaret thrived in Vienna and several theaters offered programs of melodrama, operettas, comedies, and revues. Yiddish-language theaters performed Zionist revues, and Oscar Teller and Victor Schlesinger founded a specifically Zionist cabaret. The Jewish Culture Theater (Jüdisches Kulturtheater) offered a contemporary and artistically ambitious program that included Yiddish classics.[47]

In Czechoslovakia, Czech-language theater embraced the influences of international artistic movements. For example, the directorial style of Karel Hugo Hilar, head of drama at the Czech National Theater, combined elements of expressionism and realism, and his productions, including stagings of works by Karel Čapek, won accolades across Europe.[48] In 1927, artists who were to have tremendous influence on Czech-language theatrical performance in Terezín/Theresienstadt burst onto the scene. Law students Jiří Voskovec and Jan Werich became overnight sensations with their *Vest Pocket Revue*, a series of short, satiric scenes with music, which opened in April 1927, and ran for over 200 performances.[49] As their style developed during the 1930s, the plots of their performances became more unified, but they maintained the original combination of literate good humor, commentary on local and international events, and jazz music by their legendary pianist and composer, Jaroslav Ježek. Especially popular were their improvised sequences delivered directly to the audience, the *forbiny* (from German *Vorbühne*, forestage), where they satirized, among other things, Czech nationalist chauvinism. Also in April 1927, young director E. F. Burian presented his first "voiceband" performance,

---

47 For an excellent description of Jewish theater in Vienna, see Brigitte Dalinger, *"Verloschene Sterne": Geschichte des jüdischen Theaters in Wien* (Vienna: Picus Verlag, 1998).

48 Jarka Burian, *Modern Czech Theatre: Reflector and Conscience of a Nation* (Iowa City: University of Iowa Press, 2000), pp. 24–8, 38.

49 Ibid., p. 41.

a striking choral form which blended complex recitation and non-verbal sounds with rhythmic, syncopated music.[50]

Czech theaters became increasingly politicized as Nazi Germany grew more powerful. Karel Čapek, who had concentrated on fiction rather than playwriting for 10 years, returned to the national stage in the late 1930s with two devastating plays foreshadowing the horrors of war: *The White Plague* (*Bílá nemoc*) and *The Mother* (*Matka*).[51] Voskovec and Werich, now running their own venue, the Liberated Theater (Osvobozené divadlo), performed a series of increasingly pointed yet optimistic satirical reviews. Their two final productions in 1937–38, *Heavy Barbara* (*Těžká Barbora*) and *The Eyesore* (*Pěst na oko*), played to packed houses, and reinforced audience morale with their faith in the strength of ordinary but united people.[52] Burian founded his own theater, D34, in the fall of 1933.[53] One of his most remarkable performances was *Military Service* (*Vojna*), an anti-war piece created from a montage of Czech folk texts, performed with songs and dances. In the spring of 1938, he started developing a new performance titled *Esther*. This work, based on the sympathetic portrayal of Jewish characters in a Czech-language folk play dating back to the eighteenth century, soon became politically dangerous.

German-language theater continued to thrive in Bohemia and Moravia after the First World War, especially in Prague, Brno/Brünn and in the Sudetenland. In the 1920s, there was little artistic cooperation between Czech-language and German-language theaters. Most exchanges took place internationally with other German-speaking countries and guest artists and troupes visited from Germany, Austria, and Switzerland. Since most provincial German-language theaters saw themselves as bastions of high culture, avant-garde performances were rarely imported. For

---

50 Burian, *Modern Czech Theatre*, p. 43.

51 *The White Plague* was staged in 1937 and *The Mother* in 1938, both at the National Theater in Prague.

52 Ibid., p. 51.

53 D34 stands for *divadlo* (theater) and the season in which the troupe was founded. The number was updated every year.

example, although troupes from Vienna performed contemporary scripts, they rarely used the latest methods of staging. Viennese cabaret artists like Farkas and Grünbaum, however, played in Czech cities, and brought the latest German-language comic styles with them. The New German Theater in Prague, founded in 1888, offered a rich program, their specialty being operas and operettas.

Specifically Jewish theater did not play as significant a cultural role in Bohemia and Moravia as it did in Vienna. Yiddish troupes from Vienna, Berlin, and Bucharest toured the larger cities, but a single traveling troupe based in Slovakia was the first and only Czechoslovak troupe playing in Yiddish during the interwar period.[54] A few German-language Jewish troupes were established, but they failed to gain a permanent foothold.[55]

After Hitler's rise to power in 1933, many German-Jewish artists and political dissidents sought refuge in Austria and Czechoslovakia. In Austria, these artists created a boom in the number of small cabarets in Vienna.[56] In Prague, the New German Theater was especially enriched by this influx of talent and became a center of democratic German-language culture. A few of the newly arrived artists formed their own anti-fascist troupes in Czechoslovakia; for example, Hedda Zinner's Studio 34 was heavily influenced by Burian's D34 and his voiceband recitation style. Politically oriented artists and their troupes from other countries also visited Czechoslovakia. Perhaps the best-known was Erika Mann's Swiss exile cabaret, The Peppermill (Die Pfeffermühle), which performed its antifascist programs in Czechoslovakia in 1935

---

54 Brigitte Dalinger, "Jiddisches Theater—Ein Grenzgänger zwischen den Sprachen und Kulturen," *Maske und Kothurn* 47(3–4) (2002): 89–100, see 92, 96.

55 The Young Jewish Stage of Brno (Jungjüdische Bühne Brünn), which identified itself as a "German-language literary theater with Zionism as a doctrine," remained open from 1929 to 1935. The Jewish Chamber Theater (Jüdischen Kammerspiele), established in Prague in 1935 and performing in German, lasted only a few months. See Ursula Stamberg, "Das Theaterleben der Jüdischen Bevölkerung Brünns," *Maske und Kothurn* 47(3–4) (2002): 67–81, see 78; and Dalinger, "Jiddisches Theater": 98.

56 According to laws of the time, theaters with fewer than 50 seats did not need a license.

and 1936.[57] The threat of National Socialism eventually led democratically minded Czech- and German-speaking artists to collaborate. The Club of Czech and German Stage Artists (Klub der tschechischen und deutschen Bühnenkünstler) was founded in Prague in 1936 and branches were established in Ostrava/Ostrau and Brno/Brünn. However, rising tensions between Czech and German speakers in Czechoslovakia became increasingly difficult to resolve as Hitler's power grew and as more and more German speakers in the border regions began to demand that the Sudetenland be annexed to Nazi Germany.

Austria and Czechoslovakia soon ceased to be a safe havens for Jewish artists. Austria was absorbed into the German Reich in the so-called *Anschluss* (annexation) on March 12, 1938. On September 30, 1938, representatives of England, France, and Italy signed the Munich Pact, yielding to Hitler's demand to link the Sudetenland to the Reich. On March 15, 1939, the German army invaded the remainder of Czech territory, and Bohemia and Moravia became a German-administered "Protectorate."[58] The occupation had begun.

Emigration was still possible after the *Anschluss* and from the Protectorate. There were approximately 206,000 Jews "by race" living in Austria in March 1938. By the end of November 1939, over 126,000 had emigrated, but the outbreak of war severely curtailed further opportunities to leave.[59] By June 1941, due to emigration and deportations, there were only 44,000 Jews left in Vienna. Almost half were over 60 years of age, and two-thirds were

---

57 Romana Bečvová, "'Beteiligt euch—es geht um eure Erde'. Erika Manns politisch-satirisches Kabarett 'Die Pfeffermühle' in der Tschechoslowakei," *Brücken: Germanistisches Jahrbuch Tschechien–Slowakei* 16 (2008): 229–50.

58 Czechoslovakia lost most of its Silesian territory when the Sudetenland was ceded to Nazi Germany. In March 1939, Slovakia became a nominally independent state and Subcarpathian Ruthenia became a Hungarian territory.

59 Nevertheless, another 24,500 managed to emigrate even during the war. See Botz, "The Dynamics of Persecution in Austria," p. 206.

women.[60] In March 1939, there were approximately 118,000 people in the Protectorate classified as Jews according to the Nazi racial laws; only 26,000 of them managed to emigrate before mass deportations began in the fall of 1941.[61] Those who remained represented a fairly normal distribution of age and gender.

THE TEREZÍN/THERESIENSTADT GHETTO, 1941–45

The Terezín/Theresienstadt ghetto served several functions in the Nazis' plans to exterminate the European Jews: as a transit camp, where Jews from several countries were gathered before being sent on to slave-labor and death camps; as a destination to which elderly and privileged Jews were deported; as a decimation camp, where thousands of prisoners died of "natural causes;" and as a "model ghetto" that the Nazis displayed to visitors from organizations such as the International Red Cross. The relative importance of these functions evolved over the course of the war, and changes in priorities affected all aspects of life in the ghetto, from the mortality rate to the cultural life.

The first prisoners in the Terezín/Theresienstadt ghetto were Jews from Bohemia and Moravia. In October 1941, representatives of the Prague Jewish Community, forced into negotiations with the Nazis, were made to suggest a location for a Jewish ghetto. Jewish leaders did not favor Terezín/Theresienstadt because it was far too small to hold the almost 80,000 Jews who remained in the Protectorate. However, when the Nazis selected Terezín/Theresienstadt from among various possibilities, the leaders hoped it would be a site where Jews could wait out the war, and believed Nazi assurances that they would be allowed to run it as a relatively independent Jewish town.[62]

---

60 Niklas, "... *die schönste Stadt der Welt*," p. 32.

61 Rothkirchen, "The Jews of Bohemia and Moravia," p. 59.

62 Ruth Bondy, *"Elder of the Jews": Jakob Edelstein of Theresienstadt* (New York: Grove Press, 1989), p. 241.

The precise factors that led the Nazis to select Terezín/ Theresienstadt are not known, but the site offered one obvious advantage: it was easy to guard. Terezín/Theresienstadt was established as a fortress complex in the late eighteenth century to defend what were then the northern borders of Austria against the Prussians. From the air, the complex looks like two towns, separated by the river Ohře/Eger, and each surrounded by massive, star-shaped fortress walls. The smaller of the two, called the Small Fortress, was already in use by the summer of 1940 as a Gestapo prison, mainly for political dissidents.[63] The Large Fortress, selected as the location for the ghetto, held a peacetime population of 7,000 to 8,000 soldiers and civilians. In the fall of 1941, thousands of Czech civilians were still living there.

PHASE I: IMPRISONMENT IN THE BARRACKS

The Prague Jewish Community, ordered to prepare Terezín/ Theresienstadt to house thousands of prisoners, sent transports of young men there on November 24 and December 4, 1941. The Nazis promised that those who had "volunteered" for these so-called AK I and AK II transports (from German *Aufbaukommando*, literally "building commando") would receive certain benefits (weekends at home, the transfer of their salaries to their families, etc.) which, however, never materialized. The core of the Jewish leadership of the ghetto, the so-called *Ältestenrat*, arrived with the transport of December 4. The *Ältestenrat* was headed by the *Judenältester*, Jakob Edelstein, the former deputy head of the Jewish community. As the members of AK I had already realized, the reality the leaders faced was markedly different from that the Nazis had promised. Rather than running an independent city, they would report to a Nazi commandant while taking on the

---

[63] Jews who were sent to the Small Fortress as political dissidents or for violating rules in the ghetto were treated much more harshly than the other prisoners. See, for example, the narrative of the Catholic priest Josef Miklík, *Vzpomínky z Terezína* (Prague: C.A.T., 1945).

overwhelming responsibility of day-to-day operations of the ghetto. This responsibility, however, gave Jewish leaders some room to maneuver in terms of trying to create a livable situation for the prisoners during what they all expected to be a very short war.

In the first period of the ghetto's history, which lasted from its founding till June 1942, only Jews from Bohemia and Moravia were deported to Terezín/Theresienstadt. During this period, the non-Jewish civilian population still lived in their homes but contact with them was strictly forbidden. The Jewish inmates were imprisoned in several large barracks. They left only for work, guarded by Czech gendarmes, former members of the Czechoslovak army whom the SS hired for most duties that involved direct contact with the prisoners. According to survivor testimony, most, but not all, gendarmes behaved decently towards them, treating them as fellow Czechs.

Shortly after the first transports arrived, a separate women's barracks was established and visits between men and women were forbidden. Families were divided; younger children and girls lived with their mothers, and boys aged 12 and older lived in the men's barracks. Separate children's rooms were soon established in the barracks and instructors from the Zionist youth movements were placed in charge of them.

The most shocking events to take place during this period were the executions carried out in January and February, 1942. Sixteen men who had violated prohibitions by trying to send letters to their families and buy food in the Terezín/Theresienstadt shops were sentenced to death by hanging. These were the only executions carried out in the ghetto itself. Later offenders were punished by being transferred to the Small Fortress, where most of them perished.

Jews of the Protectorate had hoped that they would at least stay in their own country, but in vain. Already in January 1942, transports began to leave Terezín/Theresienstadt. Their destination was not revealed. The prisoners only knew that the trains headed east. They lived in fear of these deportations to the unknown, even though, until the very end of the war, very few knew the full truth about extermination camps and gas chambers.[64]

The first cultural activities of the ghetto—simple and improvised programs of songs, poems, and sketches—began to take place in the barracks immediately after the first transports of prisoners arrived. Jewish leaders, apparently in an attempt to legalize these performances and ensure that prisoners would not be punished for them, requested and received permission from the Nazi commandant. They announced in the Daily Orders of December 28, 1941, that *Kamaradschaftsabende* (friendship evenings) could be held on the condition that the program be submitted in advance for approval.[65] As the cultural activities continued to expand, the Jewish leadership decided, in February 1942, to establish an administrative body to oversee them. They appointed as director of the new *Freizeitgestaltung* (Office for the Administration of Leisure Time) a young rabbi named Erich Weiner.[66]

PHASE II: CREATING THE "MODEL GHETTO"

After the last members of the civilian population left Terezín/Theresienstadt, the second phase of the ghetto's history began. On July 6, 1942, the barracks were opened, and the prisoners occupied the entire area inside the Large Fortress, except the buildings and spaces occupied by the SS.[67] The ghetto was guarded from the outside by the Czech gendarmes. Inside Terezín/Theresienstadt, the *Ghettowache*, a police force manned by the prisoners themselves, enforced rules and maintained order.

64 See, for example, the testimony of Rabbi Dr. Richard Feder, *Židovská tragedie: Dějství poslední* (Kolín: Lusk, 1947), pp. 103–4.

65 This order is quoted in Eva Šormová, *Divadlo v Terezíně 1941/1945* (Ustí nad Labem: Severoceské nakladatelství, 1973), p. 22.

66 Bondy, *"Elder of the Jews,"* p. 291. For an account written by Weiner himself, see *"Freizeitgestaltung* in Theresienstadt," pp. 209–17.

67 Fewer than 30 members of the SS were assigned to Terezín/Theresienstadt during the whole time of the ghetto's existence. See Tomáš Fedorovič, "Neue Erkenntnisse über die SSAngehörigen im Ghetto Theresienstadt," in Jaroslava Milotová, Michael Wögerbauer, and Anna Hájková (eds.), *Theresienstädter Studien und Dokumente 2006* (Prague: Sefer, 2007), pp. 234–50, see p. 236.

During the day, the prisoners were allowed to move about the town, but an evening curfew was strictly enforced. Men and women still lived separately, but visits were now allowed. Most children now lived in specially established children's homes in separate barracks. The education of Jewish children was formally banned, but their caretakers were supposed to keep them occupied with singing, games, crafts, and cultural activities. In practice, the cultural activities often constituted a curriculum that varied widely, based on the values of each instructor. As Ruth Bondy describes, "Every instructor educated his class (about forty children) in his image, and according to his world view: graduates of the Zionist youth movement did it in the spirit of Zionism; Communists looked toward a socialist revolution; Czech nationalists, toward love of the homeland."[68]

In the summer of 1942, the character of Terezín/ Theresienstadt changed again as Jews from other countries were deported to the ghetto. The first transport from Berlin arrived on June 2, 1942. Transports from German cities continued to arrive for months.[69] The basic composition of the population changed, in terms not only of nationality but also of age: the German-Jewish prisoners were substantially older than Czech-Jewish prisoners. Many of them had been told that Terezín/ Theresienstadt was a spa town where they could live out their days in comfort if they agreed to sign a housing contract that ceded all their property to the Reich. Almost all the Austrian Jews were deported from Vienna during a four-month period. From June 21 to October 10, 1942, 13 transports brought almost 14,000 prisoners; their average age was 69.[70]

Completely unprepared for the conditions in which they found themselves, the elderly German and Austrian Jews quickly

---

68 Bondy, *"Elder of the Jews,"* p. 310.

69 Karel Lagus and Josef Polák, *Město za mřížemi* (Prague: Naše vojsko, 1964), pp. 337–41.

70 After January 1943, a further 1,340 Austrian Jews were deported. See Niklas, *". . . die schönste Stadt der Welt,"* p. 90.

succumbed to exhaustion, hunger, illness, and despair. The mortality rate, which until that point had seldom exceeded 10 per day, increased drastically. Almost 4,000 prisoners died in the month of September 1942 alone, when the ghetto temporarily reached an unsustainable maximum population of almost 60,000 prisoners.[71] By the end of 1942, the rising mortality rate and further outgoing transports had reduced the population to an extremely overcrowded but sustainable level of between 40,000 and 50,000 prisoners. In January 1943, Dr. Paul Epstein from Berlin was appointed the new *Judenältester*. Edelstein and later Otto Zucker continued to represent Czech-Jewish interests as members of the *Ältestenrat*.

Although circumstances in the ghetto had stabilized somewhat by the end of 1942 and prisoners were allowed to move about freely in the town—which represented a vast improvement over confinement in the barracks—living conditions remained harsh. People were cramped into barracks and civilian homes, sleeping on roughly hewn wooden bunks, with only a small shelf for personal items. There was no privacy. Food, prepared by the "royalty" of the ghetto—the cooks—in several large kitchens, was distributed according to the prisoner's age and type of work (young people and those assigned to manual labor received increased rations). Lack of water was a grave problem. The capacity of the local waterworks, built to sustain a city of less than 10,000, could not meet the needs of a population four to five times that number. Showering was rationed by a ticket system; maintaining a basic level of hygiene was difficult; fleas, lice, and bedbugs plagued the prisoners and increased the danger of epidemics.

Tensions among the prisoners made the situation worse. For example, some of the Protectorate Jews resented the German and Austrian prisoners for overpopulating "their" ghetto; the newcomers resented Czech control of some of the more advantageous

---

71 Ludmila Chládková, *The Terezín Ghetto* (Prague: Naše vojsko, 1991), p. 48.

Freizeitgestaltung:

K/0	Leitung	Moritz Henschel
K/10	Administrative Leitung	Ratt.Dr. Weiner
K/11	Sekretariat	Dr. Hans Mautner
K/12	Programmbearbeitung	Anna Zelenka
K/13	Finanzgeb. u. Eintrittskart.	Dr. Georg Kohn
K/14	Bezirksarbeit	
K/15	Probenplan	Anna Zelenka
K/20	Technische Abteilung	Otto Spektor
K/21	Materialbeschaffung	Dr. Zd. Winter
K/22	Entwurf u. Dekoration	Architekt Franz Zelenka
K/23	Säleverwaltung	Dr. Friedner Hans
K/30	Theater	Kamill Hoffmann
K/31	Deutsches Theater	Curt Weisz
K/32	Tchechisches Theater	Gustav Schorsch
K/34	Kabarett	Kurt Gerron
K/35	Blockveranstaltungen	Myra Strauss
K/40	Musiksektion	Hans Krasa
K/41	Opern- u. Vokalmusik	Rafael Schächter
K/42	Instrumentalmusik	Gideon Klein
K/43	Kaffeehausmusik	Paul Libensky
K/44	Instrumentenverwaltg.	Paul Libensky
K/50	Vortragswesen	Dr. Franz Kahn
K/51	Allgemeine Vorträge	Prof. Dr. Emil Utitz
K/52	Jüdische Vorträge	Dr. Franz Kahn
K/53	Fremdsprachige Vorträge	Prof. Dr. Max Adler
K/54	Hebraika	Prof. Kestenbaum
K/55	Schach	Isidor Schorr
K/56	Frauenvorträge	Hana Steiner
K/60	Zentralbücherei	Prof. Dr. Emil Utitz
K/61	Allgemeine Abteilung	
K/62	Jüdische Abteilung	
K/63	Hebräische Abteilung	
K/64	Fachliteratur	
K/65	Bibliophile Abteilung	
K/70	Sportveranstaltungen	Dr. Zdeněk Winter
K/71	Fussball	Oka Hermann
K/72	Volleyball	Gustav Straschitz
K/73	Handball	Franz Kohn
K/74	Basketball	Rudolf Klein
K/75	Tischtennis	Kurt Löbl

IMAGE 1.1 **An organizational chart of the *Freizeitgestaltung* after June 1943. Divisions K/31–5 are German theater, Czech theater, cabaret, and the *Blockveranstaltungen*.**

Courtesy of the Terezín Memorial.

jobs, especially those associated with the food supply. The diversity of the ghetto increased further in 1943 when transports from Holland and Denmark began to arrive as well. Pre-war class tensions also carried over into the ghetto and were exacerbated by structures of privilege. Certain prisoners, for instance, were designated by the SS or by Jewish leaders as "prominent," and given preferential treatment, including better housing and increased rations.[72] Although many prisoners realized that both the national and class tensions were deliberately encouraged by the Nazis to keep them divided against each other, this realization was not enough to keep the tensions at bay.

Perhaps the most traumatic event during this phase of the ghetto's existence was the census. In November 1943, when irregularities were discovered in the population records, Edelstein was accused of hiding evidence of escapes. He was arrested and, on November 11, 1943, almost 40,000 people were made to march out of the ghetto onto a nearby field. They were forced to stand outside through the entire cold and damp day, not sure if they were to be counted or killed. Many prisoners died of exposure and of resulting illnesses in the weeks that followed.[73]

In spite of these hardships, Terezín/Theresienstadt cannot be classified among the most terrible extermination and slave-labor camps that the Nazis built. Although all adult prisoners were obligated to work and a small number of them were assigned to workshops manufacturing goods for the German war effort, most were occupied in jobs that supported the daily operations of the ghetto.

---

72 The "prominent" prisoners in the ghetto were divided into two groups. Group A was named by the SS; these were usually internationally known individuals or former German military officers and their families. Group B was named by the *Ältestenrat* and approved by the SS; most were professors and representatives of Jewish organizations. See Daniela Řepová, "Emil Utitz a Terezín," in Jaroslava Milotová and Anna Lorencová (eds.), *Terezínské studie a dokumenty 2003* (Prague: Sefer, 2003), pp. 169–212, see p. 184.

73 For details, see Bondy, *"Elder of the Jews,"* pp. 398–9, and H. G. Adler, *Theresienstadt: das Antlitz einer Zwangsgemeinschaft* (Göttingen: Wallstein, 2005), pp. 158–61.

Although over 33,000 prisoners died in the ghetto, there were no gas chambers. In the small crematorium outside the fortress walls their bodies were burned and their ashes placed in individual cardboard urns, which their loved ones hoped to take home after the war. The prisoners were not confronted in Terezín/Theresienstadt with the horror of mechanized mass murder—a horror that many of them faced after their deportation to other camps.

A slow improvement in living conditions was due in part to a new role assigned to the ghetto by the Nazi propaganda machine. In November 1942, the International Committee of the Red Cross, prompted by the World Jewish Congress, began requesting permission to inspect the concentration camps. After 466 Danish Jews were deported to Terezín/Theresienstadt in October 1943, Danish officials also asked to see the ghetto.[74] The Nazis realized that a carefully orchestrated visit could help them refute reports on the true situation in the camps. Berlin officials agreed to an inspection, but Terezín/Theresienstadt was first thoroughly prepared for its role as a "Jewish settlement area."[75]

The most fruitful months of the cultural life occurred during a period of relative stability in the ghetto, between November 1942 and September 1944.[76] Several "stores" had been opened in September 1942 that offered an extremely limited selection of goods and services. Nevertheless they made the ghetto seem slightly less prison-like.[77] In December 1942, a "coffeehouse" was established where prisoners, according to a ticket system, could sit for a few hours with a cup of chicory coffee and listen to music played by

---

74 Bondy, *"Elder of the Jews,"* pp. 340, 391.

75 The Nazis began to use this term in March 1944. See Anna Hyndráková, Raisa Machatková, and Jaroslava Milotová (eds.), *Acta Theresiania, sv. 1: Denní rozkazy Rady starších a Sdělení židovské samosprávy Terezín 1941–1945* (Prague: Sefer, 2003), pp. 448, 226ff.

76 Outgoing transports did not cease during this period. In May 1944, for instance, transports sent more than 7,500 prisoners to Auschwitz to ensure that Terezín did not look overpopulated.

77 See *Verschleißstellen* (glossary); Bondy, *"Elder of the Jews,"* pp. 324, 333; and Hyndráková et al., *Acta Theresiania*, p. 226.

IMAGE 1.2 **The census on November 11, 1943. By F. Bloch.**
Courtesy of Yad Vashem.

their fellow prisoners.[78] Now that public spaces had been established and the prisoners were no longer confined to their barracks, cultural undertakings took on a more public character as well.[79] They were allowed to function and, later in this period, even actively supported by the Nazis in accordance with their propaganda plans. However, they sprang, above all, from the needs of

78 Chládková, *Terezín Ghetto*, p. 48.

79 Bořivoj Srba, "Divadlo za mřížemi: Projevy české divadelní tvořivosti v pracovních, internačních a koncentračních táborech a věznicích nacistické Třetí říše," *Divadelní revue* 6(1) (1995): 9–27, see 11.

the prisoners themselves. A sample of the offerings for February 1943 provides an idea of the diversity of identities, loyalties, and affinities served by the *Freizeitgestaltung's* programming:

- **Concerts**: Jewish liturgical music, opera arias, *Journey though the Land of Music* (premiere), Raphael Schächter's Hebrew Choir (premiere)—20 performances altogether.

- **Operas**: *The Bartered Bride*, *Rigoletto* (premiere, the cultural department's anniversary performance), *The Marriage of Figaro* (premiere)—10 performances altogether.

- **Theater**: Wolker's *The Tomb* (premiere); a revue, *Youngsters not Admitted* (premiere); a cabaret within the framework of *Stolen Theater*; Cocteau's *The Human Voice*; opera evening; Thoren's *Cabaret with Skits*; evening of songs from Erben's *Flower Bouquet*; puppet theater; *Women's Dictatorship*—50 performances altogether.[80]

The theater offerings on this list, performed on various small stages around the ghetto, reveal the wide variety of the prisoner's national, linguistic, cultural, and even political affiliations. For example, the author of *The Tomb* (*Hrob*), Jiří Wolker (1900–24), was a Czech avant-garde writer who had been adopted by the communists as one of their own. *Youngsters not Admitted* (*Für Jugendliche Verboten*) was an evening of slightly racy comic songs and sketches in German; and the Stolen Theater (*Vyšlojzované divadlo*) was apparently named after the Liberated Theater of Voskovec and Werich.[81] *Flower Bouquet* (*Kytice*) by Karel Jaromír Erben (1811–70) was a Czech classic from the National Revival period, and *Women's Dictatorship* (*Diktatur der Frauen*) was a German-language three-act comedy from the early 1930s.[82]

---

80 Bondy, *"Elder of the Jews,"* p. 365.

81 Souvenir posters for *The Tomb* and for *Youngsters not Admitted* have been preserved. The Stolen Theater appears in a list of Czech-language works performed in the ghetto. See the Terezín Memorial, inv. nos. PT 4306, PT 3847, and PT 3862.

82 See the Terezín Memorial, inv. nos. PT 4304 and PT 3845.

The *Freizeitgestaltung* continued to expand; an undated organizational chart preserved in the Terezín Memorial lists more than 30 divisions, including German theater, Czech theater, cabaret, opera and vocal music, instrumental music, lectures in different languages, and chess and several sports, including soccer and table tennis.[83] In this period, the *Freizeitgestaltung* could officially employ artists and thus spare them from other forms of labor. In rare cases it even requested specific performers to be exempted from outgoing transports.[84] Its administrators scheduled the limited number of available performance and rehearsal spaces, distributed tickets, and submitted lists of works to the Nazis for censorship before performance. Performances also continued to take place in the barracks, outside of official channels.

A *Stadtverschönerung* (city beautification) in preparation for the Red Cross inspection was ordered to begin in December 1943. Throughout the spring of 1944 the renovation of the ghetto was carried out, mostly through the labor of the prisoners themselves.[85] The long-awaited visit of the commission, which included three international representatives—two Danish and one Swiss—took place on June 23, 1944. The visitors were accompanied by several SS officers, representatives from the Reich Ministry of International Affairs and from the German Red Cross. The only prisoner included in the contingent was *Judenältester* Epstein, who had received the title of "mayor" for the day and was only allowed to speak with the members of the commission in the presence of the SS. They followed a prepared path through Terezín/Theresienstadt with stops at the bakery, the bank, a performance of the children's opera *Brundibár*, and a few more sites of interest.[86] The members of the commission, in spite of certain doubts,

---

83 See the Terezín Memorial, inv. no. PT 3768.

84 See, for example, the "protection lists" and requests to remove individual artists and their families from scheduled transports in the Theresienstadt Collection, Yad Vashem, Jerusalem, file 0.64/23.

85 Chládková, *Terezín Ghetto*, p. 50.

86 Adler, *Theresienstadt*, pp. 172–8.

expressed their general approval of the standard of living in the ghetto. Dr. M. Rossel, the Swiss representative, expressed surprise in his official report over the long delay in granting the Red Cross request to visit Terezín/Theresienstadt, since there was clearly nothing to hide.[87]

Apparently inspired by the success of the visit, the Nazis created a "documentary" film about the ghetto. Prisoner Kurt Gerron, a well-known German-Jewish actor and director of the inter-war period, was ordered to direct it.[88] A partially edited version of the film, created from the footage shot in August and September 1944, has been preserved, and offers a last glimpse of hundreds of prisoners.

At the end of September 1944, the period of relative stability came abruptly to an end. A wave of transports from September 28 to October 28 carried away 18,000 people, including the majority of prisoners of productive working age and almost all the active participants in the cultural life of the ghetto. Epstein was arrested and executed, most members of the *Ältestenrat* were deported, and Rabbi Dr. Benjamin Murmelstein, a leader of the Viennese Jewish community, became the new *Judenältester*.

PHASE III: AFTER THE MASS TRANSPORTS

After these transports, the ghetto entered its last phase of existence. Only 11,000 prisoners remained, many of them elderly and ill. Those who were healthy and capable of work—mostly women—struggled to manage the most essential operations of the ghetto. The situation began to stabilize at the end of 1944. Incoming transports continued. Jews from Hungary and Slovakia arrived in

---

87 Bondy, *"Elder of the Jews,"* p. 439.

88 Karel Margry, "Das Konzentrationslager als Idylle: Theresienstadt: Ein Dokumentar-Film aus dem Jüdischen Siedlungsgebiet," in Fritz Bauer Institut (ed.), *Auschwitz. Geschichte, Rezeption und Wirkung: Jahrbuch 1996 zur Geschichte und Wirkung des Holocaust* (Frankfurt and New York: Campus, 1996), pp. 319–52.

the ghetto along with the last Czech, German, and Austrian Jews who had been protected until then for being married to "Aryans." Slowly, even the cultural life began to revive. It was clear that the war would end soon and all thoughts and hopes were pinned on that moment.

Nazi leaders, also aware of the impending defeat, negotiated the release of some of the prisoners to neutral countries. One thousand, two hundred were sent by train to Switzerland in February 1945, and the Danish Jews were released on April 15 to the Swedish Red Cross.[89] The ghetto, however, faced a last, terrible trial: on April 20, 1945, death marchers began to arrive in Terezín/Theresienstadt—starved and ill, narrating horrific accounts of their experiences. Some of the Terezín/Theresienstadt prisoners died just days before, or shortly after, the liberation, from illnesses they contracted while nursing these prisoners.

The last days of the ghetto were marked by chaotic events as the SS lost their power over the prisoners' lives and the Red Cross took over administration of Terezín/Theresienstadt. On May 3, 1945, the SS stopped trying to prevent escapes, and on May 4, a group of Czech doctors and nurses arrived to help battle the typhus epidemic that had broken out after the arrival of the death marchers. The next day the last of the SS officers left. On May 8, Soviet tanks, on their way to Prague, went through Terezín/Theresienstadt. The ghetto was liberated.[90] Two days later the Soviets took control and began repatriating the prisoners, but when the typhus epidemic could not be brought under control, they imposed a two-week quarantine. Repatriation resumed at the end of May. The last of the former prisoners left Terezín/Theresienstadt in August 1945.[91]

---

89 For an account of the Swiss transport see Vojtěch Blodig, "Poslední fáze ve vývoji terezínského ghetta," in Vojtěch Blodig and Miroslav Karný (eds.), *Terezín v konečném řešení židovské otázky* (Prague: Logos, 1992), pp. 182–90, see pp. 185–6.

90 Ibid., p. 190.

91 Chládková, *Terezín Ghetto*, p. 53.

Of the approximately 15,000 Austrian Jews deported to Terezín/
Theresienstadt, only about 1,700 survived in the ghetto or in other
camps.[92] Of the approximately 74,000 Jews deported from
Bohemia and Moravia, about 7,000 were liberated in the ghetto;
of those who were deported "to the east," that is, to various concentration and slave-labor camps, only about 3,000 returned.[93]

92 Niklas, ". . . die schönste Stadt der Welt," p. 150.

93 Of the 7,000 Czech Jews liberated in the ghetto, just over half had been
deported in the last months of the war. See Rothkirchen, "The Jews of Bohemia
and Moravia," pp. 59–60.

IVAN KLÍMA

It is significant that people become most aware of the meaning of art in moments of crisis; in moments when they come face to face with death; when they become fully aware of the irreversibility of fate. Terezín was unquestionably a place on the very border between life and death—yet people sang, recited, and performed theater there.

As a young spectator (I was 12 or 13 years old) I experienced several performances in the ghetto. I saw puppet shows and even operas: *The Bartered Bride* and Krása's *Brundibár*.[1] To this day I recall the strange atmosphere that reigned during those performances: an atmosphere full of excitement, emotion, joy, and tears. In Terezín, artists managed to stage several operas and plays. If my memory does not deceive me, the plays that were staged included *The Bear* by Chekhov, *The Marriage* by Gogol, and *Camel through a Needle's Eye by* František Langer (he escaped the fate of deportation to Terezín because he left in time for Britain, where he actively took part in our resistance movement).[2] On stage, verses by Wolker, Hrubín, and Erben were recited.[3] In December 1941, my mother and I found ourselves living in a room with 30 women. I remember how, sometimes in the evening, they sang songs.

IMAGE 2.1 *(facing page)* **A souvenir poster for** *Brundibár*, **Hans Krása's opera for children, April 1944. By Walter Heimann.**

Courtesy of the Terezín Memorial.

1 Bedřich Smetana's *The Bartered Bride* (*Prodaná nevěsta*) is considered by many to be the Czech national opera. The children's opera *Brundibár* was written by Hans Krása and Adolf Hoffmeister in 1938. See Joža Karas, *Music in Terezín: 1941–1945* (New York: Beaufort Books, 1990), pp. 24, 93–102.

2 The Czech titles are *Medvěd*, *Ženitba*, and *Velbloud uchem jehly*. Souvenir posters for these performances have been preserved. See the Terezín Memorial, inv. nos. PT 3791, PT 4302, and PT 4300.

3 The works of Czech poets Karel Jaromír Erben (1811–70), Jiří Wolker (1900–24), and František Hrubín (1910–71) had special meaning for the Terezín/Theresienstadt prisoners. Erben was a beloved writer from the Czech National Revival period; Wolker and Hrubín were communists in an era when many young intellectuals felt that communism was the only antidote to fascism.

HANS KRÁSA
FLAŠINETÁŘ
Brundibár
Walter Freund
Theresienstadt
duben 1944
DĚTSKÁ OPERA O 2 OBRAZECH
Hudebně nastudoval
A ŘÍDÍ: RUDOLF FREUDENFELD
Režie a scéna: Fr. Zelenka
TANEČNÍ SPOLUPRÁCE KAMILA ROSENBAUMOVÁ
Zpívají, hrají a tančí
DĚTI TEREZÍNSKÝCH DĚTSKÝCH ÚTULKŮ

Sometimes songs by Voskovec and Werich, sometimes folk songs or Jewish songs.[4] As they sang, someone always stood guard in the hallway, to warn the others if an SS officer approached. They sang, even though it was difficult for the women to bring themselves to sing. They sang because it was a demonstration of free life in a hopelessly unfree environment. For the same reasons, not long after, theatrical performance and even cabarets were born.

A person wonders why the rich cultural activities were more or less tolerated, or even openly allowed, during certain periods. It can be explained by the unique position of Terezín as a ghetto that was not designated explicitly as a site of extermination. (Nevertheless, hundreds of people died there every day.) Apparently the Nazis questioned from the beginning whether they should murder all Jews without exception, or save some individuals (for example, those who were awarded decorations in the First World War, members of the nobility or world-renowned individuals) at least temporarily. As the end of the war approached and the magnitude of the disaster for the Nazis became clear, some of the highly placed executors of the Final Solution began to speculate that they could exchange the lives of the survivors for money or for their own survival. For the same reason, in 1944, they allowed a commission of the International Committee of the Red Cross to visit Terezín in order to show them how well the Jews were doing in the ghetto. During that period they actively encouraged cultural activities. They even built an outdoor pavilion on the square for an orchestra that was supposed to play the music of another "racially inferior" people—jazz.

It is possible to explain the fact that the Nazis allowed things as exceptional as theater, opera, and cabaret in a concentration camp in yet another way. During the whole period, they tried to conceal their murderous intentions from the world as well as from the prisoners themselves. The fact that they allowed the prisoners to perform—that, there in the ghetto, they could even indulge in cultural activities—strengthened the impression that they were really only trying to separate the Jews from the rest of society.

---

4 See Voskovec and Werich (glossary).

IMAGE 2.2 **Women's quarters. By F. Bloch.**
Courtesy of the Jewish Museum in Prague.

Finally, even a third explanation remains. The Nazis knew well the dimensions of the Final Solution. They knew that all the interned were essentially condemned to death. Generously, and even somewhat sadistically, they allowed them to have a little fun before they were killed.

I mentioned that artists managed to stage several, mostly classic, plays. The majority were played in a hall in the Magdeburg barracks and tickets were not easy to obtain.[5]

Life in Terezín diverged utterly from the norms of society and plunged the prisoners into a situation for which no one was

[5] For a comic account of trying to obtain a ticket, see Hans Hofer's text "The Theater Ticket" in this volume.

prepared. It was life in the anteroom to the execution chamber, but thanks to news of the first defeats of the German army, hope flickered that everything would turn out well, that Hitler and his murderous mania would be overcome in a matter of weeks. It was a life in which it was hard to preserve the habits and moral norms according to which people had behaved until so recently. It was a life where one old potato or a piece of moldy bread was worth its weight in gold, where even honest people sometimes had to steal. But it was also a life where children went voluntarily to their deaths so that their parents would not die abandoned. It was a life that had lost its normal dimensions, where good and evil had lost their clear-cut forms.

All this called for original creations which would escape this strange, grimly bizarre situation yet, at the same time, portray it.

In Terezín, in addition to visual artists, actors, directors, singers, and musicians there were also many writers. Not all were capable of working in these difficult conditions, and some stayed there for such a short time that they were not able to create anything. At the same time, not everything that emerged was preserved. We can assume that most of what was written has been lost irretrievably along with its creators, of whom only a few survived.

While reading these preserved dramatic texts we must take into account that even the most veiled attempt to talk about the reality of life in Terezín, if discovered, was punishable by deportation to Auschwitz or transfer to the Small Fortress, which was, in essence, a death sentence.

I knew four visual artists: Ungar, Fritta and Haas, and the Dutch graphic artist Spier.[6] All drew and painted dozens of oppressive scenes from the lives of the interned. When the SS discovered the works of the first three they immediately took them away with their families—some to Auschwitz, some to the Small

IMAGE 2.3 (*facing page*) **Kurt Gerron's cabaret, Carousel. By F. Bloch.**
Courtesy of the Terezín Memorial.

6 For an account by Lev (né Leo) Haas himself, see "The Affair of the Painters of Terezín," in František Ehrmann, Ota Heitlinger, and Rudolf Iltis (eds.), *Terezín* (Prague: Council of Jewish Communities in the Czech Lands, 1965), pp. 157–61.

Fortress. Only Lev Haas survived and, miraculously, Fritta's son, little Thomas Fritta. Nevertheless, some of their drawings were hidden under the floorboards and preserved. To this day they bear witness to the suffering of people robbed of their freedom and dignity.

It is no different with the dramatic works. Since they were staged and performed for hundreds of spectators, one could assume that the jailors would find out about the content. Efforts to create a kind of literary cabaret, samples of which are included in this anthology, oscillated between attempts to portray reality and the desire to make light of it with a smile. The texts usually focused on apparently less meaningful details of life. For example, the story of the thermos taken away from its owner again and again illustrates on a small scale the complete injustice to which all Terezín inhabitants were subjected.[7] Other verses and short scenes remind us of what we, in the days of communist Czechoslovakia, called "communal criticism."[8] Authors made fun of the Jewish guards or the self-government, of the well-fed cooks, and of all the strange aspects of the new hierarchy.

In *Laugh with Us: The Second Czech Cabaret,* for example, we find a mention of an engagement swindler:

P. HORPATZKY. What was it that time, some kind of bigamy, wasn't it?

F. PORGES. Bigamy, that wasn't even worth talking about. That villain falsely claimed to a girl that he was a cook, and he was only a bank manager.

The cabaret artists often skirted the very edge of the possible, satirizing the stupidity or, more precisely, the criminality of the Nuremberg laws, the wearing of the Star of David, and so on.

---

7 See Hans Hofer's "The Thermos" in this volume, pp. 381–3.

8 Conscientious communists were expected to criticize themselves and their comrades in order to "exorcise all lingering demons of bourgeois thought." See Marci Shore, "Engineering in the Age of Innocence," *East European Politics and Societies* 12(3) (1998): 397–443, see 402.

Any mention of those truly guilty for the whole terrible situation, of the real criminals in SS uniforms, was unimaginable. Nevertheless, it was precisely cabaret that enjoyed the greatest interest and response among the interned. In the end, everyone knew who was truly guilty; it was not necessary to mention them. At the same time, mentions of the dishonest or egotistical behavior of their own people or the senselessness of daily life in Terezín afforded the prisoners a certain sense of satisfaction.

The works that, with the perspective of time, appear to be the deepest and most artistically remarkable are the ones which at first glance appear to speak of a completely different situation, of a different reality, but, at the same time, seek to express the despair of solitude in a world where death reigned.

I have in mind the remarkable one-act play by the young native of Teplice, Georg Kafka. Inspired by the myth of Orpheus and Eurydice, it is a poetic representation of the fate of its creator, his heart broken by death:

ALKAIOS. Why do you, Orpheus, long so much for death?

ORPHEUS. I've seen our first creations fall to ruins

What we've of late acquired, it slips away

OLD SHEPHERD. Yes, downward leads the staircase of our hours . . .

The dramatic poem ends with the death of the singer. However, in the last lines, as his friends lament over the dying Orpheus, the author raises the hope that the work will survive even the death of the poet. Georg Kafka himself was murdered at the age of 23.

Current concerns inspired yet another excellent work: the one-act play by Eliáš and Stein, *The Smoke of Home*. The authors set the play in the last days of the Thirty Years War. Three noblemen and a priest languish in a prison at Marburg castle in Hessen, forgotten by all. They dream of their homes, of the loved ones to whom they believe they will return, of life after the war which, from their perspective in prison, appears infinitely happy. When the possibility arises that two of them might be freed, a savage battle ensues in the cell over which two will have the privilege, the limitless joy, of returning home.

The play ends with an unexpected twist. The prisoners find out that the homes they dream of no longer exist. The war has destroyed everything—nothing, nothing at all, remains. There is nowhere—no one—for them to return to:

That is your smoke of home today! You want to go home? Fools! The home you left is in the past, buried in the abyss of time! There's a different world out there—beyond these walls! Do you hear? A different world!

At the very end of the play the news arrives that the war has ended; the long-awaited era of peace has finally dawned. The gates of the prison open but the four prisoners, as the authors indicate, remain seated, motionless.

This was a brave—and, unfortunately, even prescient—representation of what was actually happening in the world "beyond those walls." It contrasted painfully with the rampant and tragically unwarranted optimism that ruled among the prisoners, an optimism that undoubtedly helped them to bear the oppressive living conditions. According to survivors, the play was never staged because of this incisive but pessimistic view, even though it belongs among the best artistic creations that have survived Terezín.

In its mosaic-like nature, this anthology, which brings together serious and comic texts, couplets, songs, puppet plays, and even children's work, represents a unique view into the strange and admirable theater activities in the Terezín camp. Since many details of the life of the interned that are mentioned in the dialogues and songs would be difficult to understand today, the editor has glossed them with thorough notes and explanations. She has also managed to gather the most important biographical data about the authors and actors. The anthology deserves recognition as an important source regarding the cultural life of Terezín/Theresienstadt, which arose in spite of the difficult living conditions in the ghetto and allowed several admirable dramatic works to emerge.

PART 1

CZECH-LANGUAGE TEXTS

FELIX PROKEŠ,
VÍTĚZSLAV "PIDLA" HORPATZKY,
PAVEL STRÁNSKÝ,
KURT EGERER

RADIO SHOW

INTRODUCTION

In the summer of 2005, Zdeněk Prokeš generously granted me access to a small private collection of previously unpublished sketches, sheet music, and poems written and performed in Terezín/Theresienstadt. They were collected by his father, Dr. Felix Prokeš (né Porges), who co-authored and composed several of the works and was active in both the Czech-language and German-language cultural life of the ghetto. Two full-length Czech-language works, *Radio Show* and *Laugh with Us: The Second Czech Cabaret*, as well as several previously unknown German-language verses by cabaret artists Dr. Leo Strauss and Myra Strauss-Gruhenberg, are included in this volume. The Czech-language works were performed in late December 1942 and in the spring and summer of 1944 respectively, dates corresponding to the beginning and the end of the most fruitful period of the ghetto's cultural life.

THE AUTHORS

According to surviving lyricist and co-author Pavel Stránský, *Radio Show*[1] was written and performed by a group of young men who worked together in Block A IV, the building where the ghetto bakery and main provisions storehouses were located. They were employed in various jobs associated with the ghetto's food supply. For example, Stránský's work group, composed of about 20 men and supervised by Leo Popper, unloaded deliveries of flour and other supplies.[2]

IMAGE 3.1 (*page 45*) **The ghetto as a set design, probably for the operetta *Girl of the Ghetto*. By Adolf Aussenberg.**
Courtesy of the Terezín Memorial.

IMAGE 3.2 (*facing page*) **Interior courtyard of Block A IV, where the ghetto bakery and central provisions storehouses were located. By A. Berlinger.**
Courtesy of Yad Vashem.

---

1 I have supplied this title; there was none on the original manuscript.
2 Pavel Stránský, interview with Lisa Peschel, April 23, 2008.

According to Zdeněk Prokeš and his brothers Jan and Miroslav, their father was avidly interested in theater even as a student. However, he earned his doctorate in law. He finished his studies in Prague in 1936 and decided to attend officer-training school. On April 1, 1938, he became a member of the Union of Czechoslovak Officers but the signing of the Munich Pact on September 30, 1938, and the subsequent demobilization of the army spelled the end of his military career. Three years later, in December 1941, he was deported to the Terezín/Theresienstadt ghetto with other young Czech-Jewish workers on transport J (also known as AK II). There he was assigned to an important administrative position in the central provisions office. Because this job was critical to the ghetto's food supply, he was protected from deportation and remained in Terezín/Theresienstadt until the end of the war. He was able to preserve and bring home his entire collection of texts.

Vítěslav "Pidla" Horpatzky arrived with the same transport. He and Prokeš apparently met soon after their arrival in the ghetto, and, a year later, performed together in *Radio Show*. Their collaboration continued and, in the spring and summer of 1944, they wrote and performed

IMAGE 3.3 **Military ID of Felix Prokeš (né Porges), April 1938.**
Courtesy of Jan, Miroslav, and Zdeněk Prokeš.

IMAGE 3.4 (*left*) **Vítězslav Horpatzky in the late 1930s.** *Courtesy of the National Archives of the Czech Republic.*
IMAGE 3.5 (*center*) **Pavel Stránský in the 1930s.** *Courtesy of Pavel Stránský.*
IMAGE 3.6 (*right*) **Pavel Stránský's wedding, 1945.** *Courtesy of Pavel Stránský.*

together in *Laugh with Us: The Second Czech Cabaret*. Horpatzky was deported from Terezín/Theresienstadt to Auschwitz in the mass transports of fall 1944. He did not survive. His wife Anna, who worked in the ghetto's pharmacy, remained in Terezín/Theresienstadt until the end of the war and remarried later. According to her daughter, Eva Hirschová, Anna vividly remembered her first husband's sense of humor.[3]

Pavel Stránský, who wrote poems, song lyrics, and a few scenes for *Radio Show*, also arrived in Terezín/Theresienstadt with transport J. Although his lyrics were featured in *Laugh with Us*, he did not take part in the performance. In December 1943, he was deported to the so-called family camp in Auschwitz-Birkenau.[4] He was selected for labor in July 1944 and survived several months in Schwarzheide. In April 1945, a forced march from Schwarzheide began. The surviving prisoners reached their destination, Terezín/Theresienstadt, on the night of

3 Eva Hirschová, interview with Lisa Peschel, July 7, 2009.
4 For an account of the family camp by a survivor see Bondy, *"Elder of the Jews,"* pp. 405–47.

May 7 and 8, 1945. Stránský now lives in Prague and has two sons and four grandchildren.[5]

Little is known about Kurt Egerer (see biographical information below). He is credited with authoring the scene "Fairy Tale," a satirical history of the ghetto inspired by *Snow White and the Seven Dwarfs*.

THE SCRIPT

Radio Show consists of a loose collection of scenes recreating the broadcasts of pre-war radio station Prague 1.[6] A full outline of the performance was preserved, which established the order of the scenes. Fortunately, all the numbers listed and even the lyrics and sheet music for the original songs were found in the collection, along with three versions of the list of participants.

As Horpatzky remarks during the introduction to the performance, the show was written to mark the one-year anniversary of the group's work together in Block A IV. However, they chose an unusual way to commemorate their time in the ghetto: the performers took the audience five years back in time, to December 27, 1937. They present news broadcasts on events of the 1930s, favorite songs of the inter-war period, sports commentary based on a famous 1934 soccer match, and more scenes that recreate in great detail the social and cultural environment of 1930s Czechoslovakia. Nevertheless, in many scenes that are apparently about the pre-war past, the prisoners' Terezín/ Theresienstadt present is allegorically represented. Another thread weaves its way through almost all the scenes: veiled commentary on the state of the war, which reveals how much the prisoners knew about the international events that were to determine their fate.

---

5 See Stránský's autobiography, *As Messengers for the Victims: From Theresienstadt to Theresienstadt, with a Stop in Auschwitz-Birkenau and Schwarzheide* (Benjamin M. Block trans.) (Prague: Rekan, 2000).

6 Prague 1 was the flagship station of the Radiojournal, the inter-war network of Czechoslovak radio stations. In 1945, it was renamed Czechoslovak Radio (Československý rozhlas).

The participants in the cabaret used various nicknames and character names in addition to their real names.[7] In the following list I have tried to identify the participants, with the help of Pavel Stránský, by matching the names provided in the outline, the individual sketches, and the three lists of participants with records in the database of the Institute of the Terezín Initiative. Several of the participants arrived with transport J on December 4, 1941, and thus were among those marking a year of working together in the ghetto.

THE AUTHORS

MANUEL CHEBSKÝ, according to Stránský, was the nickname of **KURT EGERER** (Eger is the German name for the Bohemian town of Cheb). The name Manuel may be a comic reference to Egerer's profession. He owned a small business manufacturing men's ties in Prague that was located just a few blocks away from a much larger and more prestigious business: the well-known ladies' hat shop owned by Emanuel Egerer.[8] Egerer was born on July 2, 1912, and was deported from Prague to Terezín/Theresienstadt on December 4, 1941. On December 18, 1943 he was deported to Auschwitz. He survived.

VÍTĚZSLAV "PIDLA" HORPATZKY (also written as **HORPACZKÝ** or **HORPATSKY**) appears in the script as **PIDLOVSKÝ**. He was born on February 11, 1904 and was deported from Prague to Terezín/Theresienstadt on December 4, 1941. He was deported to Auschwitz on October 28, 1944. He perished.

DR. FELIX PROKEŠ (né **PORGES**) also appears in the script and on the sheet music as **JAROSLAV FELIX**. He was born on February 1, 1913, and was deported from Prague to Terezín/Theresienstadt on December 4, 1941. He was liberated in the ghetto. He died on January 15, 1982.

---

7 Nicknames were often formed by translating German names directly into Czech. For example, Fischer was translated into Rybář; both mean "fisherman."

8 In the Prague telephone directory from 1940, the businesses are listed as "Egerer and Masárek, tie factory, Na Příkopě 20," and "Egerer, Emanuel Jr., ladies' hat shop, Na Můstku 9."

PAVEL STRÁNSKÝ also appears in the script as **PAVEL JENÍK**. He was born on February 20, 1921, and was deported from Prague to Terezín/Theresienstadt on December 4, 1941. On December 18, 1943 he was deported to Auschwitz. He survived and now lives in Prague.

THE ACTORS AND THE OTHER PARTICIPANTS

ABELES is also called **SLÁVEK** and plays the roles of Rákos and Uncle Miloš. If the nickname Slávek derives from his real first name he may have been **VÍTĚZSLAV ABELES**. Born on June 1, 1920, he was deported from Plzeň/Pilsen to Terezín/Theresienstadt on January 22, 1942, and from there to Auschwitz on February 1, 1943. He survived and was liberated at Flossenbürg. After the war, he changed his name to **SKALSKÝ**.

A. FISCHER also appears as **ARNOŠT RYBÁŘ** (the literal translation of his surname into Czech). The database of the Institute of the Terezín Initiative lists 58 men named A. Fischer and 18 named Arnošt Fischer, three of whom arrived with transport J.

JOSEF FISCHER also appears as **JOSEF RYBÁŘ**. The database of the Institute of the Terezín Initiative lists 28 men named Josef Fischer. None of them arrived with transport J.

GÜNTER FÜRTH is also called Frio and plays the role of Alois Mazanec. The database of the Institute of the Terezín Initiative lists 13 men with the first name Günter and 50 with the surname Fürth, but no Günter Fürth.

KERNMAIEROVÁ-GRABOVÁ, who sang in several performances in the ghetto, is identified in most documents as **HEDDA GRAB-KERNMAYER** (variations such as **HEDVÍKA GRABOVÁ** and **HEDVÍKA KERNMAYEROVÁ** also appear). She was born on August 6, 1899, deported from Prague to Terezín/Theresienstadt on December 17, 1941, and was liberated in the ghetto.

HERRMANN appears with the group The Guinea Pigs. In the second list of participants, he is identified as **ZDENĚK HERRMANN**. The database of the Institute of the Terezín Initiative lists three Zdeněk Herrmanns who were in the ghetto in December 1942, one of whom arrived with transport J. He was born in 1919, deported on December 4, 1941, from Prague to Terezín/Theresienstadt, and transferred to the Gestapo in the Small Fortress on December 20, 1943. He perished.

HOCHNER is identified in a sketch as "**INSPECTOR RUDOLF**." The database of the Institute of the Terezín Initiative lists only one Rudolf Hochner who was in the ghetto in December 1942. He was born on May 28, 1902, deported on December 4, 1941 from Prague to Terezín/ Theresienstadt, and from there to Auschwitz on October 16, 1944. He perished.

MASÁREK also appears in the script as **DR. ERNA**; in the database he appears as **DR. ARNOŠT MASÁREK** (Arnošt is the Czech equivalent of the German name Ernst). He was born on September 1, 1910, deported from Prague to Terezín/Theresienstadt on December 4, 1941, and to Auschwitz on October 28, 1944. He was liberated in Auschwitz.

J. PICK appears with the group The Guinea Pigs. In the second list of participants his first name is given as **JIRKA** (**JIŘÍ**). There are 21 Jiří Picks in the database of the Institute of the Terezín Initiative, but only one who was deported on transport J and was still in the ghetto in December 1942. He was born on May 29, 1903, deported from Prague to Terezín/ Theresienstadt on December 4, 1941, and to Auschwitz on October 16, 1944. He was liberated in Waldenburg.

JIŘÍ POPPER appears in the script as **JIŘÍ VRCHLABSKÝ**. The database of the Institute of the Terezín Initiative includes 14 Jiří Poppers, but only one arrived with transport J. He was born on December 20, 1908, deported from Prague to Terezín/Theresienstadt on December 4, 1941, and to Auschwitz on May 18, 1944. He perished.

LEO POPPER appears in the script as Lepo and as **FRIDOLÍN KŘEČEK**. Only one Leo Popper arrived with transport J. He was born on May 7, 1908, deported from Prague to Terezín/Theresienstadt on December 4, 1941, and to Auschwitz on September 6, 1943. He perished.

SCHÄCHTER is **RAFAEL SCHÄCHTER**, a well-known conductor in the ghetto. He was born on May 27, 1905, deported from Prague to Terezín/ Theresienstadt on November 30, 1941, and to Auschwitz on October 16, 1944. He perished.

TERNER appears in the script as **PURŠL**, apparently the Czech spelling of the German nickname Burschl or Bursche (meaning "fellow," "lad," "youngster"). There are no clues to his real name in the script, but Pavel Stránský recalled that Puršl was the nickname of **ERICH TERNER**.

Terner was born on June 2, 1921, deported from Prague to Terezín/ Theresienstadt on December 4, 1941, and to Auschwitz on September 6, 1943. He survived.

WEISSKOPF appears in the script as **POLDA BĚLOHLÁVEK** (the literal translation of his surname into Czech) and plays the role of Brázda. According to Stránský this was **LEOPOLD WEISSKOPF**. He was born on December 1, 1912, deported from Plzeň/Pilsen to Terezín/ Theresienstadt on January 22, 1942, and to Auschwitz on December 18, 1943. He survived and changed his name to **LEOPOLD MAREK**.

FRANTIŠEK WEISSENSTEIN sang in *Radio Show* and also in *Laugh with Us*. He was born on February 15, 1899, was deported from Prague to Terezín/Theresienstadt on November 30, 1941 and on September 28, 1944, to Auschwitz. He perished.

THE ASSISTANTS AND THE GUESTS

MRS. NEUBRUNNOVÁ. The only woman by this name in Terezín/ Theresienstadt in December 1942 was **THERESE NEUBRUNN**. She was born on June 3, 1898, and was deported from Prague to Terezín/ Theresienstadt on July 30, 1942, and to Auschwitz on October 12, 1944. She perished.

MRS. SCHÖNBAUMOVÁ. The database of the Institute of the Terezín Initiative indicates four women with this name in the ghetto in December 1942.

MRS. KLEINOVÁ. The database of the Institute of the Terezín Initiative indicates 385 women with this name in the ghetto in December 1942.

BULLATÁ. The only woman with a similar name in the ghetto in December 1942 was **GERTRUDA BULLATY**. She was born on May 19, 1912, and deported from Prague to Terezín/Theresienstadt on September 8, 1942. She was liberated in the ghetto.

MRS. NEUMANNOVÁ. The database of the Institute of the Terezín Initiative indicates 350 women with this name in the ghetto in December 1942.

OSKAR, **MARTÍNEK** and **ŽEŽULKA**. It has not been possible to identify Oskar and Martínek. According to Pavel Stránský, Žežulka (an antiquated Czech word for "cuckoo") was his cousin **JIŘÍ FLUSSER**. He was born on July 26, 1923, deported from Prague to Terezín/Theresienstadt on December 4, 1941, and to Auschwitz on September 6, 1943. He perished.

RADIO SHOW

I. INTRODUCTION

Emcee: Vítězslav Horpatzky
Organizer: Felix Porges
Props: Microphone, "On Air" sign, Red lightbulb

EMCEE. Dear spectators, after working here together for more than a year, we meet in this space for the first time for half a day of entertainment, to which I most cordially welcome you all, and extend a special welcome to our dear guests. I have intentionally called this "half a day of entertainment," and not "celebration," as there is nothing to celebrate.

I ask you in advance not to be too critical, since this is going to be pure improvisation. In contrast to most programs here, which take their cues from the local environment, we have tried to do something different, although we know this will be more difficult. Our program is meant to be original, and in this way we want to remind you of your former normal life—that is, of the time before Terezín. We have deliberately eliminated all Terezín terms, and any requests for refunds on this account will be politely rejected out of hand.

We want to take you back five years to a time when, for example, the word *Schleuse* meant a sluice. Therefore, we cannot say in our program today that Mr. Vocásek sluiced several potatoes and, even though he is acquainted with the *Judenältester*, he has to report to the Ústí sluice.[9] At that time, you probably would not have understood.

So that's the kind of cabaret revue this will *not* be. But what kind *will* it be? I've been standing here talking forever.

---

9 The *Schleuse* (see glossary) was originally located in the Ústí barracks.

The audience must be getting impatient because they certainly didn't come to hear me lecture.

So I'd like to ask one of the organizers, initiators, authors, directors to tell me: What should I announce as the first number of the program?

(*Organizer enters.*)

So here he is. Tell me, my dear colleague, how should we start?[10] Have you taken care of the stage, the sets, the costumes? Where are the stage managers, the prompter, the prompter's box, the lighting team, the curtain operators, the extras, the stagehands? You can't just invite the audience then send me out on stage: "Now, do what you can." Is the audience going to wait for three weeks while you paint a rural countryside or a castle garden or whatever set you need for the play? How did you think this was going to work? In other shows the emcee has such an easy job; he tells a joke ("Two Jews meet . . ."),[11] announces a number, tells another joke, the audience applauds, or they say, "Well, that was crap!" But what about me? You leave me hanging up here, completely open to ridicule; what do I look like in front of all these people? For the measly two kgs of rice that I get from this storehouse once a week, I have to make a fool of myself![12] So, please tell me what I'm supposed to announce, or else I'm going home.

ORGANIZER. Don't get upset. You don't need to announce anything. You don't need to tell any jokes. Anyway, everybody has heard all of your jokes fifty times over. Forget about the props, the stage crew. I have another idea: let's listen to the radio.

---

10 This address (in Czech, *pane kolego*) was typical of the dialogues of Voskovec and Werich (see glossary).

11 In the original Czech-language script the joke is in German ("*Zwei Juden treffen sich . . .*").

12 Rice was apparently not part of the prisoners' rations. See Adler, *Theresienstadt*, pp. 344–50.

EMCEE. You've lost your mind. Radio—here? This isn't about looking foolish anymore—this is about jail time. What would we be allowed to listen to here? Maybe even . . .[13]

ORGANIZER. No, no, you don't understand. I remember hearing you promise the audience, just a moment ago, that you were going to show them something from their pre-war lives.

EMCEE. Yes.

ORGANIZER. You see, we'll just take the audience into the studio for a nice Sunday radio program. What you see here is the studio.

EMCEE. Aha, I understand—and with that my job as the emcee is over.

ORGANIZER. If you please; we should get started.

EMCEE. Gentlemen, please, the microphone, the announcer, and off we go.

IA. AFTER THE INTRODUCTION

Emcee and Organizer exit.

The lights go down and a red bulb glows showing "On Air." The lights come up again.

Lighting: A. Fischer

II. BACKSTAGE MUSIC

Harmonium: J. Fischer

"Florentine March."[14] *Several bars of the march forte, transition to piano.*

---

13 Although listening to radio broadcasts was strictly illegal, some prisoners did build radio receivers. See, for example, Bruno Häberer, "Illegale Empfänger im Ghetto von Theresienstadt," in *Radio Fernsehen Elektronik* 24(9) (1975): 282–84; and Anna Lorencová, "Židovský odboj podle vzpomínek pamětníků," in Zlatica Zudová-Lesková (ed.), *Židé v boji a odboji: Rezistence československých židů v letech druhé světové války* (Prague: Historický ústav, 2007), pp. 331–8, see p. 333.

14 The "Florentine March" ("Florentinský pochod") was written in 1907 by composer and military bandleader Julius Fučík (1872–1916).

Announcer: Masárek

Time signal: J. Fischer on the harmonium

Anouncer enters as music plays and, after several bars, begins to speak.

ANNOUNCER (*backstage*). Dear listeners, we wish you all a good morning. Today is December 27, 1937. The time is now twenty seconds to six o'clock. (*Time signal of the State Astronomical Observatory in Prague.*)

Today it has been exactly ninety years since the greatest Czech journalist, Karel Havlíček Borovský, wrote his epistles in Brixen.[15] Nothing has changed since then.

The world remains the same, it will never change;
Spit into the sea a hundred times; you cannot make
it foam.[16]

(*Interlude*)[17]

Report from the State Meteorological Institute:[18]

Temperature: −7°C, that is 3°C below normal, wind from the southeast. Air pressure adjusted to sea level: 730 mm, that is 30 mm below normal, high-pressure front south of Sicily, pressure dropping near the Black Sea. Weather forecast: changing cloud cover, sporadic showers in the west,

---

15 Karel Havlíček Borovský (1821–56) was a Czech nationalist, satirist, literary critic, politician, and one of the founders of Czech-language journalism, known for his sharp critique of the Austrian regime. On December 16, 1851, he was seized by the authorities and deported to the Tyrolian spa town of Brixen (now Bressanone in Northern Italy). He was not allowed to return to Prague until 1855. He wrote some of his best works in exile. Borovský was also known for his doubts regarding Jewish assimilation into the Czech nation. See Michal Frankl, *Emancipace od Židů, český antisemitismus na konci 19. století* (Prague: Paseka, 2007), p. 33.

16 A well-known epigram from Borovský's *The Baptism of St. Vladimir* (*Křest svatého Vladimíra*), written in exile.

17 In the original script, the interlude (probably a brief musical one) was preceded by a few lines titled "Language Advice" in which the announcer discussed an obscure point in Czech-language orthography.

18 The paragraph that follows is probably a veiled reference to the state of the war in December 1942, with "high-pressure front south of Sicily" referring to the

local precipitation in the south, slowly clearing in the east. Visibility: utterly miserable.

And the water levels on the Elbe river: Podmokly normal, Dresden –54, Magdeburg +1.50, Hamburg—no report, the situation is under investigation.[19]

IV. EXERCISE WITH US

Announcer: Masárek

Exercise and song: J. Fischer

Harmonica: Abeles

Harmonium: Terner

Accompaniment: Folk songs

Announcer opens the scene; Fischer, Terner, and Abeles enter. Fischer leads exercises to the accompaniment of a harmonica.

ANNOUNCER. The morning fitness half-hour will be led today by Brother Rybář instead of Brother Dobrman.[20] Musical accompaniment by Brother Puršl. (*Leaves.*)

RYBÁŘ. Good morning, friends. Now hop right out of bed and get ready for your morning exercise. Move all the furniture so it's not in the way. Right. First something to warm up. Hurdle race. Get ready. We will run the length of the room. Ready—go. We'll jump over the bed and crawl under the couch. So, go, go, go, go . . . What's wrong, Mr. Mareš, having difficulties? Oh my! You climbed on the top of the wardrobe and can't get down? Your wife will bring you a ladder right away.

---

seige of Malta, "slowly clearing in the east" to Soviet victories at the Battle of Stalingrad, and "visibility utterly miserable" to the impossibility of foreseeing the outcome of the war.

19 All of the cities mentioned are also the names of barracks in Terezín/Theresienstadt. "Hamburg" was the women's barracks.

20 Members of the Czech gymnastics association Sokol (see glossary) addressed each other as "brother."

So keep it up, go, go. Mr. Krákora, don't hide there behind the picture. Now stretch arms: to the sides, to the ceiling, to the back, to the front, to the floor, out the door.[21]

We'll slow down gradually, one two, one two, one two, and company halt!

Now a little exercise with this small chest of drawers. Grasp it by its legs on the shorter side and lift it as high as possible. Excellent. Now we swing it around over our heads. One two three, one two three, one two three. Faster, faster. If you swing it too slowly, the drawers come out. Oh—you see, your wife has forgotten to lock the drawer with the secret letters. Your Honor,[22] you're not doing yourself any favors by lying in bed and not exercising with us. At least make circles with your big toes so you'll get a bit of exercise.

And that's enough. Now pay attention. Stand with legs together. On "one," jump up; on "two, three," hold it; on "four," come down again. Now now, Mr. Klábosil, you are staying in the air too long. There, and now grasp the electric wire with your left hand and remain in this position until complete charring is achieved.[23] But Mr. Skočdopole, you're charring too slowly.

And now we'll exercise those organs which we kept forgetting about all through the year.

Abeles slowly moves to the back. Fischer sings, accompanied by Terner on the harmonium.

---

21 In the original, the words for these arm stretches all end with the suffix *-pažit,* and the last word is the acoustically similar *přežít* ("to survive").

22 In the original, the title used is *pane rado* (literally "Mr. Counsellor"), a title based on the Austrian title *Geheimrat* or *Hofrat.* The closest English-language equivalent is Privy Counsellor.

23 A reference to the illegal and unsafe but widespread practice of running an electrical wire from an outside power supply into the barracks to provide electricity for personal use.

THE MORNING FITNESS HALF-HOUR[24]

Stretching out our muscles will be such fun
Straightening out our bones, our whole skeleton
Muscles, sinews, tendons will be toned just fine
and be well-aligned
The internal organs we have inside
We don't think about them most of the time
But they should be tightened, strengthened, and trained.
For years and years, they've been supporting you
And now it's time to pay them some attention too.
If you don't want ill health to be your fate
then let's not delay until it's too late,
Let's work out our organs, let's exercise:

(*Refrain*) Hypophysis, larynx,
Duodenum, pharynx,
Gastriculum, ventriculum,
All veins and arteries,
Corpus callosum,
And don't abandon
your pancreas.
In everything you do,
to your own health be true
If you take care, it will be there for you.

You know that exercise serves the body well,
Without exercise you'll be plagued by illnesses
      such as nagging pains
and rheumatism, even migraines.

---

24 The song "The Morning Fitness Half-Hour" was apparently sung to the melody of the song "Long Live Cabaret!" from *Laugh with Us* (see original sheet music on p. 217 of this volume, IMAGE 7.9). However, the verses and refrains in "The Morning Fitness Half-Hour" are ordered differently. Verses 1 and 2 are sung to the melody that begins at the lyrics "Young and old alike fall in love with jazz." The refrain is sung to the opening melody that begins with the line "Ladies and gentlemen."

Sore will be your joints and your gait too slow,
Moaning and complaining where'er you go
You don't need to think twice
Just hear and take my advice
You should work out, every morning, noon, and night
Leave nothing out, if you want to do it right.
Every body part is of great concern,
each and every organ deserves its turn,
That's why to our exercise we'll return.

(*Refrain*)

Exit all.

V. ANNOUNCEMENTS FOR THE SECURITY SERVICE

Announcer: Hochner

Props: Briefcase, Glasses

ANNOUNCER. Announcements for the security service by Inspector Rudolf.

(*As Rudolf*) Attention, attention, please note:

(1) Seeking Arnošt Dostál—correction, Dostal, with a short *a*—born August 23, 1902, in Teplice-Šanov; domicile Tarnopol, Galicia;[25] last residence in Prague-Břevnov. Speaks Czech with slight Sorbian accent.[26] Has difficulty pronouncing *r*.[27] Build corpulent, hair almost none, eyes squinting

---

25 The city is located in present-day western Ukraine. Before the Second World War, almost half the population was Jewish.

26 Lusatia, a historical region in eastern Germany, is home to a Sorbian Slavic minority that has attempted to preserve its language and culture. Even in the inter-war period, the Sorbian language was so little known that it is unlikely that a Czech speaker would have been able to identify the accent.

27 In the original, the authors used the verb *ráčkovat*, which describes a rather common difficulty in Czech pronunciation. According to translator Petr Liebl, this difficulty was common among Jews in the inter-war period, and was mocked by anti-Semites.

good-naturedly, lips broad, mouth sometimes half-open, gait rolling. Identifying feature: Abhors work. He was last seen in the Black Brewery,[28] eating a triple helping of tripe soup and a plum *koláč*.[29] Was also observed to drink from his neighbor's Viennese coffee. He was wearing a grey trench coat in the shape of a kaftan, cinnamon-colored pedal pushers pulled down almost to the ankles, hobnailed work boots with the tips somewhat turned up, and a blue cap with a bill. It is assumed that, considering his talkativeness, he is being interviewed at some police station, or that it will be possible to take him into custody near one of the snack bars he frequents.

(2) Missing—Krisch Alfred, repeat Krisch Alfred; *k* as in Karl, *r* as in Rudolph, *i* as in Ivan, *s* as in Esmeralda, *ch* as in Cherub. Born October 28, 1922, in Olomouc; speaks Czech with an accent from the Haná.[30] Currently a delivery man by profession; marital status—single. Build rather tall, hair chestnut, eyes brown, clean-shaven, mouth normal, teeth healthy, nose turned-up. Identifying feature: a permanent smile. Has a special fondness for playing *čára*.[31] He was last seen wearing a short, grey jacket and long, blue work pants. In his left breast pocket he has a deposit book from the Olomouc Savings Bank, which he received as a birthday gift with an initial deposit of one thousand crowns. It is more than probable that he has already spent most of it. He was last sighted in the merry company of a robust man and the popular equestrienne Miss Joan Blondell-Bumbrlíčková at St. Anthony's fair.

This missing person is probably now in the Roudnice district.[32]

---

28 A well-known brewery and restaurant on Charles Square (Karlovo náměstí) in Prague.

29 A beloved Czech pastry. A round, flat crust of yeast dough is topped with jam or other sweet fillings.

30 A distinctive Moravian accent, considered comical by most Czechs.

31 A game in which players draw a line on the ground and, standing behind another line, throw coins. The player whose coin lands nearest to the line wins.

32 Terezín/Theresienstadt was located in the Roudnice district.

Please report any information on his whereabouts to the nearest police or gendarme station.

End of announcements for the security service.

Exit.

VI. TRAMPING SONGS[33]

Singers: Herrmann, J. Pick, A. Fischer, J. Fischer, Abeles
Accompaniment: Harmonium, Guitar

J. PICK. The Guinea Pigs[34]

Program:[35] (1) "Fort Adamson;" Guitar: Herrmann[36]

(2) "Recipe for a Tramping Song;" Guitar: J. Fischer[37]

The guitar is left on top of the harmonium.

On finishing the song, all exit.

---

33 "Tramping" was a widespread phenomenon in the inter-war period. A Czech encyclopedia from 1933 defined "tramp" as follows: "In recent times, a title for a vacationer who engages in camping which, unlike scouting, is of a very unstructured nature. Following an American model, European tramps have developed various customs and manners: singing around the campfire [. . .] organizing the camp into a settlement headed by a sheriff, etc." See *Masarykův slovník naučný: Lidová encyklopedie všeobecných vědomostí*, VOL. 7 (Prague: Československý kompas, 1933), p. 324.

34 A literal translation of the Czech title of the group, Morčata.

35 In the original script, the lyrics of the songs were provided, with no modifications specific to the ghetto.

36 The full title is "The Song about the Three Immortal Dead Men from Fort Adamson" ("Zpěv o třech nesmrtelných mrtvých z Fort Adamsonu"). The tramping settlement Fort Adamson was established in 1931 near the town of Loděnice, about 25 km southwest of Prague. For information on the history of the settlement and sheet music for this and other tramping songs, see Emanuel Sally-Prkno, *Táborák ještě nezhasíná, Ascalona a dvacet jedna dalších nejhezčích písní Emana Sallyho-Prkna* (Prague: Ivanka Luftová, Miroslav Anger, 1994).

37 This song (in Czech, "Recept na trampskou píseň") was popularized by the so-called Teachers' Choir of Kocourkov (Kocourkovští učitelé). Kocourkov is a fictional village of fools; the name was a parody of other singing groups popular at the time. See Svatopluk Káš, *Kocourkovští učitelé, jejich historie a tvorba* (Prague: Dokořán, 2008).

VII. AGRICULTURAL RADIO[38]

Announcer: Masárek

Rákos: Abeles

Brázda: Weisskopf

Props: Two pipes

ANNOUNCER. In today's agricultural radio program we bring you a conversation between neighbors[39] Brázda and Rákos.[40]

RÁKOS. Good morning, Matěj.[41] So, how'd you sleep?

BRÁZDA. Not so well, Tomáš, not so well. Ever since I got duped by that agent from Prague I haven't been able to sleep. It's been a long time since something has vexed me as much as this—and, mind you, I've done a lot of foolish things in my life.

RÁKOS. Well, I was pretty surprised. My son Franky, the one I sent off to college, said "I'm surprised that Godfather[42] Brázda fell for that; he is such a *komverzní*[43] person . . ."

BRÁZDA. Yep, you're right, Tomáš. But what can you do? What happened, happened—it can't be undone. But you'd have believed him too. He spoke like a priest on Sunday. He could talk a calf into the belly of a heifer. "Please, have a look, Sir,"[44] and so on and so forth, "I'll make you a deal—we have to go with the times—progress must be made"—and, well, I gave in. I thought—well, there certainly is something to that chemistry—and now I have a railroad car full of it and I don't need that much. What should I do with so much artificial fertilizer?

---

38 Agricultural Radio programs were initiated in 1926 by the Agrarian Party, the most powerful Czech political party of the inter-war period.

39 "Neighbor" was a traditional form of address used between wealthy farmers.

40 The characters Brázda and Rákos, played by Bohuslav Horák and Jaroslav Prokop, appeared for the first time in 1927. The name Brázda means "furrow" and the name Rákos means "cane" or "reed."

41 In the original script the characters' lines are written in a rural dialect. The phrase Rákos uses to greet Matěj is a more pious *Pozdravpámbu* ("God greet you").

42 In rural areas, a traditional form of address for an older neighbor.

43 The word *komverzní* does not exist; perhaps Rákos's son invented it to demonstrate his new level of education.

44 In the original, *pantáto*, literally "Mr. Papa," a traditional rural form of address.

Earlier, my wife and daughter and I managed to save just enough fertilizer for our fields—and then, crofter Vávra let us have some—he has plenty of children and not many fields. Now I have a railroad car full of it, and it smells too, but not as nicely.[45]

RÁKOS. Well, well, neighbor—right you are. But we all have our worries—everybody has a sore spot. I have mine too . . .

BRÁZDA. But what, what is it, Tomáš? You don't have a mortgage on your house, no illnesses in the family, so . . .

RÁKOS. But that's just it, Matěj: illness, there's an illness in the family.

BRÁZDA. But I talked with your missus[46] yesterday—she was right as rain.

RÁKOS. Thank God, the missus is healthy, but . . .

BRÁZDA. Franky?

RÁKOS. No, no—but Bessie[47] isn't doing well; she seems so nervous. And, you know, sometimes she moos so sadly, like a child wailing. You know better than anyone how an animal like that gets close to your heart. And oh, something else I almost forgot, neighbor—I have to tell you something else. You know we have that new milkmaid Mařena[48]—you know . . .

BRÁZDA. The Vána girl, right?

RÁKOS. Yep, yep, that's her. So Matěj, Mařena was milking our sweet little cow yesterday and somehow she hurt her sore finger, the one she cut when she was slicing bread, the clumsy ox. And so she winced and hit that poor little cow. I had just walked in and I stood there like I'd been struck by lightning: "You stupid cow, don't you know that this poor animal is sick?" I tell you, neighbor, people these days have no heart!

BRÁZDA. I know what you mean, Tomáš, I know exactly what you mean. It's so sad when an animal like that gets sick—it's so sad. I remember when our poor Tony was wasting away . . .

---

45 That is, as natural fertilizer.

46 In the original, *paňmáma*, "Mrs. Mama," a traditional rural form of address.

47 In the original, Stračena, a common name for cows.

48 Mařena is a diminutive of the name Marie (Mary).

RÁKOS. That ox[49] from the Styrian lands, right?[50]

BRÁZDA. Yes, yes, he was my pride—a blue-ribbon ox. The likes of him aren't even born in this country.

RÁKOS. But they are, neighbor, they are.

Exit all.

VIIA. RECORDED MUSIC

Accordion: J. Fischer

ANNOUNCER. Music from records.

VIII. NEWS FROM THE WIRE[51]

Reader: Felix Porges
Signal: Abeles and Fischer

ANNOUNCER. And now we link to Košice.[52] International and local news.

READER. (1) President Mosicki granted an audience to our envoy Juraj Slávik, who conveyed to him our wishes for the best possible cooperation between our neighboring states.[53]

---

49 In Czech, "ox" (*vůl*) is often and very colorfully used as an insult.

50 This may be a veiled reference to the first commandant of the ghetto, SS officer Siegfried Seidl. He was born in Lower Austria rather than in Styria. However, as the young men of the ghetto knew, he drove an expensive convertible, a model called the Steyer. See F. R. Kraus, *A přiveď zpět naše roztroušené* (Prague: Neumann, 1946), p. 26.

51 The following scene is written in comically poor Slovak. In both pre- and postwar Czechoslovakia, radio and television broadcasts alternated between Czech- and Slovak-language programs.

52 Košice is a city in eastern Slovakia.

53 Ignacy Mošicki was president of Poland from 1926 until the outbreak of the Second World War. According to the minutes of the Senate of the National Assembly of Czechoslovakia, Juraj Slávik's visit to Poland took place in February 1937. Slávik subsequently served as Minister of the Interior in the Czechoslovak government-in-exile (1940–45).

(2) The wonder rabbi Spira[54] from Belz[55] has arrived in Piešťany[56] with his entire entourage. All shops were immediately sold out of geese.[57] The National Guard was mobilized to receive this prominent visitor. A salute was fired, this time lasting only five minutes.[58]

(3) The development of Ruthenia[59] continues successfully. It has been reported to us that two handkerchiefs have been donated to a certain village by the vice-president of the League for Human Rights. They are now on display at the local notary public's office.

(4) The volcano Vesuvius has become active again.[60] A catastrophic explosion caused an earthquake which destroyed a modern hospital, a children's playground, and one hog out to pasture. There is no other damage. Seismographic activity was also observed in Sicily, Sardinia, and Corsica.[61] Space management[62] has ordered the evacuation of these places.

---

54 Rabbi Chaim Elazar Spira (1871–1937) was not from Belz but, rather, from Mukachevo, located in Subcarpathian Ruthenia, which was annexed to Czechoslovakia in 1920. He was respected not only by the international Jewish community but by world leaders who sought his advice.

55 Belz, a small town in the Lvov district of Ukraine (between the world wars, in the Galicia region of Poland), was a famous center of Hasidic learning. It was known to Czechs in the inter-war period as the city where Jiří Langer, brother of playwright František Langer and friend of Franz Kafka, rebelled against his assimilatory upbringing and returned to orthodox Jewishness.

56 Piešťany is located in Western Slovakia.

57 Goose is considered kosher meat, conforming to traditional Jewish dietary laws.

58 Probably an ironic reference. Slovaks, as a deeply Catholic people, were not known for their philo-Semitism.

59 Subcarpathian Ruthenia became part of Czechoslovakia after the First World War. Czech intellectuals debated whether attempts to modernize the region should be considered "development" or "colonization." See, for example, Stanislav K. Neumann, *Československá cesta: Deník cesty kolem republiky od 28. dubna do 28. října 1933. Část druhá: Karpatské léto* (Prague: Fr. Borový, 1935).

60 Vesuvius erupted in 1926 and 1929.

61 This may be a veiled reference to the Italian seige of Malta (June–December 1940).

62 In the original script, the authors use the term *priestorové hospodárstvo*, the literal Slovak translation of *Raumwirtschaft*, the title of the ghetto's department of space management. See *Selbstverwaltung* (glossary).

(5) The Paris Exposition has received one and a half million visitors to date. The guests show great interest in the Czechoslovak, Polish, and Yugoslav pavilions.[63]

(6) Preparations for the Danube Fair[64] are in full swing. Jews from the entire Levant are interested in the fair.

(7) As reported in the Tokyo Nishi Nishi Asahi Shimbun, the oceangoing ship Nagasaki Maru ran aground near the Easter Islands and sank for unknown reasons.[65]

(8) News provided by warring countries Paraguay and Bolivia regarding the Gran Chaco[66] provides a clear picture of the state of affairs. The Paraguayan General Staff announces: "The Gran Chaco is in our hands. The enemy has lost 560 planes, our own losses total one plane, which has possibly returned. The plane which was yesterday declared probably lost is now quite certainly lost." The Supreme Commando of Bolivia, on the contrary, announces: "We have shot down 899 enemy planes; on our side there were no losses. Gran Chaco is definitively in our hands."

This concludes our international and local news.

---

63 At the Paris World Exposition in 1937, the critically acclaimed Czechoslovak pavilion was designed by Jaromír Krejcar, Z. Kejeř, B. Soumar, and Ladislav Sutnar.

64 The 17th International Danube Fair was held in Bratislava in September 1937.

65 The Nagasaki Maru SS was a 5,268 ton Japanese passenger vessel built in 1922. On May 13, 1942, she struck a Japanese mine off Nagasaki and sank.

66 The Chaco War (1932–35) was the first instance of aerial warfare in the Western Hemisphere.

ANNOUNCER. Now a tenor from the foremost Prague stages, Mr. Franta Weissenstein, will present arias from *The Kiss*[67] and *Dalibor*[68] and the Dvořák song "Songs My Mother Taught Me."[69] Accompanied by Professor Rafael Schächter.

X. RADIO HALF HOUR FOR INDUSTRY, BUSINESS, AND TRADE

Editor: Fürth Günter

Administrator: Popper Leo

ANNOUNCER. In today's half-hour program the editor of the *Bakers' News*, Alois Mazanec,[70] will conduct us through the Producers' Cooperative in Josefov. Switching over to Josefov.[71]

EDITOR. We are entering the courtyard of a building in the shape of a five-pointed star.[72] Here in Josefov, the majority of the buildings have been built in this style. Walking across the courtyard, where several trucks loaded with various goods stand, is administrator Mr. Fridolín Křeček.[73] Good morning, Mr. Křeček.

ADMINISTRATOR. Your most humble servant; I bow to you, Mr. Mazanec. I'm pleased to be able to welcome you here.

---

67 Bedřich Smetana's opera *The Kiss* (*Hubička*) was performed in the ghetto. See the Terezín Memorial, inv. no. PT 4294.

68 Bedřich Smetana's opera *Dalibor* premiered in 1868.

69 The song (in Czech, "Když mne stará matka") is from the cycle *Gypsy Melodies* (*Cikánské melodie*), opus 55, no. 4, composed in 1880.

70 *Mazanec* is a special type of Easter bread.

71 Josefov/Josefstadt is the name of the Jewish quarter in Prague and also of Terezín/Theresienstadt's "sister fortress" in East Bohemia. The fortresses are practically identical in appearance.

72 The ghetto bakery and main provisions storehouse was located in Block A IV, a pentagonally shaped part of the Terezín/Theresienstadt fortifications. The entire scene is based closely upon the actual operations of the storehouse and bakery where the writers and performers worked.

73 *Křeček* means "hamster," used in colloquial Czech as a nickname for a person who hoards things.

EDITOR. It's my pleasure, and that of our listeners, who are going to enjoy a report from one of our leading cooperative enterprises.

ADMINISTRATOR. You probably mean "several enterprises," Mr. Mazanec. Because we actually have a whole group of associated enterprises here.

EDITOR. That is very interesting, Mr. Křeček. What enterprises are they?

ADMINISTRATOR. Here we have storehouses, a pasta factory, the bakery proper, and, in addition to these, we administer the district and area kitchens and distribution centers. I mention only in passing that our town is one of the most progressive. To rationalize production we supply the population directly with ready-made meals, deliciously and richly prepared, right to their homes.

EDITOR. That is wonderful! Downright fabulous, Mr. Křeček.

ADMINISTRATOR. Mr. Mazanec, our enterprises have gained popularity at home as well as abroad. Our products are being delivered to the towns Vrchlabí and Podmokly, to name only a few.[74] Our goods are also in demand in Dresden and even in Hamburg. Even the famous gourmets from Magdeburg[75] send for our elite products. What's more, even that celebrated individual, the apothecary Slováček, gets his buttery, tender turnips from us. And he is known to be extremely particular. He even weighed them in the pharmacy down to the gram.

EDITOR. And did they tally?

ADMINISTRATOR. Of course, and now he belongs to our most faithful customers.

EDITOR. This is remarkable; I'm already looking forward to the tour. So, where do we start, Mr. Křeček?

ADMINISTRATOR. Let's tour the bakery first. After all, it is the nearest. Please enter.

---

74 All the Czech and German cities and towns named here are also the names of barracks in the ghetto.

75 The most important administrative offices in the ghetto were located in the Magdeburg barracks.

(*Footsteps.*)

EDITOR. This is the smell of God's gift[76] and . . . and . . . the toilet right next to the entrance. That is truly practical . . . cleanliness everywhere.

ADMINISTRATOR. Well in a bakery that's simply a matter of course, of course, of course . . . It's a different story with our millers on the second floor, where things may occasionally be overlooked, or even get lost in the flour. Being a specialist yourself, you're already familiar with the production of bread; perhaps we should go straight to the storehouse.

EDITOR. Very true, and we'll also save some time. But I would like to ask, before we reach the storehouse, from a purely hygienic point of view: how do you store God's gift?

ADMINISTRATOR. We stack the loaves high, Mr. Mazanec; that's why we prefer to make them smaller and harder, so they can withstand the pressure.

EDITOR. Just as I expected, and what's more, your night delivery staff can transport the bread more easily when the loaves are smaller and more solid . . . And what about hygiene? The cleanliness of the carts?

ADMINISTRATOR. That is well taken care of. It is prohibited for our workers to load the bread while wearing shoes. Before loading the carts they take them off, and their gloves as well, so the bread does not get dirty. The carts are always properly cleaned after unloading and returned to the funeral parlor spotless, so they can again be used for their designated function.[77]

EDITOR. Just as it should be, Mr. Křeček. I am completely satisfied.

ADMINISTRATOR. So, here we have the storeroom for flour. The layout is modern. We don't store each kind of flour separately in rows, nor do we mark the weight or the type of flour on the sacks. That is an obsolete method. Earlier, if someone broke

---

76 In Czech, *boží dáreček*, an old-fashioned expression for "bread."

77 See *Wagenkolonne* (glossary).

into the storeroom with dishonest intentions, he was able to orient himself immediately. But today, even if such a criminal made his way in, he couldn't find his way around. Even if he wanted to steal, he couldn't, because he'd never find what he's looking for. In production this doesn't matter, because we manufacture our merchandise from a combination of flours, scientifically researched and very successful.

EDITOR. And here we have the storeroom for margarine and sugar. All a model of order, just the way I like it. But Mr. Křeček, why exactly do you keep the door locked and the window barred?

ADMINISTRATOR. It's obvious, Mr. Mazanec. Margarine today should be under lock and key. Lately people have been using it instead of butter on their heads, and the demand is growing.[78]

EDITOR. Mr. Křeček, you're joking, aren't you?

ADMINISTRATOR. Right, right.

EDITOR. And what about the rest of the storerooms?

ADMINISTRATOR. I was just getting ready to tell you about those. We manage everything in a goal-oriented way, Mr. Mazanec. As you see, we keep a limited amount of supplies here. This is the specific foundation of our modern methods: we do not store supplies but rather manufacture our products immediately and deliver them directly to the consumers. It's not like the old days, when there were such heaps of everything that they started to rot.

EDITOR. I am truly and, may I say, pleasantly surprised by the novelties and innovations I have seen here today. And before I forget, Mr. Křeček, how are things with the staff?

ADMINISTRATOR. At present we employ only professionals. We are satisfied with them and they with us. We even cover their pension plan and generally arrange everything as if they were going to stay with us for years. We prefer to pay them smaller salaries,

---

78 The phrase "to have butter on one's head" means to have a guilty conscience. From the Central European saying "He who has butter on his head should not go out in the sun."

so that we can deposit more for them in the bank.[79] A person looks forward to a quiet old age even more when he already has some kind of retirement account. But man proposes and . . . well, you know.

EDITOR. I would very much like to stay longer, Mr. Křeček. Unfortunately I must conclude today's program. But I would be happy to come again. It was truly an enormous pleasure.[80]

ADMINISTRATOR. The pleasure's been all mine, Mr. Mazanec.

XI. SONG—MRS. K.-G.

ANNOUNCER. The famous radio artist Mrs. Kernmaierová-Grabová will sing her "Song of Prague." Music and lyrics by Dr. Jaroslav Felix, accompanied by Josef Rybář.

SONG OF PRAGUE[81]

(*Refrain*) My Prague, you are my paradise, my heaven here on
    earth
And we who love you know how much those memories are
    worth
Enchanted by your silhouette
It draws me like girl's lips so red
Your beauty's like a fairy tale, it's music to my ears.
And faithful to you I'll remain for all of my life's years.

When twilight falls, the glow of day fades
Your towers casting shadows long

---

79 Although the ghetto's own currency *Ghettokronen* (literally, "ghetto crowns") did not begin to circulate until May 1943, the introduction of money was announced already in September 1942. In November 1942, a system for the payment of wages was formally introduced. See Adler, *Theresienstadt*, pp. 124–5.

80 In the original script this line was "Bylo mně skutečnými vepřovými hody" ("It was a real pork feast for me.") Such feasts take place after the slaughtering of a pig. In this context the line perhaps emphasizes the assimilation of the Czech Jews, who rarely followed traditional dietary laws.

81 See original music on p. 94 of this volume, IMAGE 3.11.

Your blossom-covered hillsides ring with
Gorgeous song.

I sing of your eternal beauty
Of Europe's cities you're the pearl
No one who's seen you can forget you
Loveliest place in all the world.

(*Refrain*)

XII. RECITATION

Recitation: Stránský

ANNOUNCER. In this brief literary interlude, Pavel Jeník will read from
his own work.

CLOWN[82]

I am welcomed everywhere,
And loved by everyone—
They welcome laughter in me
But none of them can see inside
Under the white mask
A heart wounded by love—
They want to laugh—they want to clap
For a wretched clown—idiots.

The boundaries of my life: a comedian's tent.
Daily I play, made up and powdered—
There my suffering, concealed by the laughter,
A sea of burning tears
I hide behind the grotesque.

---

82 Stránský's poems rhyme in the original Czech. I have translated them here as
free verse.

Play, let the music play, a pretty
And pleasing song—let those
Who have paid be amused—idiots.
But the clown will know mercy one day
And he, tread upon in the dust,
Shall be celebrated on high
And those whom you played for, for laughs
Shall disfigure their faces with masks
Then you will enjoy the grotesque.
Then you'll be applauding for them.
Now play for my laughter—idiots.

(*Envoi*)
I want to laugh with the mask removed,
To laugh sincerely—to see a human
Face marked by suffering laugh.
Now play for the wretched clown—idiots.

MAYFLY

You must be mine, oh night, tonight
Who knows what tomorrow will bring
Enough of this waiting—it's time.
I want to live tonight,
I want to have everything
That a woman can get out of life,
I have waited so quietly, untouched—
Today, oh night, I want to live.

No more to be like a newt in the dark
I want to see light, radiance,
Drink in all the colors, the shine . . .
I am all yours—oh dark night—
A mayfly's life I want to live,
To be happy like she is,

To know everything—to have all that she has—
I want to have tonight.

In one single night—night of nights
To feel love, passion, chills
And the heat of desire all at once
I want to be kissed, I want, night,
To drink of red wine,
Then to be crushed and prostrated
And drained by this one single night,
I want, like a mayfly, to die.

(*Envoi*)
One single night—to live all—
To be born, then to die, but fulfilled,
To have done what a woman was born for.
Mayfly, butterfly with sky-colored wings—rise and die—
It is time to go.

XIII. A SELECTION OF FOLK SONGS

Singer: Jiří Popper

Harmonium: Josef Fischer

ANNOUNCER. We now bring you several folk songs, sung by Jiří Vrchlabský. Accompanied by Josef Rybář.

FOLK SONGS[83]

1) "I Had a Dream, My Lass"
2) "Mountain so High"

---

83 The Czech titles of the folk songs are "Zdálo se mi, má panenko," "Horo, horo," "Zelení hájové," and "Tancuj, tancuj" respectively. In the original script the lyrics of the songs (except for "Zelení hájové") were provided, with no modifications specific to the ghetto.

3) "Green Groves"

4) "Dance, Dance"

XIV. FAIRY TALE

Speaker: Abeles
Overture: Melody from *Snow White*[84]
Accordion: Josef Fischer
Violin: Horpatzky
Props: Chair on the stage

ANNOUNCER. Dear children, now listen to a fairy tale about dwarfs by your Uncle Miloš.

UNCLE MILOŠ. A long, long time ago, far, far away from here, beyond seven mountain ranges and seven forests,[85] on the slope of a high mountain, lived peacefully and contentedly in their village a nation of Indians.[86]

One morning, when the people woke up, they were surprised to see a parade (*music begins*)[87] of dwarfs, with knapsacks on their backs, approaching the gates of the village. Where they came from no one knew but they disappeared into one of the biggest houses in the village.[88] On the second day there arrived a new parade of dwarfs and, again, each of

---

84 The Walt Disney film *Snow White and the Seven Dwarfs* (in Czech, *Sněhurka a sedm trpaslíků*) premiered in the US in 1937. It premiered in Czechoslovakia in the fall of 1938 as the first Hollywood film fully dubbed into Czech. See Norbert Frýd, *Lahvová pošta aneb konec posledních sto let* (Prague: Československý spisovatel, 1971), pp. 90–1, 94.

85 This is the traditional beginning of Czech fairy tales.

86 The "Indians" represent the "Aryan" inhabitants of Terezín/Theresienstadt, who still lived in the town when transports of Jewish prisoners began to arrive. The word "Aryan" refers to people speaking an Indo-European language who invaded North India in the 2nd millennium BCE.

87 That is, the song "Heigh-Ho" from *Snow White and the Seven Dwarfs*.

88 During the first few weeks of the ghetto's existence all prisoners were housed in the Sudeten barracks.

them carried a knapsack. And so it went on, day after day. The locals could not contain their curiosity and asked who these dwarfs were. They were told that those dwarfs knew various spells and charms, that they were bad people and that the villagers should be wary of them. They were also told that the new guests of the village did not like the local Indians . . . As you see, this is a fairy tale, dear children; you know that in reality all people love one another.

But the Indians began to fear the dwarfs. They packed up all their belongings and moved out of the village[89] to escape the misfortune that threatened them.[90] And so it came to be that our little dwarfs found themselves alone in the village.

They were hardworking dwarfs. They immediately elected a mayor—the two-hundred-and-eighty-four-year-old Amethyst with a long white beard. He had with him twelve wise little men, also bearded and hardworking.[91]

Amethyst immediately ordered bedsteads to be built, so that each little dwarf would be comfortable. But they soon found out that among them there wasn't a single carpenter. The sad little dwarfs prayed to God to help them. And what do you know—a miracle occurred: several little dwarfs who previously had not even known what a hammer, saw, or nail looked like learned how to be carpenters overnight. And because all the dwarfs loved each other so much that they wanted to sleep close together, they built their little beds not only close to each other but also stacked one on top of an-other, nice and high, with little ladders beside them. And because they loved animals so much, each dwarf was happy to

---

89 The last "Aryan" inhabitants left Terezín/Theresienstadt at the end of June 1942.

90 Apparently a reference to the phrase "Die Juden sind unser Unglück!" (The Jews are our misfortune!), which appeared on the title page of every issue of *Der Stürmer*, a violently anti-Semitic weekly published from 1923 until the end of the Second World War.

91 A reference to Jakob Edelstein (his name literally means "gemstone"), the first *Judenältester* of Terezín/Theresienstadt, and the members of the *Ältestenrat*.

receive a little pet to take to bed, to watch over him at night and make sure that nothing bad happened to him.[92] Amethyst also decreed that meals would be prepared for everyone so the little dwarfs would not have any extra work to do with the cooking. So tiny little cakes and pastries were baked, tiny little dumplings, and sometimes even tiny little pieces of meat. All the food was prepared in such a way so that it would not make anyone sick from overeating. You know, dear children, that dwarfs have tiny little stomachs, so this was enough for them. And everyone was happy.

Soon, however, the little dwarfs started to weep and wail that they had neither clothes nor shoes. Amethyst had only a single cobbler and only a single tailor, and they had already been working for a long time in the little office of the village. And so, again, the little dwarfs prayed and another miracle happened. Suddenly lots and lots of the little dwarfs learned how to make shoes and how to make clothes, and you would not believe, children, how well they did it. Only the cobbler and the tailor had completely forgotten how . . . It is, after all, a fairy tale.

In the village there were huge suitcases that held lots and lots of supplies—these supplies were being sorted—the better things were being set aside.[93] It would have been a shame to use them, you know. And from what was left they made new shoes and clothes for everyone, truly for all the dwarfs.

And then our little citizens had to overcome a new hardship. The road for the camel caravans that brought bread and flour ended far outside the town gates. And so Amethyst and his counselors decided that a road would be built for the camels all the way to the village well, right into town.[94] The

---

92 A reference to the bedbugs that plagued the prisoners. See *Entwesung* (glossary).

93 Items confiscated from the prisoners' luggage were sorted and those of better quality were sent to Germany.

94 A reference to the railroad spur built into the ghetto. See *Bahnbau* (glossary).

IMAGE 3.7 **Building the railroad spur into the ghetto, May 1943. By L. Haas.**
Courtesy of the Terezín Memorial.

very next morning hundreds and hundreds of dwarfs—aldermen, judges, industrialists, scribes—all, all of them streamed out of the gate, each with a little shovel on his shoulder. They worked day and night, seven days and nights and, indeed, in a *week* the road was finished. See *how fast* things work in fairy tales, dear children. Great was the rejoicing of the little citizens when on the eighth day the first camel arrived, pulling a beautiful little black carriage with columns and a canopy, decorated with silver.[95]

The little carriage, sent by a good old maharaja from the South as a gift,[96] was full of good and valuable things. And

95 The author has described one of the traditional horse-drawn funeral wagons used in the ghetto. See *Wagenkolonne* (glossary).

96 Perhaps a reference to the Jewish community offices in Prague, which continued to operate under Nazi supervision throughout the war and administered the delivery of supplies to the ghetto.

from that day onward, no one had to walk to meet the camels halfway or to wait for the caravans outside at night in the cold to help them unload. THERE WAS REJOICING EVERY-WHERE, DEAR CHILDREN.

And again Amethyst assembled his counselors. To reward the little dwarfs for their work, he ordered beautiful bazaars to be established.[97] There each little citizen could buy the things that brought joy to the heart of a little dwarf—but really the heart only of a little dwarf. He even established a tea-house with beautiful girls where, every day, new magicians performed their tricks. The little citizens truly enjoyed the tea-house; there they drank tea and coffee and were happy.[98]

But not every little dwarf had a job yet. So Amethyst decreed that every little citizen should copy down one of the

---

97 See *Verschleißstellen* (glossary). The opening of shops in the ghetto and the complex point system used to purchase goods were announced in the ghetto's daily orders on September 13, 1942. See Hyndráková et al., *Acta Theresiania*, p. 226.

98 See *Kaffeehaus* (glossary).

IMAGE 3.8 **Funeral wagons in the ghetto, 1943. By F. M. Nágl.**
Courtesy of the Jewish Museum in Prague.

fairy tales from *One Thousand and One Nights*.[99] Depending on how well each fairy tale pleased the gods, every little dwarf was assigned to a job. And behold, as if by magic, each carried out his work and fulfilled his function. We too have a saying that describes such a miracle.[100]

And finally real life began in the village. Everywhere the dwarfs were working, sawing, hammering, sewing, and writing. Plenty of writing was done, lots and lots of paper was used. Statistics and files were assembled.[101] These were ancient Indian sciences which, in our times, have unfortunately been long forgotten.

And Amethyst and all his counselors were happy.

Swift little carriages with wonderful inscriptions, drawn by the dwarfs themselves,[102] criss-crossed the village and all was as it should be. At the crossroads, and in front of the castle, stood the most handsome, specially chosen little dwarfs—a pleasure to behold for women and men.[103] They had glittering uniforms made from the finest material, were armed with short spears, and saw to it that order and discipline reigned everywhere. And so they all could have lived long and happily, if one day there had not arrived a giant caravan, and the next day another, and the next day yet another. Each one brought sacks of millet and more millet and still more millet. Nobody knew what to do with it—not even Amethyst. Finally it was proposed that with these sacks the dwarfs should build a city wall to defend the village from enemy attack. The proposal was accepted and again, hundreds and hundreds got to work.

---

99 Prisoners who wished to apply for advantageous positions in the ghetto were required to submit a resume. Information was sometimes falsified to obtain a desired job. See Hyndráková et al., *Acta Theresiania*, pp. 83, 85; and the song "Curriculum Vitae" from *Prince Bettliegend* in this volume.

100 The saying is probably "Komu dal pámbu ouřad tomu dal i rozum" ("He who receives an office from God also receives wisdom from Him," i.e. he who finds himself in a responsible position will rise to the occasion).

101 See *Zentralevidenz* (glossary).

102 See *Wagenkolonne* (glossary).

103 See *Ghettowache* (glossary).

They built great ramparts around the town under the supervision of an architect who had also become an architect as if by magic. A huge gate was built, and ramparts and towers—all from millet. But more and more caravans arrived bringing more and more millet . . . Everything would have turned out fine, if only one day there had not been an accident. The gate collapsed and the millet blocked the way out of the village. Now the little dwarfs saw that they would not be able to get out, and they were sad and they wept.

However, one day . . .

(*The Announcer interrupts with a reference to the time.*)

Dear children, next time I will finish telling you the story of how the dwarfs managed one day . . .

Gong. Finale—music "Heigh-Ho."

XV. SPORTS BROADCAST[104]

Speaker: Horpatzky

ANNOUNCER. Attention, all sports fans. We interrupt this program to broadcast live from Turin[105] the semi-finals of the World Cup in soccer.[106] At the microphone, reporter Pidlovský.

PIDLOVSKÝ. Attention, attention . . .

---

104 Horpatzky is probably imitating Josef Laufer (1891–1966), legendary Czech sports reporter of the inter-war period. Laufer was not allowed to broadcast during the war because of his Jewish origins. The following fictional semi-final match is apparently based on Laufer's most famous broadcast: that of the 1934 World Cup finals, when Czechoslovakia played Italy in Rome. The authors have incorporated additional real and fictional figures (for example, well-known Czech players who did not play in the 1934 finals).

105 The reason for setting the game in Turin rather than Rome is not clear. It may be a play on the Czech word for turnip—*tuřín*—a staple food in the ghetto.

106 Soccer was a beloved game in the ghetto. A soccer league was organized and teams played in the interior courtyard of the Dresden barracks. See František Steiner, *Fotbal pod žlutou hvězdou* (Prague: Olympia, 2009) and Adler, *Theresienstadt*, p. 604. Posters and charts of the league have been preserved in the Terezín Memorial, inv. nos. PT 4240–59.

We are broadcasting today from the beautiful stadium of the Turin soccer club, where today our national team will play in the semi-finals against the Italian national team. The weather, unlike the spectators, is as usual in our favor—not a single cloud in the sky. And I think that our golden boys, after two weeks in a local hotel, are well rested; so, all will certainly end well. *Si si signore* . . . I have just welcomed my Italian colleague . . .

Our microphone is located on the roof of the press box on the southeast side of the pitch—so, I see, as usual, both goals, one on my right and one on my left. I see the field directly before me—our team is leaving the tunnel right now—so visibility from my location is really quite good. Under the azure sky, far in the distance before me, that is, in the northwesterly direction, are the Italian mountains. At their base I see several ruins which, as you know, contribute substantially to the local tourist industry, which will certainly increase in the coming years . . . .[107] Attention attention . . . The Italian team has just arrived, to the thunderous applause of the spectators, and what do I see? . . . It was not clear until the last minute whether Cesarini would be able to play but here he is—look out, Košťálek, Cesarini is a crafty and dangerous player. He has already maimed several of our players.

The teams are already preparing for the kickoff—no, no kickoff yet—something is happening—I see a bouquet of flowers, behind it several functionaries—led by Hugo Meisl— the captain of our association,[108] accompanied by several gentlemen from the boards of the clubs Sparta and Slavia as well as from the central office. All are in very good spirits, the

---

107 Laufer was celebrated for being able to keep up an interesting commentary even when nothing was happening on the field.

108 Hugo Meisl (1881–1937), born in a Jewish family near the Bohemian city of Kutná Hora/Kuttenberg, was one of the outstanding personalities in the development of European soccer. He was, however, associated with Austrian rather than Czech soccer. The title "captain of our association" probably refers to his Jewishness. See Andreas and Wolfgang Hafter, *Hugo Meisl, oder die Erfindung des modernen Fußballs: Eine Biographie* (Göttingen: Die Werkstatt, 2007).

IMAGE 3.9 **Interior courtyard of the Hamburg barracks. The prisoners used such courtyards for cabaret performances, soccer games, and other events.**
Courtesy of the Terezín Memorial.

photographers are in place, lots have been drawn, Franta Plánička, our captain, wins the toss and the game is opened— no, the game is not opened and the referee runs to the assistant referee and borrows his whistle. In the absolute silence you can hear the singing of street musicians in the distance. Unlike in Venice, where as you know the singers sing in gondolas, here they sing in the streets.

While I have been describing this to you, unfortunately, the first goal against us has been scored. The ball went from that dangerous Cesarini from the left side all the way to the

IMAGE 3.10
A player for the ghetto soccer team Hollandia. By W. Thalheimer.
Courtesy of the Terezín Memorial.

right side to Orsi, then again to the left and to the center and then it ricocheted off one of our defenders into the net. So, I cannot tell you who scored the goal—you will find out at half-time, when I will also announce the names of our players. Well, that's all right—one goal doesn't matter. Cross your fingers and everything will be all right. We are in the twelfth minute of the first half—the ball has been kicked from the center, Sobotka has the ball, from Sobotka to Nejedlý—Nejedlý passes beautifully to Puč, but, but Tony—Tony Puč, even after that confrontation with a hot-blooded Italian after the unfortunate first goal—he did not, in fact, get the ball and again the Italians are on the offensive—I see a scrimmage some twenty-seven meters from Plánička's holy of holies[109] —one of our players is down—it's not Burger—it's not Čtyřoký—yes, it's Kolský—no, it's not Kolský, I don't see

---

109 That is, the goal that Plánička is defending.

Sobotka, yes, it's Sobotka—Sobotka is out of the fight, let's hope not for long. The free kick against us is marvelously deflected by Franta Plánička, who as you know is immensely popular here (you remember how, two years ago, someone shot him with a slingshot from behind and knocked him out of the fight). His kick, magnificently caught by Bouček, he passes it to Košt'álek, Košt'álek to Říha, Říha all the way to Nejedlý, Nejedlý to Puč, Puč passes it back, look out, now the shot—bravo!—a beautiful shot by Nejedlý—unfortunately it ends out of bounds. The ball is kicked out, intercepted by Meazza, who passes it to Feraris, he passes it to Feraris, and again to Feraris—just to clarify, there are actually three Feraris brothers playing—the youngest is twenty-one years old, the oldest thirty-six.[110]

Now an ugly situation in front of our goal is resolved by a corner—the corner is the place where the lines meet and a flag is put into the ground.[111] Look out, again that dangerous Cesarini—he shoots—Plánička is looking to the right instead to the other side—Burger throws up his hands, Košt'álek also protests, I can't tell you if there was a goal or not—yes, unfortunately there was—they're going back to the center. So I must announce to you that we are behind two–nil. Well, nothing is lost, keep your heads high, cross your fingers, a two-goal advantage can be overcome. You certainly remember how, four years ago, Hungaria was in the lead six–nil, and still we managed to finish five–one.[112]

---

110 The Italian team that played in the World Cup in 1934 included players Giovanni Ferrari and Attilio Ferraris but not three Feraris brothers.

111 The authors carry to extremes a feature of Laufer's broadcasts: commentary that made matches understandable even for non-sports fans.

112 Probably a reference to the First Vienna Arbitration of November 2, 1938 ("four years ago" from the date of the *Radio Show* performance) regarding Hungary's territorial claims against Czechoslovakia. A potentially total loss was "reduced" to a resounding defeat: arbiters from Nazi Germany and Fascist Italy forced Czechoslovakia to surrender most of the territories demanded by Hungary, but in the end they allowed Czechoslovakia to retain a few disputed western Slovakian cities.

Look out, look out, an ugly foul by one of our defense players—I won't tell you his name, you'll find out anyway in the daily papers—a penalty kick—look out—Pláničká deflects it—actually into the goal. We are losing three–nil, still our boys are holding their ground, they are fighting like lions. We're having bad luck. Back to the center, the game is mostly taking place on only one half of the field—unfortunately it is our half. But, Mr. Referee, what is this—a clear offside—I don't want to express myself more pointedly, or to express suspicion, but here, Mr. Referee, you have really done us some damage. We are losing four–nil—there are only a few minutes left until the end of the match—maybe we can at least score one goal—or they could score again—no, they are not going to score, because they already have scored, the fifth goal in a row, but guaranteed the last—because the referee has just blown the whistle. It's the end of the match and with that our fate, that is, our defeat, is sealed.

In conclusion I must say that, although we lost, we played fair, while the Italians used all possible and impossible means—I am certain they will never reach the finals.

And that concludes today's commentary on the match Czechoslovakia vs. Italy. I hope you were satisfied with the broadcast—you cannot, of course, be satisfied with the outcome of the match; neither can I. Well, let's hope that the next broadcast will bring happier news—*si si signore, **multa graci a riveren***[113]—I just thanked my Italian colleague. So, see you again in our homeland, to which I will return as quickly as possible—you'll hear from me again soon on sports radio in Prague—for now I say farewell, and long live sport!

---

[113] The mangled Italian is apparently for comic effect.

XVI. MEDLEY OF SONGS FROM THE PROGRAM[114]

Music: Josef Fischer on the accordion

VERSION 1

ANNOUNCER. Participating in today's variety show were:

Franta Weissenstein, Mrs. Kernmaierová-Grabová, Jiří Vrchlabský, Josef Rybář (song).

Tramp quartet The Guinea Pigs, Pavel Jeník (recitation of his own poetry), reporter Pidlovský (sports broadcast), Slávek and Polda Bělohlávek (agricultural radio), reporters Frio and Lepo (program for industry, business, and trade), Uncle Miloš (children's program).

Original music and lyrics for "Song of Prague" and "Morning Fitness Half-hour" written by Dr. Jaroslav Felix. Directed by Dr. Erna and Dr. Jaroslav Felix; assistant director Chebský. Musical interludes were rehearsed by bandleader Josef Rybář. Accompaniment by bandleader Rafael Schächter, Josef Rybář, and Puršl.

We conclude our program with "March of the Young," music by Dr. Jaroslav Felix, lyrics by Pavel Jeník.

All sing.

VERSION 2

Singing in today's variety show were:

Franta Weissenstein, Mrs. Kermajerová-Grabová, Jiří Vrchlabský, Josef Rybář, and the tramp quartet The Guinea Pigs: Jirka, Zdeněk, Slávek, and Arnošt Rybář.

Reciting his own poem "Clown" was Pavel Jeník.

Neighbors Brázda and Rákos were played by Slávek and Polda Bělohlávek.

---

114 Three different versions of the list of participants were preserved. All have been reproduced here in order to provide as much information as possible about the prisoners who took part.

The roles of the journalists were played by reporters Frio and Lepo and the sports reporter Pidlovský.

The original fairy tale by Manuel Chebský was told by Slávek.

Original music and lyrics for "Song of Prague" and "Morning Fitness Half-hour" written by Dr. Jaroslav Felix.

Texts for the agricultural radio and the half-hour of exercise are by Pavel Jeník.

Directed by Dr. Erna and Dr. Jaroslav Felix. Assistant director Manuel Chebský.

Musical interludes rehearsed by Josef Rybář; accompaniment: Professor Rafael Schächter, Josef Rybář, and Puršl.

Set design and construction: Dr. Erna and Manuel Chebský.

Organizational assistance with the production and refreshments were helpfully provided by Mrs. Neubrunnová, Mrs. Schönbaumová, Mrs. Kleinová, Mrs. Bullatá, and Mrs. Neumannová, and by Oskar, Martínek, and Žežulka.

As the finale of our program you will hear a song that we've named "March of the Young." The original music was written by Dr. Jaroslav Felix, lyrics by Pavel Jeník.

All sing.

VERSION 3

December 26, 1942.

Participating in today's nostalgic radio show were:

Franta Weissenstein, Mrs. Kernmaierová-Grabová, Jiří Vrchlabský, Josef Rybář, tramp quartet The Guinea Pigs.

Reciting from his own work: Pavel Jeník.

In the introduction and broadcasts appeared: Pidlovský, Dr. Jaroslav Felix, Polda Bělohlávek, Slávek, and reporters Frio and Lepo.

Original music and lyrics were written by Dr. Jaroslav Felix.

Directed by Dr. Erna and Dr. Jaroslav Felix; assistant director Chebský.

Musical interludes rehearsed by Josef Rybář, accompaniment by bandleader Rafael Schächter, Josef Rybář and Puršl.

Set designed and constructed by Dr. Erna and Chebský.

XVII. FINALE

ANNOUNCER. As our finale we'll perform a song that we've named "March of the Young."

All sing.

MARCH OF THE YOUNG[115]

We are young and our time's begun
Our day in the sun
Marching forward, proud and bold
No one keeps us from our goal
Oh our youth is our cry, it's the slogan we live by
Striding forth with heads held high
With a smile on our lips and a song in our hearts
Soon the whole world will be ours.

(*Refrain*) For ideals, for beauty we are striving
We fight for truth, oh come what may
The shield we carry bright and shining
Our sword a sword of flame
Onward we will march together
Let every brave man come with us
With our courage we will vanquish the world at once.

The End

---

115 See original music on page 95 of this volume, IMAGE 3.12.

IMAGE 3.11 **Original sheet music for "Song of Prague" ("Píseň o Praze"). Music and lyrics by Felix Porges.**

Courtesy of Jan, Miroslav, and Zdeněk Porges.

IMAGE 3.12 **Original sheet music for "March of the Young" ("Pochod mládi").
Music by Felix Porges, lyrics by Pavel Stránský.**

Courtesy of Pavel Stránský, Jan, Miroslav, and Zdeněk Porges.

LOOKING FOR A SPECTER

INTRODUCTION

The puppet play *Looking for a Specter*[1] was preserved at the end of an 800-page manuscript: the entire 20-month run of the weekly magazine *Vedem* (*We Lead*). The magazine was produced from December 1942 until the end of July 1944 in the youth home where author Hanuš Hachenburg lived with other 13- to 15-year-old boys.[2] *Vedem* was assembled once a week as a single typewritten or hand-written copy by its young editor, Petr Ginz. Every Friday evening in their room in building L417, the boys read their articles and poems aloud to each other and to invited guests. A 1995 anthology of excerpts from the manuscript and commentary by survivors acquaints readers not only with the magazine itself and the system of youth care in the ghetto but with the boys and their

IMAGE 4.1 (*facing page*) **The first page of the manuscript of *Looking for a Specter*.** *Courtesy of the Terezín Memorial.*

1 The title of this play has been translated previously as *Looking for a Monster* or *Looking for a Ghost*. The Czech noun *strašidlo* is difficult to render in English; it derives from the verb *strašit*, meaning simply "to frighten."

2 Several youth homes in the ghetto produced their own magazines. See the essay by Marie Rút Křížková and Kurt Jiří Kotouč in the chapter "Czech Literary Work," in *Art Against Death: Permanent Exhibitions of the Terezín Memorial in the Former Magdeburg Barracks* (Prague: Oswald, 2002), pp. 177–204.

Loutková hra:
HLEDÁME STRAŠIDLO
Konkurs časopisu
Vedem.
Terezín.
Ha

beloved teacher, Walter Eisinger.[3] Although Hachenburg contributed many poems and essays to *Vedem*, this was apparently his only dramatic work. An English-language translation by Terezín/Theresienstadt survivor Alisa Shek, titled *We Are Looking for a Monster*, was published in an exhibition catalog in 2001.[4]

THE AUTHOR

Little is known about Hanuš Hachenburg's life before he was deported to the ghetto. Born on July 12, 1929, he lived in Prague with his mother but never knew his father. He was sent to the Jewish orphanage on Belgická Street in Prague in 1941, where he may have been inspired by the many artists who were invited to visit the children by orphanage director Ota Freudenfeld.[5] Hachenburg was only thirteen years old when he arrived in Terezín/Theresienstadt on October 24, 1942. He soon made a name for himself in his youth home as a poet, contributing several works to *Vedem*.[6]

On December 18, 1943 Hachenburg was included in a transport that was sent to the so-called family camp at Auschwitz-Birkenau.[7] His voice was heard even there; according to survivors, a poem he wrote called "The Gong" was popular among the prisoners.[8] If he did not die

---

3 Marie Rút Křížková, Kurt Jiří Koutouč, and Zdeněk Ornest (eds.), *We are Children Just the Same: "Vedem," the Secret Magazine by the Boys of Terezín* (Philadelphia: Jewish Publication Society, 1995). The text of Hachenburg's play was not included in this publication, but pages of his original manuscript were reproduced as illustrations on the inside covers of the book.

4 See Elena Makarova, *Long Live Life! or Dance around the Skeleton* (Jerusalem: Verba, 2001), pp. 24–5.

5 See Křížková and Kotouč, "Czech Literary Work," p. 180.

6 Several of Hachenburg's poems have been published in Křížková et al., *We are Children Just the Same* (see, for example, pp. 22, 55, 82, 176, 178).

7 For an account of the family camp by a survivor see Bondy, *"Elder of the Jews,"* pp. 405–47.

8 See Křížková et al., *We are Children Just the Same*, p. 182.

of starvation, cold, or illness in Auschwitz-Birkenau his life ended in July 1944, when all the prisoners of the family camp who were not selected for labor were sent to the gas chambers.

THE SCRIPT

According to Kurt Jiří Kotouč, who lived in the same youth home and knew Hachenburg well, this was his only play. Although Hachenburg indicated on the title page that the work was written for a competition sponsored by *Vedem*, Kotouč says this was a joke on Hachenburg's part and that no such competition took place. He believes that Hachenburg wrote it simply to try out a new literary genre, perhaps inspired by the many puppet performances that took place in the youth homes.[9]

While *Looking for a Specter* is clearly the work of a young author, the dark humor of the play is at times eerily mature. In the form of a puppet play filled with both familiar and unfamiliar fairy-tale figures, Hachenburg creates an allegorical world where the bones of the elderly are collected as raw material, Death is enslaved by a dictator, and questions of guilt and innocence are impossible to resolve. Today's reader may be chilled by Hachenburg's seeming foreknowledge of events in the death camps. Kotouč, however, does not believe that Hachenburg intended to suggest that such things could actually take place. He simply took the events he had already witnessed to their logical conclusion: the banalization of death to the point where the human body became just material for collection.

Hachenburg's work has recently reached new audiences: an adaptation of the play by South African puppeteer Gary Friedman premiered in Cape Town in November 2001.[10] Although Hachenburg's sometimes brutal satire may be challenging for post-war audiences, *Looking for a*

---

9 Kurt Jiří Kotouč, interview with Lisa Peschel, January 8, 2006. Posters for several puppet performances have been preserved in the Terezín Memorial.

10 For more information, see www.lookingforamonster.com.

Specter offers a unique look into ways in which even children tried to make sense of the world of the ghetto and face it with courage.

BIOGRAPHICAL INFORMATION

THE AUTHOR

HANUŠ HACHENBURG was born on July 12, 1929 and was deported to Terezín/Theresienstadt on October 24, 1942. On December 18, 1943, he was deported to Auschwitz, where he perished.

SURVIVORS CONTRIBUTING TO THE INTRODUCTION AND ANNOTATION

KURT JIŘÍ KOTOUČ was born on February 15, 1929. He was deported from Třebíč to Terezín/Theresienstadt on May 22, 1942, and from the ghetto to Auschwitz on October 12, 1944. He was liberated in Buchenwald. Kotouč passed away in June 2008.

LOOKING FOR A SPECTER

COMPETITION FOR THE MAGAZINE *VEDEM*
TEREZÍN

Ha— [11]

CHARACTERS

Envoy
King
Policeman
Minister
Sorcerer
Peasant Woman
Honza
Grandfather
Jew/Mordechai
Mařenka
Jeníček
Death

SETS

Street
Royal hall
Sorcerer's chamber
Circus

PROPS

Microphone
Throne
Bell

---

11 Initials that Hachenburg used for his works that appeared in *Vedem*.

Act I. ROYAL HALL

KING. I don't know what to do anymore. The common people with their nasty thoughts are rebelling against me. We have to convince them that the old ways are best. Our predecessors ruled in peace and quiet and the people didn't rebel. They went about their work peacefully and obeyed the king.

MINISTER. Your Highness, I have established camps where, thanks to the success of our methods, people have stopped having such thoughts. You can see how profitable the camps are from the not-insignificant amounts of money flowing into the secret state and royal treasury in exchange for the urns of those who no longer think.[12]

KING. Enough about you and your methods! We don't need people who can't think—we need people who think what I want them to think. Otherwise who am I going to rule in my old age?

POLICEMAN. Hail to your Royal Highness! Your guards, the Savage Salami,[13] stand ready to obey your orders.

MINISTER. Excuse me, Your Highness, I have a proposition. We need a specter.

KING. A good idea.

POLICEMAN. Death. A skeleton. That's what people fear most.

MINISTER. The Savage Salami's security service could lead it around.

POLICEMAN. At your service.

KING. Excellent! I nominate you to be decorated for your most virtuous philanthropy. With the Blood Order, for instance.[14] Sir

---

12 The Nazi practice of returning urns with the remains of cremated prisoners to their families began with the introduction of crematoria at the concentration camps in the late 1930s but was later abandoned. The families were charged a fee for this "service." See Paul Berben, *Dachau, 1933–1945: The Official History* (London: Norfolk Press, 1975), p. 7.

13 In the original, *Surové Salámy*. According to Kurt Jiří Kotouč, such names were ironic references to National Socialist organizations and institutions, in this case, the SS. Interview with Lisa Peschel, January 8, 2006.

14 The *Blutorden*, established by Adolf Hitler in 1934, was the highest decoration awarded by the National Socialist Party.

Chief Commander of the Platoon, I congratulate you.[15] I will broadcast the news to my trusted followers and true believers. Bring me a microphone. (*Policeman brings a microphone. King speaks into it.*) To all my subjects: effective immediately, I decree that all old bones of any origin shall be collected by the acting authorities of the Stupid Anti-literates.[16] To be collected: all human and animal bones more than sixty years old. Whoever conceals any such person or animal subject to obligatory submission will be punished by eternal damnation in the fires of hell. I, King Anti-literate Harangue,[17] enlightened by God. (*To Minister and Policeman*) From the collected bones, my dear collaborators, I'll construct a skeleton to scare people, which will certainly meet all the requirements of modern society.

MINISTER and **POLICEMAN**. Brilliant! (*They applaud.*)

Curtain.

Act II. STREET

PEASANT WOMAN (*crying*). My grandmother, my dear grandmother! My beloved grandmother, my poor grandmother!

HONZA (*offstage*). They're coming, Grandpa, come on! (*Enters with Grandfather.*) Don't worry about a thing, Grandpa. I am proud to be getting rid of you for the good of our nation.

PEASANT WOMAN. But—your grandfather . . . my unfortunate grandmother!

---

15 This title sounds more absurd in the original Czech and may be a satire on German officers' titles. Michael Wögerbauer's German-language translation, "Herr Überoberster Oberführer der Unterabteilung," could be used to create a comic effect for English-speaking audiences. See Hanuš Hachenburg, *Wir suchen ein Gespenst* (M. Wögerbauer trans.) in Lisa Peschel, *Divadelní texty z terezínského ghetta / Theatertexte aus dem Ghetto Theresienstadt, 1941–1945* (Dalibor Dobiáš and Michael Wögerbauer trans.) (Prague: Akropolis, 2008), p. 134.

16 In the original Czech, *Spitoměli* (properly spelled *zpitoměli*) *Analfabeti*, an ironic reference to the Nazi SA (Sturmabteilung).

17 In the original Czech, *Analphabet Huba*, a reference to Adolf Hitler himself.

HONZA. Ask them if you could keep her and scare people with her yourself![18] (*Roars with laughter.*)

PEASANT WOMAN. Young man, keep your stupid remarks to yourself. My grandmother, my sorrowful grandmother . . .

HONZA. Oh! You must consign your grandmother to our king, lord and ruler, with unconcealed joy. He is lord and he can, for example, cut my grandfather into pieces, make briquettes out of him, or gunpowder, or Wiener schnitzel.

GRANDFATHER (*fainting*). Help!!

HONZA. Weakling! You don't deserve to be a son of our nation! Give up your bones with unconcealed joy! Come on, Gramps, let's go to the junkyard!

PEASANT WOMAN. You brute!

HONZA (*offstage*). Hey, junkyard! One grandfather, sixty-three years old, weight sixteen and a half kilograms, with documents and ration coupons.[19]

VOICE 1 (*offstage*). Sixteen and a half kilograms—that means the decoration of the Golden Tomcat, fourth class. I congratulate you.

PEASANT WOMAN. Oh! So there's something in it for me! I'll receive a medal and maybe I'll even be knighted.

VOICE 1 (*offstage*). Congratulations!

HONZA (*offstage*). Don't mention it. My pleasure.

Death enters.

DEATH. What a horror, madam, these bones.

PEASANT WOMAN. Help! Poli-i-i-i-i-ce!

DEATH. I'm going to turn myself in.

VOICE 2 (*offstage*). And why don't you go gather bones at the battle-front? There are heaps of them there!

VOICE 3 (*offstage*). Hands up! (*Fires a shot.*) You are sentenced to life in an improvement camp.

---

18 That is, the grandmother already looks frightening enough to be used as a specter.

19 Ration coupons were introduced in the Protectorate of Bohemia and Moravia in October 1939.

DEATH. These are strange times.

PEASANT WOMAN. Police!!!

> *Policeman enters.*

POLICEMAN. *Was hier? Halt!*[20] Aha—my dear lady Death! We've been searching for you; we need you. Come with me!

DEATH. I wouldn't even think of it.

POLICEMAN. You are under arrest. Come with me immediately. (*Puts his hand on Death's shoulder.*)

> *Exit.*

Curtain.

Act III. ROYAL HALL

Policeman enters, leading Death.

POLICEMAN. Here is Death.

KING. Pleased to meet you. (*To Policeman*) I see you've been hard at work.

POLICEMAN. Yes, I certainly have. I ran after her for three whole hours and used up lots of bullets.

MINISTER. That's irresponsible. Such expensive goods . . .

KING. I appoint you to be my state specter. My guards, the Savage Salami, will lead you around and the people will be afraid of you. We'll immediately determine your field of service based on the advice of my cabinet ministers.

MINISTER. We propose the area from the prime meridian, longitude 0°, all the way around to the prime meridian, longitude 0°.

KING. Indeed. I approve. Take her away.

Curtain.

---

20 Ungrammatical German for "What's going on here? Stop!"

Act IV. STREET

VOICE. Three years later . . .

MAŘENKA (*baby talk*).[21] Look, Jeníček, Death is coming this way. And some man with lots of medals is leading her. They come here every day at four o'clock. They've been doing it three years already.[22]

VOICES (*backstage*). Hurrah! Here she comes! Look at that scrawny lady, Vašíček![23]

Death enters with Policeman.

DEATH (*making ghostly noises*). Whooo-ooo-oooo! Booooo! Fee-fi-fo-fum! Boo boo boo![24]

HONZA. Well this is like the haunted house at the county fair.

GRANDFATHER. Now I've seen everything! Ha ha ha ha.

DEATH. Boo boo boo!

POLICEMAN. *Rechts um! Links um!*[25]

JENÍČEK (*to Policeman*). Sir, you are an idiot.

DEATH. Boo boo!

POLICEMAN (*to Jeníček*). You're under arrest!

MAŘENKA. Hee hee hee! What are you talking about, you old geezer? You'll never catch him!

POLICEMAN. You're under arrest too.

Peasant Woman runs in.

PEASANT WOMAN. My God! My children. The little Lord Jesus and the Virgin Mary in heaven! (*Policeman chases Mařenka. Jeníček*

---

21 The unconventional spelling of this passage in the Czech original suggests that Mařenka is a child.

22 Mařenka (little Mary) and Jeníček (little Johnny) are common names in Czech fairy tales. Mařenka and Jeník are also the names of the main characters in the Czech opera *The Bartered Bride* (*Prodaná nevěsta*), which was performed in the ghetto.

23 The character Vašíček or Vašek also appears in *The Bartered Bride*.

24 In the Czech original, Death makes sounds typical of Czech fairy tales: "Bubububububu! Búúúú! Chlemst chrup chlamst! Bububu! Búúú!"

25 German for "Right face! Left face!"

IMAGE 4.2 **A doll made in the ghetto representing a *Ghettowachmann* (member of the Ghetto Guard).**

Courtesy of the Terezín Memorial.

runs after him and hits him on the back. Death haunts them all.) My children!

HONZA. Leave that girl alone!

POLICEMAN. I am an officer of the state.

DEATH. Boo! boo!

Mařenka and Jeníček run away while Honza holds Death.

HONZA. So! Now everything is all right. (*Leaves with Grandfather.*)

GRANDFATHER. Good afternoon, Mr. Secret Service! (*Exits.*)

Curtain.

KING. Dear Mr. Sorcerer! I have come to you for advice.

SORCERER. Hmm—for advice. Well, do you have any money?

MINISTER. As soon as we are victorious, dear Doctor of Law.[26] I guarantee it.

SORCERER. I'll take your word for it. Please, have a seat. (*Pause*) Oh, there are no chairs here! Aha! So, well, please stand for a while.

KING. My people, dear Doctor, are harboring rebellious thoughts.

SORCERER. AHA!

MINISTER. Yes—and listen to this! Yesterday when I went out into the streets to investigate the situation, people were treating Death like some figure from the county fair and making rude remarks!

SORCERER. May I ask—my dear clients—what kind of remarks?

KING. Well, for instance: "Hey lady, give me your beef-bones for broth!" Somebody put up a huge poster: "Preserve your bones, little bones, and aspic, little aspic, in denatured alcohol. Available for 3.50 crowns a liter in Anna Vodenková's drugstore, 9 Újezd Street, entrance under the arcade."

SORCERER. Hmm, hmm. A serious offense.

MINISTER. And so, our favorite Doctor of Law and Witchcraft, what is His Excellency, our King Anti-literate Harangue, supposed to do? The people must fear something in our kingdom, something in our regime—so who is supposed to scare them—if not death? What's the best kind of specter?

SORCERER (*thinks for some time*). You, Your Excellency!

Pause.

KING. And will people consider me a specter?

SORCERER. Of course. You are the greatest specter of our time.

KING. Oh—well—hmm—thank you. This is quite an honor.

---

26 In the original script the Minister addresses the Sorcerer as *judr* (pronounced "YEW-der"), from the Czech abbreviation for doctor of law, JUDr. Jokes about greedy lawyers were popular during this period.

MINISTER. Success! The king thanks you! I mean, the country thanks you!

KING. If you ever need anything, please, don't hesitate to ask! But only after we win!

King and Minister leave. Sorcerer shakes his head in worry.

Curtain.

Act VI. ROYAL HALL

King sits on his throne. Policeman enters.

POLICEMAN. Your Majesty, one of your subjects is waiting outside!

KING. I'm not surprised. What does he look like?

POLICEMAN. Very fat. And, well, a few details: his pants are full of holes, and he has a nose—well, it's hard to describe—and sidelocks.

KING. All right, bring him in.

Mordechai[27] enters.

MORDECHAI. *Gitn tag!*[28] (*Bows thrice.*)

KING. Speak!

MORDECHAI. Oh King! Hear me or rather the words of my unworthy mouth! The mouth of your most humble, truest, and poorest slave in this world.

KING. I said you can say whatever you please.

Policeman comes in but stops at the door.

MORDECHAI. Oh! My heart is seized by a terrible pain! Oy vey! My greatest King, chosen by Jehovah, why do you collect bones like this?

KING. Well, for God's sake, how am I supposed to collect them? Nobody will hand in his relatives voluntarily!

---

27 The character of Mordechai embodies many negative Jewish stereotypes. It is possible that Hachenburg intended to satirize members of the Jewish Council of Elders, whom some prisoners viewed as excessively servile.

28 From the German *Guten Tag* (good day). The unconventional spelling in the original suggests Yiddish or distorted German pronunciation.

MORDECHAI. *Selpsferstendlich.*[29] My great King is always right about everything. But a righteous man is filled with sorrow to see those bare bones, completely uncovered. Oh, King! Have mercy! Let the bones of your humble subjects be covered by skin!

KING. So be it!

MORDECHAI. Oy oy—*um Gottes willen,*[30] tears come to my eyes and my soul is burdened by great sadness. Oh—oh! Bare skin unprotected from frost, bad weather, and prying eyes—oh King, hear my distraught weeping! Let the weak flesh be covered at least by humble rags discarded by the people, if not by decent clothes. Ach, ach! My God! (*Beats his breast.*)

KING. You have a point. So be it!

MORDECHAI. And now, my King, let me serve you body and soul and allow me to collect those rags, bones, and skin all over the length and breadth of your glorious lands—for, believe me, I have had long years of practice.[31]

KING. Officer!

POLICEMAN. At your service.

KING. This man will be the state director for the collection of waste and persons older than sixty years of age. And you, Sir . . .

MORDECHAI. Israel ben Cohen ben Isaac Yehuda ben Mordechai Karpeles.

KING. Well, Mr. Karpeles, go forth and carry out your duties. You'll receive a beige uniform with the appropriate markings, decorations and side stripes in our state dispensary.

MORDECHAI. Blessed be our good king who hears his children in their misery and helps them to fill their purses. Amen. (*Exits.*)

Envoy enters.

ENVOY. Praise be to the Lord Jesus Christ. I have been sent to address legal matters of concern to the One Holy Catholic and Apostolic Church.

---

29 In the original, *sälpsferständlich,* from the German *selbstverständlich* (of course).

30 German for "for God's sake."

31 Mordechai here represents a further Jewish stereotype: the rag picker.

KING. I am listening.

ENVOY. Yesterday your authorized officials broke into the Church of the Virgin Mary the Macabre and, from a silver reliquary depicting the Virgin Mary washing the underdrawers of St. Joseph, they stole three ribs and one marrow-bone of St. Sebastian of Blessed Memory.[32] The flock rebels against it and demands that at least the marrow-bone—with its contents—be returned no later than 6 p.m. to the monastery of the Shining Mercy, where thirty liters of soup will be cooked from it for the poor and unemployed. The rest will be sent express registered back to the Church of the Virgin Mary the Macabre.

KING. I acknowledge your church as the one true church but I can't give that bone back. I need it urgently.

ENVOY. Well for God's sake, then, at least give me back the marrow! Your Excellency, I beseech you to remember your devoted and hungry flock.

KING. All right, all right. Take the marrow. But I need the bone. I just ran out of glue.

ENVOY. Oh horrors! Did St. Sebastian of Blessed Memory have hooves instead of his revered and holy feet that his bones should be boiled for glue?

KING. Yes, from this empty marrow-bone I'll make glue, adding goats' droppings and water. I always find some substitute in hard times. I suggest you to do the same; you must have lots of old holy teeth and other junk, and teeth make fabulous glue.

ENVOY. As you wish, Your Highness. But I warn you that, as a result, a great misfortune will certainly be visited upon your person.

KING. You may leave my presence.

ENVOY. Thank you!

Curtain.

---

32 This may be a joke on Hachenburg's part. The phrase "of blessed memory" is a direct translation of the Hebrew expression *zichrono livrachah,* used for deceased loved ones and respected Jewish historical figures—but not for Catholic saints.

Honza, Mařenka, Jeníček, Peasant Woman. A sign: "Circus of History, Fate, and Co."

JEW.[33] Venerable gentlemen! Now for the main event![34] Here comes the king, the debauchee, who collected bones with impunity! He dances here with Death, who crushes him to his last breath!

MAŘENKA (*baby talk*). Here they come, Jeníček!

DEATH and KING. I can't stand it!

KING. It's terrible!

DEATH. It's your fault!

KING. It's your fault!

DEATH. It's my fault? It's your fault!

KING. Not mine, you monster, but yours!

DEATH. Mine? It's yours, buddy! Yours!

Audience applauds; King and Death quarrel with increasing speed.

KING. It's your fault.

DEATH. It's your fault.

KING. It's your fault.

DEATH. You beast, it's your fault.

KING. You moron, it's your fault.

DEATH. It's not my fault!

KING. It's not my fault!

JENÍČEK. It's not their fault!

JEW. And that's the end of our show. We invite you to come again tomorrow, at five minutes to midnight, admission is free.

Curtain.

The End

---

33 Since there is only one "Jew" listed in the cast of characters, this figure is probably Mordechai from the previous scene.

34 In the original, *Hauptattración*, from German *Hauptattraktion* (main attraction).

IMAGE 4.3 **A souvenir poster for a marionette theater performance.**
Courtesy of the Terezín Memorial.

„PRINZ BETTLIEGEND"

AUTOR:	JOSEF LUSTIG
TEXTY:	FRANT. KOVANIC
VÝPRAVA, KOSTÝMY:	OTA NEUMANN
HUDBA:	Jaroslav JEŽEK

KOUZELNÍK	OTA NEUMANN
BUBENÍK	MILAN KLINGER
DÁMA	GERTA WEINBERGOVÁ
KRÁL	EVŽEN FEURSTEIN
PRINCEZNA DIENSTFREI	TRUDA POPPEROVÁ
MINISTR FINANCÍ	FRICEK GROSS
MINISTR ZDRAVOTNICTVÍ	EGON KRAUS
ORDONANC	OTA BAUER
MENAGE - DIENST	OSKAR SOBOTA
PRINC „BETTLIEGEND"	JIRKA REICH
PLAČÍCÍ SLEČNA	ZDENKA FANTLOVÁ
HOKUS	JIŘÍ SPITZ
POKUS	JOSEF LUSTIG

DOPROVÁZÍ:	JIRKA HORNER
REŽIE:	JOSEF LUSTIG
SVĚTLA:	JINDRA WEIL

FRANTIŠEK KOWANITZ

Songs from the Revue
PRINCE BETTLIEGEND

INTRODUCTION

Prince Bettliegend was one of three revues performed in the ghetto by a group of actors that formed around the comic duo Josef Lustig and Jiří Štefl (né Spitz). Their fellow prisoner František Kowanitz wrote the song lyrics; most of them were set to popular melodies by Jaroslav Ježek, the legendary composer for the Liberated Theater of Voskovec and Werich.[1] The texts included here were found in the archives of the Jewish Museum in Prague. According to a note on the typescript, they were copied from a manuscript in the possession of survivor Dr. Josef Bor in March 1970.[2] Although all were preserved in a file for *Prince*

IMAGE 5.1 (*Facing page*) **A souvenir poster for the revue *Prince Bettliegend*.** *Courtesy of the Terezín Memorial.*

1 See Voskovec and Werich (glossary).

2 Josef Bor (né Josef Bondy) was born on July 2, 1906. He was deported from Kolín to Terezín/Theresienstadt on June 5, 1942, and to Auschwitz on October 28, 1944. In the 1960s he published two works based on his experiences in the ghetto: *The Abandoned Doll* (*Opuštěná panenka*, 1961) and *Terezín Requiem* (*Terezínské rekviem*, 1963). He died on February 5, 1979.

Bettliegend, the sheer number and variety of the texts suggests that some may have been written for the duo's other revues. In 1993 the song lyrics were published in an appendix to Ludmila Vrkočová's book *Requiem for Themselves*, an account of the cultural life of the ghetto based mainly upon survivor testimony from the 1980s.[3]

The texts are published here with the intention of restoring them to their original setting within the plot of a theatrical revue. None of the three scripts has been discovered but survivor testimony enables at least a partial reconstruction of the plots.

THE AUTHORS AND THE SCRIPTS

Little biographical information has been preserved about Lustig, Štefl, and Kowanitz. However, documents preserved in the archives of the Terezín Memorial in the Czech Republic and survivor testimony allow us to trace their theatrical activities in the ghetto.

Lustig and Štefl may have worked together for the first time in late May 1942, when theater artist Karel Švenk[4] organized a performance to mark the six-month anniversary of the first transport to Terezín/Theresienstadt, AK I.[5] Also participating in that production was actor Evžen Foltýn (né Eugen Feuerstein), who provided vivid descriptions of some of the scenes in *Prince Bettliegend* in his testimony.

Štefl himself described how their performances were conceived:

The idea was born to do theater in the style of the Liberated Theater. The first attempt in the fall of 1942 was titled *Let's*

---

3 Ludmila Vrkočová, *Rekviem sami sobě* (Prague: Arkýř, 1993), pp. 154–62, 165–6. Vrkočová obtained the lyrics from a songbook preserved by survivor Marta Fantlová-Neumannová.

4 Švenk was one of the most active Czech-language cabaret artists in Terezín/Theresienstadt. See Rebecca Rovit, "A Carousel of Theatrical Performance at Theresienstadt," in Anne D. Dutlinger (ed.), *Art, Music and Education as Strategies for Survival: Theresienstadt 1941–45* (New York: Herodias, 2001), pp. 122–43.

5 A poster for the performance that lists the actors' names has been preserved in the Terezín Memorial, inv. no. PT 4308.

IMAGE 5.2 **A souvenir poster for a cabaret by Karel Švenk marking the six-month anniversary of the arrival of the AK I transport.**

Courtesy of the Terezín Memorial.

Meet at Philip's. It was the first theater that made fun of the situation in which people in Terezín lived.[6]

Kowanitz was already collaborating with them at this point, writing original texts to Ježek's melodies. According to Dr. Eva Šormová, whose work on the ghetto is based on testimony she gathered from over forty survivors in the 1960s, the revue was about a group of former Terezín/Theresienstadt prisoners who meet several years after the war.[7]

Lustig and Štefl's first fully staged revue, *Prince Bettliegend*, satirized certain aspects of life in the ghetto.[8] *Bettliegend*, literally "bedridden," indicated a person who, having been prescribed bed rest due to illness, did not have to work.[9] Such an official designation could also exempt a prisoner from outgoing transports. Terezín/Theresienstadt doctors sometimes assigned this designation even to a healthy prisoner in order to protect a friend or family member or in return for a bribe.[10]

As Štefl recalled, Lustig wrote *Prince Bettliegend* as a satirical fairy tale to criticize this kind of favoritism and corruption. The first scene took place in a wizard's workshop; the actors stood behind a screen so that only their shadows were visible. The wizard inadvertently revealed that he has cast a spell on a prince who, as a result, could not get out of his bunk. The wizard's helpers, Hocus and Pocus, played by Lustig and Štefl in the style of Voskovec and Werich, decide to try to free him.

The second scene took place at the king's palace. The set for this scene had a canopy supported by four decorated columns from a funeral wagon.[11] Instead of a coat of arms it was decorated with an ace of spades.[12] Foltýn, who played the king, remembered this scene vividly:

---

6 Jiří Štefl, interview with Eva Šormová, May 2, 1963.

7 See Šormová, *Divadlo v Terezíně*, p. 50.

8 A souvenir poster for the performance has been preserved in the Terezín Memorial, inv. no. PT 4305.

9 Luděk Eliáš, interview with Lisa Peschel, March 1, 2005.

10 See Adler, *Theresienstadt*, p. 285.

11 See *Wagenkolonne* (glossary). The decorative columns of the funeral wagons were usually sawed off to make the loading of cargo easier; they would have been easy to obtain as set pieces.

12 In the Czech card game *Černý petr* (Black Peter), the player who draws this card loses the game.

IMAGE 5.3 **Spectators standing on a funeral wagon to watch an outdoor perform-ance. The columns of the wagon have been removed. By A. Aussenberg.**
Courtesy of Yad Vashem.

The play began like puppet theater. I sat in an armchair as if on a throne and Truda Popperová sat next to me on the ground. We were frozen in awkward positions like abandoned marionettes. The curtain rose and we corrected our postures, like when the puppeteer lifts the strings. King: "And know, my royal daughter, Princess Dienstfrei,[13] that you will take as your husband anyone who can free the prince from the spell." Everything was accompanied by puppet-like movements. Princess: "And why, royal father, am I not allowed to marry the man my heart desires?"[14]

13 *Dienstfrei* in German means "free of service," that is, someone with no obligation to work.

14 Vrkočová, *Rekviem sami sobě*, p. 111.

According to Štefl, this opening was a parody of the ghetto's "puppet" self-government.[15] In spite of their critical intentions, however, the song "The Royal Speech" reveals a great deal of sympathy for the difficult situation in which the Jewish leaders found themselves. Soon after the opening of the scene, the actors ceased the puppet-like movements and acted and spoke normally. The plot continued in this vein, with the king and other characters looking for a means to break the spell on the prince.

Survivors recalled only scattered details of the remaining scenes. Foltýn remembered one in which the prince lay on a bunk, propped up to make him visible to the audience, quoting Hamlet:

> He recited from the famous monologue "to be or not to be" and took from his dish a real Terezín dumpling. And then he said, "To be or not to be. A dumpling. Should I eat you?" The audience went wild.[16]

Štefl remembered a young lady in the audience who did not like the sad ending. The actress playing the young lady, Zdenka Ehrlich-Fantlová, recalled her role:

> At that point a young girl in the audience burst into tears over the prince's plight. Hearing this, the clowns [Lustig and Štefl] invited her up on stage and assured her that the Prince would stay bedridden and everything would turn out fine.[17]

According to Štefl, it is at this point that the prince announced that he could not get out of bed because he had formally been classified as *bettliegend*, and an inspection would get him into trouble. The play, from a Terezín/Theresienstadt point of view, ends happily: no one manages to break the spell on the prince and he remains bedridden. In the last scene, Lustig and Štefl stepped out of their roles and, in the style of Voskovec and Werich, they commented on the play and talked about current events with each other as well as the audience.[18]

---

15 See *Selbstverwaltung* (glossary).

16 Vrkočová, *Rekviem sami sobě*, p. 111

17 Zdenka Ehrlich-Fantlová, "The Czech Theater in Terezín" (Deryk Viney trans.), in Rebecca Rovit and Alvin Goldfarb (eds.), *Theatrical Performance During the Holocaust* (Baltimore, MD: Johns Hopkins University Press, 1999), pp. 231–49, see p. 234.

18 Jiří Štefl, interview with Eva Šormová, May 2, 1963.

The last play that Lustig and Štefl worked on together, *Ben Akiba Lied*,[19] was written in the summer of 1943 but not performed until the summer of 1944.[20] Dr. Sormová summarized the plot as follows:

> The entire play was basically a theatrically expanded debate about Rabbi ben Akiba's saying "everything has happened before."[21] The spectators were guided through a series of scenes by two Terezín prisoners who argued about the truth of Ben Akiba's pronouncement. They returned to various historical periods and places—to ancient Rome, to the time of the persecution of the Christians, to Mount Olympus. And in the conclusion of the play they tried to explain to the founders of Terezín, Joseph II and Maria Theresa, the new function of their city, but their imperial highnesses did not understand. [22]

Štefl and Fantlová, who played the role of Aphrodite, provided further details. For example, in the scene about the persecution of Christians, actors playing a lion and a tiger talked about how they have eaten so many Christians that they cannot stand to see another one.[23] One of the victims cast into the arena, Mordechai Pinkas, argues that, since he is a Jew and not a Christian, there must be some mistake; eventually he persuades the lion and tiger to let him go free.[24]

IMAGES 5.4 and 5.5 (*pp. 122, 123*) **Illustrations for *Ben Akiba Lied*.**
Courtesy of the Terezín Memorial.

---

19 Preserved posters feature only illustrations and do not include the names of the cast or the dates of the performances.

20 Jiří Štefl, interview with Eva Šormová, May 2, 1963. He also recalls that they performed the play approximately 10 times before Czech-language theater was forbidden late in the summer of 1944.

21 Akiba ben Yosef (*c.*50–*c.*135 CE), or simply Rabbi Akiba, was a great authority in matters of Jewish tradition and is considered one of the founders of rabbinical Judaism.

22 Šormová, *Divadlo v Terezíně*, p. 50.

23 Jiří Štefl, interview with Eva Šormová, May 2, 1963. He also provides details about the set and costume design for this scene: "On one barrel sits a terrible monster dressed in a striped gold T-shirt, on its head a round hatbox, on the box a cat-head and whiskers [a tiger]. The lion had sand-colored clothing, on its head was a similar box."

24 Ehrlich-Fantlová, "The Czech Theater in Terezín," p. 238.

J.LUSTIG: Ben Akiba lhal.

J.LUSTIG: Ben Akiba lh al.

The scene with the Olympian gods, according to Štefl, was "a satire on the Council of Elders and on the German Reich."[25] Fantlová describes the scene, where the gods all argue with each other and fail to come to any kind of agreement, as meant to "echo the divisions within both the Council of Elders and the German political leadership."[26]

In the final scene, which featured Empress Maria Theresa and Joseph II looking down upon the ghetto, "two Jewish souls come floating up, straight from Terezín, and offer to give the empress and her son a detailed account of events down there. Their majesties reject it out of hand."[27] The two arguing prisoners played by Lustig and Štefl finally agreed that, since nothing like Terezín/Theresienstadt had ever happened before, Ben Akiba lied.

Josef Lustig did not live to see the premiere of *Ben Akiba Lied*. He died of an illness in the ghetto at the end of January 1944. In September 1944 Štefl and Kowanitz were deported to Auschwitz. Only Štefl survived.

BIOGRAPHICAL INFORMATION

The names of all the participants in *Prince Bettliegend* were listed on the poster for the performance preserved in the Terezín Memorial.

AUTHORS

JOSEF LUSTIG directed *Prince Bettliegend* and played the role of Pokus in addition to writing the play. He was born on January 11, 1911, was deported from Prague to Terezín/Theresienstadt on May 15, 1942, and died there on January 28, 1944.

FRANTIŠEK KOWANITZ (also written **KOVANIC**) was born on April 16, 1910. He was deported from Prague to Terezín/Theresienstadt on December 4, 1941, and to Auschwitz on September 28, 1944. He perished.

---

25 Jiří Štefl, interview with Eva Šormová, May 2, 1963.
26 Ehrlich-Fantlová, "The Czech Theater in Terezín," p. 239.
27 Ibid.

OTA NEUMANN played the role of the Magician and also created the sets and costumes. Unfortunately, it is not possible to identify him more closely. In the database of the Institute of the Terezín Initiative, the name Ota or Otakar Neumann appears eight times and the name Otto Neumann eighteen times.

MILAN KLINGER played the role of the Drummer. He was born on September 13, 1917, deported from Prague to Terezín/Theresienstadt on November 24, 1941, and to Auschwitz on October 23, 1944. He perished.

GERTA WEINBERGOVÁ (probably **GERTRUDA WEINBERGEROVÁ**) played the role of the Lady. She was born on April 2, 1921. On December 14, 1941, she was deported from Prague to Terezín/Theresienstadt and on October 28, 1944 to Auschwitz. She returned to Terezín/Theresienstadt on a death march and was liberated there.

EVŽEN FOLTÝN (né **EUGEN FEUERSTEIN**) played the role of the King. He was born on April 7, 1914, deported from Prague to Terezín/Theresienstadt on November 24, 1941 (with transport AK I), and was liberated there.

GERTRUDA (TRUDA) POPPEROVÁ (stage name after the war: **JANA ŠEDOVÁ**) played Princess Dienstfrei. She was born on February 26, 1920, and deported from Prague to Terezín/Theresienstadt on December 14, 1941. She was liberated in the ghetto.

BEDŘICH (FRICEK) GROSS played the role of the Minister of Finance. He was born on June 5, 1906. On November 24, 1941 he was deported from Prague to Terezín/Theresienstadt, and on September 6, 1943, to Auschwitz. He perished.

EGON KRAUS played the role of the Minister of Health. He was born on April 28, 1906. On December 4, 1941 he was deported from Prague to Terezín/Theresienstadt and on September 28, 1944, to Auschwitz. He perished.

OTA BAUER played the role of the Orderly. He was born on December 1, 1921. On November 24, 1941 he was deported from Prague to Terezín/Theresienstadt and on October 1, 1944, to Auschwitz. He perished.

OSKAR SOBOTA played the role of the Food Service Worker. He was born on May 18, 1912. On November 20, 1942 he was deported from Prague to Terezín/Theresienstadt and on December 18, 1943 to Auschwitz. He perished.

JIŘÍ (JIRKA) REICH played the role of Prince Bettliegend. He was born on July 1, 1924. On December 10, 1941, he was deported from Prague to Terezín/Theresienstadt and on September 28, 1944 to Auschwitz. He perished in Dachau on March 14, 1945.

ZDENKA FANTLOVÁ (after the war, **EHRLICH-FANTLOVÁ**) played the role of the Crying Girl. She was born on March 28, 1922. On January 22, 1942, she was deported from Plzeň/Pilsen to Terezín/Theresienstadt, and on October 16, 1944, to Auschwitz. She survived and now lives in London.

JIŘÍ ŠTEFL (né **SPITZ**), born on May 3, 1913, was deported from Prague to Terezín/Theresienstadt on February 8, 1942, and to Auschwitz on September 28, 1944. He was liberated in Auschwitz.

JIŘÍ (JIRKA) HORNER performed the musical accompaniment. He was born on September 15, 1923. On December 10, 1941, he was deported from Olomouc/Olmütz to Terezín/Theresienstadt and on October 12, 1944, to Auschwitz. He survived.

JINDŘICH (JINDRA) WEIL operated the stage lights. It is not possible to identify him more closely. In the database of the Institute of the Terezín Initiative there are three men named Jindřich Weil who were in the ghetto in the spring of 1943.

SONGS FROM THE REVUE
PRINCE BETTLIEGEND

THE ROYAL SPEECH
Melody: "A Young Man Rides on his Horse"[28]

Hear, oh Nation, I address you, speaking as your King
See the signs of age that the attempt to serve you brings
You know how to take my tribute; God forbid you should contribute
What I ask of you.

I will always stand behind you, even though, Nation mine,
All my government's work for you, you openly criticize
While struggling to do our best, slaps in the face are all we get
We are undermined.

I'm aware you're not contented, what you're hoping for
Is that somewhere else for you there's happiness in store
You love the country of your past, your brave young hearts are
    beating fast
You long for something more.

What you want is entertainment, dancing, theater
Eating dumplings, pork, and cabbage, drinking Pilsner beer.
You would like more room for living, better coats, and boots, and
    clothing
Than you receive here.

---

28 These lyrics are sung to the melody of the song "A Young Man Rides on his Horse" ("Jede mladík na svém koni"), one of only two melodies in *Prince Bettliegend* not written by Jaroslav Ježek. This composition for men's chorus was written by Peter Jirge (1819–79).

You would like to earn more money, want to gather wealth
Live in greater comfort than is possible in my realm
Maybe you want central heating, couches, armchairs for your
     meetings
Your wants, they overwhelm.

Don't believe that elsewhere lies a better life for this folk
"Over there the grass is greener," don't believe such a joke.
Fortune anywhere can meet you, anywhere your foes can beat you
Until you croak.[29]

He who now is well provisioned, he who has enough
Eats so much he's sleeping badly, 'til he's overstuffed.
He who only fills his trap can't know when he will get a slap
Or greetings from above.[30]

Keep in mind that with your head you won't knock down a wall,
All your swearing and complaining won't help you at all,
Don't expect security, there's nowhere you'll find certainty
I hope you will recall.

Finding peace in this world is as hard as if you would
Make a resolution that you'll cross the sea on foot.
Don't shake your fist at the weather, try to keep your wits together
Where you can, do good.

If you have to bow and bend 'til your whole body's sore
Keep in mind there aren't any roses without thorns
All the thorns will fall someday, he'll still be standing who his fate
With self-control has borne.

Oh my Nation, this I tell you, I who am your king
So instead of ruling I will try to give you strength

---

29 In the original, *chcípnout* (to kick the bucket), usually used for animals.

30 A "greeting from above" has various possible meanings—for example, a bomb, or a summons from the commandant.

You'll bear your burdens with my help, just don't lose your faith in
    yourselves
You'll endure everything.

THE SUITCASE AND ME

Melody by Jaroslav Ježek: "The World Upside Down"[31]

Just a number, not a name, thin skin covering a frame
In weather foul or fair, delivered here and there
That's my suitcase—and that's me.
Used to bearing frequent blows, inspected by cold hands
    unknown,
Packed up and then we're shipped off again
That's my suitcase, and that's me.

What could be inside, packed in that thin hide
Maybe all that's left are memories
Happy memories of better times
Just like what remains in me
Maybe there's a prayer in the corner there
Maybe one last crust of bread
Maybe hopes to start anew somewhere
Like those going through my head.

A hard shell to take shocks aplenty, that's what you should have
Fragile frames spelled the end of many who had the right to live.
A thorny uphill path, a long road full of hurt for my suitcase, me
    as well
If I'm lucky I'll just lose my shirt, if I'm not I'll lose myself.

---

31 These lyrics are sung to the melody of the song "The World Upside Down"
("Svět naruby") from the Voskovec and Werich revue *Rag Ballad* (*Ballad z hadrů*,
premiere 1935).

HOCUS AND POCUS INTRODUCE THEMSELVES
Melody by Jaroslav Ježek: "One Hundred Percent Men"[32]

We are two artists who're known 'round the world for
    scamming
He who falls under our spell, soon to our tune he's dancing
Just mention "Hocus" or his friend "Pocus"
And it's a clear case of flim-flamming.

Our specialties are smuggling, tricks and swindle
We like to *schleuse*[33] you more than just a little
With just a touch of *šmelina*[34]
That is our bread and butter.
Gambling and cheating, trickery, delusion,
Reading the future, lies and great illusions
The greatest con men all around the whole globus
We're here for you,
The firm "Hocus and Pocus."

THE THREE ERAS OF SWINDLELAND
Melody by Jaroslav Ježek: "Civilization"[35]

As you can find out in books on history
There was once a very famous dynasty[36]
They chose, out of fear of foreign conquerors

---

32 These lyrics are sung to the melody of the song "One Hundred Percent Men" ("Stoprocentní muži") from the Voskovec and Werich revue *Golem* (premiere 1931).

33 See glossary.

34 *Šmelina*: fraud. See *šmé* (glossary).

35 These lyrics are sung to the melody of the song "Civilization" ("Civilizace") from the Voskovec and Werich revue *Ass and Shadow* (*Osel a stín*, premiere 1933).

36 Emperor Joseph II of the Habsburg dynasty decreed the founding of the Terezín/Theresienstadt fortress.

To build a fortress city shaped just like a star.
Then to make their country harder to invade
All around the town, huge barriers they made
Not just trenches wide, but ditches side by side
And enormous hollow walls where many troops could hide.
In them they made holes through which their men could
    shoot their guns
Filled the town with generals and plenty of cannons.

The inhabitants, they were elite soldiers
They ate steak and sausage, sometimes pork shoulder
And they had pubs and restaurants and interesting things to do
With that town they wanted to scare their neighbors too.

Many years have passed and since those olden days
The world has change a lot in big and little ways
No one's intimidated by the fortress moats
And certain people had a star sewn on their coats.
By the thousands they moved in; to house them all
The soldiers' quarters served, until the barracks all
Were filled up to the eaves, then they used the factories
Then shops and pubs and inns and schools became dormitories.
Soon enough they found out all the exits had been sealed,
They were happy when they got a one-potato meal.

They had nothing else, there was a state of crisis
No drop of alcohol, cash did not exist
And then they started advertising, soon the town was in the
    news
Not only in the papers, but in the movies too.[37]

---

37 There were two attempts by the Nazis to make propaganda films about the ghetto. The directors of both were prisoners. The first, directed by Irena Dodalová, was filmed in 1942, and the second, directed by Kurt Gerron, in 1944. Only fragments of both films survive. See Karel Margry, "The First Theresienstadt Film (1942)," *Historical Journal of Film, Radio and Television* 19(3) (1999): 309–37; and Margry, "Das Konzentrationslager als Idylle."

All of these aforementioned conditions meant[38]
They had to have a brand new type of government
Brand new types of leadership for night and day
Brand new ways of organizing work and play.
The basis of all work is called the *Hundertschaft*
Who cares for your well-being? Why the *Raumwirtschaft*,
Verteilungsstelle for the fashionable fella
At *Bettenbau*, they build your bunks and make sure you sleep well.
For cleanliness of body, turn for help to *Entwesung*
Cleanliness of spirit, the *Freizeitgestaltung*.

With points from the *Bezugsscheinstelle* you can buy what they are
    selling
Spedition will get you there, from *Kleiderkammer* clothes to wear
Glimmerspaltung, that's demanding, rumors of Pürglitz
    are spreading[39]

---

38 The following verses feature the Czech Jews' ghetto argot. Some words are adopted unmodified from the German; others are modified, sometimes in comic ways, based on the rules of Czech grammar, spelling, and word construction. Unless otherwise indicated, definitions have been taken from the glossary in Adler, *Theresienstadt*, pp. XXIX–LIX.

39 *Hundertschaft*: a group of 100 workers. See Hyndráková et al., *Acta Theresiania*, p. 63. ***Raumwirtschaft***: Department of Space Management. See *Selbstverwaltung* (glossary). ***Verteilungsstelle***: locations where essential goods such as clothing were distributed to prisoners. These were later replaced by the ghetto "shops." See *Verschleißstellen* (glossary). ***Bettenbau***: a workshop where the three-tier bunks where the prisoners slept were built. See Hyndráková et al., *Acta Theresiania*, p. 78. ***Bezugsscheinstelle***: locations where coupons for purchasing wares in the ghetto "shops" were distributed to the prisoners. See *Bezugsschein, Verschleißstellen* (glossary). ***Spedition***: Department for Transport of Goods. ***Kleiderkammer***: a storehouse for confiscated clothing, from summer 1942 located in the Ústí barracks. ***Glimmerspaltung***: a workshop for the splitting of mica, used in optical equipment. ***Pürglitz***: in Czech, *Křivoklát*. In the spring of 1942, approximately 1,000 women from Terezín/Theresienstadt were sent there to labor in the forest. See Pavla Zemanová, "Die Theresienstädter Außenkommandos" (Blanka Papešová trans.), in Miroslav Kárný, Jaroslava Milotová, and Michael Wögerbauer (eds.), *Theresienstädter Studien und Dokumente 2001* (Prague: Academia, 2001), pp. 75–105.

Arbeiterbetreuung must see to the helpings of *zubussy*
O.D. opens gates again and employs older gentlemen
The *Putzkolonne* cleans your closet, *Wärmeküche* heats your food up
Baureferat clears the yards, the *Klowache*, the toilet guards
Oh, all our plates are full and then some thanks to the *Menage*
    commission.

The *Landwirtschaft* has plowed the park, the *Lichtkontrolle*'s in the
    dark
The *Zentrallager*, goods it handles, *Materiallager*, candles
Einlauf, Auslauf, makes things speedy, *Säuglingsheim*, where
    baby's feeding
How the post works, it's a winner, *Menagedienst* can't get to
    dinner
Against theft and deception it's *Sicherheitswesen*
If you're blocked or got the trots the *Gesundheitswesen*.[40]
Bahnbau's just completed the greatest modern railroad track,
So the journey's easier to Prague on the way back.

---

40 **Arbeiterbetreuung**: the office responsible for the welfare of workers in the ghetto. **Zubussy**: extra rations of food for workers performing heavy labor. From German *Zubuße*. **Putzkolonne**: groups of female prisoners assigned to cleaning work in the ghetto. **Wärmeküche**: small kitchens for heating food were established in most barracks and houses. **Baureferat**: a division responsible for construction work; for example, they pulled down the walls that divided up the courtyards of buildings in the ghetto. **Klowache**: guards who kept order in the long lines for the toilets and outhouses. **Menage commission**: a three-member body supervising the use of provisions and distribution of food in each kitchen. **Landwirtschaft**: the Agricultural Department that cultivated vegetables and other crops outside the walls of the ghetto. These crops were intended for the SS, not for the prisoners. **Lichtkontrolle**: lights in the prisoners' living quarters had to be turned off by a certain time at night. See Adler, *Theresienstadt*, p. 92. **Zentrallager**: central storehouse, administered the distribution of goods to the smaller warehouses such as the *Materiallager*. **Einlauf, Auslauf**: some divisions of the *Selbstverwaltung* (see glossary) had "inboxes" and "outboxes" for internal mail delivery. **Säuglingsheim**: locations in the ghetto where nursing infants were cared for. Over 200 children were born in the ghetto. See Adler, *Theresienstadt*, p. 524. **Menagedienst**: food service workers who marked the prisoners' meal tickets and distributed rations. **Sicherheitswesen**: between the summers of 1942 and 1943, this was a separate division for safety and security in the ghetto. **Gesundheitswesen**: Department of Health.

AN OPTIMISTIC SONG ACCORDING TO SOLAR: THINGS WILL WORK OUT

Melody by Jaroslav Ježek: "He Who Looks at the World"[41]

Although your body's aching, your bones feel like breaking
Your courage is unshaking, just hold your head up high
The more the wind is blowing, the beatings keep going,
The more your hunger's growing, the more you can defy.
When the winter ends, spring melts the ice,
And those who've persevered will find their paradise
He who bears this torture with faith in the future,
Who knows he will endure here, will reach with us the prize.

But he who's always sighing, and "only if I"-ing
Who in advance is shying away from sweet sunshine
Who loses his sense of humor
His life will end sooner
You'll laugh off all the rumors
If a smile is your lifeline.
Good cheer will be your shield, a joke, your sword,
You'll conquer all the world, a sweet life will be yours
So, friends, don't cede the day if things don't go your way
It all will be okay if we only stay the course.

THE LITTLE LOUSE AND THE LITTLE FLEA

Melody by Jaroslav Ježek: "Aesop and the Anteater"[42]

Long, long ago in a town that you know lived a pretty louse girl
Lovely to see but filled with conceit, she snubbed the whole world
Louse-men tried to give her kisses, asked her to be their missus,
The louse girl just sniffed and then proudly lifted her proboscis.

---

41 The actual title of the song is "What I Like in the World" ("Co na světě mám rád"), a foxtrot from the Voskovec and Werich revue *Heavy Barbara* (*Těžká Barbora*, premiere 1937).

42 These lyrics are sung to the melody of the song "Aesop and the Anteater" ("Ezop a brabenec"), from the Voskovec and Werich revue *Caesar* (premiere 1932).

One day there came across her path
A manly flea, he was so handsome, handsome
That in a flash her affections were won.
Her heart, it started beating fast
With burning love, that'd only begun, begun
And grew and grew for the flea so handsome.

Lovelorn, she watched her flea-man from the evening 'til the dawn
Then struck great misfortune—with one big jump he was gone.
So the louse, she came to know the pain, the pain of love,
When love's rejected, rejected
He disappeared before she could object.

Now since that day, the louse's life's changed, she's slowly fading
Spends her time moping, vainly hoping, always waiting
The lice warn her frequently such love's never won easily
Dissuade her they can't, for she loves a man of a different species.

But . . . she's smart as well as fair
She knows on skin is where the flea has his lair
To see him elsewhere's exceedingly rare
She seldom steps out onto bald skin so bare
To see if flea-man is there
He rarely visits a place where there's hair.
When a flea bites, he leaves a pimple, like a little raised spot,
When the louse bites, with all her effort, she makes only tiny dots.
So until the end of time
She looked and looked but never saw him again
A lousy life was her unfortunate end.

THERE IS A SAYING THAT GOES AS FOLLOWS . . .

Melody by Jaroslav Ježek: "Nine Crafts"[43]

There's a proverb wise that tells us habits we develop start to seem
  just natural
Saying this of profiteering, can we make a virtue of necessity as well?
As conditions here get tougher day by day
It's harder for a guy to maintain moral ways
Soon all that he cares about is stealing for himself and what a deal
  will bring him.

Certain tactics seem to work in theory, not in practice
But the simple fact is stolen goods can be the most attractive
Hurry, buy it while it's hot
I'll sell it if it's mine or not.
Got tomatoes? I'll trade you potatoes, for a baguette,
Give you cigarettes, well, cigs—how many? cost a pretty penny
Things that used to be quite pricey
Now sell pretty dicey.

What we're seeing,
Hoarding goods and profiteering, racketeering, all our honesty is
  disappearing
But it's stealing
And we know that to the victims it's unfeeling and deserves our
  condemnation really
And moreover he who spends his days rolling in clover
What's over his shoulder? comes a moment, when the fun is over
All the worry and the flurry
Ends in a big hurry.

---

43 These lyrics are sung to the melody of the song "Nine Crafts" ("Devět řeme-sel") from the Voskovec and Werich revue *World Behind Bars* (*Svět za mřížemi*, premiere 1933).

CURRICULUM VITAE[44]

Melody: "If People Didn't Make Mistakes"[45]

Oh what a great day
When we were told to hand in curriculum vitae
And in order to obtain a safe position
They had to be the most outstanding works of fiction.

That piece of paper
If it inspires confidence, then you'll be safer
You will have pulled off quite a caper—then you'll
Have to put your plan in motion
Got to get the magic potion
Called *Protektion*.[46]

Because your talents, even those you weren't given
To write them all on your CV, it is permitted
Include all that you've ever studied
What you've learned from all your buddies
Put it at the disposition
Of your favorite institution—they will match you
That's if a sudden change of climate doesn't catch you.

Of course, it's not enough to have recommendations
Just hope your pals can make some well-placed interventions,
If you are starting from the bottom
Oh, some help from friends is common
If they put in a good word

---

44 Prisoners who wished to apply for advantageous positions in the ghetto were required to submit a resume. Information was sometimes falsified to obtain a desired job. See Hyndráková et al., *Acta Theresiania*, pp. 83, 85.

45 The actual title of the song is "People Learn from their Mistakes" ("Chybami se člověk učí"). The original melody is a rumba by the American composer Herman Hupfeld titled "When Yuba Plays the Rumba on the Tuba." The song was featured in the Voskovec and Werich revue *Robin the Bandit* (*Robin zbojník*, premiere 1932).

46 Favoritism or nepotism.

Then your CV a fine job for you has procured
That's even if they know your CV is absurd.

Each gets the work spot
That he deserves, not
Based on his wisdom
But nepotism.

But let's not take away from people their illusions
Let them continue filling CVs with delusions
'Cause there's a stone for each glass house
There waits a cat for every mouse
And also waiting is the guy[47]
Who gets the last laugh though he doesn't even try
And a CV for that laugh he won't have to write.

FINAL SONG FROM PRINCE BETTLIEGEND
Melody by Jaroslav Ježek: "March of the Neutral Ones"[48]

An evil, unexpected fate has met each of us here
There's no doctor who can heal us, that's perfectly clear,
No, for all of our worries, time's the only cure,
Time, it marches on and the outcome is sure.

Once more, beaten by their might
You take a fall but bear it all
As bravely as you can
Once more, you join in the fight
On your feet, there's no defeat
Shake off the dust again.

---

47 That is, Death.

48 These lyrics are sung to the melody of the song "March of the Neutral Ones" ("Pochod neutrálů") from the Voskovec and Werich revue *North against South* (*Sever proti Jihu*, premiere 1930).

In every struggle he shall be victorious
Who can hold out just five minutes more,
And what you've refused to yield
Will be forever yours.

ZDENĚK ELIÁŠ and JIŘÍ STEIN

THE SMOKE OF HOME

INTRODUCTION

The manuscript of *The Smoke of Home*, a historical drama about four men imprisoned during the Thirty Years War, came to light in the spring of 2006 based on information provided by Professor Jiří Franěk (né Frischmann) in Prague.[1] As a friend of co-authors Zdeněk Eliáš (né Eckstein) and Jiří Stein in Terezín/Theresienstadt, Franěk remembered the play and even after more than 60 years was able to describe the plot in detail. After Zdeněk Eliáš left Czechoslovakia for Germany and then the United States, Franěk maintained contact with him and was able to provide me with the US address of his second wife, Kate Elias. When I contacted her, she confirmed that a copy of the play was in her possession and sent me a photocopy.[2]

THE AUTHORS

Much information about the life of co-author Zdeněk Eliáš has been provided by his surviving family members: his younger brother Luděk Eliáš, who performed in several plays in the ghetto; his widow, Kate; and his daughter, Dorothy.[3] Zdeněk and Luděk grew up in the Bohemian town of Slaný, about 35 kilometers northwest of Prague. As Zdeněk related to Kate, their grandmother was still observant, but their parents were Freethinkers and forbade her to provide the boys with any kind of Jewish religious education.[4] According to Luděk, their father

---

IMAGE 6.1 *(facing page)* **A set design, probably by Bedřich Fritta for *The Golden Chain* by J. L. Perez.**
Courtesy of the Terezín Memorial.

---

1 *The Smoke of Home* was the title recalled by Jiří Franěk. There was no title on the manuscript.

2 Testimony by several survivors from the authors' circle of friends in Terezín/Theresienstadt establishes that the play was written in the ghetto itself, but that Eliáš most likely reconstructed the version preserved in the manuscript immediately after the war.

3 Zdeněk is also survived by a daughter, Katherine, and a son, Peter.

4 Unpublished essay by Kate Elias, March 2010.

was deeply committed to the notion that a person who considered himself a member of a particular nation should conform to its ways. Although their parents spoke both Czech and German, they gave their sons Czech names and sent them to Czech-language schools.[5]

When transports to Terezín/Theresienstadt began, Zdeněk was being treated for an illness in a Prague hospital. He was deported to the ghetto in July 1942, five months after Luděk and their parents. There Zdeněk soon got to know his co-author, Jiří Stein. Věra Eliášová (née Kaudersová), who after the war became Zdeněk's first wife, was a member of their circle in the ghetto. She described the young men's friendship in a passage of her memoirs that also provides insight into the way of life of the young Czech Jews in the ghetto:

> Zdeněk and his friend Jiří invited me to come and see their loft; together they were building a little partitioned corner of an attic for themselves. [. . .] As I got to know them better, I saw that they complemented each other very well. Jiří, an engineering student, was more realistic, Zdeněk, a philosophy student, more lyrical. Zdeněk treated us to Shakespeare's sonnets which he memorized and recited with great feeling. Jiří solved the problem of lighting in their loft. Together these two friends wrote a play. Its action took place in the Thirty Years War.[6]

Jiří and Zdeněk's collaboration came to an end when Zdeněk's name appeared on a transport list. He was deported to Auschwitz along with Luděk, who volunteered for the transport because his girlfriend, Eva (née Langerová, later Eliášová), was also on the list, in May of 1944. Both men were selected for labor and sent to Schwarzheide, a satellite camp of Sachsenhausen. When the camp was evacuated in April of 1945, Zdeněk was too ill to join the forced march. Even though the Nazis threatened to shoot those who could not walk, he remained in the infirmary with several other wounded and ailing prisoners—including Jiří Franěk, who had also been deported to Schwarzheide and

---

5 Luděk Eliáš, interview with Anna Lorencová, October 18, 1994.

6 Věra Eliáš, *On My Good Days I Feel That I am a Cupboard* (Seattle: Peanut Butter Publishing, 1992), p. 53.

had been injured in a bombing raid.[7] They were liberated when Soviet and Polish troops arrived on April 22 and eventually returned to Prague, where Zdeněk spent some months in a rehabilitation facility. Luděk survived a death march that arrived at its destination—Terezín/Theresienstadt—the night of May 7 and 8, 1945. Zdeněk and Luděk's parents were no longer there. They had been deported to Auschwitz in October 1944 and did not return.

After the communist rise to power, Zdeněk fled the country and became a correspondent for Radio Free Europe in Germany and the US. Luděk remained in Czechoslovakia and worked with several theaters, eventually becoming involved in radio and television broadcasting as well. The brothers were able to meet twice in Austria in 1964, when Luděk was sent as a correspondent to the Innsbruck Olympics. Luděk and Eva were allowed to visit the US in the early 1980s, but Zdeněk could not return to visit his homeland until after the collapse of communism in 1989.

Co-author Jiří Stein also wrote poetry in the ghetto; some of his works have been preserved in private collections and in the archives of the Jewish Museum in Prague. Two of his poems, "The Letter" ("Dopis") and "To the City" ("Městu"), were published in the original Czech with a German translation in 1985.[8] Little is known about his life. He was born on August 23, 1920 and deported from Prague to Terezín/Theresienstadt with one of the first transports to the ghetto on December 4, 1941. He was deported from Terezín/Theresienstadt to Auschwitz four months after Zdeněk, at the end of September 1944. Of that transport of 1,500 young men, approximately half were selected for labor but only 79 survived until the end of the war. Jiří Stein died in Dachau in December of 1944.

---

7 According to Franěk, Zdeněk saved his life by persuading him to stay in the infirmary rather than trying to join the forced march. Jiří Franěk, interview with Lisa Peschel, March 6, 2006. "Let them shoot me," he said when Franěk reminded him that laggards would be shot. "I'm practically dead already." Jiří Franěk, conversation with Kate Elias, May 2000.

8 Jarmila Skochová, "Literarisches Schaffen erwachsener Häftlinge im Konzentrationslager Theresienstadt," *Judaica Bohemiae* 21(1) (1985): 29–31.

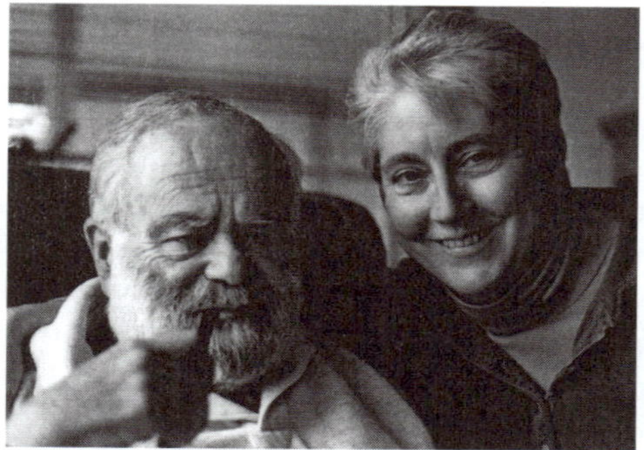

IMAGE 6.2 (*below*) **Zdeněk Eliáš' pre-war university identification card, showing his post-war name change.**
Courtesy of Kate Elias.

IMAGE 6.3 (*left*) **Zdeněk Eliáš (left) with Kate Elias, 1999.**
Courtesy of Kate Elias.

IMAGE 6.4 (*facing page*) **Jiří Stein.**
Courtesy of Dorothy Elias.

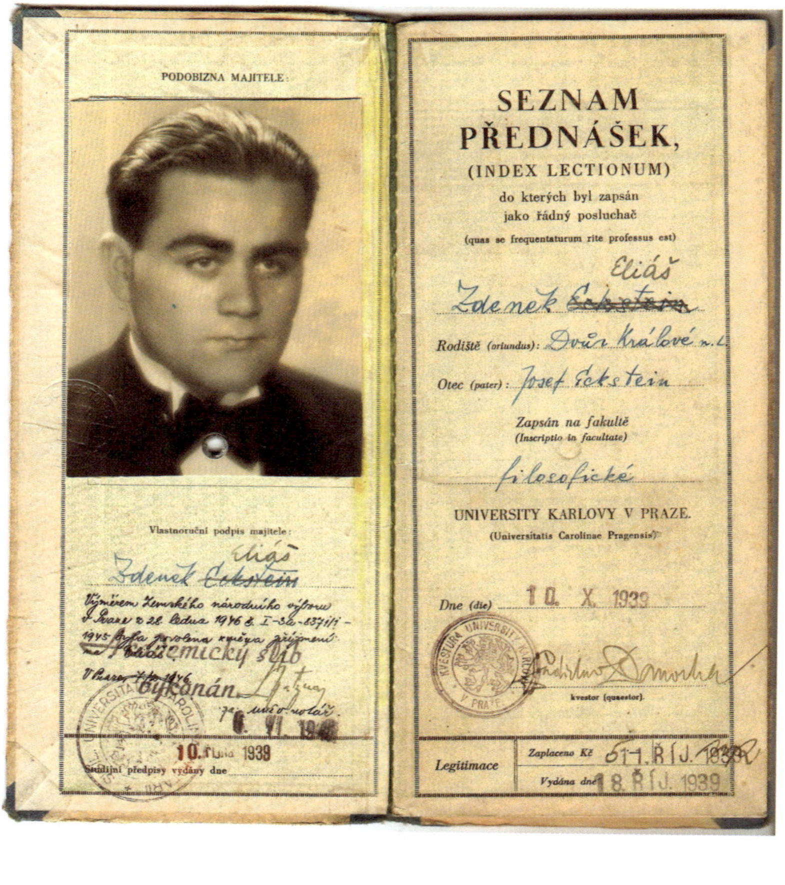

PODOBIZNA MAJITELE:

Vlastnoruční podpis majitele:

Eliáš
Zdeněk ~~Eckstein~~

Akademický slib vykonán

10. října 1939
Studijní předpisy vydány dne

SEZNAM PŘEDNÁŠEK,
(INDEX LECTIONUM)
do kterých byl zapsán
jako řádný posluchač
(quas se frequentaturum rite professus est)

Eliáš
Zdenek ~~Eckstein~~

Rodiště (oriundus): Dvůr Králové n. L.

Otec (pater): Josef Eckstein

Zapsán na fakultě
(Inscriptio in facultate)

filosofické

UNIVERSITY KARLOVY V PRAZE.
(Universitatis Carolinae Pragensis)

Dne (die) 10. X. 1939

KVESTURA UNIVERSITY KARLOVY V PRAZE

kvestor (quaestor).

Legitimace	Zaplaceno Kč
	Vydána dne 18. ŘÍJ. 1939

According to Luděk, the play was inspired by a Czech translation of Rainer Maria Rilke's *The Song of Love and Death of the Cornet Christoph Rilke*. Zdeněk apparently heard the work recited by the young director Gustav Schorsch during one of the seminars he conducted for young actors in the ghetto. The first paragraph of *The Smoke of Home*, titled "In Place of a Prologue," closely follows the language of the introduction to *The Song of Love and Death*. The character of Christian, like Rilke's main character Christoph, is a young cornet (standard-bearer), and both works take place against a historical backdrop: for Rilke, a seventeenth-century battle between the Austrians and the Turks; for Eliáš and Stein, the Thirty Years War.[9] There, however, the similarities end. *The Smoke of Home* is a work that thoroughly reflects the immediate concerns of its young Czech-Jewish authors.

Setting the play in the Thirty Years War (1618–48) enabled the co-authors to draw parallels with their own wartime situation; it also increased the works' dramatic impact due to the intensely emotional significance of this event for Czechs. In popular historical conscious-ness, the defeat of Czech and allied forces at the Battle of White Mountain in 1620 was viewed as the event that had brought an end to hard-won religious freedoms and ushered in "three hundred years of darkness"—that is, Germanization and forced re-Catholicization under their Austrian rulers—that ended only with the establishment of inde-pendent Czechoslovakia in 1918.[10] The war began as a religious conflict, with the Catholic rulers of the Holy Roman Empire—most promi-nently Habsburg Austria and south Germany, along with Habsburg

---

9 Bertolt Brecht's *Mother Courage* is also set at the time of the Thirty Years War and the protagonist, like the character of Veronika in *The Smoke of Home*, is a trader who follows the troops, selling goods to the soldiers. There is little possibil-ity of direct influence. Brecht wrote his play in exile in 1939 and it premiered in Zurich in 1941, long after Brecht's works had been banned in territories occupied by the Nazis.

10 Ladislav Holý, *The Little Czech and the Great Czech Nation: National Identity and the Post-communist Transformation of Society* (New York: Cambridge University Press, 1996), p. 39.

Spain—allied against the North German Protestant states and Sweden. However, in the later years of the war during which the play takes place, Catholic France forged an alliance with Sweden, joining the Protestant forces in an effort to limit the power of its Habsburg rivals. By the time the Peace of Westphalia was negotiated the war had wrought enormous devastation all over Europe. In the Czech lands the population declined by a third due to the expulsion of Protestant Czechs and the casualties of war, disease, and famine.

The authors, however, did not make the obvious choice of selecting Protestant figures as their protagonists. Rather, the characters in *The Smoke of Home* were fighting on the side of the Catholics. The cavalry officer von Waldau and the cornet Christian von Stetten were from the Swabian region of Bavaria and had been fighting there in support of the imperial army of the Holy Roman Empire when they and Father Anselm, a Catholic priest from the same region, were taken prisoner. Their captors brought them back to Hessen, a Protestant German state, where they were imprisoned. Another officer with the Catholic forces, Casselius, was imprisoned with them in the winter of 1647. Waldau, Christian, and Anselm spend most of the play fervidly anticipating their release and homecoming until Casselius's devastating monologue reveals to them that there will be no return to the life they remember.

According to all the survivors who remembered the script—not only Luděk Eliáš, Jiří Franěk, and Věra Eliášová, but Věra's sister Alena Sternová (née Kaudersová) and their friend Eva Musilová (née Hirschová)—*The Smoke of Home* was never performed in the ghetto, apparently because the Terezín/Theresienstadt public needed hope above all else. As Luděk explained, however, it was not the goal of the authors to write a popular play:

> Those boys, with a certain strange clear-sightedness, allowed for the possibility that the home people were looking forward to, the home they dreamed of, was only a chimera, that there would be nothing left. To come to that conclusion required a certain clarity of perception which very few people had. And I think that it was the need to express exactly that possibility,

rather than an attempt to write a play which would be staged in Terezín, which led to its creation.[11]

Franěk agreed that the authors belonged among the few in the ghetto who realized that a very different life awaited them after the war:

> *The Smoke of Home* is a play completely reflecting our existence in the concentration camp. [. . .] A great number of people lived only for their memories of home, a home they very much idealized. They spent hours talking about it: who they had been, what it was like, what they had achieved. All those naive recollections were related to a notion of home which was unchanging. Only a few were able to look the truth in the eyes, a truth which was already apparent even in the camps: none of us would return to the same home we left. Eliáš and Stein were able to face that possibility.[12]

BIOGRAPHICAL INFORMATION

THE AUTHORS

ZDENĚK ELIÁŠ (né **ECKSTEIN**) was born on May 28, 1920 and was deported from Prague to Terezín/Theresienstadt on July 16, 1942. He was deported to Auschwitz on May 18, 1944, where he spent some weeks in the so-called "family camp" at Auschwitz-Birkenau.[13] He was selected for labor and sent to Schwarzheide, a satellite camp of Sachsenhausen. He was liberated there in April 1945. He died in Seattle on February 2, 2000.

JIŘÍ STEIN was born on August 23, 1920 and was deported from Prague to Terezín/Theresienstadt on December 4, 1941. He was deported to Auschwitz on September 29, 1944 and perished in Dachau on December 19, 1944.

---

11 Luděk Eliáš, interview with Lisa Peschel, October 20, 2006.

12 Jiří Franěk, letter to Lisa Peschel, June 18, 2006.

13 For an account of the family camp by a survivor see Bondy, "*Elder of the Jews*," pp. 405–47.

JIŘÍ FRANĚK (né **FRISCHMANN**) was born on November 24, 1922. He was deported from Pardubice to Terezín/Theresienstadt on December 5, 1942 and to Auschwitz on December 15, 1943, where he spent several months in the family camp at Auschwitz-Birkenau and was eventually selected for labor. He was liberated in Sachsenhausen in April 1945. He died on December 30, 2007.

LUDĚK ELIÁŠ (né **ECKSTEIN**) was born on July 29, 1923. He was deported with his parents from Kladno to Terezín/Theresienstadt on February 26, 1942, and to the family camp at Auschwitz-Birkenau on May 18, 1944. He was selected for labor and sent to Schwarzheide, a satellite camp of Sachsenhausen. He survived a death march from Schwarzheide and was liberated in Terezín/Theresienstadt. He and Eva (née Langerová, born on February 28, 1927) married after the war. She died on February 19, 2007. He currently resides in Ostrava/Mährisch Ostrau.

VĚRA ELIÁŠOVÁ (née **KAUDERSOVÁ**) was born on October 30, 1922. She was transported from Prague to Terezín/Theresienstadt on July 13, 1943, and was liberated in the ghetto. She died on February 16, 1997.

ALENA STERNOVÁ (née **KAUDERSOVÁ**) was born on April 18, 1925. She was transported from Prague to Terezín/Theresienstadt on July 13, 1943, and to Switzerland on February 5, 1945.[14] She lives in Munich.

EVA MUSILOVÁ (née **HIRSCHOVÁ**) was born on January 24, 1925. She was transported from Prague to Terezín/Theresienstadt on March 6, 1943 and remained there until the liberation. She died in the spring of 2009.

---

14 For an account of this unique transport see Blodig, "Poslední fáze ve vývoji terezínského ghetta," pp. 185–6.

AK II 651
VILLA WILLINGER

TRANSLATED BY DOROTHY ELIAS

IN PLACE OF A PROLOGUE

On the third day of August in the year of our Lord 1645, two officers of the emperor's army and a priest were captured by Hessian troops at the battle of Allerheim. They were taken to Marburg castle in Hessen, then under the rule of Princess Amalie Elizabeth, and were imprisoned for three long years. They were forgotten. A fourth prisoner was added to their number during the winter of 1647, an officer under the imperial army's General Holzapfel, who was besieging Marburg. The emperor's armies withdrew and our prisoners endured further long months in captivity. On October 26, 1648, in the early morning hours . . .

A prison cell. A barred window in the background. Night. Waldau, Father Anselm, and Casselius are lying in the cell, sleeping on straw. Christian stands at the window. Waldau mumbles sleepily and sits up.

CHRISTIAN (*turns around*). Can't sleep either, Waldau?

WALDAU. I can't sleep.

CHRISTIAN. Are you thinking of home, too?

WALDAU. No, I'm not. I'm cold. And I can't get the taste of that horrible buckwheat porridge out of my mouth. For three years all they've been feeding us is that sickening slop . . . Listen, Sir Christian, when I finally leave this place, I'll drown Princess Amalie Elizabeth and that new[15] marshal of hers in buckwheat porridge! You can bet that Marshal Gaspard Cornelius

IMAGE 6.5 (*facing page*) **A bunk built by Lev Willinger, 1943. By F. M. Nágl.** *Courtesy of the Jewish Museum in Prague.*

15 The term used in the original Czech script, *přivandrovalý*, means literally "newly arrived from somewhere else" and implies lack of experience and perhaps lack of competence in the new environment.

Mortaigne de Potelles had something better for dinner![16] And you can bet that he didn't wash it down with tepid water that's been standing in a jug all day! (*Pause*) Roast venison! Were you used to eating roast venison at home, Sir Christian?

CHRISTIAN. Home! Dinner at home, Waldau . . . The family around the table . . .

WALDAU (*enthusiastically*). And with it a Mosel or a Rhine wine in pewter tankards . . . pointless words, dammit! Buckwheat porridge, tepid water—yuck!

CHRISTIAN. When's the last time you were home, Waldau?

WALDAU. The last time? (*Ponders*) Wait—that time after Breitenfeld . . . That was six years ago. You weren't even in the army then. See this scar? I got this one at Breitenfeld. That was a pretty scuffle! We were stuck in the mud like sitting ducks, and Torstenson was on us before we knew it. Lucky for me a friend got me out of there on a hay wagon . . . Why, even Piccolomini had a narrow escape there . . . Then I was laid up at home for half a year till I recovered. I had it good there . . . then back into the field. Who knows what's been going on at home since then.

CHRISTIAN. Waldau . . . you lived hardly a half hour's ride away from us, and we didn't even know each other. Sometimes I used to ride around there with Eleonor. I remember that once someone pointed you out to me in the Rain[17] church—the old warrior. Did you come to hear Father Anselm preach?

WALDAU. Almost every Sunday, Sir Christian. After all, I am a Catholic. In fact, I still remember you as a young boy, how you used to sit with your parents in Lord Stetten's pew.

CHRISTIAN. What do you suppose is happening in Bavaria? What's happening in Rain? Maybe there's peace there now . . .

---

16 In 1647, Mortaigne de Potelles transferred from Swedish service to become commander-in-chief for the Swedes' Protestant allies in Hesse-Cassel. See William P. Guthrie, *The Later Thirty Years War: From the Battle of Wittstock to the Treaty of Westphalia* (Westport, CT: Greenwood Publishing, 2003), p. 112.

17 Pronounced "Rhine."

(*Excitedly*) You probably haven't heard—last night—that's right, you were asleep already—Casselius spoke with that new guard of ours in the hall, that Walloon soldier.

WALDAU (*livens up*). What did he say? Where are our troops? Why didn't you wake me? What about our General Werth? Dammit! How does it look for us?

CHRISTIAN. They've probably forgotten about us completely, Waldau . . . Besides, Casselius didn't tell us all that much. Werth and Holzapfel withdrew our troops to Bohemia, and General Wrangel joined up with Turenne and they're probably encamped somewhere in Swabia.[18] He didn't know much else . . . The Swedes and the French . . . our poor country . . .

They are silent for a moment.

WALDAU (*quietly begins to sing an old soldier's tune*). God, be at hand
Death has entered our land . . .
(*louder*) Hey! death has entered our land . . .

The singing wakes Casselius and Father Anselm. Casselius sits up and rubs his eyes.

ANSELM. No God-fearing man would make so much noise at night! A man shuts his eyes for a minute and you don't show him any consideration!

WALDAU. Don't give yourself airs! We're not in your Rain parsonage here, Father Anselm.

ANSELM. When you sleep, you snore like a wood saw; when you're awake you make a racket.

WALDAU. Be quiet! You'll have a good, long sleep soon enough . . . soon enough to regret it.

CASSELIUS (*with his usual mildly sarcastic smile*). Gentlemen—an argument? At this late hour, when all creatures are sleeping the sleep of the just?

ANSELM. So why is he disturbing the midnight peace, the heathen?

WALDAU (*growls*). The devil wished you on us, you Bible-thumper!

---

18 Carl Gustaf Wrangel (1613–76) and Vicomte de Turenne (1611–75) were commanders of the Swedish and French forces respectively.

CASSELIUS. Waldau, honestly, I'm surprised at you. Where is your Christian forbearance, Father Anselm? It seems that people have to make their already miserable lots even harder for each other. What do you say, Christian?

CHRISTIAN (*at the window*). How many more nights will I watch the heavens through these bars? What if I never see you any other way, you heavenly lights? In any case, Casselius, the stars shine just the same here as they do at home—above Rain. Maybe Eleonor is watching that reddish one twinkling above the horizon, just as I am. Maybe our gazes are meeting at that point this very instant . . . What does that star mean, Casselius? The light of better days—or maybe a period marking the end of our lives?

CASSELIUS. No such thing, friends. You're seeing the planet Mars, the fourth planet in our solar system. Master Johannes Kepler wrote about it at length in his excellent work *Prodromus*. A great man, Christian . . .

ANSELM (*impassioned*). You're always brandishing your Keplers, Galileos and Copernicuses . . . the Earth apparently spins about the Sun in a circle . . . what kind of laws are you inventing that aren't written in the Good Book? Don't you fear God, blasphemer?

CASSELIUS. Father Anselm, it is precisely in these laws that it's possible to discern God's greatness. What's more, the planets don't circle the Sun, but travel in ellipses, whose axes . . .

ANSELM (*interrupts him*). You're spreading pagan heresy! You sneer at Scripture. All the calamities on earth are—thanks to you and your ilk—righteous punishment for your heresies!

CASSELIUS (*gently*). You know, Father, there are two kinds of people. One kind knows, the other kind believes. You believe.

ANSELM. " . . . And I saw a beast of prey, climbing out of the sea, that had seven heads and ten horns, and on its horns ten crowns, whose names were heresy!"

CASSELIUS. Precisely, Father Anselm. Revelations of St. John, Chapter 13. A beautiful spot . . . "Et bestia, quam vidi, similis erat pardo et pedes eius sicut pedes ursi, et os eius sicut os leonis . . ."

WALDAU (*to Anselm*). Yes! And you're spreading out again, just as if you were at home in the parsonage! Move over a bit!

ANSELM. This is my spot. You're not going to lecture me about where I can lie down! It's your fault that I'm awake.

Waldau grumbles unhappily.

CASSELIUS (*to Christian*). Are you still thinking about Eleonor, Christian?

CHRISTIAN. Eleonor—and home . . . My thoughts are always with them. In fact, I'm only living for the moment when I can return to Stetten. Eleonor, Casselius . . .

WALDAU (*interrupts him*). I know, Sir Christian, how easy it is to talk about Miss Eleonor now! Now you can't help being faithful . . . but you weren't always that way . . . Don't you remember? Veronika? Freiburg?

CHRISTIAN. Veronika! God, I wonder where the wind has carried her off to? I never told you about her, Casselius.

CASSELIUS. A young lord's romantic encounter? Do tell . . .

CHRISTIAN. She was a good girl! She took care of me . . . maybe she even saved my life . . . she liked me.

WALDAU. Liked him! She was crazy about him! She would have followed him into burning hell fires!

CASSELIUS. A noble young lady?

WALDAU. Oh no, she ran one of the canteens for the troops[19] . . . nice girl . . . from somewhere in Saxony. She was following Werth's divisions. That time at Freiburg Christian caught a fever . . . and that Veronika didn't stir from his side after either battle. Were you at Freiburg, sir?

CASSELIUS. That was four years ago, right? No, I was still at the Spanish court then.

---

19 The word used in the original Czech script, *markytánka*, identifies a profession like that of the protagonist in Brecht's *Mother Courage*: a trader who follows the troops, selling goods to the soldiers.

WALDAU. You really missed something there! That was in the summer . . . All of a sudden one morning—bang! There were the French, and on us like a storm! No getting into our formations. That time Werth's cavalry didn't even engage. For safety's sake we retreated closer to Freiburg right after the battle—and that move made Christian worse. We had hardly made camp, then suddenly on the third day an alarm! Turenne and that duke were there again! You've never seen such a fray, gentlemen! Infantry with light and heavy artillery attacking us . . . but we held our own! It cost them four thousand men! Our General Mercy lost his brother there. Sir Christian was laid up feverish in the tent and that girl Veronika always at his side . . . she took care of him like his own mother—until he got better. And then she stuck with us for a whole year . . .

CASSELIUS. Hm. Nice, Christian. And during that year . . . ?

CHRISTIAN. Yes, but I didn't have a clear conscience about it. I knew we'd have to part one day. I think even she was quietly reconciled to that. It didn't end till Allerheim—exactly a year after Freiburg. There we just lost sight of her in all that confusion— then they captured us—and we haven't seen Veronika since.

CASSELIUS. A nice tale . . . but you won't tell Miss Eleonor about it, will you?

CHRISTIAN. No, I won't hide it from her, Casselius . . . when we're together again . . . strolling through the old park in the evenings . . . riding on outings into the countryside . . . to services at the Rain church . . . Why so quiet, Father Anselm?

ANSELM. Well . . . you've reminded me . . . our countryside . . . I long for a bit of peace and quiet after all this conflict and confusion . . . a bit of solitude . . . home . . . I too have a home, you know . . . the Rain parsonage! The parsonage, the garden, the church of St. Boniface—it means as much to me as Stetten does to you. God willing, we shall all return home in good health.

WALDAU (*to Casselius*). You were speaking with that Walloon guard yesterday, Sir . . . When the hell are we going home? We've been rotting here for such a long time . . .

CASSELIUS. Friends, God disposes according to a different measure than we might wish . . . This is all merely a brief episode. Even your Rain . . . all our lives . . . it's all just a moment. The only question that remains is how we live it.

WALDAU. Come visit us at Waldau—I'll show you how we live it! During the day we'll ride out after deer, or into the fields after rabbit—we have the best horses in all of Bavaria at Waldau—let me drop dead if I don't manage to return to the life befitting a nobleman! And in the evening, Sir Casselius, you'll see feasting at Waldau! Do you like smoked venison? With a burgundy, of course!

CASSELIUS. Love it to death, my friend! You're right, that's also a solution.

CHRISTIAN. You're laughing, Casselius! Life—an instant . . . but how to really deal with it?

CASSELIUS. Don't worry about it. Somebody else will always be solving this question for us, regardless of what we call Him. *Silence.*

CHRISTIAN. This weighs me down, Casselius. The air is oppressive here . . . in Hessen . . . maybe all over the world . . . Why is that? What have we wrought? We or our fathers—whose sins are we atoning for?

CASSELIUS. Don't complain so much! At least you're alive . . . You'll never be satisfied in any case, not in a cell in Marburg prison, nor by the hearth at home in Stetten . . . we always want more than is granted us.

CHRISTIAN. But what do we want, Casselius? We ask for so little! A little peace . . . and then maybe those we love . . . Only to open our eyes for once and not have to see these horrors, broken faces, empty eyes, shattered walls, smoking ruins . . . not to have to hear the beat of heavy footsteps, marching to the sound of fife and drums, the hoarse voice of a drunken sergeant shouting senseless commands . . . Only to open our eyes to see . . . an apple tree in blossom beneath the bedroom windows at Stetten, a cat purring before a bowl of milk, a wide unmown field of ripening grain in the afternoon sun . . . Rain in the midst of green meadows . . . Peace and quiet, Casselius . . . like up there among the stars . . . Are we asking too much?

CASSELIUS. Apparently so—and mainly too soon. Because we'll only be granted peace and quiet in our last hour—and then we'll have them eternally. You don't have the right to ask for them as long as you're alive. And the more eventfully, the more fully you live, the more easily you'll go there—into the quiet.

WALDAU (*softly, petulantly*). To hell with all this! I want to go home—to Waldau! (*Lifts his head, stands up slowly and goes to the door.*)

CHRISTIAN. No, don't say this, Casselius. There has to be something else on this earth that we can turn to with our hopes and dreams. Father Anselm constantly imagines his church and parsonage in Rain. Waldau keeps seeing the comfort and plenty of his family estate. I, Casselius, see the small white castle shining in the dusk among old trees . . . and a girlish figure, running toward me between the rows of trees . . . And you, Casselius, where is your haven?

Casselius smiles and gestures to imply a circle round himself.

WALDAU (*turning suddenly, shouts*). No, no, and no! I won't wait! I don't want to die here like a caged rat! Let me out! I need to get out! I need air! Why are you standing there? Why aren't you tearing out the bars? Why aren't you battering down the door? Me—I'm a soldier! By his majesty's grace, Captain of the Horse Regiments von Waldau reporting! Cavalry! Mount! After me, on the double! To Rain—to Waldau . . . (*Collapses by the door and sobs uncontrollably.*)

ANSELM (*reaches for a crucifix with commanding gesture*). On your knees! You have forgotten your Lord, unbelievers, who suffered for you, who was crucified for you! Pray humbly to your God that He might hear you! (*Leads a prayer; Waldau and Christian kneel and repeat after him.*) Hear, my Jesus, I approach Your throne and pray—for day is done and night descends—receive my heart and soul—let me number the days Your mercy will grant me—my heart will be filled by You—all torment will leave me. For there, where You are . . .

CHRISTIAN (*stands, repeats*). . . . for there, where You are . . . where are You?

ANSELM (*continues*). . . . light and day of our lives . . .

CHRISTIAN. Light? It's night! We're born in the dark, live in the dark, die in the dark! Why are you telling me about light when I can't see it? Why are you telling me about God when He doesn't reveal Himself to me in His deeds? How can I praise Him who turns His face from me without cause? Where is your God? Maybe in the smoking ruins, on dozens of bloody battlefields? Are the burning cities perhaps the eternal flames at His altar? Did He let His son preach brotherly love so that He could cause brother to savage brother like hungry wolves? I have no faith! Do you hear? There is no God!

ANSELM (*lifts his face to the heavens*). Lord who Thou art; Thou, whose mercy is endless as the sea, curse not the sinner and forgive him, for he knows not what he does!

CHRISTIAN (*despairing*). Do you exist? If You do, relieve my doubts so that I might have faith again! Show Yourself—in word or deed—like You appeared to the Israelites in the desert! Show Yourself!

ANSELM (*exclaims*). Don't blaspheme!

CHRISTIAN. Give me a sign! (*Silence.*) Give me a sign!

Pause. A handful of pebbles falls through the window. Christian and Waldau stare. Anselm falls to his knees. Casselius strides to the window.

VERONIKA. Christian!

CASSELIUS (*surprised*). Hey! Someone is calling you!

VERONIKA. Sir Christian!

CHRISTIAN (*goes hesitantly to the window and looks out. Then, joyfully*). Veronika! Is that you!?

WALDAU (*rises*). Veronika? Where did she come from?

VERONIKA (*overjoyed*). Sir Christian!

CHRISTIAN. Veronika! You came after me? Are our troops here? Where is Werth's cavalry?

All is quiet. Only Christian's silhouette, as he speaks with the unseen Veronika, is visible against the barred window. Day begins to dawn.

VERONIKA. I'm here alone, Sir Christian, without our troops . . . I've been searching for you for so long! For a year after Allerheim I rode with the imperial troops, asking for you everywhere— and nothing, not even a rumor . . . And then I set out on my own. Oh, if you only knew all the places I've looked for you!

CHRISTIAN. Is it really you? God has really sent you to me?

VERONIKA. I traveled with the Swedes for half a year; I was with the French . . . and I searched everywhere . . . doesn't anyone know the Cornet von Stetten? . . . it was as if the earth had swallowed you up . . . all I knew was that you had been cap- tured at Allerheim—and nothing since then. Not our men, not the French, no one could tell me anything . . . Oh, what haven't I tried these last few years—there's too much to tell!

CHRISTIAN. What's happening at home? What are the Bavarians doing? Have you been to Rain?

VERONIKA. I walked through all of Lorraine, I was in Württemberg, in the Palatinate, I looked for you in Brunswick . . . I walked from city to city, from camp to camp . . . always asking about you . . . What suffering I've endured through it all! Maybe you won't find me pleasing anymore!

CHRISTIAN. Veronika, you good—

VERONIKA. Sir Christian!

CHRISTIAN. And were you in Bavaria? Were you in Rain? In Stetten?

VERONIKA. I was, I was there too. That was the first place I went after I left the imperial army.

CHRISTIAN. What about my parents? Are they alive? And . . . (*pauses*) Eleonor?

VERONIKA. I didn't talk with them. I asked the servants about you— and they had no news of you . . .

CHRISTIAN (*disappointed*). So you can't tell me anything about them?

VERONIKA. And then I set out on the road again . . . only thinking of you . . . Do you have enough to eat? Are you sleeping on the ground? Did that fever come back? And now I've finally found you! Sir Christian!

CHRISTIAN. And how did you find us?

VERONIKA. I arrived here last night. I was asking some soldiers down in the tavern . . . like I always ask . . . and a Hessian soldier told me, "They say there are four imperial soldiers up there in the castle; been there a long time already." My heart stopped. Right away I suspected . . . And then I went with him, but he had to promise me that he'd help me. And this morning he confirmed that it was you! Oh, Sir Christian, I can't tell you how glad I am to be talking to you!

CHRISTIAN. Veronika, God Himself has sent you! We really thought that everyone had completely forgotten us!

VERONIKA. Wait a minute, Sir Christian—he's signalling. Someone's coming!

CHRISTIAN (*steps away from the window*). Friends—perhaps God is offering us a helping hand!

WALDAU. He's[20] got to help get us out of here, Sir Christian— home!—to Rain!

ANSELM. Lord, You heard the prayers from the desert! Now I believe that, soon, I'll be able to give thanks to You at the altar in Rain! (*Prays.*)

CHRISTIAN (*joyously*). I'll gallop past Rain, the wind will race me up to Stetten—from the crossroads at the three firs I can already see a thread of smoke—the smoke of home . . .

VERONIKA. Sir Christian! (*Christian hurries back to the window.*) I have to be quick—they're hurrying me. We have to get you out of here, Sir Christian.

CHRISTIAN. How?

VERONIKA. I've arranged everything. Be ready. Tomorrow the guards will change shifts at one hour past midnight. My friend will be in the new shift . . .

---

20 In the original Czech script it is ambiguous whether Waldau means "she" (Veronika) or "he" (God).

CHRISTIAN. But . . .

VERONIKA. Don't be afraid, Sir Christian, everything is ready . . . The horses will be waiting—you'll travel as a Hessian trader . . . to Fulda . . . then on—past Kulmbach—to Cheb—and into Bohemia . . . and from there we'll go wherever we want!

CHRISTIAN. But—there are four of us, Veronika!

VERONIKA. Four! That's impossible, Sir Christian. You alone . . .

CHRISTIAN. It has to be possible! I can't leave without them.

VERONIKA. Wait!

Silence for a while.

WALDAU (*joyfully*). Sir Christian! Home! Home, do you hear? (*Kicks the food dish.*) Buckwheat porridge! (*Laughs.*) I can already taste it on my tongue—smoked venison—juicy—and we'll drink it down with Rhine wine, Sir Christian!

CHRISTIAN. Casselius, aren't you excited? You'll be my guest at Stetten, for as long as you like. You'll see Eleonor . . .

Casselius presses his hand.

VERONIKA. Sir Christian!

CHRISTIAN. So—when?

VERONIKA. You and one other. We can't take more. Don't ask . . .

CHRISTIAN. Veronika—isn't there some other way?

VERONIKA. I have to go. They're hurrying me. Till tomorrow—an hour past midnight. God keep you!

CHRISTIAN. Veronika! (*Silence.*) She's gone!

ANSELM. No, God won't allow us to perish here; we'll escape from this prison like the Israelites from the land of Egypt . . . He'll protect us from all evil along the way. We'll go without fear, my son.

WALDAU. Tomorrow at midnight . . . as traders . . . who ever would have thought we'd be traveling together as Hessian traders in a canvas cart, Sir Christian . . . Rattling along with cart horses. But somewhere past Fulda we'll get fast horses, and then we'll push on into Bavaria like Werth's knights . . . Hell of a girl, that Veronika . . .

ANSELM. Wait, my son. The woman said just two.

WALDAU. Two, Father, I heard.

ANSELM. But you just said you're going. If I go with Christian, then you can't!

WALDAU. You? But who said anything about you, Father? Of course I'm going home with Sir Christian, and that's that! No one mentioned you at all!

ANSELM (*wrathfully*). And you think that God sent us salvation in the shape of this young woman so that you could be liberated, while I, His servant, will be left here in the hands of the enemy?

WALDAU. Look at him, Sir Christian! So he thinks he's going! So I, captain of Werth's cavalry, the best rider and swordsman in his gracious majesty's army, I, gentleman from Waldau, nobly born, should rot here in this hole . . . while he, little preacher, goes home! The people of Rain probably can't wait to hear his pious platitudes! By thunder, anything but that, brother in Christ! I'm going!

ANSELM. Fear God, lest He strike you down with His lightning! What are you going to achieve on this earth? Laze about at Waldau, chase rabbits by day, and indulge in drunkenness and gluttony by night? For this God should liberate you?

WALDAU. That's none of your business! You can be sure I won't be living a monk's life—not after these three years here.

ANSELM. Christian, my son, recall that it was I who baptized you, who acquainted you with the words of God in the years of your youth. And surely it was no accident but God's will that back there at Allerheim I was thrown into the same wagon in which you were lying, unconscious, that I might watch over you.

CHRISTIAN. Friends, calm yourselves! I will make it my first task—if we can't all leave here together—to ransom you from captivity.

WALDAU (*stubbornly*). And . . . who knows how the escape will turn out? All kinds of riffraff wander the roads today—you get hit by a musket ball and we can wait to be ransomed till Judgment Day. You don't know what you might encounter along the way; my right arm will protect you better than Father Anselm's pious bleating!

ANSELM. Enough! I appeal to you, Christian, and God knows I have a right to this, that you choose me to accompany you, and pay no attention to this godless blasphemer. Under the protection of the Highest we'll reach home safely.

WALDAU. Home! Home! And you want to keep me from returning home, you black crow!

ANSELM. Silence, you son of a dog! You would insult a priest? You'll burn in hell fire!

WALDAU (*beside himself*). Stay here because of you? Eat this slop because of you? While at home, at Waldau—

ANSELM. You're going to hell, and not to Waldau! I'm going! To Rain, to St. Boniface—

WALDAU (*shouting*). You'll have to kill me first!

ANSELM (*compassionately*). I shall pray for your soul, heathen. You and I are going, Christian.

CHRISTIAN (*suddenly decisive*). You come with me, Casselius!

Casselius shrugs; simultaneously Waldau throws himself at Father Anselm.

WALDAU. You're not going!

ANSELM. Murderer!

CHRISTIAN. Stop it!

Casselius has been watching the argument with growing unease. He jumps between them and separates them.

CASSELIUS. Fools! Get a hold of yourselves! Blind, thoughtless fools! (*Pauses, then quietly*) Should I have told you after all what that Walloon actually said to me? Should I have told you that, three weeks ago, General Wrangel's brother was killed when they were defeated near Dachau, and that in vengeance he tore through Bavaria like death incarnate, sowing all the horrors of war? That he torched your towns and villages? That even the cynical Walloon who marches back and forth in front of our cell still recalls with horror the havoc that was wrought by the Swedes and the French? There are no stones left standing in your Rain—today your church and parsonage, Father Anselm, are shattered ruins—

WALDAU (*after a pause*). . . . and Waldau?

CASSELIUS. Waldau? It has long since stopped smoking amidst the trampled and ruined fields! And you, Christian, were you to go from Rain up to Stetten, at the crossroads by the three firs you would see a thread of smoke from the conflagration where Stetten used to stand! That is your smoke of home today! You want to go home? Fools! The home you left is in the past, buried in the abyss of time! There's a different world out there, beyond these walls! Do you hear? A different world! There won't be any comfort, leisure or carousing at Waldau, there won't be time for pious meditation in a quiet corner of your little parsonage garden, Father Anselm! Your romantic dreams will remain unsatisfied, Christian . . . There won't be time! Do you hear? There won't be time!

CHRISTIAN (*listens*). Wait! What's that? Listen . . .

ANSELM. Bells!

From outside, where morning has broken, there is the uproar of a growing crowd and tolling bells; sound of shouting; all four listen transfixed.

SHOUTS. Peace!—Peace! The lords in Münster have agreed to a final peace! It's over! It's over! Peace for all time!21

The doors are flung open and from outside the guard's voice is heard.

GUARD. Peace! Do you hear, emperor's men? Go home! You're free! (*Receding*) It's over! Go home!

All four sit frozen.

WALDAU (*in a strangled voice*). Home . . . ?

Casselius bursts out in convulsive laughter.

---

21 The Treaty of Münster, signed on October 24, 1648, was the last of a group of treaties comprising the Peace of Westphalia that marked the end of the Thirty Years War.

SMĚJTE – SE S NÁMI

Režie: Dr. Felix Porges

Napsal: Dr. Felix Porges,
V. Hornatzky, Pavel Weisskopf

Hudba: Dr. Felix Porges

Hudebně nastudoval a doprovází:
Kurt Mayer

Hrají:

Karel Beermann,
Franta Weissenstein,
V. Hornatzky,
Dr. Felix Porges,
Pavel Mayer,

Elly Bernsteinová-
Porgesová
Hanka Ledererová
Ing. Frant. Beran
Hanka Krauskopfová

FELIX PROKEŠ,

VÍTĚZSLAV "PIDLA" HORPATZKY,

PAVEL WEISSKOPF,

and PAVEL STRÁNSKÝ

LAUGH WITH US
The Second Czech Cabaret

INTRODUCTION

In the summer of 2005 a text came to light which had long been considered lost: *The Second Czech Cabaret*, also titled *Laugh with Us*.[1] Several sources confirmed that the work had been performed in Terezín/Theresienstadt: prisoner Josef Taussig's notes for an essay he planned to write on cabaret in the ghetto, and a poster, song lyrics, and related documents preserved in the Terezín Memorial in the Czech Republic.[2] Survivors and their heirs have provided me with two separate versions of the cabaret.

IMAGE 7.1 *(facing page)* **A souvenir poster for *Laugh with Us*.**
Courtesy of the Terezín Memorial.

---

1 The title on the script is *The Second Czech Cabaret*. The title on the archival documents described below is *Laugh with Us*, which is one of the first lines of the cabaret's opening song.

2 Josef Taussig, "O terezínských kabaretech," in Miroslav Kárný, Jaroslova Milotová, and Eva Lorencová (eds.), *Terezínské studie a dokumenty 2001* (Prague: Academia, 2001), pp. 310–46; and the Terezín Memorial, inv. nos. PT 3826–31. Specific verses quoted by Taussig and the close correspondence of the names on the poster with the names of the participants listed in the text confirm that the two titles refer to the same cabaret.

One of the versions was preserved by the family of co-author Felix Prokeš (né Porges).[3] The text is typewritten and extensive notes are written onto the manuscript; the handwriting, according to his sons, is Prokeš's own. The notes include corrections and additions to the dialogue as well as notes on entrances, exits and other stage directions. The handwritten sheet music for the songs Prokeš composed for the cabaret was also preserved in the collection.

The version of the text published here was provided by Hana Lojínová (neé Ledererová) who received it from Prokeš in the ghetto for her role as a dancer. Only a few notes in pencil were written on the manuscript, also apparently in Prokeš's handwriting. This manuscript appears to be the later version; corrections that had been written by hand in the Prokeš manuscript were incorporated into the typewritten Lojínová manuscript, and in it the authors joke about events that took place later in the spring and summer of 1944.[4]

THE AUTHORS

Three of the authors of the cabaret—Prokeš, Horpatzky, and Stránský—had worked together previously on another performance, *Radio Show*, also published in this volume.[5] About the fourth author, Pavel Weisskopf, very little is known: he arrived in the ghetto in December 1942, on the same transport as Porges and Horpatzky, and was deported to Auschwitz with the mass transports in the fall of 1944.

Much more is known about a figure who played an important role in the cabaret and in Prokeš's life: Elly Prokešová (neé Bernsteinová). In her hometown of Jihlava/Iglau she acted in numerous Czech- and

---

3 For more information on the collection, see the introduction to *Radio Show* in this volume.

4 For example, the first scene in the Prokeš manuscript includes an April Fools' Day joke. In the Lojínová manuscript that joke has been removed and in a new sketch the performers refer to *Announcements* (*Mitteilungen*), the new name given to the *Daily Orders* (*Tagesbefehl*) on April 15, 1944.

5 For more information on these authors, see the introduction to *Radio Show* in this volume.

German-language performances.[6] After her deportation to Terezín/ Theresienstadt in May 1942 she participated in the theatrical life of the ghetto, performing, for example, the title role in the original operetta *Girl of the Ghetto*.[7] She and Prokeš became acquainted in the ghetto and were married there on December 26, 1943.[8] They performed together in their own Czech-language cabaret and also appeared in the German-language cabarets of Leo Strauss and Myra Strauss-Gruhenberg.

Felix and Elly Prokeš were not deported further; they were liberated in Terezín/Theresienstadt and returned to Prague. Since weddings in the ghetto were not legally recognized, they married again in 1945. Prokeš's experience in the central provisions office of the ghetto enabled him to assume a position at the Ministry of Agriculture. Elly employed her talent for languages as a tour guide and a simultaneous interpreter for films. After the war, neither of them was active in theater. Their sons Miroslav, Jan, and Zdeněk were born in 1946, 1947, and 1950 respectively.

THE SCRIPT

As Taussig wrote, Porges and Horpatzky's cabaret was one of three Czech cabarets in Terezín/Theresienstadt that "knew and admired the Liberated Theater."[9] Their dialogues are clearly modeled on those of that theater's beloved comedy team, Jiří Voskovec and Jan Werich. In Prokeš and Horpatzky's first script, *Radio Show*, they and their fellow performers took their audiences back to their pre-war lives. In *Laugh*

---

6 The Prokeš family preserved several clippings from her pre-war performances.

7 A poster for the operetta (in the original German, *Ghettomädel*) and several songs have been preserved. See the Terezín Memorial, inv. nos. PT 3853 and PT 3899–3902. For an account of the performance see Philipp Manes, *Als ob's ein Leben wär: Tatsachenbericht Theresienstadt 1942–1944* (Ben Barkow and Klaus Leist eds.) (Berlin: Ullstein, 2005), p. 178.

8 The Prokeš family has also preserved wedding cards given to them by their friends in the ghetto.

9 Taussig, "O terezínských kabaretech," p. 313.

IMAGE 7.2 (*above*) **Felix Prokeš and Elly Bernsteinová's wedding, 1945.**
Courtesy of Jan, Miroslav, and Zdeněk Prokeš.

IMAGE 7.3 (*facing page, top*) **Vítězslav Horpatzky with his wife Anna, 1930s.**
Courtesy of Eva Hirschová.

IMAGE 7.4 (*facing page, bottom*) **Vítězslav Horpatzky's transport card, showing the second transport to Osvětím (Auschwitz).**
Courtesy of the United States Holocaust Memorial Museum.

ÚSTŘEDNÍ KARTOTÉKA — TRANSPORTY.

R. č. 16470

Horparzky Liegfried
Vítězdar

Rodná data: 11/2 1904

Adresa před deportací: Praha XII, Soběslavská 2250.

1. transport	2. transport
dne: 14. XII. 1941	dne: 26. 10. 1944
J	číslo: EV – 1464
č. 637	do: Osvětim

I.

with Us: The Second Czech Cabaret they employ the opposite strategy: they take them into the post-war future. In the script, they and their friends from Terezín/Theresienstadt have returned to Prague and can look back on their experiences from a safe distance. Using particularly aggressive satire they trivialize even the most dangerous aspects of the ghetto, making them appear—at least for a short time—less terrifying. By selecting other experiences from the ghetto as ones they might indeed remember fondly, they weave even Terezín/Theresienstadt itself into a narrative that projects their own survival.

BIOGRAPHICAL INFORMATION

The names of the participants were listed on the script and on a poster for the performance preserved in the Terezín Memorial.

THE AUTHORS

For biographical information on **HORPATZKY**, **PROKEŠ**, and **STRÁNSKÝ**, see pp. 51–2 of this volume.

PAVEL WEISSKOPF was born on June 7, 1906. He was deported from Prague to Terezín/Theresienstadt on December 4, 1941, and from there to Auschwitz on September 28, 1944. He perished.

THE ACTORS AND OTHER PARTICIPANTS

ING. FRANT. (FRANTIŠEK) BERAN appears on the poster but not in the script. He was born on March 21, 1901, deported to Terezín/Theresienstadt from Prague on April 9, 1943, and to Auschwitz on September 28, 1944. He perished.

KAREL BERMAN (sometimes written Bermann; on the poster his name is spelled **BEERMANN**), was born on April 14, 1919. He was deported from Prague to Terezín/Theresienstadt on March 6, 1941, and on September 28, 1944, to Auschwitz. He was liberated in Allach.

ELLY PROKEŠOVÁ (née **BERNSTEINOVÁ-PORGESOVÁ**) was born on September 7, 1917. She was deported from Třebíč to Terezín/Theresienstadt on

May 18, 1942, and remained there until the liberation. She died on
January 29, 1975.

HANA KRAUSKOPFOVÁ, born on April 17, 1925, was deported from Prague
to Terezín/Theresienstadt on March 9, 1943, and on October 1, 1944,
to Auschwitz. She was liberated in Mauthausen.

HANA (HANKA) LOJÍNOVÁ (NÉE LEDEREROVÁ), born on October 3, 1923, was
deported from Prague to Terezín/Theresienstadt on September 12,
1942, and remained there until the liberation.

KURT MAIER (sometimes written Meyer; on the poster his name is
spelled **MEIER**), born on February 17, 1911, was deported from Prague
to Terezín/Theresienstadt on December 4, 1941, and on October 1,
1944, to Auschwitz. He survived.

PAVEL MAIER (sometimes written **PAUL MAYER**), born on August 17, 1919,
was deported from Brno/Brünn to Terezín/Theresienstadt on January
28, 1942, and on September 28, 1944, to Auschwitz. He perished in
Dachau on January 24, 1945.

FRANTIŠEK WEISSENSTEIN, born on February 15, 1899, was deported from
Prague to Terezín/Theresienstadt on November 30, 1941, and on
September 28, 1944, to Auschwitz. He perished.

THE SURVIVORS CONTRIBUTING TO THE INTRODUCTION AND ANNOTATION

LUDĚK ELIÁŠ (né **ECKSTEIN**) was born on July 29, 1923. He was deported
from Kladno to Terezín/Theresienstadt on February 26, 1942, and to
Auschwitz on May 18, 1944. He was selected for labor and sent
to Schwarzheide, a satellite camp of Sachsenhausen. He survived
a death march from Schwarzheide and was liberated in Terezín/
Theresienstadt. He currently resides in Ostrava/Mährisch Ostrau.

JAN FISCHER was born on July 19, 1921. He was deported from Prague
to Terezín/Theresienstadt on December 4, 1941, and to Auschwitz-
Birkenau on September 28, 1944. He was selected for labor and was
liberated at Blechhammer. He currently resides in Prague.

DORIS GROZDANOVIČOVÁ (née **SCHIMMERLINGOVÁ**) was born on April 7, 1926. She was deported to the ghetto from Brno/Brünn on January 28, 1942. She was liberated in the ghetto. She resides in Prague.

MARIANNE FOLTÝNOVÁ (née **MÜLLEROVÁ**) was born on October 19, 1922. She was deported from Prague to Terezín/Theresienstadt on February 8, 1942, and was liberated there. She currently resides in Prague.

HANA REINEROVÁ was born on April 19, 1921. She was deported to Terezín/Theresienstadt on July 5, 1943, and to Auschwitz on October 1, 1944. She was liberated in Mauthausen. She died on June 1, 2007.

LAUGH WITH US
The Second Czech Cabaret

CAST

Franta Weissenstein
Karel Bermann
Kurt Meier
Elly Bernsteinová
Felix Porges
Pidla Horpatzky
Hanka Ledererová
Pavel Meier
Hanka Krauskopfová
Pavel Weisskopf

PROGRAM

1. OPENING: F. Porges

2. "LONG LIVE CABARET" (Song): E. Bernsteinová

3. FIRST DIALOGUE: F. Porges, P. Horpatzky

4. THREE FOLK SONGS: P. Meier
     a. "I Had a Dream, My Lass"
     b. "Tovačov"
     c. "On the Lord's Meadows"

5. SECOND DIALOGUE: F. Porges, P. Horpatzky

6. BAR SCENE
     a. ECCENTRIC DANCE ("Pink Crinoline"): H. Ledererová
     b. TWO SONGS: E. Bernsteinová
             I. "Andalusian Nights" (Tango)
             II. "Abandoned" (Slow foxtrot)
     c. DUO: E. Bernsteinová, H. Krauskopfová

I. Express foxtrot

II. "Tavern in Odessa" (Tango)

III. "Merry Multiplication" (Foxtrot)

d. ACCORDION SOLO: K. Meier

I. Second Hungarian Rhapsody by Lizst
in a jazz arrangement

II. Variations on the song

7. THIRD DIALOGUE: F. Porges, P. Horpatzky

8. TWO OPERA ARIAS: F. Weissenstein

a. Jeník's aria from *The Bartered Bride*

b. Aria from *Dalibor*

9. FOURTH DIALOGUE: F. Porges, P. Horpatzky

10. CZECH AND SLOVAK DANCES: E. Bernsteinová, H. Ledererová

11. FIFTH DIALOGUE: F. Porges, P. Horpatzky

12. TWO SONGS: K. Bermann

a. Friml: "In Quiet Nights"

b. Blodek: "Spring Song"

13. SIXTH DIALOGUE: F. Porges, P. Horpatzky

14. SEVENTH DIALOGUE AND COUPLET: F. Porges, P. Horpatzky

15. EPILOGUE: F. Porges, P. Horpatzky

1. OPENING

PORGES. Ladies and gentlemen, welcome to our second original Czech cabaret. We intend to offer you a cheerful evening. We want, we want . . . but why should I give you a long explanation; you'll find out what we really want from this little song I wrote. So that it stays in the family, my wife will sing it to you. Accompanying her, and the rest of the program, Kurt Meier.

2. "LONG LIVE CABARET" [10]

Lyrics: Pavel Stránský and Felix Porges
Music: Felix Porges

E. BERNSTEINOVÁ. Ladies and gentlemen,
Come laugh with us again
We're glad to have you at our show
We welcome all of you
You know that after
A dose of laughter
You'll feel renewed.
Boys, girls of every age
Fans of the cabaret
All friends from far and near
We're glad you're here.

Young and old alike fall in love with jazz,
When they hear the music, they start to dance
Everyone who's young at heart
Picks up the beat and wants to take part.

---

10 See original music for "Long Live Cabaret" ("Ať žije kabaret") on p. 217 of this volume, IMAGE 7.9.

Everyone who shares our philosophy
And tries to look at life optimistically
Hurry friends come quickly
And join us under our flag.

You young folks, so full of vitality,
And all those, who love rhythm and melody
Calling everybody, whose pulse beats fast
At the thought of sharing in song and dance
Old and young, oh all hear
The call to arms.

Spectators, fans and friends
Don't miss a single second 'cause we promise
    you'll have fun
Something for everyone
We'll entertain you
With the refrains you
Love oh so well.
Once more before we start
We wish you from the heart:
Let a *happy-end*[11] befall you
One and all.

3. FIRST DIALOGUE

In the rear a backdrop of City[12] *on Wenceslas Square.*

WEISSKOPF (*in the voice of a newspaper boy, backstage*). Evening,
evening edition of *Czech Word*, tomorrow morning's *A-Z*,

---

[11] In the original Czech script the English expression "happy-end" (written with a hyphen) is used.

[12] City was the name of a clothing store on Wenceslas Square, the heart of Prague's business district. The wide sidewalk in front of the store was a favorite meeting point. Jan Fischer, interview with Lisa Peschel, March 9, 2006.

special edition of the *Telegraph*: Murder of a police inspector in Ostrovní street.[13]

Porges and Horpatzky enter with newspapers in their hands.

HORPATZKY (*reading*). New maximum prices: Pork—13 crowns 45 hellers; white bread—25 hellers. You know, my dear colleague,[14] you never read such things in Terezín; there the most-read section was the lost and found. Do you remember? A person kept reading that some bridge had lost its head.

PORGES. That a bridge lost its head? What kind of nonsense are you talking about?

HORPATZKY. Well, a bridgehead[15] got lost, sometimes initiative got lost, even airplanes got lost, every day.[16]

WEISSKOPF (*in the newspaper-boy voice*). Special edition: Murder of a police inspector.

HORPATZKY. Or you know, a nice pork chop there cost a thousand crowns, but on the other hand, no one murdered any police inspector.[17]

PORGES. Surprising, isn't it. You know, though, things were altogether different there than they are anywhere else.[18] I'm qualified to judge. I know the world well enough; I have been here, there and everywhere.

---

13 The film *Murder in Ostrovní Street* (*Vražda v Ostrovní ulici*, 1933) was based on an actual murder case. Luděk Eliáš, interview with Lisa Peschel, May 30, 2010.

14 This address (in Czech, *pane kolego*) was typical of Voskovec and Werich.

15 In the Czech original the authors use the German word *Brückenkopf* (bridgehead). The word has the same military meanings in German as in English: a type of fortification allowing for control of a bridge or an advanced position seized in hostile territory.

16 These veiled references satirize Nazi military defeats, news of which had reached the ghetto by the summer of 1944.

17 According to all accounts there was virtually no violent crime among the prisoners. See Adler, *Theresienstadt*, pp. 486–7.

18 The dialogue that follows (through Horpatzky's line "Prague, ah") was apparently inspired by a dialogue between Voskovec and Werich from their revue *Golem* (1931). A recording is available on the CD *Osvobozené divadlo 2* (Prague: Ultraphon 1994), track 6.

HORPATZKY. I've been to those places too.

PORGES. So you understand, don't you. You know, so often there I reminisced: Ah, Prague.

HORPATZKY. Not me; for me it was more like: Prague, ah.[19]

PORGES. You're a different sort of person, there's nothing to be done about that. But how everything has changed since then—it's hard to believe, most of all the people. For example that peculiar fellow—what was his name? yes, that Federer,[20] how he scrambled for an extra helping of food[21] there, even though there was only barley, now of course he only goes to Šroubek's[22] and when they have only forty-eight dishes on the menu he loses his temper because they don't have that forty-ninth dish, just the one he has a taste for. Now his favorite is that Czech-Jewish dish.

HORPATZKY. What is that?

PORGES. Don't you know? It's pork with *šoulet*.[23] All the same he had to wait a long time until his most fervent wish was fulfilled. It never happened in Terezín, not until now.

HORPATZKY. What wish?

PORGES. To get to know one of the lady cooks. But they just don't have the same appeal now as they did before.

HORPATZKY. Or that fellow who was in charge of one of the barracks—how he put on airs in front of those poor people.[24]

---

19 In Voskovec and Werich's recording, although the two accentuate their differences, "Ah, Prague" and "Prague, ah" are practically identical expressions of nostalgia.

20 Sixteen men with the surname Federer were deported to Terezín/Theresienstadt. It is unclear whether the authors are referring to a specific individual or are using the name as the Czech-Jewish equivalent of "John Doe."

21 The word used in the original Czech script, *náchšup* (also spelled *nášup*), is derived from the German word *Nachschub*, "extra portion."

22 U Šroubků was a large, elegant, and popular restaurant inside the Grand Hotel Šroubek on Wenceslas Square. The hotel is now named Hotel Evropa.

23 *Šoulet* is a kosher dish. See *scholet* (glossary). The joke probably refers to the level of assimilation of the pre-war Czech Jews who rarely observed traditional dietary laws.

Now he's back in Brno[25] and travels selling underwear for the firm Murmel and Stein.[26] But some of them still can't get used to the new conditions. You know what kind of unpleasantness I have with my wife. When a new maid moves in with us—we have a maid again now, you don't get anyone to work for free anymore like they did back then,[27] now you have to pay health benefits and so on—my wife immediately lunges at the poor woman's suitcases and rifles through them.[28]

PORGES. Force of habit, right?

HORPATZKY. My wife was in the Ústí barracks[29] for a long time. Very unpleasant.

PORGES. Do you remember, by any chance, a young man from Terezín? He sang folk songs in the courtyards there.[30] What was his name again? He was kind of smallish big.

HORPATZKY. Well, which was he? Smaller, big, bigger, small?

PORGES. Well, middle-sized, I'm not going to argue with you.

HORPATZKY. Aha, you probably mean Pavel Meier. He used to be a court singer; now he's become a chamber singer.

PORGES. And in which chamber does he actually sing?

---

24 In the Czech original, the spelling of certain words in this paragraph indicates that Horpatzky is satirizing the pronunciation and grammatical mistakes of a German speaker trying to speak Czech.

25 In the original script the authors used "in Prin," a Czech phonetic spelling of "in Brünn," the German name for the Moravian city of Brno. Many of the members of the Jewish community in Brno/Brünn were German speakers.

26 A joke based on the name of Rabbi Dr. Benjamin Murmelstein, a leader of the Jewish community of Vienna and the third *Judenältester* of the ghetto.

27 Possibly a reference to the *Putzkolonne* (cleaning crew), a group of female prisoners assigned to cleaning work in the ghetto.

28 In the original script the word used for "search" is *prošlojsovat*. See *Schleuse* (glossary).

29 During this period, the Ústí barracks were used as a central storehouse for suitcases and clothing confiscated from the arriving prisoners.

30 The barracks where most prisoners were housed were built around large open courtyards where performances, soccer games, etc., sometimes took place.

HORPATZKY. In none, he's a *Kammersänger*.[31] But you know, he still sings those folk songs.

PORGES. I'm surprised he isn't fed up with them by now.

4. THREE FOLK SONGS[32]

Singer: P. Meier

    A. "I Had a Dream, my Lass"

    B. "Tovačov"

    C. "On the Lord's Meadows"

5. SECOND DIALOGUE

Porges hums to himself: "On the Lord's Meadows."

HORPATZKY. You're in a good mood. But did you know that we also had a lord's meadow in Terezín?

PORGES. I didn't know about that.

HORPATZKY. It was called Bohušovice Hollow. There was a massive event there, a beautiful public demonstration.[33]

PORGES. Aha, I know, there was that international Sokol rally.

HORPATZKY. And I remember—there was another person who, when

IMAGE 7.5 *(Facing page)* **A folk dancer in the ghetto wearing the Czech national colors. By C. Burešová.**
Courtesy of Yad Vashem.

---

31 This joke depends on the double meaning of the German-language titles *Hofsänger* and *Kammersänger*. They literally mean "court singer" and "chamber singer," but also indicate the level of proficiency and recognition a singer has attained.

32 The Czech-language titles of the songs are "Zdálo se mi, má panenko," "Tovačov," and "Na těch panských lukách" respectively.

33 The Bohušovice/Bauschowitz Hollow is located just outside the ramparts of Terezín/Theresienstadt. A census of the ghetto took place there on November 11, 1943. See introduction to this volume, p. 28.

they questioned him, said that he found that ducat, and he got two months for it.[34]

PORGES. That was a so-called *šmé* if you can still manage to recall that expression. Those happened there all the time. Like that huge trial with the engagement swindler. Certainly you remember that; that was such a *šmelina en gros*.[35]

HORPATZKY. What was that? I don't remember anymore.

PORGES. Didn't you used to go to the courthouse all the time?[36]

HORPATZKY. No, I went out of my way to avoid the courts.

PORGES. But you were put on trial once, weren't you?

HORPATZKY. Me? Oh please. That was some other short dark-haired fellow. What was it that time, some kind of bigamy, wasn't it?

PORGES. Bigamy, that wasn't even worth talking about. That villain falsely claimed to a girl that he was a cook, and he was only a bank manager.[37]

HORPATZKY. That's downright wickedness. But I've noticed that Terezín always follows you. I run into reminders all the time. There I was in Lucerna[38] and who didn't take the stage but that star from Terezín, that Hanka Ledererová. You remember her, right?

---

34 In the folk song "On the Lord's Meadows," the singer finds a golden ducat and tries to decide how to spend it. In Terezín/Theresienstadt, owning such a valuable item would have been an offense punishable by imprisonment in the ghetto jail.

35 That is, an enormous fraud.

36 There was a civil court in Terezín/Theresienstadt under the auspices of the *Selbstverwaltung* that tried minor crimes such as libel, theft, and fraud among the prisoners. See Bondy, *"Elder of the Jews,"* pp. 306–9; Adler, *Theresienstadt*, pp. 453–92; and the play *The Insult—But Unintended* in this volume, pp. 361–9.

37 The elevated status of cooks in the ghetto is a recurrent theme in the cabaret. This particular joke is sometimes credited to Terezín/Theresienstadt prisoner and author Karel Poláček. See Ludmila Chládková, "Karel Poláček v Terezíně," *Terezínské Listy XXVI* (1996): 55–70, see 63.

38 The Lucerna building, located just off Wenceslas Square, includes a large hall that can seat up to 4,000 spectators, a cinema, coffeehouses, etc.

PORGES. Of course. She had it really good back then; she had that Aryan grandmother.[39] But now it causes her problems at every turn—because of that they don't even want to let her into Palestine.[40]

HORPATZKY. Those grandmothers, they were always causing trouble. You know, my ninety-three-year-old grandmother had to sign a formal agreement that she did not intend to have any more children.[41] But what am I saying? Why don't we go to Lucerna and see Hanka Ledererová; we don't have anything else to do. That Elly Bernstein-Poržé[42] will be performing there too.

PORGES. I don't know her.

HORPATZKY. Oh, come on, don't tell me that you don't remember her from Terezín.

PORGES. Actually no, I knew all kinds of people there, but not her.

---

39 Prisoners with non-Jewish relatives had certain advantages; for example, they were occasionally allowed to receive packages of food and other supplies from them. See František Beneš and Patricia Tošnerová (eds.), *Pošta v ghettu Terezín / Die Post im Ghetto Theresienstadt / Mail Service in the Ghetto Terezín* (Petr Liebl and Dagmar Lieblová trans.) (Prague: Profil, 1996).

40 I have left out of the translation the following three lines which contain a complex German–Czech pun:

> **HORPATZKY**. Of course they won't let her into Palestine if she's so *zasypovaná*. [*Zasypovaná* is the literal translation into Czech of the German word *versippt*. Jews in mixed marriages with a non-Jewish partner and their children were classified as *arisch versippt*, that is, with Aryan family ties, and were protected to some extent from transports to the ghetto and from the ghetto to further camps.]

> **PORGES**. Maybe you mean *zasypaná*. [Porges, confused, asks whether Horpatzky means to use a phonetically similar Czech word meaning "buried" or "overwhelmed."]

> **HORPATZKY**. No, I mean *zasypovaná, versipovaná*. [Horpatzky finally uses the more common Czech translation of *versippt*.]

41 Horpatzky literally says ". . . that she did not intend to round the number of her descendants upward," that is, to the nearest unit of 10. As a consequence of the Nazi plan to reduce the Jewish population, Jewish women were forced to sign agreements that they did not intend to give birth to more children.

42 The Czech transliteration of the French pronunciation of "Porges."

HORPATZKY. That would be a match for you.

PORGES. I'm not even curious. Come on; let's go.

HORPATZKY. We'll stop at the automat on the way for a *chlebíček*.[43] So let's go. Wait, where are you heading? Are you trying to get to Vodičkova street by way of Dejvice? Here, through the Stýbl passage; watch out for the tram so you don't get run over.[44]

6. BAR SCENE

A. ECCENTRIC DANCE ("Pink Crinoline")[45]
Performed by H. Ledererová

PORGES. So what should we have?

HORPATZKY. Waiter, Martel cognac, and twenty Egypt cigarettes but mild.[46]

BERNSTEINOVÁ. I will now sing you two songs by Dr. Felix Porges to lyrics by Pavel Stránský.

B. I. "ANDALUSIAN NIGHTS" (Tango)[47]

Nights in Andalusia,
Rich like the poetry of
Les poetes maudits,[48] ringing in my ears

---

43 A *chlebíček* is a typical Czech open-faced sandwich. Horpatzky is probably referring to a well-known establishment and great novelty in inter-war Prague: the automated snack bar on the ground floor of the Koruna building at the base of Wenceslas Square. On the insertion of a coin the automat dispensed a *chlebíček*.

44 Horpatzky tries to keep Porges from going the wrong way. One entrance to Lucerna is located on Vodičkova street, just off Wenceslas Square. Dejvice is a neighborhood in the western part of the city.

45 The dance was performed to the popular song "Pink Crinoline" ("Růžová krinolína") composed in 1942 by František Svojík.

46 Very expensive brands of cognac and cigarettes.

47 See original music for "Andalusian Nights" ("Andaluzské noci") on pp. 218–19 of this volume, IMAGES 7.10 and 7.11.

Breezes orange scented,
Placid pools so tempting
Fate has brought me here.

(*Refrain*) Hypnotic rhythm of castanets and mandolins
Not for millions, no, I never would exchange them
They mean much more to me than their weight in gold
Their melodies sound so deeply in my soul.
A senorita's arms are the softest bed you'll ever find
A life's dream realized, a lovely dream I had to leave behind
Now home again, when dark night overcomes me
I feel the hot sun above me
Enchanted by its power.

Nights in Andalusia,
Sweet as a melody that
Fills up my senses like a rare perfume
The lovely girl I'm missing
Her red lips were made for kissing
I long to be there too.

(*Refrain*)

B. II. "ABANDONED" (Slow foxtrot)[49]

Alone out here upon the wharf I moan
And tell the sea of all my woes
Moonlight reflected on the sea tonight
Oh I entrust to it my plight.

The stars, oh they glitter so far away
I sing to them of my pain.
Alone out here upon the wharf I moan
of my heartbreak and memories.

---

48 Stránský uses the phrase *prokletí básníci* (accursed poets), the Czech translation of the French *les poetes maudits* (Baudelaire, Rimbaud, Verlaine, etc.).

49 See original music for "Abandoned" ("Opuštěný") on pp. 220–21 of this volume, IMAGES 7.12 and 7.13.

IMAGE 7.6 **One of the ghetto *Verschleißstellen*: the "grocery store." The jars in the foreground are labeled *Senf* (mustard). By F. Bloch.**

Courtesy of Yad Vashem.

Oh Ocean, can't you see how I suffer
Ocean, sing to me of faithless lovers.

Alone and lonely through the night I roam
And hold your image in my soul.
It seems, that all that I can do is dream,
That's all fate has in store for me.

The breeze that fans my feverish brow
Will carry you my song somehow.
Ah, ah, ah.

PORGES. My dear colleague, here, take a look at the program—look what's up next.

HORPATZKY. Just a moment. Next: the duo Bernsteinová and Krauskopfová—aha, she's the one from that Terezín Lippert.[50]

PORGES. That's right, the one with the mustard and pickles.[51] What are they going to sing?

HORPATZKY. "Express Foxtrot," "Tavern in Nikolayev," no, that's gone, "Tavern in Odessa," well, that'll be quite a mess,[52] and "Merry Multiplication."

---

50 Lippert was a famous Prague delicatessen. Porges and Horpatzky may be referring to the shops that opened in the ghetto in September 1942 (see *Verschleißstellen* [glossary]). One was a "grocery store" that sold an extremely limited selection of goods. See Hyndráková et al., *Acta Theresiania*, p. 226.

51 Survivors recall a mustard-like spread as one of the few food items that could be purchased in the ghetto.

52 Hopatzky is probably referring to events on the Eastern Front. The strategically important port of Nikolayev in southern Ukraine was destroyed in battles between the Soviet and German armies. Many parts of Odessa were damaged during the Red Army's siege and recapture of the city.

C. DUO[53]

Performed by E. Bernsteinová, H. Krauskopfová

    I. "Express Foxtrot" (Malina)

    II. "Tavern in Odessa" (Dobeš-Brom)

    III. "Merry Multiplication" (Traxler-Rychlík)

HORPATZKY. The band wants a drink—waiter, something for the musicians. Hey, Mr. Bandleader, play us a song.

PORGES. That's going to cost you something.

HORPATZKY. That doesn't matter.

D. ACCORDION SOLO

Performed by K. Meier

    I. "Second Hungarian Rhapsody" by Liszt in a jazz arrangement

Horpatzky gives Meier a banknote.

    II. Variations on the song

7. THIRD DIALOGUE

PORGES. I tell you, that was almost as nice as the coffeehouse in Terezín.

HORPATZKY. Only the coffee wasn't as strong.

PORGES. Certainly you must have visited that great establishment as well.

HORPATZKY. Of course. I was an avid visitor of all the establishments of the free time.

PORGES. Of what?

HORPATZKY. Of the free time—the *Freizeit*.[54]

PORGES. Aha, why didn't you say it in Czech right away?[55]

---

53 The Czech-language titles of the songs are "Expres-fox," "Krčma v Oděse," and "Veselá násobilka."

54 Horpatzky uses the Czech words meaning "free time," the literal translation of *Freizeit*, the prisoners' nickname for the *Freizeitgestaltung*.

55 Porges satirizes the prisoners' propensity to incorporate German words into the Czech language.

IMAGE 7.7 **The coffeehouse in the ghetto. By L. Haas.**
Courtesy of the Terezín Memorial.

IMAGE 7.8 **A poster for the opera** *The Bartered Bride* (*Prodaná nevěsta*) **featuring F. Weissenstein and K. Berman, with an image of Kecal, the marriage broker.** *Courtesy of the Terezín Memorial.*

HORPATZKY. Everyone there was so nice, so friendly . . . and how perfectly everything worked out with those tickets.[56]

PORGES. What do you mean? Things worked out fine with the tickets; I couldn't complain.

HORPATZKY. You worked for the *Freizeit*, didn't you?

PORGES. No, but sometimes I had a bit of bread to spare; so . . . you know.[57]

HORPATZKY. Of course. Those doormen at the theater were so helpful.

PORGES. Yes, but once they threw you out, I remember that.

HORPATZKY. Do you have to talk about that here, in front of all these people? You're a scandalmonger. It was when they played Smetana's "The Moldau"—I tried to use my bath ticket to get in.[58] And now you have to go and tell everyone.[59]

PORGES. Well they know worse things about you than that. You know, I just remembered another remarkable event. Once I went to the coffeehouse and they actually performed the program they were supposed to; strange, isn't it?[60]

HORPATZKY. That really is an odd coincidence. Say, did you know that I was supposed to join the *Freizeit*?

PORGES. As a ticket-taker, right?

HORPATZKY. Of course not, I beg your pardon, such an important function.[61] As a—quick, what do you call that, that thing you use to climb up?

---

56 A satirical comment on favoritism in the distribution of tickets to cultural events. See Hans Hofer's "The Theater Ticket" in this volume.

57 That is, as a bribe to obtain a ticket.

58 Due to the shortage of water, prisoners had to bathe according to a ticket system. Horpatzky apparently tried to use his bath ticket for admission to a performance of composer Bedřich Smetana's "Vltava" ("The Moldau"), a symphonic poem about the river that runs through the center of Prague.

59 In the original script this passage ended with the line "Now all we have to do is build you a *pavlač*." A *pavlač* was a type of interior balcony in Central European buildings where women met to gossip.

60 The musical program in the coffeehouse apparently rarely matched the program that had been posted.

61 Ticket-takers' access to the cultural activities of the ghetto meant that theirs was a high-status position.

PORGES. A stepstool.

HORPATZKY. Ladder, in German.

PORGES. *Leiter*.[62]

HORPATZKY. Yes, leader. There were already fifteen of them; I was supposed to be the sixteenth. One of them noticed how well I know how to give orders, to organize things, and he immediately said that I should be the sixteenth leader. So I went there, they looked at my birth certificate, *na rodný list* . . .

PORGES. Why did they need the *Národní listy* for that?[63]

HORPATZKY. What do you mean *Národní listy*? They looked at my birth certificate, my, *meine*, birth, *Geburts*, certificate, *Liste*,[64] and said, "Aha, nothing can come of this, you're already over eighteen, so you can't be a leader."[65] But let's leave that alone, those were still beautiful and touching moments when, for the first time in a long time, we heard *The Bartered Bride* again.[66]

PORGES. You're right, that was a kind of spiritual escape attempt,[67] I would call it. I can still hear Jeník's beautiful aria. It's one of my favorites; do you know it?

HORPATZKY. Of course I know it; I sing it too.

---

62 The joke is based on the two meanings of *Leiter* in German: ladder and leader.

63 This pun is based on the acoustic similarity between the Czech phrase *na rodný list* (at my birth certificate) and the title of a right-wing Czech newspaper, *Národní listy* (*National Pages*), which published anti-Semitic articles.

64 Horpatzky clarifies by translating every word from Czech into German, perhaps satirizing the fact that many of the Prague Jews spoke only German or were bilingual.

65 Some of the most important administrative positions in the ghetto were occupied by very young men. See the example of 23-year-old Egon Redlich in Bondy, *"Elder of the Jews,"* p. 255.

66 The Terezín/Theresienstadt performances of Bedřich Smetana's opera *The Bartered Bride* (*Prodaná nevěsta*), considered by many to be the Czech national opera, are recalled with exceptional emotional intensity by many of the Czech-Jewish survivors. Horpatzky refers to the opera by its nickname, *Prodanka*. Directed by prisoner Rafael Schächter, the first performance took place at the end of November 1942 and it was performed about 35 times. See Karas, *Music in Terezín*, p. 24.

67 Porges uses the German word *Fluchtversuch* (escape attempt), a term well known to the prisoners due to the Nazis' intensive efforts to prevent such attempts.

PORGES. What?

HORPATZKY. Yes, but only at home, in the shower.

PORGES. I remember it well . . . back then it was sung by, I think, Franta Weissenstein, right?

HORPATZKY. Of course, of course, Franta Weissenstein.

8. TWO OPERA ARIAS[68]

Performed by F. Weissenstein

> A. Jeník's aria from *The Bartered Bride* ("How Could He Believe")
> B. Aria from *Dalibor* ("When My Zdeněk")

9. FOURTH DIALOGUE

PORGES. You know, everything would be great, everything would be just fine, if only we didn't have those thirty-two political parties again.[69] A person got so used to that consensus in Terezín, to that unanimity. Nobody knew what favoritism was there, no one knew what corruption was. When by chance there was a shortage of something, then they replaced it right away with something else, to make it up to you. They ran out of potatoes, so you didn't have to salute anymore.[70] Something for something.[71]

---

68 Both operas are by Bedřich Smetana. The Czech titles of the arias are "Jak možno věřit" and "Když Zdeněk můj."

69 A reference to the pre-war multiplicity of political parties.

70 The order that prisoners must salute all Nazi officers was abolished on March 6, 1944, as part of the *Stadtverschönerung* (see glossary) in preparation for the visit of the International Red Cross Commission. See Hyndráková et al., *Acta Theresiania*, p. 415.

71 I have left out of the translation the following three lines:

> HORPATZKY. That was equivalent.
>
> PORGES. Potatoes, not equivalent.
>
> HORPATZKY. I mean equivalent; you're weak with those foreign words.

The pun depends on Porges not knowing the word "equivalent" (in Czech, *ekvivalent*) which, being a Latin-based word, is foreign to Czech speakers.

HORPATZKY. Then there were those darker rolls; for that we got a city band with a pavilion.[72] You know, there was *Essensverschlechterung, Stadtverschönerung*,[73] things always balanced each other out. There were all kinds of different proposals. Do you remember later they wanted to cut the bread ration in half and in exchange install telephones in all the rooms? But that didn't work out.

PORGES. I remember; that was sometime in the winter of 1950. You know, those are real problems; they're not so easy to solve.

HORPATZKY. Please, don't worry your head about that. I have enough other worries.

PORGES. Like what?

HORPATZKY. I don't know where to go tonight.

PORGES. You have terrible worries.

HORPATZKY. I don't like going to Zámečník's;[74] they have bad cognac. At the Balkan-Grill that *čevapčiči*[75] just doesn't taste good to me anymore.

PORGES. Oh, you've just had it so much that you're tired of it.

HORPATZKY. I would go to Juliš's;[76] there they still have the same headwaiter as before the war.

PORGES. You still owe him money, don't you?

HORPATZKY. To the cinema? *The Great Dictator*,[77] I've already seen that three times, they're playing *All's Well that Ends Well* for

---

72 The establishment of a city band to perform on the town square was another project of the *Stadtverschönerung*. See Hans Hofer's "The Main Square" in this volume.

73 Horpatzky invents the German word *Essensverschlechterung* (literally, "food worsening") after the example of *Stadtverschönerung*.

74 U Zámečníka was a nightclub on Wenceslas Square.

75 A typical Balkan dish made of ground meat and vegetables.

76 U Juliše, a famous pre-war establishment. On the lower level was a Viennese-style pastry shop; on the upper level was a dance hall.

77 Charlie Chaplin's film premiered in October 1940 and was banned in Germany and all countries occupied by the Nazis.

the seventeenth week.[78] At the Alhambra[79] there are only brunettes. I'm not so keen on them; I like blondes, you know?

PORGES. Yes, I remember. But you know what, if you like blondes, I can help you. I'll take you somewhere where there are two very nice buxom blondes.

HORPATZKY. And what do they do?

PORGES. They dance our folk dances.

HORPATZKY. Our folk dances? You're going to laugh, *Sie werden lachen*.[80]

PORGES. Why, *warum?*

HORPATZKY. I know them from Terezín too, from the Strauss-Ensemble.

PORGES. A person can't surprise you with anything; it's terrible.

10. CZECH AND SLOVAK DANCES

Performed by E. Bernsteinová, H. Ledererová

11. FIFTH DIALOGUE

PORGES. So how did you like the girls?

HORPATZKY. Very pretty, it's true, but please, don't drag me anywhere else, you're all just fun and games, ready for a good time but no serious work.

PORGES. You really look ready for some serious work.

HORPATZKY. Well, appearances can sometimes be deceiving. A person simply has to educate himself a little too, right?

---

78 This reference to the Shakespeare play is apparently a joke based purely on the literal meaning of the title.

79 Alhambra was a well-known night club with entertainment on Wenceslas Square.

80 Horpatzky and Porges begin to translate their lines into German, perhaps because the Strauss-Ensemble was a German-speaking cabaret group. Some of the cast of *Laugh with Us* also performed with them. See *From the Strauss Cabarets* in this volume.

PORGES. Right, of course, so let's go somewhere and inebriate our-selves.[81] What do you like to drink, *slivovice*?[82]

HORPATZKY. Not inebriate, educate. You know, I'd like to go, oh, to a museum or to the library or somewhere like that.

PORGES. What, are you feeling all right? What's the matter with you? Wait, I've just thought of something that'll do. Wouldn't you like to listen to the radio for a while? I've got a beautiful new set, a Telejiskra.

HORPATZKY. What?

PORGES. Well, Telefunken, I'm translating it.[83]

HORPATZKY. What a chauvinist.[84]

PORGES. A very nice television set.

HORPATZKY. Aha, the kind of set you can't listen to and can't watch either.[85]

PORGES. Well come on, I live right here around the corner . . . So we're already here. What should we watch?

HORPATZKY. Say, could you get Tel Aviv for me? I would run home to get my son. You know he's never seen so many Jews together in one place and he can't even imagine it.

PORGES. It's not working; the signal's scrambled somehow.

HORPATZKY. So try something else. That Moravian station, that Přerov or whatever it was called, the one people used to listen to so much . . . but maybe that's not so interesting anymore.[86]

---

81 The original pun is on *vzdělávat* (to educate oneself) and *zdělat* (tie one on).

82 *Slivovice* (plum brandy) is a popular spirit in many countries of Central and Eastern Europe.

83 Telefunken was the first company in Germany to manufacture television sets. Porges translates the brand name literally into Czech (*jiskra* and *Funken* both mean "spark").

84 Horpatzky here refers to "language chauvinism," a form of Czech nationalism so exaggerated that even foreign brand names were translated into Czech.

85 Probably a reference to the fact that listening to the radio was severely restricted during the war.

86 The prisoners understood Přerov as a veiled reference to the neighboring town of Kroměříž, which is pronounced similarly to the phrase *kromě říše* (outside the Reich). Thus this joke is a reference to the illegal practice of listening to radio stations like the BBC, broadcasting from outside Nazi-occupied Europe. Hana Reinerová, interview with Lisa Peschel, February 20, 2006.

PORGES. No, that's not current anymore, but what if we could get Prague?

WEISSKOPF (*backstage*). Hello, hello Prague, we continue our variety show with songs performed by a member of the opera of the National Theater, Karel Bermann.[87]

HORPATZKY. Well let's watch, Karel Bermann, Kecal.[88]

PORGES. And how.[89]

WEISSKOPF (*backstage*). Karel Bermann with "In Quiet Nights" by Rudolf Friml and "Spring Song" by Vilem Blodek.

PORGES. Good, and now let's get him on camera, so we can see him too. There, it's working. Look, as if he were right here with us.

12. TWO SONGS[90]

Performed by K. Bermann

    A. "In Quiet Nights" (by R. Friml)
    B. "Spring Song" (by V. Blodek)

13. SIXTH DIALOGUE

Weisskopf brings a sign: "Park." Two chairs, between them a sign: "Bench." Horpatzky enters, sits on one chair, behind him a sign: "Retiree." Porges enters, sits on the second chair, behind him a sign: "Gentleman." They greet each other. Horpatzky begins to play with his star; he sighs.

PORGES. Please excuse me for disturbing you, but I would really like to know what kind of an insignia you have there or what it might mean.

HORPATZKY. You don't know?

---

87 Karel Bermann (after the war, Berman) actually became a member of the opera of the National Theater in Prague in 1953.

88 Berman played the role of Kecal the marriage broker in some of the Terezín/Theresienstadt performances of *The Bartered Bride*.

89 Porges refers to the literal meaning of the name Kecal: "he talked nonsense."

90 The original Czech titles are "Za tichých nocí" and "Jarní píseň."

PORGES. I really can't recall ever having seen it before.

HORPATZKY. Then you are a fortunate man; I envy you. This was once a great fashion. People wore it a lot, on jackets, on overcoats, on trousers, on underwear and I don't know where all else.

PORGES. And what if it didn't look good on some people? For example, if that ugly color didn't go with their complexion?

HORPATZKY. That didn't matter. It was simply decreed, I think according to some grandmothers,[91] and it had to be worn. And that brought the whole club together for you. We even left with it.

PORGES. On tour?

HORPATZKY. Of course not.

PORGES. On an excursion?

HORPATZKY. No. That was at the time of the housing and food crisis, there wasn't much to eat and it was expensive, so we signed up and they transported us away for free.

PORGES. But where?

HORPATZKY. Now what was that town called, named after some German poet, Schillero? No, something else. Who were the other German poets?

PORGES. Heine, Heino? Uhlando?

HORPATZKY. No, it started with G.

PORGES. Grillparzero?

HORPATZKY. No, not him either. What is this called in German? (*Points to his fist.*)

PORGES. *Hand*.

HORPATZKY. No, this part.

PORGES. Aha, the part at the top. *Faust*.

HORPATZKY. Yes, yes, and who wrote *Faust*?

PORGES. Well, Goethe.

HORPATZKY. Yes, correct, it was called ghetto.

---

91 An allusion to the Nuremberg laws that decreed who was classified as a Jew by race.

PORGES. Ghetto, ghetto? Wait, I read about that once in my school reader. But that was in the Middle Ages.

HORPATZKY. Absolutely, and I lived through them as well.

PORGES. Certainly. And now you're going to tell me that you are about five hundred and ninety-eight years old.

HORPATZKY. Oh, no, these were modern Middle Ages with trains, tractors, telephones.

PORGES. Aha, that's something else altogether. That really interests me; you must tell me something about it. You know, I have such strange ideas about it. The way I imagine it, there were only laws, orders, rules, prohibitions, commands, directives, instructions, regulations, etc.

HORPATZKY. All those things were there. We even had our own self-government. But otherwise it was actually an ideal city. You know, no one there had to think.

PORGES. That would be something for me.

HORPATZKY. Now that I take a closer look at you, that's for certain.

PORGES. Don't get personal right away.

HORPATZKY. There other gentlemen thought for you. You didn't have to worry about anything. Everything was prescribed: food, housing. But otherwise, people could do whatever they wanted. There a rabbi was a dramaturge,[92] another rabbi was the minister of health, a doctor worked as a baker, only lawyers remained at their craft.

PORGES. At the court?

HORPATZKY. No, they had a *Schleussmannschaft*, as they called it.[93] Some dentists also stayed in their own profession, touching a

---

92 The head of the *Freizeitgestaltung* was Rabbi Erich Weiner. See his own description of the ghetto's cultural activities in Weiner, "*Freizeitgestaltung* in Theresienstadt."

93 Jokes about greedy lawyers were popular during this period. The so-called *Schleussmannschaft* was the team of prisoners assigned to work in the *Schleuse* where incoming and outgoing deportees and their luggage were processed and items were often stolen.

nerve there too. Why, we even had a bandleader from the radio[94] who worked there as a cook.[95]

PORGES. And how did that work out? Did he conduct in the kitchen?

HORPATZKY. Well, you know. While dishing out food he conducted, like so, and everything flew . . .

PORGES. That must have been truly beautiful.

HORPATZKY. So it shouldn't come as a surprise to you that when news got out about how beautiful life was there, people started to arrive from all over Europe, like for an international Sokol rally.

PORGES. Then what language did they speak? How did they understand each other?

HORPATZKY. Well, it was very difficult to understand each other there. Of course, people from Prague, they had it good, they just kept speaking German,[96] but otherwise as time went on we cultivated a peculiar . . .

PORGES. Cultivated epiculiar? Is that some kind of grain?

HORPATZKY. No, we cultivated a peculiar . . .

PORGES. Is that like buckwheat? or millet? or . . .

HORPATZKY. No, we cultivated a peculiar, homegrown, original, authentic language.[97]

PORGES. I can't even begin to imagine that. Could you describe it for me?[98]

---

94 In the original script, Radiojournal, the inter-war Czechoslovak radio network.

95 In the 1930s, Karel Ančerl, who worked as a cook in the ghetto, had conducted the orchestra of Voskovec and Werich's Liberated Theater, and later the orchestra of the Radiojournal. He continued to conduct in the ghetto. After the war he became head conductor of the Czech Philharmonic.

96 Many of the Prague Jews spoke only German or were bilingual.

97 In the original script the pun depends on the acoustic similarity between the Czech word Horpatzky utters, *svébytnou* (peculiar), and the phrase Porges hears, *svoji bytnou* (our landlady).

98 In the following paragraph the Retiree demonstrates the Czech Jews' ghetto argot. Some words were adopted unmodified from the German; others were modified, sometimes in comic ways, based on the rules of Czech grammar, spelling, and word construction. Unless otherwise indicated, definitions have

HORPATZKY. Well, for example, a friend came to me one morning and said *šahoj*, man, I was left out of the *Hundertschaft*, I lost my *eskartu*, I already polished off my *dekádu* and I haven't gotten any *cubusy*. I'm completely *zíchouš*.[99] If they don't request[100] to transfer me from *Bahnbau* to *Ges.-Wes.*, *Küwa*, or MTK, [101] I'll go crazy.[102] And then the *Raumwirtschaft* didn't give me an *Übersiedlungsverfügung* for *Entwesung*. Well, if I could at least get up onto the ramparts for *Körperertüchtigung*, I'd have *reko* and *cuzac*.[103] I wanted them to let me out[104] of the *Einsatz*, but the *Zimmerältester* said that the *grupouš* would have to go to the *gebojdovi*, but the *Blockältester* said that

---

been taken from the glossary in Adler, *Theresienstadt*, pp. XXIX–LIX, with additional contributions by survivor Doris Grozdanovičová.

99 Šahoj (pronounced "SHAH-hoy"): a combination of "shalom" and the Czech greeting *ahoj*. The expression *šahojist* indicated a Czech-assimilated Jew who opportunistically pretended to be a Zionist. See Bondy, *"Elder of the Jews,"* p. 277. **Hundertschaft**: a group of 100 workers. See Hyndráková et al., *Acta Theresiania*, p. 63. **Eskartu**: meal ticket, from German *Esskarte*. **Dekádu**: an extra ration of food distributed to prisoners who performed certain types of labor during a *Dekade* (a 10-day labor period). **Cubusy**: extra rations of food for workers performing heavy labor, from German *Zubuße*. **Zíchouš**: an ailing person, from German *Siecher*.

100 In the original script the authors use *neanfordrovat*, a "Czechified" version of the German verb *anfordern* (to request).

101 Ges.-Wes.: Department of Health, an abbreviation for the German *Gesundheitswesen* (see *Selbstverwaltung* [glossary]). **Küwa**: the guard unit responsible for preventing theft in the kitchens, from German *Küchenwache* (kitchen guard). **MTK**: the meaning of this abbreviation is not clear.

102 In the original script the authors use the verb *zcvokatit*, derived from the Czech word *cvok*, an insane person.

103 Raumwirtschaft: Department of Space Management. **Übersiedlungsverfügung**: a relocation order. **Entwesung**: disinfestation (see glossary). Here Horpatzky refers to the fact that prisoners were temporarily moved out of their quarters from time to time so that buildings in the ghetto could be disinfested in an attempt to control the spread of fleas, lice, and bedbugs. **Körperertüchtigung**: physical strengthening. In the period before the visit of the commission of the International Committee of the Red Cross, exercises were held on top of the ramparts surrounding the ghetto to improve the prisoners' health. **Reko**: extra rations for those recovering from illness, from German *Rekonvaleszenten-zubuße*. **Cuzac**: extra rations, from German *Zusatzskost*.

104 In the original script the authors use the verb *freištelovat*, a "Czechified" version of the German verb *freistellen* (to release).

without the *Bezirksältester*'s permission he wouldn't do it, so it went to the *Ältestenrat*, to the Leitung, and the *Judenältester* turned it down. The same old *dré*,[105] same old *šmé*, nothing gained,[106] no *šlojs*, at best I'll get the bunker.[107]

PORGES. For God's sake, what sort of incomprehensible words are you babbling? Could you translate that for me into some kind of standard English?

HORPATZKY. Well, it would mean something like: You know, I'd really like to get a decent meal around here sometime.[108]

PORGES. That's a complicated language, for sure.

HORPATZKY. Well, at the time, it meant something quite important to that person; for him it meant that, that day, he would have to cut loose.

PORGES. What did he have to cut? [109]

HORPATZKY. I don't mean he had to cut some *thing*, I mean he had to cut loose his own moral scruples . . .

PORGES. Cut loose, is that like to cut bait?

HORPATZKY. No, no, he had to cut himself loose of his . . .

---

105 *Einsatz*: short for *Arbeitseinsatz* (labor assignment). *Zimmerältester*: head of a room in the prisoners' quarters. *Grupouš*: head of a section of the prisoners' quarters (part of a barracks or several civilian houses), from German *Gruppenältester*. *Gebojdovi*: the head of a barracks building, from German *Gebäudeältester*. *Blockältester*: head of a group of civilian houses (see *-ältester* [glossary]). *Bezirksältester*: head of one of the four *Bezirke* or administrative sectors of Terezín/Theresienstadt. *Leitung*: the leadership of the *Selbstverwaltung*. *Dré*: trick, from the German *drehen*, to turn or to twist.

106 In the original script the authors use the word *vejvar*, a Czech slang expression for profit or proceeds.

107 In the Czech original, *nejvýš z toho kouká bunkr*. *Bunkr* (bunker) was slang for the ghetto jail; thus the phrase approximately means "the most I can hope for from this is a few days in jail."

108 The original Czech is a bit more earthy: Horpatzky employs a verb used for animals, *nažrat se* (to feed).

109 In the original, the first pun is based on the acoustic similarity between the phrases *mít odvaz* (to cut loose, to release one's inhibitions) and *mít od Vás* (to get [something] from you).

PORGES. Aha. Well why didn't you say that right away. Of course those people there would have had to cut loose if they were tied up.[110]

HORPATZKY. For God's sake, who was tied up?

PORGES. Well, you just said that person had to cut himself loose, i.e. he must have been tied up, if he had to cut himself loose.

HORPATZKY. He was neither *i* nor *e* nor tied up. The guy was hungry, he wasn't a manager of provisions,[111] he didn't have an uncle on the Council of Elders, he wasn't an elder of any kind,[112] he went to one office then another, they didn't give him anything, so he had to cut loose his own inhibitions, his own moral scruples, and just take something, and that was his cutting loose. Do you understand now?

PORGES. Yes. You know, it's so strange, a person knows the words but everything has a different meaning.

HORPATZKY. Yes, even Czech words meant something quite different there. For example, two important men met and the first said, "Good day, my dear colleague, it looks to me as though it will rain." Immediately the second started to analyze what he meant by that, that today it will rain, what could lie concealed behind those words, what the hidden message might be. He was beside himself—and he only calmed down when it actually started to rain that day.

PORGES. Those were really very intelligent people.

HORPATZKY. Certainly. They also spoke a lot of Latin; people there were quite extraordinary. Today, or before the war, people said, "Our grandmother's short of breath, she has the trots and we're afraid that she's going to kick the bucket on us." Not

---

110 The second pun is based on the similarity between the phrase *mít odvaz* and the verb *odvázet se* (to free or untie oneself).

111 Horpatzky makes a subtle dig at his fellow actor: Felix Porges was a manager of provisions in the ghetto.

112 The title "elder" was given to prisoners in leadership positions in the ghetto. See *-ältester* (glossary).

there. There they said, "Grandma has pneumonia, it is feared that she will contract enteritis, we hope it will not be complicated by icterus, for she has latent encephalitis, we must give her an intravenous injection, so that she does not expire."

PORGES. Excuse me, something else just occurred to me. Could you tell me how people lived, when there were so many people there together?

HORPATZKY. For that we had our own ministry of space management that tried to arrange the space in the most economical way—mainly others' space, less so with their own. That ministry was very flexible. In one day they fixed a three-family home to hold sixty-eight families, and they didn't even move them into the gutters and chimneys. Anyway, some of them lived on Q, the others lived on L.[113]

PORGES. And no one lived on the beds?

HORPATZKY. I'm telling you, some lived on Q, the others lived on L, L went to visit Q, Q went to visit L.

PORGES. Aha, those were like two addresses, Q and L. The mailman had it easy if there were only two addresses.

HORPATZKY. There everything was numbered. So, for example, the mailman got a letter with the address: Mr. Josef Novák—there were a lot of them there—AAAQ . . .[114]

PORGES. You stutter. I didn't notice that before.

HORPATZKY. That's an address.

PORGES. That's stuttering.

HORPATZKY. Mr. Josef Novák, AAAQ, slash 985, Block E IIIa, Q407, F II 325, slash 013, and immediately he knew that it's the second building around the corner.

---

113 See L, Q (glossary).

114 Novák is a very common name among Czechs but not among Czech Jews. There were only four prisoners named Novák in the ghetto during its entire history.

PORGES. Well, but what if that equation and that slash and q to the second power or whatever you said didn't work out and he didn't find that person?

HORPATZKY. What equation? But even in that case there was another possibility. We had an unusually large building, the ministry; we called it the castle. It was full of offices and in each of those offices there were several card files, of course there had to be a central card file for those several card files, so as to know where each card file was.[115] So when you were looking for someone, you went to that central card file, there they told you in which card file you would possibly find the card, you went to the first office, to the second, to the third, to the fourth, until you found that card file, you looked and . . . no card. So you went down and called O.D.[116]

PORGES. OD? Who OD'd? The postman?

HORPATZKY. What are you talking about?

PORGES. You said OD; who overdosed?

HORPATZKY. Not that kind of O.D. For us, O.D., that was kind of an all-purpose go-to, it was our security service. When a slap was heard somewhere, the O.D. was called, when people had to stand in line, the O.D. was called, when there was a fight somewhere, O.D.

PORGES. Aha, that was some kind of Salvation Army.[117]

HORPATZKY. The O.D. said, "I don't know," and sent you to the *Orientierungsdienst*[118] and there they told you, that Josef Novák, that name you must certainly still remember, left by transport.

PORGES. You mean maybe by train or by car.

HORPATZKY. No, transport.

---

115 See *Zentralevidenz* (glossary).

116 See O.D. (glossary). In the original script, the pun is based on the similar pronunciation of the initials O.D. and the Czech preposition *od* (from).

117 The Salvation Army expanded its activities to Czechoslovakia in 1919.

118 See *Hilfsdienst* (glossary).

PORGES. What is that for a means of transportation?

HORPATZKY. Transport, that was a magic word. Children there weren't afraid of the bogey-man or witches,[119] there they simply said, "a transport is going," and you should have seen it, how that shook each of them, how all were immediately well-behaved and obedient; it's not surprising, since only selected people were allowed to leave on such a transport.

PORGES. And how were they selected? There must certainly have been great interest.

HORPATZKY. For that there were special commissions that, including relatives, probably had about 1,500 members.[120] They selected certain groups, while other groups were protected. It was simple enough. For example, first the AK and the G.W. were protected, then the rules changed to the complete opposite. For example my brother stayed there because he was AK, while my cousin had to go because he was AK. My step-brother didn't go because he was G.W., while my brother-in-law, who joined the G.W. so he wouldn't have to go, had to go. It was different though, when AK went to K.[121] They did that to get S-bread.[122]

PORGES. S-bread. Is that what you baked with that buckwheat, or millet, or whatever you were cultivating?

HORPATZKY. No, there there was S-bread, also L-bread, N-bread, K-bread.[123]

---

119 In the original, Horpatzky names traditional Czech fairy-tale characters: *bubáky, polednice,* and *klekánice.*

120 Workers in the transport division (*Transportabteilung*) and certain groups of prisoners in the ghetto were protected from outgoing transports until the fall of 1944 and could extend that protection to family members.

121 K, for German *Kistenbau,* the building of crates, was considered heavy manual labor and earned increased rations. See Bondy, "*Elder of the Jews,*" p. 385.

122 In the original, Horpatzky means the initial S, but Porges understands the Czech preposition *s* (with).

123 These letters indicate different categories of bread rations: S for "*Schwerarbeiter,*" those workers performing manual labor, N for "normal," L for "*leicht*" (light), and K for "*krank*" (ill). See *Brotkategorie* (bread categories) in Adler, *Theresienstadt,* p. XXXV.

PORGES. I've never eaten such bread before.

HORPATZKY. So an AK, in order to get S, went to K. Is that clear?

PORGES. Well, not very. I am completely flabbergasted. But how was it for you?

HORPATZKY. I had it good.

PORGES. Were you that K or whatever it was called?

HORPATZKY. No, but sometimes one of the higher-ups came to our place for dinner.

PORGES. Aha, so, a little corruption here and there.

HORPATZKY. Please. Corruption? There wasn't any money there, so you couldn't bribe anyone, even if you wanted to.[124]

PORGES. Without money that wouldn't work, I understand.

HORPATZKY. You know, all kinds of things didn't exist there. There were no tobacco shops but people still smoked; there were no directors but theater played on and on.

PORGES. And what about actors; were there any there?

HORPATZKY. Well, there were plenty of them. There everyone knew how to play comedy.

PORGES. Say, I've noticed that you're quite willing to talk about this. Could you also tell me if there were any schools there?[125]

HORPATZKY. Schools there developed very slowly. Jules Verne would have loved it; there his two years' holiday finally became a reality.[126] But the pupils there were very gifted. I knew the son of one head cook who finished the entire elementary school in

---

124 As Porges, Horpatzky and their audiences in the ghetto knew, an economy based on Terezín/Theresienstadt's own currency, *Ghettokronen*, had been introduced in May 1943. See Adler, *Theresienstadt*, pp. 124–5.

125 Structured education for the children of the ghetto was forbidden, but the caretakers in the children's and youth homes assembled programs of songs, games, lectures and cultural activities that to a certain extent made up for the lack of formal schooling.

126 A reference to a popular adventure novel by Jules Verne that has been published in English under various titles, including *A Long Vacation, Adrift in the Pacific*, etc.

fourteen days and with honors. Those children of the cooks were all very gifted. On the other hand children had it rough. You know, before the war or today, when a child brings home an F in math he can say "This grade is not fair; the teacher picks on me because he's an anti-Semite." There that didn't work. There the only thing to do was to come home and say "Dad, what a mess, an F, do we have some bread? Please, smooth things over; go iron it out."[127]

PORGES. And was education organized somehow? Was there some kind of Central School Foundation?[128]

HORPATZKY. Of course. Everything was done there according to the slogan "youth for worry."[129]

PORGES. There must be some mistake. You probably mean "youth for joy."

HORPATZKY. No, no. Youth for worry. *Jugend für Sorge*.

PORGES. You're a funny guy. But listen, I remember those were such unsettled times; did you get any news there about events?

HORPATZKY. Well, of course. On one hand we had our own illustrated news agency, *Announcements*,[130] but mainly we made up the news ourselves. The most popular news at that time was about Turkey; it entered the war every week. Until the Turks found out and said to themselves, "What? You're not going to tell us what to do," and they didn't enter the war at all. Invasions, we had those five times a week, like dumplings.

---

127 That is, to bribe the teacher with bread.

128 The Central School Foundation (Ústřední matice školská) played an important role in the development of Czech national identity. It was established in Prague in 1880 as the Czech counterpoint of the German School Association (Deutscher Schulverein) which supported German-language schools in Bohemia and Moravia.

129 A mistranslation of *Jugendfürsorge* (see glossary).

130 On April 15, 1944, in anticipation of the visit from the International Red Cross Commission, the title of the bulletin used to communicate with the prisoners was changed from *Daily Orders* (*Tagesbefehl*) to *Announcements from the Jewish Self-Government* (*Mitteilungen der Jüdischen Selbstverwaltung*). See Hyndráková et al., *Acta Theresiania*, pp. 40–2.

And the speed with which the news spread. Early in the morning someone in the Sudeten[131] mentioned something, and at 10 a.m. when I got to Dresden, they already knew about it.

PORGES. Wait, you didn't tell me—that town was in the Sudetenland?

HORPATZKY. Why would it be in the Sudetenland?

PORGES. Well, you just said that you went from Sudeten to Dresden, so it would have had to be in the Sudetenland.

HORPATZKY. But you don't understand me, Sudeten, those were the Sudeten barracks. So when I went from Sudeten to Dresden to check out the girls . . .

PORGES. But weren't there any girls there, that you had to walk all the way to Dresden?

HORPATZKY. Sometimes I even walked to Hamburg to check out the girls.

PORGES. Hmm, aren't you exaggerating just a bit? You walked that far?

HORPATZKY. That's nothing. I knew one person, he walked from Hannover to Magdeburg every day to iron things out.[132]

PORGES. Well, certainly, someone would walk 500 km to do his ironing.[133] Who are you going to tell that one to?

HORPATZKY. What do you mean, 500 km?

PORGES. Well, from Hannover to Magdeburg. It sounds suspicious to me.

HORPATZKY. But you don't understand me, Hannover is the Hannover barracks, Magdeburg is the Magdeburg barracks. You know, I got so used to those names. Until this day when

---

131 The Sudeten regions were the border areas of Czechoslovakia, mostly populated by ethnic Germans.

132 The most important administrative offices in the ghetto were located in the Magdeburg barracks.

133 Horpatzky means "iron out" in the figurative sense of trying to solve a problem or disagreement; Porges takes the expression literally.

I travel by train and the conductor shouts "Podmokly," I stick my head out the window and look for the armory.[134] I'm back at my old office job now and when my boss says, "in the afternoon we're going to register," I'm completely thrown off track and in the afternoon I certainly won't be back in the office.[135] But you wouldn't understand that.

PORGES. Say, since it's just between us, I would like to ask one discreet question, in confidence, of course: were the people there honest?

HORPATZKY. You wouldn't have had to lead up to the question like that. Things were very honest there. There were so many institutions that ensured honesty. Each person was supervised by twenty-six to thirty-one administrative departments which saw to it that each received his own. And they also received their own. Immediately upon arrival, they took care of your luggage.

PORGES. Some kind of travel agency?

HORPATZKY. No, the *Transportleitung*.[136] It was responsible for luggage and even actually got the luggage.[137] There they made sure that people did not fall into temptation. That's why they came up with the idea of coloring the food so that it would be unappealing. But they didn't color boiled barley; that was already repulsive enough all by itself.

PORGES. Well that's a great idea; some clever fox must have thought that up.

---

134 Podmokly/Bodenbach is now part of the Bohemian city of Děčín. The Podomkly barracks in Terezín/Theresienstadt were located across from the armory.

135 Registration of the Jewish population, carried out on Nazi orders by the Jewish congregations, took place in the Protectorate in the fall of 1941. The lists were subsequently used to assemble transports. Registration also took place in the ghetto itself before some outgoing transports. See Bondy, *"Elder of the Jews,"* pp. 225, 318.

136 The *Transportleitung* was responsible for the administrative work associated with incoming and outgoing transports (registering newly arrived prisoners, searching luggage, etc.).

137 This joke may mean that members of the *Transportleitung* kept prisoners' suitcases instead of returning them to their owners.

HORPATZKY. No, cc-fox.[138] Forgive me, I sputtered a bit. But then they realized that it was deadly poisonous, so they gave it up.

PORGES. And how did they figure that out?

HORPATZKY. Well, about six hundred cooks were seriously poisoned by it. Then ladies started using it like lipstick; it was called *Fuchsrot*.[139]

PORGES. You don't say. And what about family life, was that maintained as well?

HORPATZKY. Family life there was on a point system.

PORGES. On a point system? You're joking, right?

HORPATZKY. Those were the so-called *Zulassungsmarke*. At first those were for packages.[140] By the way, with those packages it was so interesting; each person there had some unknown sponsor in the Sudetenland. Most packages were sent by a Portuguese firm; the firm must have had relatives there.[141] After that, when there weren't any more packages, those *Zulassungsmarke* were for family life. Otherwise family life was maintained well enough—the father of one family with the mother of a second family, but it was family life.[142] All the same, after the war, everything went back to normal.

---

138 According to a survivor who worked in one of the ghetto kitchens, "fox" (in Czech, *liška*) is a veiled reference to *jíška*, a roux made of butter and flour that was frequently stolen from the ghetto kitchens. As an attempt at preventing theft red food color was added to the *jíška*; it was intended to stain the mouth and thus reveal the identity of the thieves. Marianna Foltynová, interview with Lisa Peschel, November 25, 2006.

139 *Fuchsrot*: German for "fox red."

140 Starting in July 1943, prisoners were allowed to send *Zulassungsmarke* (admission stamps) to friends and relatives in the Protectorate, which gave the recipient the right to send a package to the ghetto. See Beneš and Tošnerová, *Mail Service in the Ghetto Terezín*.

141 In the spring of 1943 the International Red Cross began sending packages of food to Terezín/Theresienstadt. Since parcels could not be sent from Switzerland to countries under German rule, the packages were sent from Portugal. See Bondy, *"Elder of the Jews,"* p. 341.

142 The forced separation of families (men, women, and children lived in separate housing) led to the collapse of some marriages and the emergence of new relationships.

WEISSKOPF. We're closing, gentlemen.

PORGES. Well, there's some kind of draft here, they should close this place. Listen, the way I hear you talk about it, it must have been a total madhouse there. I'm surprised you didn't try to escape.

HORPATZKY. That wasn't necessary; it was dissolved. So let's get going. Please, allow me to introduce myself. I'm Wiley.[143]

PORGES. Pleased to meet you. I'm Hungry.[144]

HORPATZKY. Me too, let's go somewhere for dinner.

PORGES. I already ate, but I'm Hungry.

HORPATZKY. Well, if I haven't eaten either, let's go.

PORGES. But you don't understand me, I'm full.

HORPATZKY. So are you Full or Hungry?

PORGES. I'm full, and I am Hungry.

HORPATZKY. Listen, it seems to me you would have fit right in in that madhouse.

14. SEVENTH DIALOGUE AND CLOSING COUPLET

PORGES. Well I'll tell you, Pidla, today's cabaret went really well. You know, I already heard a rumor[145] next door. They said that we said that we're all about to go home already.

HORPATZKY. Of course not—in six weeks at the earliest.

PORGES. Well, for what it's worth, it would be nice if we could talk about it at home already:

(*They sing "Couplet."*)[146]

There was once a group for artists
The *Freizeit* was its name

---

143 The name in the original script, Vykutálenej, means "sly."

144 The name in the original script, Nevečeřel, means "he who has not dined."

145 The word Porges uses here is *bonke* (see glossary).

146 See original music for "Couplet" ("Kuplet") on p. 222 of this volume, IMAGE 7.14.

HORPATZKY. There every budding talent had its fair shot at fame

PORGES. Intrigues amongst the members, such things were unknown there

HORPATZKY. And each one gladly helped the other, everything was fair.

PORGES. In spite of this and more

HORPATZKY and **PORGES**. We wish for no encore.

> (*Refrain*) Those old days in Terezín
> Now we see them differently
> Just a memory
> Though we feared catastrophe
> It passed without calamity
> Now it's history.
> They won't believe you when you try to describe
> Just what an absurd thing was Terezín life.
> In a hundred years we'll bet
> When the whole world reads of it
> All they'll do is laugh.

PORGES. The artists were all humble, each knew his proper place

HORPATZKY. They solved their disagreements with patience and grace

PORGES. They never ever argued, they never put on airs

HORPATZKY. They never fought amongst themselves, the ideal atmosphere.

PORGES. And now we must admit

HORPATZKY and **PORGES**. That this description doesn't fit.

> (*Refrain*)

15. EPILOGUE

The "Castaldo March" plays. After several bars—[147]

PORGES. Ladies and gentlemen,

HORPATZKY. We wish you goodnight again

PORGES. We hope you enjoyed our show

HORPATZKY. We're sorry you have to go

PORGES. We thank you for your indulgence

PORGES. And together we wish you

HORPATZKY and **PORGES**. Good night.

The End

---

147 The "Castaldo March" was composed by Rudolf Nováček in 1890.

IMAGE 7.9 **Original sheet music for "Long Live Cabaret" ("Ať žije kabaret"). Music by Felix Prokeš, lyrics by Pavel Stránský and Felix Prokeš.**

Courtesy of Pavel Stránský and Jan, Miroslav, and Zdeněk Prokeš.

IMAGE 7.10 **Original sheet music for "Andalusian Nights" ("Andaluzské noci").** **Music by Felix Prokeš, lyrics by Pavel Stránský (version 1).**

Courtesy of Pavel Stránský and Jan, Miroslav, and Zdeněk Prokeš.

IMAGE 7.11 **Original sheet music for "Andalusian Nights" ("Andaluzské noci"). Music by Felix Prokeš, lyrics by Pavel Stránský (version 2, using their pen names Jaroslav Felix and Pavel Jeník).**

Courtesy of Pavel Stránský and Jan, Miroslav, and Zdeněk Prokeš.

IMAGE 7.12 **Original sheet music for "Abandoned" ("Opuštěný"). Music by Felix Prokeš, lyrics by Felix Prokeš and Pavel Stránský (version 1).**

Courtesy of Pavel Stránský and Jan, Miroslav, and Zdeněk Prokeš.

IMAGE 7.13 **Original sheet music for "Abandoned" ("Opuštěný"). Music by Felix Prokeš, lyrics by Felix Prokeš and Pavel Stránský (version 2, using their pen names Jaroslav Felix and Pavel Jeník).**

Courtesy of Pavel Stránský and Jan, Miroslav, and Zdeněk Prokeš.

IMAGE 7.14 **Original sheet music for "Couplet" ("Kuplet"). Music and lyrics by Felix Prokeš.**

Courtesy of Jan, Miroslav, and Zdeněk Prokeš.

PART **2**

GERMAN-LANGUAGE TEXTS

LITERARISCHES STRAUSS
BRETL
Dr. Leo Strauss
Myra Strauss
Otto Skutecký
Edith Baum
Irene Gottlieb
Elly Bernstein-Porges
Dr. Felix Porges
Hanka Lederer
Olga Zwicker
Fränkl Lea
Paul Mayer
Fränkl. Mirjam
Isaak Hannelore
Hernlicht Eveline

LEO STRAUSS
and MYRA STRAUSS-GRUHENBERG

From the STRAUSS CABARETS

INTRODUCTION

Many of those interested in the cultural life of Terezín/Theresienstadt are already familiar with the name Leo Strauss and especially with his best-known song, "As If" ("Als ob"). Several of his songs and poems preserved in the archives of the Terezín Memorial in the Czech Republic have been published.[1] Now newly discovered works by Strauss and his wife, Myra Strauss-Gruhenberg, the only female author represented in this volume, can be added to the repertoire.[2] The texts came to light in the collection of survivor Felix Prokeš, who performed with the Strausses in German as well as in his own Czech-language cabaret.[3] In addition, two essays

---

IMAGE 8.1 (*page 223*) **The ghetto as a set design, probably for the operetta *Girl of the Ghetto*. By Adolf Aussenberg.**
Courtesy of the Terezín Memorial.

IMAGE 8.2 (*facing page*) **A souvenir poster for the *Literary Strauss Cabaret*.**
Courtesy of the Terezín Memorial.

---

1 See, for example, Ulrike Migdal (ed.), *Und die Musik spielt dazu: Chansons und Satiren aus dem KZ Theresienstadt* (Munich: Piper, 1986); and Tania Golden, Alexander Wächter, and Sergei Dreznin (eds.), *Chansons und Satiren aus Theresienstadt* (Vienna: Rabenhof, 1992).

2 Another poem written by Myra Strauss-Gruhenberg, "The Yellow Star" ("Der gelbe Stern"), is published in Manes, *Als ob's ein Leben wär*, p. 87.

3 For more information on the Prokeš collection, see the introduction to *Radio Show* in this volume.

written in the ghetto itself shed light on a little-known aspect of the couple's work and the cultural life of the ghetto overall: theatrical performances organized as a social service. The *Blockveranstaltungen* (performances in the housing blocks) administered by Myra Strauss-Gruhenberg brought desperately needed relief into the quarters of the ill and the elderly.

THE AUTHORS

LEO STRAUSS (born on January 21, 1897), the son of operetta composer Oscar Straus, was born in Teplice-Šanov/Teplitz-Schönau.[4] According to a brief biography recorded in the diary of fellow prisoner Philip Manes, apparently provided by Strauss himself, he published his first poems in a school newspaper at the age of eight. His family moved constantly, but he completed secondary school in 1915 and earned a doctorate at the University of Vienna in philosophy and law.[5]

He and his wife **MYRA STRAUSS-GRUHENBERG** (born on July 14, 1900) were deported from Vienna to Terezín/Theresienstadt on October 1, 1942, and immediately became involved in the cultural life of the ghetto. In addition to writing and performing in their own cabarets, the Strauss Ensemble (Strauss-Ensemble) and the Literary Strauss Cabaret (Literarische Strauss-Brettl), they performed in play readings organized by Philipp Manes.[6] Leo Strauss also wrote texts for and performed in renowned German-Jewish actor Kurt Gerron's cabaret Carousel (Karussell).[7]

---

4 Oscar Straus (1870–1954, real name Oscar Nathan Strauss) apparently changed the spelling of his name to avoid confusion with operetta composer Johann Strauss.

5 Manes, *Als ob's ein Leben wär*, p. 465.

6 Souvenir posters for both cabarets are found in the Terezín Memorial. See inv. nos. PT 4079 and PT 4080. For a list of the Manes Group's activities, see inv. no. PT 3981.

7 See the Terezín Memorial, inv. no. PT 3933. Gerron's cabaret has been described in several works about the cultural life of the ghetto. See Rovit, "A Carousel of Theatrical Performance at Theresienstadt"; and Karas, *Music in Terezín*, pp. 146–8.

In a diary entry from late summer 1944 Philipp Manes vividly described one of the Strauss's outdoor *Blockveranstaltungen*:

> The light muse has moved out into the courtyards; the posts and boards have been set up. It is the Strausses, those steadfast bringers of merriment, who with their ensemble have provided the elderly with two entertaining and often contemplative hours over two thousand times. They bring a colorful jumble of music, dance, seriousness and cheer, and above it all sounds the accordion, this rescuer of those in need of difficult-to-arrange accompaniment.[8]

On October 12, 1944, not long after celebrating their two thousandth performance, the Strausses were deported together to Auschwitz. Both perished.

THE SCRIPT

Leo Strauss's works range from comic songs to sonnets.[9] Although his style is whimsical, his works occasionally have a dark and even despairing edge. With lines like "we are buried here alive" in a poem about the crowded conditions of the ghetto, he confronts the truly desperate nature of the prisoners' situation. Other pieces, however, appear unrelated to Terezín/Theresienstadt, or engage with life in the ghetto in a much lighter way. Perhaps these works were written for the *Blockveranstaltungen*, where their suffering audiences needed no reminder of the miserable conditions in which they lived. Instead, as Myra Strauss-Gruhenberg wrote in her own essay published here, the most urgent need was "to distract the old and the sick as soon as possible from their cares." Her single poem in this collection, "The Last Cigarette," describes a moment of calm enjoyed by a woman who, by all accounts, was the center of a maelstrom of creative activity. The two

---

8 Manes, *Als ob's ein Leben wär*, p. 356.

9 I have translated Strauss's three sonnets ("Sleepless Night," "April Weather," and "The Angel") as blank verse.

IMAGE 8.3 (*left*) **A caricature of Leo Strauss from 1944 by Aloe Durra.**
Courtesy of the Terezín Memorial.

IMAGE 8.4 (*right*) **A drawing of Myra Strauss-Gruhenberg by an unknown artist, labeled "Myra in 1935."**
Courtesy of the Terezín Memorial.

essays on the *Blockveranstaltungen* and the statistics they provide—a thousand performances had taken place by the end of 1943, and the number had exceeded two thousand by the end of summer of 1944—testify to her organizational skill and determination to ease the suffering of the most unfortunate prisoners in the ghetto.

BIOGRAPHICAL INFORMATION

The names of the authors and performers appear on posters for the Strauss Ensemble and the Literary Strauss Cabaret.[10]

THE AUTHORS

DR. LEO STRAUSS, born on January 21, 1897, was deported on October 1, 1942 from Vienna to Terezín/Theresienstadt and on October 12, 1944 to Auschwitz. He perished.

MYRA STRAUSS-GRUHENBERG, born on July 14, 1900, was deported on October 1, 1942 from Vienna to Terezín/Theresienstadt and on October 12, 1944 to Auschwitz. She perished.

THE ACTORS AND THE OTHER PARTICIPANTS

For the actors listed on the posters as Hanka Lederer, Paul Mayer, Dr. Felix Porges, Elly Bernstein-Porges, and Pavel Weisskopf, see the biographical information for Hana Lojínová, Pavel Maier, Felix Prokeš, Elly Prokešová and Pavel Weisskopf in *Laugh with Us: The Second Czech Cabaret* in this volume, pp. 172–4.

EDITH BAUM (also **DITTA BAUM**) was born on June 17, 1921. She was deported from Vienna to Terezín/Theresienstadt on February 25, 1943 and to Auschwitz on October 9, 1944. She perished.

GERTRUDE FRANKL was born on June 11, 1912. She was deported from Vienna to Terezín/Theresienstadt on September 10, 1942 and to Auschwitz on October 19, 1944. She perished.

LEA FRÄNK(E)L (born on November 22, 1931) and **MIRJAM FRÄNK(E)L** (born on March 18, 1933) were deported together on October 9, 1942 from Vienna to Terezín/Theresienstadt and on October 19, 1944 to Auschwitz. They perished.

---

10 See the Terezín Memorial, inv. nos. PT 4079 and PT 4080.

STRAUSS-Ensemble

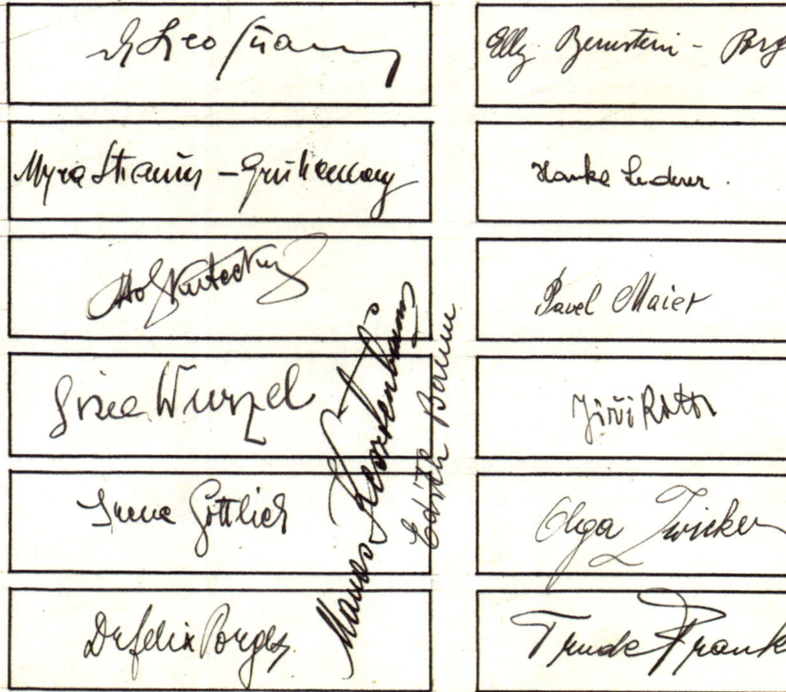

ALŽBĚTA (ELISABETH) GLASER-SCHÖN does not appear on the posters but is perhaps the Lisa Glaser mentioned in the essay. Born on March 16, 1921, she was deported from Prague to Terezín/Theresienstadt on December 12, 1942, and to Auschwitz on October 16, 1944. She was liberated in Kurzbach.

IRENE GOTTLIEB was born on May 8, 1924. She was deported from Vienna to Terezín/Theresienstadt on October 1, 1942 and to Auschwitz on May 16, 1944. She perished.

HANNELORE ISAAC, born on May 28, 1930, was deported on July 22, 1942 from Düsseldorf to Terezín/Theresienstadt and on October 9, 1944 to Auschwitz. She perished.

MANAS KESZTENBAUM was born on August 31, 1909 and deported on December 4, 1941 from Prague to Terezín/Theresienstadt. On October 28, 1944 she was deported to Auschwitz. She survived.

JIŘÍ ROTH (mentioned as **GEORG ROTT** in the following essay), born on February 3, 1920, was deported from Prague to Terezín/Theresienstadt on November 20, 1942, and to Auschwitz on September 28, 1944. He perished.

OTTO SKUTECKÝ was born on August 5, 1907. He was deported from Prague to Terezín/Theresienstadt on November 30, 1941 and to Auschwitz on September 28, 1944. He was liberated in Kaufering.

EVELINE STERNLICHT, born on June 1, 1931, was deported from Moravská Ostrava/Mährisch Ostrau to Terezín/Theresienstadt on September 30, 1942 and was liberated in the ghetto.

GISELA WURZEL was born on April 15, 1902. She was deported from Vienna to Terezín/Theresienstadt on September 10, 1942. She was liberated in the ghetto.

OLGA ZWICKER, born on October 26, 1909, was deported on January 28, 1942 from Brno/Brünn to Terezín/Theresienstadt. On October 6, 1944 she was deported to Auschwitz. She was liberated in Mauthausen and after the war took the name **HAVLOVÁ**.

IMAGE 8.5 *(facing page)* **Signatures of the members of the Strauss Ensemble.** *Courtesy of the Terezín Memorial.*

DEVELOPMENT OF THE *BLOCKVERANSTALTUNGEN* THROUGH THE END OF 1943[11]

MYRA STRAUSS-GRUHENBERG

Late in the autumn of 1942 the *Blockveranstaltungen*—that is, performances in individual *Blockhäuser*[12] and in the infirmaries—came into being. At first all necessary prerequisites were missing. Instruments were not available, artists could not be found, sheet music and texts were lacking, and there was no overview of the rooms and houses to be played for. Because the purpose of these performances—namely, to distract the old and sick as soon as possible from their cares—did not bear any delay, the performances began pell-mell with the most primitive means. A singer or reciter stood in one of the small rooms between the bedridden people and performed whatever he could draw from his memory that could serve as a repertoire.

The first months were devoted above all to meeting the huge demand quantitatively. All artists that one ran across or discovered were prevailed upon; music and texts were found or feverishly written. Card files for the individual rooms, including information on the residents and their special needs, were rapidly assembled under the most difficult conditions—at first only in the third sector,[13] where most of the old and sick were housed. After three months of work the situation had developed to the point where there was a performance at least once a week in all the houses. Three to five artists participated in each individual performance and so a full hour could be filled with varied entertainment. An average of 50 performances a week were presented during this period.

Once the quantitative demand had been met it was possible to address the qualitative aspects that until this time had had to take

---

11 The original German-language text was found in the archives of Yad Vashem in Israel, file 0.64/075. It was apparently submitted as a report to the leadership of the *Freizeitgestaltung*.

12 The plural of the German word *Blockhaus*: one of the former civilian houses in the ghetto, as opposed to the large barracks buildings.

13 The ghetto was divided into four administrative sectors or *Bezirke*.

IMAGE 8.6 **A hospital in the ghetto, 1943. By J. Ullmann.**
Courtesy of the Terezín Memorial.

second place. Participants were more rigorously selected, the reper-toires were reviewed and brought up to date with texts written here, the groups were no longer put together at random but according to the artists' artistic approaches. Decisive in this regard was permission to have accordion accompaniment; fixed ensembles formed around indi-vidual musicians and no longer performed unprepared but rehearsed more and more carefully. The coming of warmer weather also posi-tively affected the quality of the performances. It was possible to move the performances from the small rooms out into the large courtyards, where artists could perform not for forty to sixty people but for three hundred spectators or more. As a result the number of performances was reduced and they could be lengthier and more carefully prepared.

At this time an important change took place in the leadership of the *Blockveranstaltungen*, in that the former leader Professor Utitz was called upon for another position. His constant assistant, Myra Strauss, took over not only his post in the third sector but also leadership of the *Blockveranstaltungen* for all of Theresienstadt. This expansion to all four sectors was possible only as a result of the large capacity of the courtyards and the one-and-a-half to two-hour programs of the individual ensembles. Of course the small infirmaries were in no way neglected. They profited from the overall improvement in that the ensembles performed their very best pieces there. It was possible to achieve the goal of playing in each courtyard at least once a week during the warm

IMAGE 8.7 **A performance in one of the interior courtyards. By L. Haas.**
Courtesy of the Terezín Memorial.

seasons with about forty performances per week. However, the out-going transports ripped bigger and bigger gaps in the groups of artists. In October 1943, under the leadership of Myra Strauss, the participating ensembles—the Variety Group, the John Group, the Steiner Group,[14] the Strauss Ensemble and the Literary Strauss Cabaret—celebrated a thousand *Blockveranstaltungen*.

The coming of cold weather meant a sudden end to this improvement. It was no longer possible to perform in the courtyards, but a return to the overcrowded small rooms was out of the question. The decreasing numbers of artists, the fewer remaining accordions and the ever greater number of illnesses caused a drastic reduction. Still, by building a stage specifically for the *Blockveranstaltungen* where performances were held on an ongoing basis, the artistic needs of a great part of the public could be met for a while. But when this stage had to be closed because it could not be heated, and in addition the difficulties of providing entertainment in the coffeehouse (for similar reasons: illness, transports, lack of instruments) forced the artists of the *Blockveranstaltungen* to help out, the performances were radically limited. Qualitatively, the end of 1943 has seen often very cheering and even astonishing accomplishments, but quantitatively, performances are taking place at the insufficient rate of only about twenty a week. These are distributed among the infirmaries and the blocks—mainly the newly erected barracks.

---

14 The German names of the ensembles were Bunte-Gruppe, John-Gruppe, and Steiner-Gruppe. For posters of the John and Steiner groups, see the Terezín Memorial, inv. nos. PT 4098 and PT 4178.

THE LITERARY STRAUSS CABARET:
On the Fourteen Hundredth Cabaret Performance in Theresienstadt[15]

PRESENTED BY ARNO NEUMANN[16]

> Motto: In the literary cabaret, as opposed to the non-literary cabaret, the meanings of the jokes are not completely obvious.
> They have to be sought.
> Sometimes they are even worth the trouble . . .
>
> *Freely quoted from Dr. Leo Strauss.*

For over a year I have been closely following the development of the Theresienstadt *Kleinkunstbühnen*—as the Germans have named their cabaret. This form did not arise, as did most institutions—the largest ones in the ghetto—in response to need—no. Rather it arose from the drive to make art—the provider of joy, comfort, distraction, and diversion—available as well to the ill and elderly bedridden, who cannot reach the new attic performance spaces. Concern for these poorest of the poor by some noble philanthropists led them to organize the first *Blockveranstaltungen*. Mrs. Myra and Dr. Leo Strauss were among the first. The number quoted above speaks louder than any words of what has been achieved through their efforts, through their exemplary willingness to sacrifice, their refusal to be dissuaded by the danger of epidemics, by the lice in the old people's homes,[17] by the stale air in the narrow, overfilled infirmaries where the artists must go to reach their listeners.

---

15 This undated essay was preserved in the Prokeš collection. For more information on the collection, see the introduction to *Radio Show* in this volume.

16 Arnošt Neumann was born on January 17, 1902, deported from Prague to Terezín/Theresienstadt on November 30, 1941, and to Auschwitz on October 1, 1944. He died on February 9, 1945, in Dachau. For further information on Neumann, see Elena Makarova, Sergei Makarov, and Victor Kuperman (eds.), *University over the Abyss: The Story behind 520 Lecturers and 2,430 Lectures in KZ Theresienstadt 1942–1944* (Jerusalem: Verba Publishers, 2004), p. 495.

17 See *Entwesung* (glossary).

Only he who has witnessed with them countless times the touching, heartfelt scenes, who has listened to the words of gratitude, seen the quivering handshakes and looks full of emotion with which these often already half-dead people thank the performers for a last moment of pleasure, can judge just how much good and noble work the groups of artists around Mrs. Myra and Dr. Leo Strauss have accomplished through their dedication and love for their fellow man.

The critics at first focused more on good intentions than actual accomplishments and viewed every means as justified by the end. But the leaders of the variety hours constantly attempted to improve their programs, the selection of the performers, the milieu of their offerings (the summer stages in courtyards and gardens, and finally the coffeehouse and the halls in the Cavalier and Magdeburg barracks). The previous relative view is no longer necessary; the present cabaret groups may be subjected to more objective criticism. The three groups currently active under the organizational leadership of the Strausses, the Strauss, Steiner and John cabarets, will be addressed here.

The Literary Strauss Cabaret represents the best form of literary cabaret. Trademark: Vienna, during the last decade of peace. We find here the spirit, jokes, esprit, charm and grace that we appreciated and loved in the Vienna of Peter Altenberg, Schnitzler, Auernheimer, Zweig and all of the others up to Karl Kraus. Dr. Leo Strauss, the ideal creator of form and content, the most amusing and highly intellectual host of his ensembles, seems inexhaustible. The most recent program, with the exception of the Czech songs, was from a literary point of view completely his own work. The sketches "Spa Music," "Marriage Dialogue," and "Pierre Puts Everything in Order," the meditative monologue "The Desk"[18] about the gained and lost million, his lyrical poems, recited well by Georg Rott, the couplets "The *Menage* is Coming" and "The Package (Theresienstadt Currency),"[19] interpreted by the most spirited performers of the ghetto, Mrs. Myra Strauss and Mrs. Trude Frankl, the songs "Theresienstadt Tango" and "Theresienstadt Waltz," that the blond Ditta

---

18 These sketches and monologues have apparently not been preserved.

19 These two couplets have been preserved. See Migdal, *Und die Musik spielt dazu*, pp. 71, 75.

Baum presented expressively and with great musical purity, as well as the new program number "Theresienstadt Questions,"[20] a humorous and current number performed by the blondest Ditta Baum and the most dark-haired lady of the ensemble[21] all have their source in the workshop of this apparently inexhaustible person. I don't know how well the good doctor's luggage managed to pass through the *Schleuse* into the ghetto, but his intellectual equipment and his great, purely Viennese talent remain undamaged. We ourselves are witnesses, in all this misery and struggle, to the ways both have grown in breadth and depth. No bursts of laughter are heard in response to his subtly pointed patter. But a subtle, dreamy smile, seemingly inspired by a reverie far away from Theresienstadt, reflects the effect that he elicits again and again. Thanks and recognition are due to him in the first place.

In the Theresienstadt cabarets Mrs. Myra Strauss is, in addition to the liveliest and most expressive interpreter, an administrative dynamo—a high-voltage wire but not fatal—with the ability to overcome countless and unforeseen difficulties with ease. One meets her daily during the earliest work hours in the *Freizeit*,[22] accompanied by the members of her troupes, who agreeably assist so that everything functions smoothly. She administers close to fifty performances—the variety hours, the performances in the infirmaries, in homes for invalids, in the housing blocks—and, in many cases, performs in them herself. She is always in good spirits and willing to offer advice and help—drop her a line and she will visit immediately.

The third in the artistic and administrative leadership is band leader Skutecký.[23] He is responsible for musical rehearsals. He accompanies the singers on the piano as well as on the accordion and plays the incidental music. He is also the musical inventor, composer, and arranger of many frequently performed melodies.

---

20 Of the three songs mentioned, two have apparently been lost. The third, "Theresienstadt Questions," has been preserved. See ibid., p. 87.

21 Probably Irene Gottlieb (see next page).

22 See *Freizeitgestaltung* (glossary).

23 One of Skutecký's compositions, the music to the song "Drunt im Prater ist ein Platzerl," has been preserved. See the Terezín Memorial, inv. no. PT 4090. For the lyrics, see Migdal, *Und die Musik spielt dazu*, p. 65.

Grouped around this triumvirate is a circle of expressive and capable ladies. The blond Ditta Baum I have already mentioned. A year ago Mrs. Strauss brought her right from the *Schleuse* to the stage. Like her gold-blond hair, at the time her accordion was also a rarity in the ghetto. Since then Miss Baum has set the accordion aside to focus on her singing and acting; the hair color she has kept. One sees and hears her at least once a day on stage. The second blond of the ensemble is Mrs. Bernstein. She completes the Viennese ensemble through her fine performances of Czech songs. She is almost the only one of her kind, and therefore even more welcome, acclaimed and applauded.

Mrs. Wurzel performs as an actor in the sketches: a very talented, precise interpreter, who so easily finds the good-humored Viennese tone and performs it convincingly (for example, in the "Marriage Dialogue"). The black-haired Mrs. Gottlieb has until now been the expressive singer of songs in Yiddish. In this new program, for a change, she has a comic part in the "Theresienstadt Questions." Each of her verses, well focused and heartily interpreted, elicits a salvo of laughter from the audience.

Mrs. Trude Frankl currently sings "The Package" by Dr. Strauss. She accompanies herself on the accordion. As with every piece in her repertoire, she also performs this one with great success. One must not only hear it but see it. In outer appearance she creates the impression of a well-painted poster: classy, bubbly, and lively. And the tempo, the play of glances, the expression . . . she represents a high class of performing artist.

The final number, "Theresienstadt Waltz," sung as a solo by Miss D. Baum, is enlivened by a dance number by the graceful Lisa Glaser and the five young tap dancers Hannie, Gucki, Mirli, Putzi, and Uschi, because dance belongs unconditionally to the Viennese.[24] And this program, in its best numbers, is just as Viennese as its creator and most of its interpreters.

---

24 These are probably the nicknames of the young women listed at the bottom of the poster for the *Literary Strauss Cabaret* with accompanist Paul Mayer (Pavel Maier).

AN UNREAL PLACE[25]

I know a town, a small one,
A small town, oh so nice,
Its name—I will not say it,
That would not seem so wise.

This funny place in fact is
Quite unreal as it were
And only chosen creatures
Are allowed to enter there.

I think the life they live there
Wouldn't seem a life to you,
I'm told they are enjoying
Rumors that won't come true.

The streets are always crowded
People hurrying to and fro—
The chief thing's not to work there,
But to pretend doing so.

A smart cafe's to be seen there,
Much like Cafe Savoy—
The papers and the music
Make you feel a regular guy.

Some people there are sometimes
On others pretty hard—

---

25 This English-language version by an unknown translator was preserved in the Prokeš collection. The text was sung to the melody "Two from Ottakring" ("Zwei aus Ottakring") by Alexander Steinbrecher.

At home they were no big bugs,
Here they begin to start.

They get their as-if-coffee
Twice a day to drink—
It wouldn't be a Saturday
without as-if-meat, I think

They queue up for thin soup
With naught in it, I guess
Of vitamins a hotbed
A turnip is, no less.

They lie down on the rough floor
As if it were a bed,
And think of their beloved ones
Whose news they have not read.

They bear their sorrows just so,
As if there were no sorrow—
They talk of a better future,
As if it were tomorrow.

BAD TIME

Time, it came to stay with me
For much too long a visit
No book helped; though I tried to read
There was no way to pass it.

Time would not stop plaguing me
No matter how I willed it
In all its relativity
At last the clock delivered me
It struck the time—and killed it.

LEO STRAUSS, MYRA STRAUSS-GRUHENBERG

SLEEPLESS NIGHT

I lie awake, my head upon the pillow
And envy all the friends who, lost in sleep
Have left me here alone in quiet darkness
To listen to the soft sound of their breath

To know that now they're free of all the struggles
That constitute our daytime destiny
They glide away from evening that released them
Approaching sudden morning in soft flight.

Now I alone must walk this weary pathway
From evening toward the sluggish morning grey
I stumble, breathing hard, through thorny bushes

And helplessly in circles seem to turn.
But chimes of the clock tower offer milestones
That stand, devoted, faithful at their posts.

OUR WORLD HAS GOTTEN SO MUCH SMALLER

Our world has gotten so much smaller
On foot you cross it very well—
Nothing lies 'tween south and north
Except nine Qs and then six Ls.[26]

Fifty thousand people packed
Onto a crowded carousel,
They must obediently cram into
Nine Qs only and six Ls.

The sun tempts us outside to wander
Back to lands we love so well—

---

26 See L, Q (glossary).

But no road here will take us further
Than to nine Qs and six Ls.

World that we have long abandoned
Wide, free world, adieu, farewell—
We are buried here alive
Inside nine Qs and then six Ls.

THE CVOK[27]

At home my friends affectionately
Used to call me "Schmuck,"
Here however I've advanced,
They address me as "the *cvok*."

When a Jew arrives in Terezín
He gets quite a shock,
But me, I like it here just fine,
So they think that I'm a *cvok*.

In the ghetto life is busy,
People working 'round the clock
I like my peace and quiet,
So they think that I'm a *cvok*.

I don't get very hungry
Sitting home here in our block
So I turn down my N-ration[28]
They think that I'm a *cvok*.

I like to hear the rumors
Such interesting talk

---

27 See glossary.

28 Letters indicated different categories of bread rations. "N" stood for "normal." See *Brotkategorie* (bread categories) in Adler, *Theresienstadt*, p. XXXV.

But I don't believe a single word[29]
They think that I'm a *cvok*.

To get some outdoor exercise,
I take long, healthy walks
Ten times across the town and back—
They think that I'm a *cvok*.

And it seems to me ideal
To sit down at five o'clock
Without my paper or my pipe—
They think that I'm a *cvok*.

My friend told me that his new bride
Is the eldest of her block[30]
"The oldest one!" I cried out loud,
"Well maybe you're the *cvok*."

And for a bet of lentil soup[31]
Sometimes we play tarock[32]
I always do my best to lose—
So they think that I'm a *cvok*.

Each Friday carefully I brush
my one good Sabbath-frock—
I'm more pious than I was at home—
So they think that I'm a *cvok*.

Sometimes those I've offended
Try to put me in the dock

---

29 The word used in the German-language original is *kec*, a Czech slang expression for senseless talk.

30 The *Blockältester* was the head of a group of civilian houses.

31 Lentil soup, made of a synthetic lentil powder, was one of the least favorite foods in the ghetto.

32 One of a family of popular European card games played with the tarot deck.

Their charges never seem to stick[33]
Luckily I'm just a *cvok*.

APRIL WEATHER

The sun, she shines her beams through woven cloudthreads
The rain, he slants across the sun's bright face
Like two children bathing in a hurry
Eager once again to start their games.

Time and time again they shift the light
Each one trying to surprise the other
They have not yet fathomed their own truth:
Isolation long and duties strict.

Later on they'll find themselves in far-off
Summerland, where they'll become accustomed
To the earnest work of being sun and rain

They'll celebrate their ever rarer meetings,
Crowning them with their own arch triumphant
Grandly built of many vibrant colors.

THE ANGEL

That once an angel to the elders came
Seemed unlikely. One knows how old folks natter.
Their children wished to see him to believe it
And saw him not, who stood by sorrowful.

---

[33] There was a civil court in Terezín/Theresienstadt that tried minor crimes such as libel, theft, and fraud among the prisoners. See Bondy, "*Elder of the Jews,*" pp. 306–9; Adler, *Theresienstadt,* pp. 453–92; and *The Insult—But Unintended* in this volume.

And with their doubts they never ceased to wound him
Til he withdrew his image from their sight
The miracles he'd wrought, shamefaced now,
He hid in the relentless laws of nature.

They listened closely, straining hard to hear
Not noticing the song of nightingales.
They did not grasp that once the sun stood still

But saw that it continued in its path.
And failed to hold in high regard the pledge,
The miracle that every mother knows.

THE BONKEL-UNCLE[34]

Today our uncle's feeling spry
A gleam of mischief in his eye
He jokes to a stranger whom he meets
On the corner of the street:
"How come you're just standing there?
Can it be you're unaware?
A whale's escaped from the zoo
He's swimming this way now—it's true!"

The man's jaw drops down to the ground
Then he starts canvassing the town
Keeping everyone abreast
Of the news our uncle meant in jest
In fifteen minutes, north to south,
The news has spread by word of mouth:
"A whale's escaped from the zoo
He's swimming this way now—it's true!"

---

34 See *bonke* (glossary). Strauss adds a Viennese twist with the diminutive *l*.

Soon a lady comes to call
She tells Uncle the news that all
The people of the town, they went
To see the whale, the grand event.
Our uncle chortles merrily:
"It's just a joke—how could it be
That a whale could escape from the zoo?
How could such a thing be true?"

Then yet another guest arrives
A third, a fourth, and number five
Can already provide details:
From afar, the crowd has seen the whale!
Our uncle ponders for a bit
Then reaches for his walking stick.
"Who knows, then, what a whale can do?
He's swimming here—maybe it's true!"

MAYBE I AM A DON JUAN

I.

It was a day in springtime
My favorite start-a-fling time
I came to visit you.
We sat all three together
Outside, in balmy weather
Your husband read a letter
His eyes began to droop.
He nodded off, oh finally,
But his leg was blocking my way
There was nothing I could do.
I thought we had a good chance
At a legendary romance
But the tale has stayed as clean as
A nursery rhyme at school.

(*Refrain*) Maybe I am a Don Juan
It never quite comes through
The ladies, they come on to me
With just a glance they summon me
Let's have a rendezvous.

I put on my best gloves and then
I go to the rendezvous—
There I wait one, two hours and then
Three hours and then—
Four—hours and—then . . .
Maybe I am a Don Juan
It never quite comes through.

II.

It doesn't always end well.
With Pepi for example
I really had it rough.
Sweet milkmaid I was wooing
But her cow was my undoing
It always started mooing
When I tried to speak of love.
And I must say it displeased me
That her dog, he was so beastly
What an insolent young pup.
Though I gathered up my courage
It vanished like a mirage
When a hen joined our entourage
I'd finally had enough.

(*Refrain*)

THE LAST CIGARETTE

Myra Strauss-Gruhenberg

The day is filled with situations dire
But evening brings a few hours light and free
A brief escape from what imprisons me
I stretch contentedly. I am so tired—

What do I care that day will once more come?
Into the hiding place beside my bed
I reach and find it, my last cigarette
I am so happy: I am so in love—

And blissful 'til the last ember stops glowing
On gentle drift of dreams along I glide . . .
Already knowing I'll be, in the morning,
So angry with myself. I realize
The cigarette that I was just enjoying
Was one I'd saved for morning's baleful skies.

THE TREASURE
A Puppet Play in Ten Acts

ARTHUR ENGLÄNDER

INTRODUCTION

Arthur Engländer has been known to US audiences for decades as the character of the father in one of the most popular English-language plays about the Holocaust, *I Never Saw Another Butterfly*.[1] It now appears he may have authored plays in Terezín/Theresienstadt as well. A file containing the puppet play *The Treasure* was preserved among materials related to the ghetto in the archives of the Yad Vashem Holocaust Memorial in Jerusalem.[2] No author's name appears on the scripts themselves, but since the file is devoted solely to Arthur Engländer's work and he clearly authored the other items in it, it is likely that he wrote the puppet plays as well.

IMAGE 9.1 (*facing page*) **Designs for marionettes.**
Courtesy of the Terezín Memorial.

1 Celeste Rita Raspanti, *I Never Saw Another Butterfly: A Play* (Woodstock, IL.: Dramatic Publishing, 1971).

2 File 0.64/075 includes two versions of *The Treasure* and an English translation of one version by Carol F. S. Edelman and her parents Martin and Rita Stern. The translation published here is of the second version.

Efforts to confirm the script's authorship and whether or not it was written and performed in the ghetto led to interviews with Arthur Engländer's daughter and his three nieces, who related to me the remarkable story of the three Engländer brothers and their puppet theater. Raja Žádníková, Arthur's only child, lives in Prague. His nieces in Israel, Rahel Ardon[3] and Shulamit Amir, are the daughters of Arthur's older brother Otto (in Czech, Otakar), who was a fervent Zionist and helped to establish the Jewish youth club Blue-White (Blau-Weiss).[4] Otto's daughter from his second marriage, Deborah Vietor-Engländer, lives in Germany. All three of Otto's daughters remember the youngest brother, Viktor, as a lovable uncle with an apartment full of fantastic inventions but also as a terrible businessman who often let his brothers take responsibility for his debts.

In 1922, Arthur and Otto, who had both completed degrees in engineering, went to Palestine. They were accompanied by Otto's wife Margarethe, who was originally from Vienna, and their three-year-old daughter Rahel. Otto had been offered the position of municipal engineer for the city of Tel Aviv.

According to Raja, Arthur was not a passionate Zionist like his brother. However, he accepted a position in the town of Afula as a water-well engineer because, during the period of economic crisis in Europe, opportunities in his area of specialty were scarce. In Palestine he met Rosa, a young Zionist from Vienna. They married and their daughter Raja (in Hebrew, "friend") was born in 1929. Arthur probably learned Arabic, which appears in the script, during his years in Palestine. Otto's second daughter Shulamit was also born in Palestine in 1927.

During a visit to Prague, Otto discovered that his father's health was failing and decided to take over the family fur-import business.

---

3 Rahel Ardon passed away in May 2008.

4 After the First World War, the club's German-language name Blau-Weiss was replaced by the Hebrew name Tekhelet-Lavan (both mean blue-white). Although it was not explicitly Zionist, the future of Palestine was one of its members' central concerns. See Bondy, *"Elder of the Jews,"* p. 26.

Otto and Arthur and their families returned to Prague in 1930. Three-year-old Shulamit went to a German-language kindergarten and eleven-year-old Rahel to a Czech-language school; they also learned Czech from their maid, Jarmilka.

Rahel and Shulamit both vividly recalled the marionette theater in their apartment in Prague. As Rahel described it,

> We had a big flat, and two of the rooms were separated by large doors. My father had the theater specially built so that you could set it up in that doorway and hang a curtain above it, so that the puppet operators could not be seen. Our dad used to write the stories and compose the music, and Viktor's wife was a piano teacher, so she played the music.[5] The three brothers operated the marionettes and did the voices.[6]

The folding puppet theater had features such as electric lighting, a trap door and several sets, including mountains with snow made of cotton. Rahel recalled about thirty different puppets, including typical fairy-tale characters such as the witch and the king but also more unusual figures, like the Loch Ness Monster and a bird that could blow smoke from its nose and ears.[7] Shulamit recalled that, although Otto had the puppet heads made by artists, they spent hours dressing the marionettes and making the scenery. She especially remembered the performances to celebrate her birthdays:

> This was almost an institution; it was not usual in those days to have a birthday party. I can still see this picture of all the children sitting on the floor, they got lemonade and cookies.

---

5 Shulamit also recalls that it was their father who wrote the plays the brothers performed in Prague. He died just a week before a collection of his stories was published. See Otakar Engländer, *Geschichten aus der Geschichte meines Lebens* (Mainz: Selbstverlag, 1971).

6 Rahel Ardon, interview with Lisa Peschel, October 25, 2007.

7 The puppet theater itself may have been preserved. Shulamit recalled that her father's partner, a non-Jewish Czech named Zirnfuss who became the official owner of the fur-importing business when all companies were required to be "Aryanized," agreed to store it in his basement. Three of the puppets—Spejbl, the Queen, and a Peasant—were shipped to England and are still in the possession of Deborah Vietor-Engländer.

[. . .] They were absolutely fascinated; it was the talk of my class, this puppet theater. [. . .] The greatest excitement I remember from those days was a play in which a puppy took part in the story, and suddenly a real puppy appeared on the stage, and that was my birthday present.[8]

Although the family spoke German at home the plays were written in Czech, since the invited audience consisted largely of the girls' Czech-speaking classmates.

Shulamit's eleventh birthday, in 1938, was the last one celebrated with such a puppet show. Soon thereafter a series of crises caused the family to disperse. During a trip to Palestine in 1937 Rahel had married.[9] She was visiting in Prague when the Munich Pact was signed but returned to Palestine immediately after the Czech border regions were occupied and remained there for the duration of the war. When the Nazis invaded the rest of Czech territory in March of 1939, Otto was coincidentally on a business trip in Scandinavia. Persuaded by friends that, as a Zionist, he would be in danger if he returned, he moved to London and eventually worked with the Czechoslovak government in exile. Viktor managed to escape to England and then emigrated to Buenos Aires. Shulamit's mother, who had been ill for several years, expended the last of her energy to obtain a place for her daughter on a *Kindertransport* so that Shulamit could join her father in London.[10] Her mother died in Prague in 1942.

Arthur, Rosa, and Raja Engländer were all deported to Terezín/ Theresienstadt in January 1942. There Arthur worked as a manual laborer and Rosa was a caretaker in the children's home where Raja lived. Raja, whose experiences in the ghetto inspired the play *I Never Saw Another Butterfly*, was ill with typhus for several months and did

---

8 Shulamit Amir, interview with Lisa Peschel, October 17, 2007.

9 Her first husband Nehemiah Argov later became foreign minister in the government of David Ben-Gurion.

10 These transports were a rescue effort in which the United Kingdom took in nearly 10,000 predominantly Jewish children from Nazi-occupied territories. They have been described in dozens of survivor memoirs and portrayed in films, including Mark Jonathan Harris's Oscar-winning production *Into the Arms of Strangers: Stories of the Kindertransport* (2000).

IMAGE 9.2
**Arthur Engländer
in the 1930s.**

*Courtesy of
Raja Žádníková.*

CIRKUS
Text: Jar. Dubský
Loutky: Walter Freud
Technická výprava: Ing. Art.
                        Engländer
Kulisy: Ausenberg
Kostýmy: Orienter

not recall her father's involvement in the cultural activities of the ghetto.[11] However, preserved documents reveal that he gave lectures about topics ranging from *Cities in Palestine* to *Descartes and his Contemporaries*.[12]

He was also actively involved in puppet theater and worked with Walter Freud, author of the play *Purimspiel* in this volume, on several performances.[13] However, no documents have been found that confirm his authorship of *The Treasure* and whether the play was performed in the ghetto.

Rosa and Raja survived in Terezín/Theresienstadt until the liberation. Arthur perished after his deportation from the ghetto to Auschwitz in October, 1944.

THE SCRIPT

The plot of the play is similar in the two versions of the script that have been preserved. Two children and the clown Kašpárek/Kasperle travel to Africa in search of a treasure, live with an Arabic-speaking tribe in the village of Aljanin, and return to Europe with a discovery that saves even the poorest from hunger: the potato. It is unlikely that Engländer

IMAGE 9.3 *(facing page)* **A souvenir poster for the marionette theater performance** ***Circus*. Arthur Engländer is listed as responsible for technical aspects of staging.** *Courtesy of the Terezín Memorial.*

11 Part of the play is set during the period of Raja's illness. Engländer devised an unusual strategy to help his daughter recover at a point when she had lost her will to live: he sent her math problems to solve (Raja Žádníková, interview with Lisa Peschel, October 6, 2007). Arthur's letters to Raja are reproduced in Deborah Vietor-Engländer, "'Festung meiner Jugend'. Bisher unbekannte Mädchentagebücher aus Theresienstadt und ihre Umsetzung im Unterricht der Mittelstufe," in Barbara Bauer and Waltraud Strickhausen (eds.), *"Für ein Kind war das anders." Traumatische Erfahrungen jüdischer Kinder und Jugendlicher im nationalsozialistischen Deutschland* (Berlin: Metropol Verlag, 1999), pp. 408–20.

12 See Makarova et al., *University over the Abyss*, p. 449.

13 Engländer's name appears on several posters preserved in the Terezín Memorial. See, for example, posters for the puppet shows *Johnny's Kingdom* (*Honzovo království*) and *Circus* (*Cirkus*), inv. nos. PT 3860 and PT 3885.

himself did not know that the potato was brought to Europe from South America, but by placing the story in Africa he was able to employ his language skills to characterize the Arabic-speaking Africans.

The scripts differ most in the names of their characters. In the version published here, the characters have names more familiar to Czech speakers. For example, the clown figure is identified by his traditional Czech name, Kašpárek, and the play features the famous Czech puppet characters Spejbl and his son Hurvínek.[14] This version also includes Czech-language expressions and grammatical features. In the other version, a boy named Wendelin and his teacher Fleissig appear instead of Spejbl and Hurvínek and the clown figure is called by his German name of Kasperle. The two versions also differ in minor plot points. For example, this version ends with the announcement that the story will be continued in a subsequent puppet play. The version featuring Wendelin and Fleissig concludes with Kasperle's appeal to the king to treat children and the poor more justly and ends with a puppet ballet.

Although the notion of finding a new source of food was clearly relevant to the prisoners' situation in the ghetto, *The Treasure* has few other connections with the world of Terezín/Theresienstadt. Perhaps it served what one survivor called the most important function of theater for children: "We needed to divert them. So that they would simply forget about everything around them. Because when a person simply fixated on what was happening in front of him, he forgot about all the rest."[15]

---

14 The Theater of Spejbl and Hurvínek was founded as a professional puppet theater in 1930 and is still operating today. See www.spejbl-hurvinek.cz.

15 Hana Reinerová, interview with Lisa Peschel, December 9, 2004.

THE AUTHOR

ARTHUR (in Czech, **ARTUR**) **ENGLÄNDER** was born on January 16, 1891. He was deported to Terezín/Theresienstadt on January 30, 1942 and to Auschwitz on October 1, 1944. He perished.

THE SURVIVORS CONTRIBUTING TO THE INTRODUCTION AND ANNOTATION

RAJA ŽÁDNÍKOVÁ (née **ENGLÄNDEROVÁ**) was born on August 25, 1929. She was deported to the ghetto with her parents on January 30, 1942. She and her mother Rosa (in Czech, Růžena) were liberated in Terezín/Theresienstadt. She lives in Prague.

THE TREASURE

A Puppet Play in Ten Acts

CHARACTERS

Vojan, a farmer
Mrs. Vojan
Liese, their niece
Vávra, a policeman
Spejbl
Hurvínek, his son
Kašpárek
Medicine woman
King
King's messenger
City man
City woman
Bambo, an African chief
Villagers, city people, Africans

THE ACTS

Act 1 *At the Edge of the Forest near the Village*
Act 2 *Vojan's House*
Act 3 *Village Square in Libric*[16]
Act 4 *Deep in the Forest*
Act 5 *Africa, near the Village Aljanin*
Act 6 *Oasis*
Act 7 *Village*
Act 8 *Enchanted Forest*
Act 9 *City*
Act 10 *King's Palace*

---

16 Perhaps the village of Libřice, near Hradec Králové.

Farmer Vojan comes from work with a rake over his shoulder.

VOJAN (*singing*). Tra la la, my work is done
I'm walking home in the setting sun
The grain is mowed, the fields are clear
My heart is bursting with good cheer, hurrah!
(*Addresses the audience.*)

Well it's been hard work in the fields this year; you wouldn't believe what has to be done to put a loaf of bread on the table. First plowing the fields—not everyone knows how to do that, the whole day back and forth, pull, little horse, pull—the horse doesn't want to go any further, or a big stone gets stuck in the plow. You come home in the evening exhausted.

For the grain to grow well, the field has to be fertilized. So you drive and drive and drive, loading manure from the manure pile, and then unloading it in the field, again you plow, and go over it with the iron comb, the harrow.

Now comes the good part—the sowing. All day I walk through the field and scatter golden grain upon the ground— my Lord, I should get home now, my wife is waiting with dinner—but I still have to tell you—now the grain grows. That means making sure that the birds don't eat the young grain. Those sparrows have a lot of nerve! You hit a sheet of tin with a stick, tap tap tap and finally the grain can grow in peace. Let enough rain fall, let the sun shine again, but God willing, let there be no hail!

And when the grain turns a beautiful golden, then out early with the scythe and ritch, ratch, mow it fast, till my bones creak. My wife says I talk too much; tell me children, do you think so too? But we can't finish the play so soon, so I must continue my tale. That's why I have to tell you more.

So, where did I stop? Good Lord . . . where was I . . . wait, I've got it—so in the spring, after you've plowed . . . no,

I already told you that—please, children, where did I stop? Mowing . . . yes, that's it . . . now I remember. The grain is mowed, I'm just coming now from the mowing. It has to dry for a few days, so tomorrow I'll stack the grain in sheaves.[17]

Then you haul it into the barn, the little horse runs, I just hope it doesn't rain! Thank God it didn't rain, the barn is full. Now comes the thresher, puff puff rat-a-tat, by George, it has a huge stomach, it eats everything, then gives us back beautiful grain. You take it to the mill, the stones grind it into flour, then the baker takes the flour and he makes bread out of it.

So now you know how much work I had to do for you to eat bread and butter. Boy am I hungry now; I'll hurry home. But wait, who's coming this way? Liese, my dear niece, is that you?

Liese enters.

LIESE. Good day, dear Uncle Vojan, I'm glad to see you here, it's already getting dark—how are you and how's my aunt?

VOJAN. I'm fine, it's just that I'm terribly hoarse.

LIESE. Hoarse? Why, do you have a cold?

VOJAN. From talking.

LIESE. From talking? But there's nobody here.

VOJAN. What do you mean nobody? Look, there's a crowd of children sitting out there. I've just explained to them how bread is made. But now tell me—how is my sister, your mother, my brother-in-law, your father, and all my friends in Libric?

LIESE. Thank you for asking. Everyone's well and although we have a lot of work we're happy and have a lot of company. Old Sojka with the red nose visits us all the time and tells so many jokes, he always wears a green scarf and thinks it's his handkerchief; he always blows his nose into it.

VOJAN (*laughing*). Ha ha ha! That's funny!

---

17 In the original German, the stacked bundles of grain are called *Puppen* (dolls). I have left out of the translation Vojan's explanation, ". . . not the kind you dress and take for a walk in a doll buggy; we make grain dolls."

LIESE. And old lady Brabec comes, too; she never goes anywhere without her thick sheepskin coat, even in the summer, when we run around in our bathing suits. And she shivers with cold when she sees us and knits us warm things. Even for her goats she knits little woolen vests, the poor animals have to go around in sweaters.

VOJAN. That is really crazy, ha ha ha.

LIESE. And just yesterday we had a visitor from the city, a young man named Kašpárek. He acts terribly mysterious, as if he's looking for something special. Supposedly there's a treasure buried around here somewhere.

VOJAN. I don't mean to make fun of him, but while he's hunting for his treasure he'll probably fall in the manure pile. Come on, Liese, let's go home, mother will be impatient already.

Both exit singing "Merry is the Gypsy Life."[18]

ACT II. VOJAN'S HOUSE

MRS. VOJAN. Now where is my husband? Dinner's getting cold and I'm so hungry I could faint. He must have finished with the mowing long ago. I hope nothing's happened to him, for God's sake . . . (*Weeps.*) No, nothing will happen to him—now I'm going to count to three, and if he doesn't come home by then, I'm going to start eating alone. So . . . one, two, half past two, a quarter to three, five minutes to three . . . THREE. (*A knock.*) Hooray, there's Mr. Vojan!

VÁVRA (*stumbles in*). A good evening to you all.

MRS. VOJAN. Oh no, it's only you. I'm waiting for my husband.

VÁVRA. Yes, it's me, officer Vávra, come to visit you. I'm tired of walking back and forth, back and forth between the water pump and the mayor's house. When I was young, yes, life was certainly much more interesting.

---

18 The German title is "Lustig ist das Zigeunerleben."

MRS. VOJAN. It's true, your wife is very interesting.[19]

VÁVRA. When I was young I sailed on a ship, I went to Egypt, and there I rode on a camel to the pyramids. Those are stone houses, two thousand years old, and twenty times taller than your house.

MRS. VOJAN. How many times? I'm hard of hearing.

VÁVRA. Yes, and there we hunted the crocodiles that swim in the river, it's called the Nile, like goldfish in an aquarium. I was in India and rode on elephants, there's a very thick forest there, it's called the jungle, and lions and tigers live there, just like in the zoo.

MRS. VOJAN. You're right, she does look good in blue.

VÁVRA. The animals roar the whole night long so you can't sleep, and it's hot as an oven. Yes, I could tell you some stories. (*Begins to sing "When Someone Takes a Trip."*)[20]

Vojan and Liese enter.

VOJAN. Well isn't this a cheerful scene! Good evening everyone. I've kept my old lady waiting, haven't I dear, but I'll make it up to you: I've brought a welcome guest. Liese's here for a visit.

VÁVRA. Good, Liese's here, greetings, dear sister.

LIESE. Have you been drinking?

VOJAN. I'm hungry as a lion; bring dinner or I'll collapse!

They eat and say "the food is good," etc. Hurvínek and Spejbl enter.

SPEJBL. Good evening, Mr. and Mrs. Vojan, we've taken the liberty of coming for a visit. How is the grain? Are you done with the mowing?

VOJAN. Certainly, it's all cut, and we'll bring it in on Saturday.

HURVÍNEK. Papa, look, there's a girl; she's pretty.

---

19 As Mrs. Vojan reveals a few lines later, she is hard of hearing and her replies to Vávra are often non sequiturs. I have translated for acoustic similarity rather than preserving the meaning of her original lines.

20 The German title is "Wenn einer eine Reise tut."

SPEJBL. Well of course it's a girl; ask her her name.

HURVÍNEK. Hello, girl, what's your name?

LIESE. My name is Liese and I'm the niece of my uncle Vojan and I'm here from Libric for a visit.

HURVÍNEK. So people live there too?

SPEJBL. Well you're not so bright; what else would you expect to find there?

VÁVRA. Rabbits, geese, pigs, cows, horses, ha ha ha.

MRS. VOJAN. Why is he laughing? I'm hard of hearing.

VOJAN. Vávra just said something funny.

MRS. VOJAN. Why are you calling him Sonny?

Everyone laughs.

LIESE. A very nice young man came to Libric yesterday. His name is Kašpárek and he's been telling us about things in the city. But in Libric they don't believe a word of it.

HURVÍNEK. Papa, I want to see him. I can also tell very interesting stories. May I go to see him?

SPEJBL. If you're good you can go to Libric with Liese tomorrow to see Kašpárek.

VOJAN. I'm curious myself; when you come back you'll have to tell us everything.

VÁVRA. Don't forget to ask Kašpárek's real name; I'm leery of a person who doesn't . . .

MRS. VOJAN. Well I'm also feeling cheery; I'm in the mood to sing.

VÁVRA. Sing, sing, that we could do; listen everyone, I'm going to sing a Czech song. (*Sings "When the First Cobbler was Born," etc.*)[21]

Everyone shouts "Bravo."

VOJAN. Now Liese should sing!

Liese sings "I Have Loaded My Wagon Full."[22] Everyone dances to end the scene; Vávra falls down.

---

21 The Czech title is "Když se první švec narodil."

22 The German title is "Hab' mein Wagen voll geladen."

Kašpárek speaks to the villagers.

KAŠPÁREK. And I tell you, there are things in the city that you've never seen before. Here in the village, if you want light, you have to fill up the oil lamp, take off the glass chimney, light a match, light the lamp, put the chimney back on, and only then does the lamp begin to burn. In the city you push a button, the electric lamp turns on right away, and you never even see a flame.

VILLAGERS. He's lying; there's no such thing.

KAŠPÁREK. It gets even better. When you want to travel, you have to harness up the horses, giddyup, little horse! But the horse doesn't feel like it, you shout hey and ho and snap the whip, finally the horse begins to move and your wagon creeps along at a snail's pace. In the city: no horses, no oxen, in the city it's electric. You only see the people getting in, then ring ring, the man turns a wheel and off we go. Or a car that goes by itself, chug chug chug, faster than a greyhound can run.

VILLAGERS. Nonsense, it's not possible.

KAŠPÁREK. Do you know about the telephone?

VILLAGERS. What is that?

KAŠPÁREK. You are way behind the times; where are you living? On the moon? Just imagine—this box is a telephone. I speak into it and in the city my father hears my voice. Of course you don't know about radio either: one man speaks, sings, laughs and thousands of people in Africa and America hear his voice coming out of a little box.

VILLAGERS. The boy's a swindler, it's ridiculous, don't believe him!

KAŠPÁREK. Oh, they are blockheads. You've probably never even seen running water. I turn on the faucet and the water flows out all by itself, but you have to go to the pump. You have to use a stove if you want your room to be warm; I turn on the central heat and I'm already sweating. We turn on the sunlamp and get a tan in the winter, in the summer we make ice in the icebox, we don't climb the stairs, but take the elevator. And that people can fly in the sky, certainly you've heard of that?

VILLAGERS. You're going to fly soon if you don't stop with your lies.

KAŠPÁREK. You are so dumb; apparently not one of you has ever set foot out of this village. You should read newspapers and books; you'll find all of this there. You should go to the city and look around for yourselves. Yes, people can fly. There is a bird made of steel and aluminum; it's called an airplane. A man gets in, vroooom like the fastest bird, in four hours he flies from here to Paris.

And I want to tell you what a cinema is: everything that I do and say can be photographed with a film camera and tomorrow the people in the city can go to the theater and see you all on screen. They can also hear everything I've told you and they'll realize how dumb you all are.

VILLAGERS. He's got a lot of nerve; this liar deserves a beating!

Villagers come after Kašpárek; he runs. Liese and Hurvínek enter.

LIESE. What's going on here? You want to beat up a guest? What did he do to you?

VILLAGERS. He told us terrible lies.

LIESE. Maybe he's lying, and maybe there are things in the world that you don't know about. Shame on you; go home.

Villagers slowly disperse, muttering "impudence," "nonsense," etc.

KAŠPÁREK. Dear courageous girl, my thanks; you have saved me. I really only told them about things in the city, but these people have learned nothing and know nothing about the world. What is your name?

LIESE. My name is Liese. You're right, so often I've tried to tell these people about the things I've read—but enough about that or I'll get annoyed all over again. Here is my friend Hurvínek. I've brought him along from the neighboring village. He wanted very much to meet you.

KAŠPÁREK. I'm glad that someone in this small town is interested in me. Because you're so nice, I would like to let you in on a big secret. I live in an old house in the city and in the attic I found a box full of books. I love reading; I lie down on my stomach in the morning with a book in front of my nose and in the evening I stand up, very stiff, but I've read the whole book.

HURVÍNEK. A person like that is called a bookworm—my father says that he eats the books up and not a scrap remains. Show me; do you have paper in your stomach?

KAŠPÁREK. Ha ha ha, I'm very ticklish, stop that!

LIESE. Kašpárek, tell us more; Hurvínek, leave him alone![23]

KAŠPÁREK. Once I found a story in an old book, and there it said that here in Libric in the forest on a mountain there is a treasure. I found a map too.

HURVÍNEK. Show us the map—hurrah, there's a treasure in the woods! A treasure!

KAŠPÁREK and LIESE. Have you gone crazy? The treasure is a secret; nobody is supposed to know!

Hurvínek cries.

KAŠPÁREK. You're a baby. Here, see, everything's shown on this map and tonight we're going up to the mountain to look for the treasure.

HURVÍNEK. At night? Oh, I'm afraid. I'm not going with you; at night people are supposed to sleep, that's what my father says.

LIESE. So stay here then. I don't know what you're afraid of. I'll go with you, Kašpárek, we'll search for the treasure.

HURVÍNEK. If you say there's nothing to be afraid of, then I'm not afraid either. And if someone comes, I'll punch him in the nose.

Exit all.

---

23 Liese employs a feature of Czech grammar in the German-language text. Using the vocative case, she addresses Kašpárek and Hurvínek as "Kašpárku" and "Hurvínku."

Kašpárek, Liese, Hurvínek.

ALL. Quiet, quiet, quiet, if this treasure map is good,
　　Quiet, quiet, quiet, we'll find it in this wood
　　Quiet, quiet, quiet, let's hope as we come near
　　Quiet, quiet, quiet, it doesn't disappear.

HURVÍNEK. Ouch, I ran into something—why did I have to come with you crazy people? Wouldn't it be nicer to be lying in bed, reading a story? I'm so afraid. (*Cries.*)

KAŠPÁREK. Quiet, you chicken, no one's hurting you. Think instead about the treasure we want to find; then we'll all be rich.

HURVÍNEK (*shouts*). Oh God, look over there, a witch is coming; she has fiery eyes and she's going to put a hex on us.

LIESE. You should be ashamed of yourself, such a big boy and you're acting like a baby in diapers. But wait—something really is coming this way. Who's there?

MEDICINE WOMAN. Greetings to you all; what are you children looking for alone in the forest? Aren't you afraid?

HURVÍNEK. Thank God, finally somebody who understands me. Oh, I'm terribly afraid; help!

MEDICINE WOMAN. What are you doing here then?

HURVÍNEK. These two brought me along. They're looking for some kind of treasure.

MEDICINE WOMAN. A treasure? That's strange; these children want to find a treasure. Oh, how heavy it is for me to carry this wood.

LIESE. You know what, let's help this old woman carry the wood home.

They take the wood from her.

MEDICINE WOMAN. Children, because you're so good, I'm going to tell you something. Around here they call me a witch.

HURVÍNEK. There you have it, I knew it, she's going to turn us into monkeys now.

MEDICINE WOMAN. Don't be afraid; witches only appear in silly children's stories. I gather herbs and help the poor people of the village when they get sick. Once, many years ago, a sailor was ill and got lost in the woods. I took him home and helped him get well. In gratitude he left a little chest with me, but there were only papers in it. I can't read so I buried it here in the forest.

LIESE and **KAŠPÁREK.** Show us the box and we'll read what's written there.

MEDICINE WOMAN. Because you have been so good to me, you shall have it. I'll dig it up. (*Digs up a box; it glows.*)

KAŠPÁREK, LIESE, and **HURVÍNEK.** Hurrah, the treasure. Now we are rich. Gold ducats, jewels.

MEDICINE WOMAN. Don't get too excited; I told you, there are only papers inside it.

KAŠPÁREK. Well that's too bad, I was already so excited and planning to buy myself a new puppet theater. But who knows, maybe these papers will be good for something. Who can read?

HURVÍNEK. I can read wonderfully; show me those papers. (*Reads.*) Brumba, golo, werde, tolo, soja, funny stuff.

KAŠPÁREK. You're holding it upside-down; let me try. (*Reads.*) Who, that do is no, let . . . no one will learn anything from this.

LIESE. It seems to me that neither of you learned much in school. Now I'm going to have a try. (*Reads.*) Whoever finds these papers can make his fortune if he travels to Chief Bambo in the village of Aljanin near Yemen in Africa.[24] Show him the ring and Bambo will show you a treasure.

KAŠPÁREK. Now that's interesting. Where is the ring?

HURVÍNEK. Here is a little iron ring. Hurrah, we're going to Africa, who's going along, you, Liese?

LIESE. I'm going along, and you, Hurvínek?

HURVÍNEK. I don't know yet. I have to ask my father first.

KAŠPÁREK. We don't have time. If you want to come, you have to do it right away. So decide.

---

24 This description places the village of Aljanin somewhere in the Horn of Africa, across the Red Sea or Gulf of Aden from Yemen.

Medicine woman has disappeared. In her place there stands a bleating goat. The sun slowly rises; it becomes bright.

HURVÍNEK. Where is our medicine woman? She's gone; she's turned herself into a goat. I think . . . I think she really was a witch. I'll go with you. Papa will certainly allow it.

All sing "Must I Leave the Little City."[25]

Exit all.

ACT V. AFRICA, NEAR THE VILLAGE ALJANIN

Liese, Kašpárek, Hurvínek, later Bambo with his little son.

LIESE. That was quite a trip; I never dreamed that someday I would travel all the way to Africa. The beautiful trip through Italy, then over the sea, and now: we're in Africa. Here, see all the palm trees, the beautiful golden sand, monkeys are playing here and there, and there stands a heron. I think I'm dreaming and yet it's all real. How lucky I am.

HURVÍNEK. And the heat, the crocodiles, the flies, the spiders and the strange food, only dates, figs, olives, yuck, how unhappy I am. It's been so long since I've had plum dumplings! What will my papa say? Oh, it's so hot!

KAŠPÁREK. Hurvínek, don't act like an old lady and stop complaining or we'll leave you here to roast in the sand. Children, we're in Africa, hip hip hooray, we three from Bohemia. But now we have to find the village of Aljanin and chief Bambo. Ah, here comes someone.

HURVÍNEK. Oh no, the devil is coming to get us! That man is all black and the little one looks like a chimney sweep.

LIESE. Hurvínek, you're so dumb; those are black Africans.[26]

---

25 The German title is "Muss i' denn, muss i' denn, zum Städtle hinaus."

26 In the following scenes I have attempted to remain faithful to the language of the original script, which reflects racial attitudes of the inter-war period. However, theater artists planning to perform the play today may wish to alter these scenes significantly.

Chief Bambo enters with his little son, behind him some animals, a calf, hens, etc., which cluck, cackle, and low.

BAMBO. *Ahlem, sahlem, chawadscha. Kif halak, schu esma?*[27]

HURVÍNEK. What is that black man saying? Does he think we're scoundrels? I don't like being insulted.

KAŠPÁREK. That's a funny language. My Lord, how can someone talk like that?

LIESE. Now wait a minute, children; that's Arabic, a language like any other. Once I learned a little from a book and now it's going to come in handy.

HURVÍNEK. My God, what a girl; she knows everything.

LIESE. *Kattir, cherek, hamdulilah, kif inti, esmi Liese.*[28]

BAMBO. *Taib, sitt, schu lasem hon?*[29]

LIESE. He's asking what my name is and what we want here. Kašpárek, show him the ring! (*Bambo sees the ring, shouts for joy, and begins to dance, crying "Allah, akbar, talu, talu."*[30] *The animals make noise.*) He is inviting us to his village, where we will be his guests.

KAŠPÁREK. The people back at home will be amazed. Imagine, we will be guests of the chief.

Exit all.

---

27 Arabic for "Greetings, honored ones. How are you? What are your names?" The transliteration of Arabic has been preserved from the original German-language script in order to retain potentially meaningful irregularities (comically intentional errors, indications of lack of knowledge of the language on the part of the character or the author, etc.). Only obvious inconsistencies have been corrected. *Sch* should be pronounced like the English *sh*, *j* like the English *y*, *th* like the English *t*, and *z* like the English *ts*. For more information, see the pronunciation guide for German in this volume.

28 Arabic for "Thank you, praised be Allah, how are you? My name is Liese."

29 Arabic for "Fine, miss. What do you want here?"

30 Arabic for "God is great, come with me, come with me."

Liese, *Kašpárek*, *Hurvínek*, *Bambo*.

LIESE, **KAŠPÁREK** and **HURVÍNEK** (*exclaiming*). Oh, how beautiful, this glorious oasis, these flowers, wonderful!

BAMBO. Dear my children friends, I many weeks, you guests of mine, your language learn a little. Girl beautiful, white with my Arabic, will marry me. Then I treasure show.

LIESE. Oh no, this is getting strange, this black man, he is certainly a good person, but I don't want to marry him!

KAŠPÁREK. But Liese, we have to find the treasure. Why did we come to Africa? You have to marry him.

LIESE. What good will this treasure do me then? You'll go home and leave me here alone with this black man. (*Weeps.*) Oh, I'm a poor unhappy girl.

HURVÍNEK. Kašpárek, be reasonable. I won't let Liese stay here. What would my father say? The flowers and the whole wonderful oasis don't make me happy any more. But we have to find the treasure. Stop, Liese, don't be sad. I have an idea. Tell him that you'll marry him and when we have the treasure, we'll figure out what to do next.

LIESE. All right, Bambo, when you show us the gold, rings, chains and precious gems, then I'll marry you, isn't that right, Kašpárek?

Kašpárek and Hurvínek speak simultaneously.

KAŠPÁREK. *Aiwa*.[31]

HURVÍNEK. *Ano*.[32]

BAMBO. Not all understand, what treasure gold precious ring are, but young lady my wife, good. Here dig secret. (*Digs a small box out of the earth.*)

---

[31] Arabic for "Yes."

[32] Czech for "Yes."

LIESE, KAŠPÁREK and **HURVÍNEK.** *Hamdullila,*[33] hurrah, *zaplat'pánbůh,*[34] the treasure is found! What is it? There are apples in there—that's no treasure!

LIESE. You call this a golden treasure, Bambo? Those are only apples or pears. The wedding is off. It's over between us.

KAŠPÁREK. What a swindle. We made such a long trip for a few apples—ha ha, the joke is on us. Curse that witch.

BAMBO. Now whole village invite, treasure give, girl marry.

LIESE. You can forget about that. Children, let's run away!

HURVÍNEK. And what are we supposed to do with these apples; play soccer with them? They can stay here along with the rest of the whole stupid treasure. Bambo can eat them up all by himself until he gets a stomachache.

LIESE (*shouts*). No, take everything along, we have no idea what kind of fruit they are.

BAMBO. I no understand, girl mine marry, stay here. (*Tries to hold on to her; Kašpárek and Hurvínek hit him and he falls down. Kašpárek, Hurvínek and Liese run away, taking the fruit. Bambo lies on the ground.*) Oh, bad people, got treasure, now all gone, my white miss. *Inalabuk, inaldinak, jachribetak, achmar!*[35]

ACT VII. VILLAGE

People are gathered, waiting. Officer Vávra tries to keep order.

VÁVRA. Please don't crowd, ladies and gentlemen, there is plenty of room here.

VILLAGERS. You should make room . . . wait, here they come, see, our heroes are here, hurrah, hurrah, *nazdar.*[36]

---

33 Arabic for "Praised be Allah."

34 Czech for "Thank God."

35 Arabic for "Cursed be your father and your faith. May your house burn, you donkey."

36 The Czech expression *nazdar* (to success) can mean "hello," "goodbye," or "hurrah."

Kašpárek, Hurvínek and Liese enter. Liese carries palm leaves; the others carry exotic fruit and a box containing the new fruit.

VOJAN. Finally you've come back; we all were so worried about you. So this is Kašpárek, who started the whole thing.

HURVÍNEK. Mr. Vojan, I won't let anyone say anything bad about my friend Kašpárek. Papa, we were in Africa, you read about that already in the newspaper. We saw lions and tigers and we lived in an African village and I boxed the black chief there on the ear.

SPEJBL. A chief? For God's sake, weren't you afraid?

HURVÍNEK. When he wanted to marry Liese I was so furious that I knocked him right to the ground.

VOJAN. Well that's really something! Tell us, how is it in Africa?

KAŠPÁREK. We lived among the natives, black and brown. They live in huts, eat dates, and drink the milk of the coconuts that grow on the trees there. Here are a few dates. And we searched for a treasure.

VÁVRA. Where is the treasure? I've never been in such suspense.

LIESE. Well, things with the treasure didn't work out like we planned. We've only brought back some fruit—apples or pears. Take a look.

VOJAN. Those aren't apples or pears; that's something completely new. I've never seen anything like it.

VÁVRA. Throw them away; I'm sure there's a curse on them.

KAŠPÁREK. No, no, Liese brought them, she should keep them as a reminder. You can dry them, then they won't go bad.

LIESE. I'm going to plant these fruits in the forest and see what grows.

SPEJBL. Now I invite all of you to my home; you must tell us about everything you've experienced.

Exit all.

ACT VIII. ENCHANTED FOREST

Kašpárek, Liese, Hurvínek; later Spejbl, Vávra, Vojan, King's messenger.

KAŠPÁREK. Ho ho ho, what have we here? This is an enchanted forest; Liese, what have you done? A month ago you planted the fruits from Africa in this field and now it's like a fairy tale.

HURVÍNEK. Golly, we've brought a piece of Africa back with us. I just hope that black guy, Mambo or Bambo or whatever his name was, doesn't come out from between the trees. I'd curse him: *Inalabuk, abuk, sei sift.*[37] It makes me furious whenever I think of him.

KAŠPÁREK. Hurvínek, I don't even recognize you anymore. What's happened to you? You used to be such a coward.

LIESE. Yes, that whole business with the marriage made him ferocious. But children, look, we can't do anything with all these dumb plants. Wait, over there in the corner, something very ordinary-looking is growing; let's see what it is.

KAŠPÁREK. This plant only has leaves, but let's taste them. Blech, that's bitter. And now the other leaves, ewww, so sour! We were certainly taken in by this treasure.[38]

LIESE. Wait a minute, I want to see what's underground. (*Pulls bulbs out.*) Hey, this is amazing, those are exactly the same fruits that we saw in Africa.

KAŠPÁREK. So let's take a bite. Ech, it doesn't have any taste at all, like *Schkubanken.*[39]

LIESE. Should we try to roast them, then see how they taste?

HURVÍNEK. Yes, great idea, we'll build a fire and I'll blow like a locomotive.

They roast the fruits. Hurvínek blows into the fire, coughing and sneezing.

---

37 Arabic for "Cursed be your father and your father's father, you dirt."

38 In the original, Kašpárek sings two lines from a folk song here: "Now adieu and good night, now we have reached the end" ("Ade nun zur guten Nacht, jetzt wird der Schluss gemacht"), and then adds the phrase "with the treasure."

39 A bland pasta-like dish made of potatoes, flour, and butter.

LIESE, KAŠPÁREK and **HURVÍNEK.** Oh, they taste delicious, just like bread.

HURVÍNEK. Maybe you can make dumplings out of them too. But what should we call this plant?

LIESE, KAŠPÁREK and **HURVÍNEK.** A name, a name . . . / I'm for African pear / I vote for black apple.

HURVÍNEK. Stop; we won't get anywhere like this. Let's take our time and think about it. So, where does the plant grow?

KAŠPÁREK. It grows in the earth and it looks like an apple. (*Ceremonially*) Let's call it the earthapple[40]—or in English, the potato. And Momba, Bomba, Bambo, that makes it *brambor* in Czech.

HURVÍNEK and **LIESE.** Hurrah, we brought the *brambory* back with us, we'll go down in history.

They dance and sing. Spejbl, Vojan, Vávra enter.

VOJAN. Where have you children been? The whole town has been looking for you and everyone is worried about you.

VÁVRA. Nothing can happen to you as long as I, Officer Vávra, am with you. I'll protect you with my sword.

KAŠPÁREK. We don't need you, you bigmouth, we can protect ourselves.

SPEJBL. Where did this wonderful forest come from? I've never seen trees like these before. It's a miracle.

VOJAN and **VÁVRA.** How strange, fabulous, magnificent!

LIESE. See, this is what's become of the fruit we brought back from Africa.

VÁVRA. This forest should become a zoo. Bring in a few more animals—lions, tigers, elephants—and people will come in droves.

VOJAN. Bravo, children, soon we'll have a zoo here with the most beautiful plants.

KAŠPÁREK. And we've brought something else back as well; taste this.

---

40 A literal translation of the German *Erdapfel*.

VÁVRA. My God, that tastes good, it's like bread. What is this plant called?

LIESE. We've named it earthapple or *brambory*. It grows in the earth, and now everyone, even the poorest people, can grow earthapples and they won't be hungry anymore, even if they don't have any bread. I think that this is a greater treasure than the gold ducats we brought back. Poor Bambo.

Messenger enters.

MESSENGER. The king has heard of your wonderful trip and invites you to come to his palace and show him the treasure that you have brought back.

KAŠPÁREK. Oh, even the king wants to see us. Let's go, let's go to see him. But we can't take this wonderful garden with us. He will have to come down from his throne and see it for himself. But we can send him some of these earthapples or *brambory*. He should roast them and taste them.

MESSENGER. Earthapples, *brambory*, what is that? Perhaps you're still a bit disoriented after your trip to Africa. (*Exits.*)

HURVÍNEK. And now, quickly, let's go see Mrs. Vojan. She can make us some fine earthapple dumplings.

They sing "A cup of tea, sugar and coffee."[41]

Exit all.

ACT IX. CITY

Kašpárek and people from the city.

CITY MAN. Kašpárek, you're now a famous man, all the newspapers write about you, about how you were in Africa and brought back a new plant. Now the poor people have something to eat.

---

41 This line (in the original German, "eine Tasse Tee, Zucker und Kaffee") is apparently from the folk song "Morgen marschieren wir zu dem Bauern in das Nachtquartier."

CITY WOMAN. I've also planted it; it grows everywhere, even in the worst soil. I thank you from the bottom of my heart; my children are not hungry anymore. What good fortune!

KAŠPÁREK. I'm glad that old Bambo didn't lie to us, but it was actually Liese, the girl from Libric, who brought the earthapple. By the way, tomorrow we're all going to see the king. He wants to hear about our adventures; I must tell him all about it.

ACT X. KING'S PALACE

King, Princesses, Spejbl, Hurvínek, Liese, Vojan, Vávra, Kašpárek.

KING. I, the king, am glad, am glad . . . what did I want to say . . . aha, yes, I am glad, that Kašpárek has brought us such a new and beautiful plant, which, which . . .

KAŠPÁREK. My king, don't exert yourself so much, everyone knows that hunger is now a thing of the past. I read about the treasure in a book, but this girl Liese almost had to marry old Bambo in Africa.

HURVÍNEK. I was there too, and I boxed his ear so hard that he fell over, and Liese took the earthapple and we ran away.

KING. But I don't understand, the newspapers only mention Kašpárek and now there are three of you.

KAŠPÁREK. Then the newspapers should mention that these two were there as well.

KING. All right, now I know what I wanted to say. You three good children have brought us great happiness because you have brought us such a useful fruit. Now we wish to reward you. What do you wish for, Hurvínek?

HURVÍNEK. I have to ask my papa first: Papa, what do you allow me to wish for?

SPEJBL. My God, what a silly boy; wish for whatever you want.

HURVÍNEK. Then I wish that, when I'm bigger, I'll be able to marry Liese without asking my father's permission.

KING. That is a wonderful wish. If Liese will have you, you shall have her. And you, Liese, what would you like?

LIESE. With Hurvínek there's still time. I wish for a big field, and there I will plant grain, vegetables, and the new earthapple.

KING. You shall have it. Bravo, I like that girl. Give her a big field. And now you, Kašpárek, what would you like most?

KAŠPÁREK. I would like—well, what would I like? I'm not sure yet, but I'll tell you in the next play.

The End

WALTER FREUD
PURIMSPIEL

In the *Purimspiel* (*Purim Play*) we hear a voice rarely represented in the theatrical life of the ghetto: the voice of a young Zionist. This script, preserved in Walter Freud's file at Beit Terezín in Israel,[1] is the only work authored by him that has so far come to light.[2] The play appears to end in mid-scene and it is likely that the final pages were lost. Although it is not possible to say definitively whether the extant manuscript was preserved from the ghetto or reconstructed after the war, a poster preserved in the archives of the Terezín Memorial in the Czech Republic confirms that a *Purimstück* (*Purim Piece*) written by Walter Freud was performed in Terezín/Theresienstadt in March 1943.[3] Survivor Jiří Shmuel Bloch, living today in Zichron Yaakov, Israel, confirmed that the text published here corresponds to the poster. Even before perusing the script, he recalled that his good friend Dov Révész, one of the actors listed on the poster, sang the parody of the aria "La donna e mobile" that appears in the final act.[4]

IMAGE 10.1 (*page 281*) **The synagogue in the Cavalier barracks. By E. Neugebauer.**
IMAGE 10.2 (*facing page*) **A souvenir poster for the *Purimstück*. By Walter Freud.**
Both images courtesy of the Terezín Memorial.

---

1 Archives of Beit Terezín, file 338. There is no information regarding how the script reached their archives.

2 Freud wrote at least two more original works: a German-language revue, *What Was Mordechai Like?* (*Wie war Mordechai?*) and a Czech-language Hannukah play called *Menorah*. See the Terezín Memorial, inv. nos. PT 8413 and PT 8420.

3 See the Terezín Memorial, inv. no. PT 4041.

4 Jiří Shmuel Bloch, interview with Lisa Peschel, October 24, 2007. The aria is from the first act of the opera *Rigoletto* (1851) by Giuseppe Verdi.

MÄRZ 1943

PURIMSTÜCK

VON WALTER FREUD

REGIE, – AUSSTATTUNG :

WALTER FREUD

MITWIRKENDE:

Revezs Dov.
Erich Huppert,
Hans Epstein,
Frant. Weiss,
Karel Fleischer,
Walter Freud,
u. Jugendliche der Heime Q 710, u. L 410
3 Wiederholungen BV 241

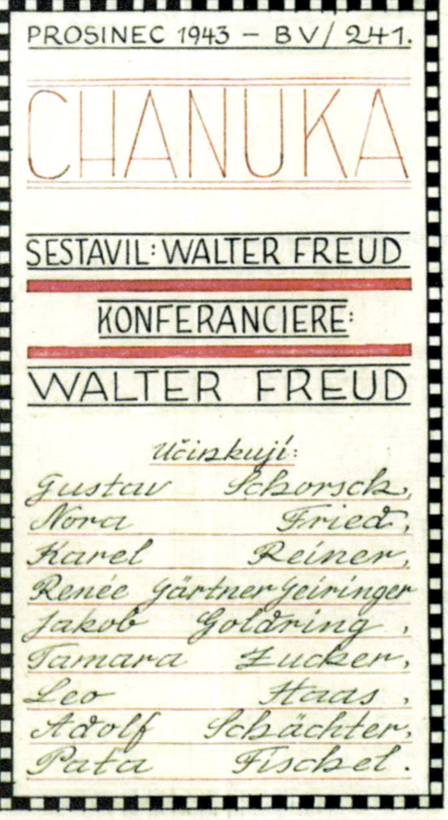

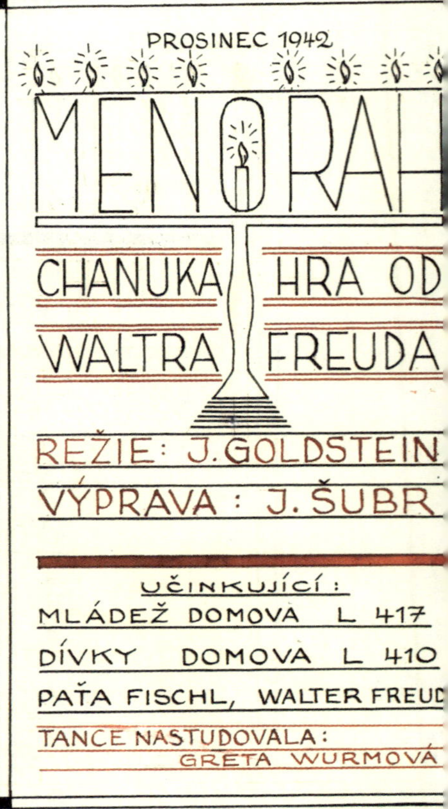

IMAGE 10.3 (*left*) **A souvenir poster for a Hanukkah celebration in December 1943, organized and hosted by Walter Freud.**

IMAGE 10.4 (*right*) **A souvenir poster for *Menorah*, a Hanukkah play by Walter Freud performed in December 1942.**

Both images courtesy of the Terezín Memorial.

Walter Freud perished after his deportation to Auschwitz. His wife Ruth survived, and thanks to letters she wrote to Beit Terezín in 1995[5] and a 1997 interview with Elena Makarova,[6] as well as testimony by Terezín/Theresienstadt survivor Michal Beer,[7] much is known about his life.

Walter was born in 1917 in Vienna but grew up in Brno/Brünn. During the occupation he was employed by the Jewish congregation as a *shaliach*[8] and traveled widely in Moravia, delivering lectures on Jewish topics. As Ruth described his work, "He was not pious, but he wanted Jewish youth to know their history."[9] He traveled frequently to the town of Strážnice to work with a large Maccabi youth group.[10] There he met Ruth, and they were married on December 7, 1941.

At the beginning of 1942 Walter was named head of the Jewish orphanage in Brno/Brünn. Ruth, who in the meantime had completed a training course as a children's nurse, worked there with him. In March 1942, the 80 children of the orphanage and all their caretakers were deported to Terezín/Theresienstadt. In the ghetto, Walter and Ruth were assigned to work in the girls' youth home L410. Posters preserved in the Terezín Memorial reveal how he immersed himself in the cultural life of the ghetto and especially in work with youth.[11] He organized

---

5 Her letters and a wedding photo are preserved in the archives of Beit Terezín, file 338. Unless otherwise indicated, the letters are the source of all the biographical information below. Dates have been confirmed with information from the database of the Institute of the Terezín Initiative.

6 Makarova et al., *University over the Abyss*, p. 405.

7 Michal Beer, interviews with Lisa Peschel, October 15 and 16, 2007.

8 In the Zionist movement, the *shaliach* devoted himself above all to educating youth and preparing them for emigration to Palestine.

9 Makarova et al., *University over the Abyss*, p. 405.

10 Maccabi groups were branches of an international Jewish sports organization. The first Czechoslovak chapter was founded in 1919. See Ruth Bondy, *Mezi námi řečeno: Jak mluvili Židé v Čechách a na Moravě* (Prague: Nakladatelství Franze Kafky, 2003), p. 90.

11 In addition to the *Purimspiel* and the two works mentioned earlier, Freud organized an evening of works by Scholem Aleichem (Terezín Memorial, inv. no. PT 3916), a children's revue titled *A Girl Travels to the Promised Land* (*Ein Mädchen reist ins gelobte Land*, PT 4014), and several more performances.

several performances on Jewish and Zionist themes for adults as well as for young audiences. Judging by the *Purimspiel* itself and the comic titles of some of his other works, it is perhaps not surprising that he participated in the lecture series of the ghetto with a talk titled "Jewish Humor."[12] He also helped young people adapt their favorite fairy tales and stories for the stage.[13] He was even able to indulge his passion for puppet theater, sometimes working with another author represented in this collection, Arthur Engländer.[14] Survivor Hana Reinerová, the caretaker for a group of boys in home Q609, recalled that he taught her young charges to make marionettes.[15]

Because they both worked in the girls' youth home, Walter and Ruth Freud were one of few married couples in the ghetto who were able to live together.[16] A year after their arrival, however, they suffered a terrible loss: the death of their child. Ruth was already expecting a baby when they arrived in the ghetto. Although the doctors in Terezín/Theresienstadt recommended that she terminate her pregnancy, Ruth refused, believing that the war would be over by the time the child was born. Their daughter, Eva, nicknamed "Yanika," was born in November 1942 but contracted whooping cough and died when she was only four months old.[17] As Ruth wrote, "Walter himself built a small white coffin and we accompanied the little one to the crematorium."

Walter was deported to Auschwitz on the first of several mass transports in September and October 1944. According to Ruth, the SS

---

12 Makarova et al., *University over the Abyss*, p. 456.

13 See, for example, posters for a Czech-language performance of *The Pied Piper of Hamelin* (*Krysař hamelský,* Terezín Memorial, inv. no. PT 4310) and a German-language performance based on Erich Kästner's children's novel *Emil and the Detectives* (*Emil und die Detektive,* Terezín Memorial, inv. no. PT 3848).

14 See, for example, posters for two Czech puppet plays, *Johnny's Kingdom* (*Honzovo království*) and *Circus* (*Cirkus*), in the Terezín Memorial, inv. nos. PT 3860 and PT 3885.

15 Hana Reinerová, interview with Lisa Peschel, August 31, 2006. A poster for a puppet play staged by her boys lists Walter Freud as one of the artistic supervisors. See the Terezín Memorial, inv. no. PT 3857.

16 Michal Beer, interview with Lisa Peschel, October 15, 2007.

17 According to survivor Michal Beer, the Freuds derived the nickname from the letters Y N K. In Hebrew, when different vowels are added to the three-letter verb root, these letters form several words related to the verb "to suckle."

IMAGE 10.5 **A souvenir poster for *The Pied Piper of Hamelin*, adapted by Walter Freud.**

Courtesy of the Terezín Memorial.

claimed that the transport was being sent to build a new ghetto and Walter volunteered to help.[18] Ruth and approximately five hundred other women from Terezín/Theresienstadt volunteered for a transport leaving just a few days later that would supposedly reunite them with their men. She never saw Walter again. At Auschwitz she was selected for labor; she was liberated in Kudowa, a subcamp of Gross Rosen.

THE SCRIPT

With this work Freud perpetuated the long tradition of Purim plays: performances that contribute to the festive atmosphere of the holiday. Purim commemorates events that took place during the Jewish diaspora in Persia, in the capital city of Shushan, in the fifth century BCE. The Purim play traditionally features several figures from the biblical Book of Esther. The Persian king, Ahasuerus, is not an evil character but has been deceived by the villain Haman into agreeing to the murder of the Jews. Haman, the king's minister, begins to plot against the Jews after Mordechai, Ahasuerus's Jewish doorkeeper, refuses to bow to him (as a Jew, Mordechai bows only before God). Haman tells Ahasuerus that the Jews are disobeying the king's laws and requests a decree granting the enemies of the Jews the right to kill them all on the designated day. The king agrees, not knowing that Esther, his second wife, the young and beautiful queen, is a Jewish orphan and Mordechai's niece.[19] When Esther reveals Haman's plot to the king, Ahasuerus sentences Haman to death. Although he cannot annul his own royal decree, he issues a second decree granting the Jews permission to defend themselves and they triumph over their enemies. Vashti, the first wife of King Ahasuerus who was banished from the court for her disobedient behavior, often plays a role in the Purim play as well.

---

18 Makarova et al., *University over the Abyss*, p. 406.

19 Esther is tradionally referred to as Mordechai's niece; in the Book of Esther she is identified as the daughter of Mordechai's uncle.

Freud's text freely combines elements of the traditional Purim play with influences from the prisoners' daily life: a cabaret song about rampant gossip in the ghetto, a scene about the young Zionists' theoretical love of manual labor, etc. It culminates in a comic opera sung by Esther, Haman, Mordechai, and the King.[20] The work provides us with insight into Freud's own personal brand of "Jewish humor" and also with a rare look into the daily activities of young Zionists in the ghetto: how these young people, most of whom came from very assimilated families, learned about Jewish history and holidays, struggled to learn Hebrew, and prepared for a future in Palestine.

BIOGRAPHICAL INFORMATION

THE AUTHOR

WALTER FREUD was born on May 25, 1917. He was deported to Terezín/ Theresienstadt on March 31, 1942 and to Auschwitz on September 28, 1944. He perished.

THE ACTORS

The following actors are listed on the *Purimstück* poster:

DOV RÉVÉSZ appears in the database of the Institute of the Terezín Initiative as Pál Révész. He was born on January 7, 1922 and registered in Plzeň/Pilsen. He was deported from Prague to Terezín/ Theresienstadt on May 15, 1942. According to the database he was released from the ghetto on March 15, 1944 as a Hungarian citizen. This conflicts with information provided by Jiří Shmuel Bloch, who testified that Révész was deported to Auschwitz and subsequently perished.

ERICH HUPPERT, born on February 7, 1925, was deported on January 28, 1942 from Brno/Brünn to Terezín/Theresienstadt and on September 28, 1944 to Auschwitz. He was liberated in Buchenwald.

---

20 See sheet music on pp. 320–31 of this volume, IMAGES 10.6–17.

HANS or **HANUŠ EPSTEIN** was a common name in the ghetto. There are ten listed in the database, but only two appear to be of the right age. One was born on March 20, 1924. He was deported on January 22, 1942 from Plzeň/Pilsen to Terezín/Theresienstadt and on September 6, 1943 to Auschwitz where he perished. The other was born on March 17, 1925, deported from Brno/Brünn to Terezín/Theresienstadt on April 8, 1942, and to Auschwitz on December 18, 1943. He perished on April 21, 1945 in Schwarzheide.

FRANT. (FRANTIŠEK) WEISS was a common name in the ghetto. In the database of the Institute of the Terezín Initiative it appears eleven times, but there is only one who was approximately the same age as the other actors. Born on May 24, 1926, he was deported on January 28, 1942 from Brno/Brünn to Terezín/Theresienstadt and on September 28, 1944 to Auschwitz. He perished.

KAREL FLEISCHER, born on July 2, 1925, was deported on April 8, 1942 from Brno/Brünn to Terezín/Theresienstadt and on September 28, 1944 to Auschwitz. He perished.

The youth of homes Q710 (the Zionist youth home) and L410 (the girls' home where Freud worked) also participated in the play. One of the girls from the youth homes apparently played the role of Esther; all of the actors named on the *Purimstück* poster were male.

THE SURVIVORS CONTRIBUTING TO THE INTRODUCTION
AND ANNOTATION

MICHAL BEER (née **MAUD STECKLMACHEROVÁ**) was born on April 7, 1929. She was deported to Terezín/Theresienstadt from Olomouc/Olmütz on July 4, 1942 and was liberated in the ghetto. She now lives in Tel Aviv.

RUTH FELIX (née **FREUD**) was born on June 14, 1924. She was deported to Terezín/Theresienstadt on March 31, 1942 and to Auschwitz on Octo-ber 1, 1944. She was liberated in the slave-labor camp Kudowa.

JIŘÍ SHMUEL BLOCH was born on May 3, 1926. He was deported from Plzeň/Pilsen to Terezín/Theresienstadt on January 22, 1942 and to Auschwitz on September 28, 1944. He was liberated in the slave-labor camp Blechhammer. He now lives in Zichron Yaakov, Israel.

HANA REINEROVÁ was born on April 19, 1921. She was deported to Terezín/Theresienstadt on July 5, 1943 and to Auschwitz on October 1, 1944. She was liberated in Mauthausen. She passed away on June 1, 2007.

PURIMSPIEL

CHARACTERS[21]

> Director of the Theater Troupe
> King, also Ahitofel and A
> Haman, also Bal Marduk and B
> Esther
> Vashti (a man) and C
> Mordechai, also Nisibist and D
> The People of Shushan
> E

ACT I

The entire theater troupe, with the Director, enters through the audience and takes the stage, singing a Huha Horra.[22]

DIRECTOR. Now all you players, gather 'round
Look what an audience we've found
To watch the scenes that you'll perform:
Women, plain and fair of form,
Men, both poor and prosperous
The miserly and the sponsorous.
Bakers, cobblers, cooks, and jailers
Clerks and locksmiths, brokers, tailors

---

21 The cast list on the *Purimstück* poster names six actors (including Walter Freud himself) and the youth from homes Q710 and L410. This list of characters in the script also suggests a core cast of six (the Director and A, B, C, D, and E) and additional actors to play the smaller roles (Esther and the "People of Shushan"). Details regarding the characters are provided at the beginning of each scene.

22 Huha Horra: probably the hora (also spelled horah), a dance that originated in the Balkans and played an important role in the development of Israeli folk dance. It is often performed to the Hebrew folk song "Hava Nagila," which is perhaps the song the actors are singing as they enter. The significance of "Huha" is unclear; perhaps it is just a comic twist on the name of the dance.

All are gathered here today.
Quickly now, what shall we play?
Wait—where's Ahasuerus, our royal?

KING. Here, among his subjects loyal.

DIRECTOR. Would you please stop embarrassing me—
Is this how you earn your salary?
Get up here, drop the pretense
Those chairs are for the audience.

KING. I'll tell you why I'm here, to wit:
I'm looking for a place to sit.

DIRECTOR. Whatever has come over you?
The first two rows, as usual,
Are set aside for VIPs.

KING. Well, as the king, I'm one of these.

DIRECTOR. They're for the Jewish Council members
Not for stateless kings, remember . . .
Off-stage, you have no commonweal.

KING. And they—no robes, no crowns—are real?

DIRECTOR. Enough. We've got a packed-full house

MORDECHAI. As if we were playing *Die Fledermaus*![23]

DIRECTOR. So let's begin our tale sublime
Or we might just run out of time.
To all our honored guests:
A welcome unreserved.
We bring to you the very best
That human ears have ever heard,
That human eyes have ever seen,
If you don't like it, you can leave.
For those of you who choose to stay,
We'll gladly now present our play:

---

23 The operetta *Die Fledermaus* by Johann Strauss was performed in the ghetto under the direction of Hans Hofer, another author featured in this volume. See the Terezín Memorial, inv. no. PT 4045.

A *Purimfest*.
Wait—I mean a *Purimspiel*.
Guests, forgive me, please don't feel
Offended by these small delays
Soon we'll be *in medias res*.

MORDECHAI. That's Latin; it means, "in the middle of things."[24]

DIRECTOR. My players travel from ghetto to ghetto
With Nathan the Wise and Rigoletto[25]
For our spectators, what's the greatest hit?
They love it when we play that Shylock.[26]
But what today we'll represent
Are true, historical events
From long ago.
The Jews in Persia, as you know,
Were not at all well loved by the regime.

MORDECHAI. They were probably being blamed for some defeat.[27]

DIRECTOR. I'm the director; my company:
The king . . .

The King steps forward and bows.

KING. Ahasuerus, that's me.
Eternal sovereign on the stage,
I've ruled these boards for many an age
Returning faithfully once a year
For Purim, as you see me here.

---

24 More specifically, *in medias res* indicates the narrative technique of beginning a story in the middle of the action rather than at the chronological beginning of the events.

25 Gotthold Ephraim Lessing's work *Nathan the Wise* (*Nathan der Weise*) was performed several times in Terezín/Theresienstadt as a staged reading, and *Rigoletto* was one of several operas performed in the ghetto. See the Terezín Memorial, inv. nos. PT 3981 and PT 3923.

26 The break in the rhyme scheme is intentional. In the original script this verse reads "Und unser allergrößter Reißer / ist der vielgerühmte Scheilock."

27 The *Dolchstoßlegende* (stab-in-the-back legend) that circulated in Germany after the First World War relieved the military of responsibility for the defeat and blamed the loss on sabotage by socialists, Bolsheviks, and Jews. This legend was exploited by Hitler to turn public opinion against these groups.

DIRECTOR. Here is Vashti, looking good,
    A credit to modern womanhood.

VASHTI. I'm Vashti, proud and beautiful
    Just between us . . . the king's a fool
    He didn't know how to deal with me
    So I left the court and now I'm free.

DIRECTOR. In the Bible, it's explained differently.

HAMAN. In this group, I am number three
    But I'll conceal my evil intents,
    Cloaking them in deep silence.
    My defeat each year is nothing new
    But I'm still dead set against the Jews
    For the court bows down as I pass by—

DIRECTOR. Except for the old Jew Mordechai
    A central figure in the tale.

MORDECHAI. Before no power do I quail.
    I remain what I've always been,
    The uncle to the Jewish queen.

ESTHER. My name is Esther,
    And to the letter, my king fulfills my every wish.
    On his guard, always standing by
    Is my dear old uncle Mordechai.

DIRECTOR. And all the rest whom you see here
    They play the folk of Shushan.[28]
    The outcome of the tale's not clear
    For those who live in Shushan.
    Yes, every man is in suspense
    Inside the fortress Shushan.
    He can't know how the story ends
    He feels so small in Shushan
    But in his tales, he's twice his size[29]

---

28 In this passage, Shushan becomes an allegory for the ghetto itself.

29 Many survivors have described the widespread phenomenon of Terezín/Theresienstadt prisoners exaggerating the importance of their pre-war positions. See, for example, Utitz, *Psychologie života v terezínském koncentračním táboře*, pp. 22–3.

The little man in Shushan.
Though without omens, without signs,
The hopeful folk of Shushan
Believe Haman will get the noose
Then, oh, what joy in Shushan
Sometimes they're in a foul mood,
The rabble's roused in Shushan,
But what's to tell—we know them well,
The nasty folk of Shushan.

KING. Long live the folk of Shushan! (*He goes to the Director, puts the crown on his head.*) There—you have my crown. You play the king today; I won't do it.

ALL. What's going on, what's happening?

KING. I've been in the theater for years and I always play the king, the same king Ahasuerus every year! Always the same *Purimspiel*—I've had enough!

VASHTI. He's right. I'm not going to play Vashti anymore. (*The actor takes off his dress and bra and gives them to the Director.*)[30] You can play Vashti yourself.

DIRECTOR. But ladies and gentlemen, the audience!

KING. The audience knows the tale by heart already.

HAMAN. I'm not going to play Haman anymore either. (*Gives Mordechai the dagger.*) Mordechai can play Haman if he wants.

MORDECHAI. I know some Jews who gladly try to play the role of Haman, but I'm afraid you won't find anyone who wants to play the Jew!

DIRECTOR. But ladies and gentleman, the audience!

ESTHER. What about them? Always "the audience." Why does only the audience have the right to have fun on Purim? We have our rights too. The audience always laughs at the actors; today we'll laugh at the audience.

ALL. Bravo, bravo!

---

30 The list of characters indicates that this role is played by a man.

MORDECHAI. The laugh's on the audience—good idea; how should we begin?

DIRECTOR. But ladies and gentleman, the audience!

HAMAN. We don't give a damn about the audience. We're playing for ourselves today.

KING. But I'm not going to play the king.

VASHTI. And I'm not playing Vashti.

HAMAN. I won't play Haman either.

MORDECHAI. Then, my worthy fellow actors, I suggest you play, for once, the people of Shushan.

KING. That's an idea—we'll play the folk of Shushan, not the life of the court and castle.

HAMAN. Yes, that's an idea—I will play a simple man of the people.

DIRECTOR. Ladies and gentleman, the audience! (*The players leave the Director alone, rush to a box, pull out costumes and start to dress as pious Jews. The Director turns to the audience.*) Ladies and gentlemen, the actors . . .

Two actors grab him, stick him in the box of costumes and close the lid. The curtain falls.

ACT II[31]

In front of the curtain.

Herr Fröhlich, Herr Schön, Herr Popper, Frau Kohn, Frau Zwicker, Frau Müller.[32]

---

31 This act is based on the song "Goodbye, Herr Fröhlich" ("Auf Wiedersehen, Herr Fröhlich"), which was a popular cabaret number in the inter-war period. The *Purimspiel* version, however, may have been recited rather than sung; the German-language verses in the original do not appear to fit the melody. Another Terezín/Theresienstadt version of the song has been published in Migdal, *Und die Musik spielt dazu*, pp. 98–9. It was probably performed in the ghetto by cabaret artists Bobby John and Ernst Morgan. See Volker Kühn, "Kabarett im KZ," in booklet to the CD/DVD set *Totentanz: Kabarett im KZ* (Neckargemünd: Edition Mnemosyne, 2000), p. 45; and the Terezín Memorial, inv. no. PT 4099.

32 These six characters were probably played by the "people of Shushan," i.e. the youth from homes Q710 and L410. I have retained the German "Herr" and "Frau" instead of using "Mr." and "Mrs." in this translation to preserve the rhythm of the original text.

HERR FRÖHLICH. Herr Schön, have you heard?

HERR SCHÖN. Heard what, Herr Fröhlich?

HERR FRÖHLICH. There's something up in Shushan.

HERR SCHÖN. Well, well, you don't say? And where, Herr Fröhlich?

HERR FRÖHLICH. Now I don't know exactly, but probably at the castle.

HERR SCHÖN. The castle? *Auf Wiedersehen*, Herr Fröhlich.

HERR FRÖHLICH. *Auf Wiedersehen*, Herr Schön.

HERR SCHÖN. Herr Popper, have you heard?

HERR POPPER. Good day, Herr Schön. What's going on?

HERR SCHÖN. There's something up in Shushan at the castle.

HERR POPPER. Well, you don't say, and what, Herr Schön?

HERR SCHÖN. Now I don't know for sure, but what else could it be? It's very likely something with that Haman.

HERR POPPER. So something's up with Haman in Shushan?

HERR SCHÖN. *Auf Wiedersehen*, Herr Popper,

HERR POPPER. *Auf Wiedersehen*, Herr Schön.

HERR POPPER. Oh, what luck to see you here, Frau Kohn.

FRAU KOHN. Oh, my dear Herr Popper! What's happening?

HERR POPPER. There's something up in Shushan at the castle—and certainly it's something with that Haman.

FRAU KOHN. With Haman? and what, Herr Popper?

HERR POPPER. What else could it be? He's surely gotten mixed up in some quarrel.

FRAU KOHN. *Auf Wiedersehen*, Herr Popper.

HERR POPPER. *Auf Wiedersehen*, Frau Kohn.

FRAU KOHN. Frau Zwicker, Frau Zwicker!

FRAU ZWICKER. My word, I haven't seen you in so long.

FRAU KOHN. Now, have you heard the news, Frau Zwicker?

FRAU ZWICKER. I don't have to hear it all to know it all.

FRAU KOHN. There's something up in Shushan, Haman's gotten mixed up in some quarrel at the castle, that's all that I can tell you—

FRAU ZWICKER. Do you have this from a reliable source?

FRAU KOHN. Am I perhaps an unreliable source?

Auf Wiedersehen, Frau Zwicker.

FRAU ZWICKER. *Auf Wiedersehen*, Frau Kohn.

A brief pantomime, where all whisper softly and only the word "Shushan" is heard.

FRAU MÜLLER. Herr Schön, Herr Schön!

HERR SCHÖN. What's going on, Frau Müller?

FRAU MÜLLER. Haven't you heard the news?

HERR SCHÖN. I know, there's something up in Shushan!

FRAU MÜLLER. And how, Herr Schön!!

HERR SCHÖN. Do you know?

FRAU MÜLLER. Hmph, do I know . . . that Haman's gotten mixed up in some quarrel at the castle, with the king and the queen, and the king will see him hang.

HERR SCHÖN. Is it really so?

FRAU MÜLLER. Of course, and now we'll go free; the fourteenth of Adar has been cancelled!

HERR SCHÖN. *Auf Wiedersehen*, Frau Müller.

FRAU MÜLLER. *Auf Wiedersehen*, Herr Schön!

ACT III

The curtain opens. Five men are bent over their books, studying.[33]

A, B, C, D, E, Herr Schön.

---

[33] This act perpetuates a traditional aspect of many Purim plays: scenes satirizing *pilpul*—the seemingly endless, minute analysis of Jewish law.

A. The matter is as follows: you need two witnesses to convict a man according to eyewitness testimony. Now the two witnesses testified that they saw Reuben kill Simeon[34] on such and such a day, in such and such a place. Now two new witnesses appear and say to the first two: you've committed perjury. On that day you weren't even there, but somewhere else with us. The law says: the first witnesses gave false testimony and they must be condemned to death. When they are executed, they will be executed together, because one cannot be executed alone. If one of them dies in the meantime, then you must let the other live, because one alone cannot bear false witness—testimony from one person means nothing; you need the testimony of two witnesses.

B. So both of them sinned together and therefore they can only be punished together.

C. But how can the first two witnesses be punished based on the testimony of the two new witnesses? Here are two witnesses and there are two witnesses. Two against two. How do we know that the new witnesses are telling the truth?

D. This question is nothing new. Many sages have already spoken of it—Rashi[35] and others as well. The matter is as follows: each of the first two witnesses is interrogated alone so one doesn't hear what the other says, and now the two new witnesses testify against one of them at a time, so each time it's two against one.

E. All right, and this means that, if one of the false witnesses dies, the other can't be executed. Now I ask you: what happens if they are going to the place where they will be executed, and on the way, one picks up a stone and kills the other. So he has

---

34 Reuben and Simeon, the eldest sons of Jacob and Leah, were two of the patriarchs of the twelve tribes of Israel. In this scene they are significant simply as biblical names; Reuben the patriarch did not murder Simeon.

35 Rashi (Rabbi Shlomo Yitzhaki, c.1040–c.1105): a medieval French rabbi who authored one of the best-known and most beloved commentaries on the Torah.

to be set free, because they must be executed together. By killing the other, the first one saves himself. Is this possible?

A. What a question. He will still be executed because he murdered the other witness.

B. This answer is no answer. He cannot be executed for killing the other witness, because it isn't murder.

C. And why not? Why shouldn't it be murder?

B. Because it is written: only he who destroys life commits a murder. However, he who kills a dead man, that is, a man who is as good as dead and who cannot be saved, he who kills such a person commits no murder. Here a man has to be executed, he is already on the way to his execution, thus he is, for all practical purposes, already dead. How can they execute the other for killing him? He has killed a dead person.

D. It is true that he who is being led to his execution is practically dead, so whoever kills him does not commit murder and thus cannnot be punished for murder. He is free, and he cannot be executed for his false testimony because one witness alone cannot be executed. He is therefore truly free. If the one false witness kills the other false witness, he frees himself.

E. That's impossible. A criminal escapes his punishment by committing another crime? That's impossible. The second witness, who for all practical purposes is dead, since he is on the way to his execution, is in the same position as the other. Both are being taken to their executions. Both are lost. Now the one kills the other and for that he should go free?

A. Well, if one can do it, the other can too. If the other, the second witness, had killed the first, he would have gone free. Thus the other had the means to save himself, so he wasn't really lost, he wasn't as good as dead, he wasn't dead but alive. Thus the first witness would have killed a living man, would have committed a real murder, so he can be executed for that and the whole matter doesn't help him at all.

B. If that's the case, if it doesn't help the first witness to kill the second one, if he will still be executed, then it wouldn't help the second witness to kill the first. He would still be executed. So if he has no way to save himself, if he will be executed anyway, then again he is as good as dead and the first witness kills not a living man but a dead man and he is free.

HERR SCHÖN (*rushing in*). Friends, we are saved, the decree of the fourteenth of Adar has been overturned!

A. *Scha*[36]—don't bother us, can't you see we're working?

HERR SCHÖN. What will you do now? Everything is back the way it was, Haman is no more, Mordechai will be a minister, friends, think about it, what will you do now? Celebrate, be glad!

A. Don't bother us now; we have more important things to discuss. So, my friends, the matter is apparently not yet resolved. Let us begin again from the beginning.

Curtain.

ACT IV[37]

A (Ahitofel),[38] *B (Bal Marduk),*[39] *C, D (Dardanalus),*[40] *E (Eshpruta the Nisibist),*[41] *Herr Fröhlich, a platoon of soldiers, and their leader.*

---

36 Yiddish for "shhhh."

37 The characters in this scene represent conflicts (class tensions, anti-Semitism even among converted Jews, etc.) between various social groups in inter-war Central Europe and within the ghetto itself.

38 Ahitofel (also spelled Ahitophel) was an advisor to King David of Israel who conspired with David's son Absalom to overthrow the king. The plot failed and Ahitofel committed suicide.

39 Bal Marduk was a god worshipped in ancient Mesopotamia and patron deity of the city of Babylon. By the late 2nd millenium BCE he was regarded as head of the pantheon of Babylonian gods.

40 Perhaps Dardanus. In Greek mythology, Dardanus was a son of Zeus and Electra. He founded the city of Dardania on Mount Ida in the Troad. According to some accounts, he came to the Troad after surviving a great flood.

41 The School of Nisibis, founded in 350 CE, was an important spiritual center of the early Church of the East, which belonged to the Syriac tradition of Eastern

B. Well aren't you a sight, Mr. Ahitofel. You have certainly seen better days, Mr. Ahitofel—you were a soap factory magnate from the land of the Nile, Mr. Ahitofel and his donkeys' milk,[42] you didn't even recognize me, Bal Marduk; you didn't even give me the time of day!

C. Be quiet, Bal Marduk. Why are you always looking for trouble? Now we are all equal, the same fate awaits us all, now we are all workers, ordinary workers with ordinary shovels.

B. And with several thousand Thalers[43] hidden away with some Persian.

A. You talk about the Persians, Bal Marduk, as if they were strangers. I am a Persian too and what's it to you if I've given my brother a sum of money for safekeeping? I am a worker now, all the same.

D. You a worker? You will always be the famous Ahitofel Ltd., manufacturer of soap—and swindler.

A. What? My soap received first prize for Persian-made products and was used by the former queen Vashti . . . Queen Esther washes in the *mikveh*,[44] but she probably uses my soap too. You speak out of jealously, Mr. Dardanalus, because your Astarte[45] toothpaste was for sale only at flea-markets.[46]

Christianity. Nisibis, the ancient city where it was founded, is now known as Nusaybin and is located in modern-day Turkey. The meaning of the name Eshpruta is not clear.

42 Donkey's milk has been recognized since the time of Cleopatra for its cosmetic properties.

43 Clearly an anachronism: the first Thaler coin, the Joachimsthaler, was minted in the sixteenth century from silver obtained from St. Joachim's Valley in Bohemia.

44 Jewish ritual bath.

45 The goddess Astarte appeared in Ancient Egypt along with other deities of the northwest Semitic peoples. She was worshipped especially in her aspect as a warrior goddess, and was also associated with fertility and sexuality.

46 In the original, *Einheitströdelmarkt*, a term combining *Einheitsmarkt* (standard market) with *Trödelmarkt* (flea market).

D. You are mistaken, Mr. Ahitofel. Do you know Poseidon, Greek god of the sea, who wields a trident with three teeth? Yes—he cleans those teeth only with Astarte toothpaste.

E. You Jews, always quarreling amongst yourselves . . . Jewish rabble.

All laugh.

C. And what are you, if I may ask?

E. I am a Nisibist.

B. Followers like you surely make the goddess Nisibis very happy.[47] Why are you here with us then? The decree of the thirteenth of Adar applies only to us Jews.

E. I know that. I'm here by mistake.

A. It was always my ideal to become a Nisibist—Ahitofel is my name.

E. Eshpruta—nice to meet you.

A. At the next possible opportunity we will become co-religionists; of that you can be sure.

D. In the meantime, pay attention to your ditch-digging—a little faster now!

A. How dare you? Don't you know who I am? Haven't you seen my chariot? The axles made of gold, the seat of cedar wood— now the mayor of Shushan drives around in it and I'm suppo- sed to take orders from you on how to do my work—besides, I'm a worker just like you, what do you have against . . .

B. Stop it. Workers don't quarrel amongst themselves.

A. That's right. So why does he act so spitefully toward me? Why is he always trying to oppress me? You are no better than I am, if not worse.

C. What are we working on, anyway? Really, what is this for, what is it supposed to be?

D. Do you need to know what all the work they assign you to is for?

---

47 There is no goddess Nisibis; Freud's reference is probably for comic effect. The Nisibist probably represents a Jewish convert to Christianity.

E. It's terrible, the way you treat each other! It serves you right that they chose the thirteenth of Adar for you—what did our sort do to deserve this, that by mistake we have to spend our lives with rabble like you?

HERR FRÖHLICH (*rushes in*). Gentlemen, haven't you heard? Why do you still have those shovels in your hands?

A. Because we are workers.

HERR FRÖHLICH. Stop! we're free again—the whole thing's been resolved—the decree of the thirteenth of Adar is cancelled—Esther and Mordechai have taken care of everything—we're free!!

D. That's impossible!

A. We are free, workers, we are free.

B. Our time has come!

D. We need a rallying cry.

E. Long live the goddess Nisibis.

C. Long live Persia.

B. A slogan, quickly, a slogan. The rallying cry of the liberated worker!

A. Give us back our factories, give us back our factories! (*Hangs a poster with the slogan "Vashti is better."*)

> *All the others exit, chanting their slogans. D comes back, sees Ahitofel's poster, tears it down and hangs up his poster, "Astarte is even better." The chanting of slogans fades away in the background. Troops march in with brooms in their hands. The end of each broom-stick is wrapped with a rag. Their leader marches in front, and all wear paper hats. Herr Fröhlich enters from the other side.*

HERR FRÖHLICH. Have you heard? We're finally free!

LEADER. What's that? What did you say?

HERR FRÖHLICH. It's true; Mordechai will be a minister.

LEADER. Well, brothers-in-arms! This is news for us; now we will be able to help our people, old Mordechai will negotiate with the king—we will make our demands! Our discipline and our weapons will determine our future.

HERR FRÖHLICH. Tell me, why have your soldiers wrapped the ends of their weapons?

LEADER. Very simple. Since we belong to the faithful, we know the power of God the Almighty: If God wills it, a broom can shoot![48] (*Calls one person out of the ranks and whispers to him*) Attention!

HERR FRÖHLICH. How can they hear and obey orders when you speak so quietly?

LEADER. Don't worry; word will get around.[49]

HERR FRÖHLICH. Well trained.

LEADER. See for yourself!

HERR FRÖHLICH. Left face!

No one moves; only one person asks: "Where are we going?"

LEADER. Not like that; no one will understand. *Gen misrach*![50] (*All make the appropriate turn. More commands of this type:* Schmone essre, *i.e. three steps back.*[51]) Yes sir, we don't negotiate, we demand *lech lechha*![52] Company—march!

Exit.

ACT V

The characters are digging a pit.[53]

---

48 A proverb, variously identified as Yiddish or Russian.

49 Perhaps a satirical reference to gossip in the ghetto. See *bonke* (glossary).

50 *Gen* is apparently based on the German verb *gehen* (to go), and *misrach* in Hebrew means "east."

51 Pious worshipers take three steps forward at the beginning of the *Shmoneh Esrei* (as it is spelled in English), the key prayer of the worship service, and three steps backward at its conclusion, approaching and departing from God's throne without turning their backs.

52 In the Book of Genesis, *lech lechha* (Hebrew for "go" or "leave") was God's commandment to Abraham to leave his native land and his father's house for the Promised Land that God would show him.

53 This act represents members of the Zionist youth movement in the ghetto.

A, B, C, D, E, the Zofeh,[54] *Herr Fröhlich.*

All sing "Anu nihje harishonim."[55]

A. What are we building here, anyway?

B. The foundation for a barracks.

A. A foundation? A foundation—aha, an economic foundation![56]

B. No, a foundation made of concrete.

A. A concrete foundation? That's not possible. That can't be!

C. Why not?

A. Concrete foundation? Ridiculous! There is nothing in the world that is not based on an economic foundation—are you trying to convince me that barracks constitute an exception and are based on a concrete foundation?

C. Of course.

A. Reactionary!

D. *Chaverim, chaverim. (Looks at his watch.) Anachnu muchrachim, anachnu medabrim rak ivrith achschav!*

E. *Ken, ken rak ivrith!*[57]

---

54 *Zofeh,* from the Hebrew word for "see," here means "scout," a nickname for the youngest members of the Zionist movement.

55 A Hebrew song sung by Zionist youth. The lyrics mean "We will be the first" (that is, the first pioneers in Palestine). See Jakob Schönberg (ed.), *Shire Erets-Yisrael* (Jerusalem: Hozsaah Ivrith Ltd., 1947), p. 40.

56 In the original, *ökonomische Grundlage* (sometimes translated as "economic basis"), a term from Karl Marx's *Outlines of the Critique of Political Economy* (1858).

57 *Chaverim, chaverim*: Hebrew for "Friends, friends" (that is, fellow Zionists). The transliteration of Hebrew has been preserved from the original German-language script in order to retain potentially meaningful irregularities (comically intentional errors, indications of lack of knowledge of the language on the part of the character or the author, etc.). Only obvious inconsistencies have been corrected. *Sch* should be pronounced like the English *sh, j* like the English *y, th* like the English *t,* and *z* like the English *ts.* For more information, see the pronunciation guide for German in this volume, pp. xxii–xxiii. ***Anachnu muchrachim, anachnu medabrim rak ivrith achschav*:** Hebrew for "We must, we will now speak only Hebrew!" ***Ken, ken rak ivrith*:** Hebrew for "Yes, yes, only Hebrew!"

C (*whispers to Aaron*). I just met someone today—I'm telling you, Aaron, a girl . . . beautiful . . .

E. *Rak ivrith chaverim, rak ivrith!*[58]

C. *Jesch li naarah jaffa meod, jesch li naarah jaffa meod, hoi hoi jefejfija. (He is silent for a moment.)* Halleluja Halleluja . . .

D. *Chaverim, chaverim—jesch li—jesch li . . .*

E. *Gam naarah?*

D. *Lo lo, jesch li, jesch li.*

ALL. *Mah jesch lechah?*

D. *Jeschli ha ha (bursts out) ha definita!*

E. *Ha definitionah? Ejze definitionah?*

D. *Mah ze chaluz? Ata mevijn?*

---

58 The following few lines are in Hebrew. The translations are as follows. *Rak ivrith chaverim, rak ivrith*: "Only Hebrew, friends, only Hebrew!" *Jesch li naarah . . . jefejfija*: "I have a very pretty girl, I have a very pretty girl, *hoi hoi* a beauty." This is a line from a Hebrew folk song. As Jiří Shmuel Bloch suggests, perhaps C's Hebrew is so poor that the only way he can express himself is by quoting this line from the song. Interview with Lisa Peschel, February 10, 2008. *Chaverim, chaverim—jesch li—jesch li*: "Friends, friends, I have, I have . . ." *Gam naarah?*: "Also a girl?" *Lo lo, jesch li, jesch li*: "No, no, I have, I have . . .". *Mah jesch lechah?*: "What do you have?" *Jeschli ha ha ha definita*: (Hebrew and Latin) "I have a . . . a . . . a . . . definition!" D apparently does not know the Hebrew word for definition, *hagdarah*, and instead uses the Latin word *definita*. *Ha definitionah? Ejze definitionah?*: "You have a definition? What definition?" *Mah ze chaluz? Ata mevijn?*: "What is a *chaluz*? Do you understand?" That is, D has learned the word *chaluz* (pioneer) and is asking the others if they know what it means. *Lo ani mi-Berlin!*: "No, I am from Berlin!" This joke is based on the similarity of the Hebrew phrases "Do you understand?" and "Are you from Wien (Vienna)?" *Chaluz jachol . . . beli nekud*: "A *chaluz* (pioneer) can read without points, but not live without points." A joke based on a double meaning of the word "points." In the first phrase, "points" indicates the system of dots, known as *niqqud* or *nikkud*, used as diacritical marks to represent vowels or distinguish between alternative pronunciations of letters of the Hebrew alphabet. The second phrase refers to ghetto-specific point systems. Manual laborers received extra bread for hard labor, night labor, etc., and their work was measured with a point system. Prisoners could also obtain coupons worth a certain number of points (see *Bezugsschein* [glossary]) that could be traded in for items in the ghetto shops. See Hyndráková et al., *Acta Theresiania*, pp. 158–9, 226.

E. *Lo ani mi-Berlin!*

D. *Chaluz jachol likroh beli nekudoth, aval ejno jachol lichjoth beli nekud.*

E (*looks at his watch*). *Dajenu!*

B. Well, that was a wonderful definition.

A. He only does that because he thinks there'll be something in it for him. Later, in exchange for his words of wisdom, he'll demand a *vatikim* certificate.[59]

B. That's not true. His ideas are brilliant. He will definitely play a leading role in *ivrith* propaganda. For example, yesterday at the rabbis' meeting he proposed that the sentence in the Haggadah, *Leschanah haba bi jeruschalajim* should be changed, for propaganda reasons, to *leschavuah ivri haba bijeruschalajim*.[60]

C. Look out, here comes a *zofeh*!

All begin to work and sing "Anu nihje . . ."

ZOFEH (*to a member of the group who is working clumsily*). Pardon me, can I help you?

E. So you too want to experience the joys of manual labor?

Dajenu!: "Enough for us!" A reference to the prayer sung in the Passover Haggadah.

59 In the inter-war period the British government distributed a limited number of certificates for immigration to Palestine. The *vatikim* (veterans), as senior members of the Zionist movement, were the first to receive such certificates.

60 Ivrith **propaganda**: this may be a reference to the Propaganda Department of the Jewish National Fund (JNF [in Hebrew, Keren Kayemet LeYisrael, KKL]). The JNF was founded in 1901 to buy and develop land in Palestine for Jewish settlement. The Propaganda Department concerned itself with disseminating the symbols, knowledge, and ideas that gave Zionism its meaning. See Yoram Bar-Gal, *Propaganda and Zionist Education: The Jewish National Fund, 1924–1947* (Rochester, NY: University of Rochester Press, 2003). **Haggadah**: the Jewish religious text that sets out the order of the Passover Seder, commemorating the Jewish liberation from slavery in Egypt as described in the Book of Exodus. **Leschanah haba bi jeruschalajim**: Hebrew for "Next year in Jerusalem." A pious refrain used at the end of the Passover Haggadah. **Leschavuah ivri haba bijeruschalajim**: Hebrew for "The next Hebrew week in Jerusalem." That is, he encourages other Jews not to wait until "next year" for emigration to Palestine.

ZOFEH. No, I am from Yad Tomechet[61] and when we happen to encounter someone who is old or unfit for work, we are supposed to try to be helpful, and I've been watching you for a while . . .

D. But Jochanan, what are you thinking, this is a *chaver* . . .

ZOFEH. David, is that you? I didn't even recognize you!

C. Aaron—Yad Tomechet, I just remembered, excuse me for leaving early, I almost forgot, I have a *sichah*[62] for Yad Tomechet.

ZOFEH. Is it hard, working like that with a shovel?

D. What an idea, Jochanan! For us, for whom work is a maxim and a categorical imperative,[63] we who, with the workers . . .

E. *Lav medabern vor dem jeletl!*[64]

D. Oh, sorry, I though he was over sixteen.[65] Well, Jochanan, to work is very nice, and healthy for the body and the spirit . . .

ZOFEH. David, you must have forgotten, you're supposed to have a *sichah* with us now. Come on or it will be too late.

D. That's right—Aaron, please excuse me, I have a *sichah* right now with the *zofim* . . . come on, let's go.

A. Well, of course . . .

B. We'll take care of your part of the work, we'll just have to dig a bit harder . . .

---

61 Yad Tomechet (Hebrew for "a helping hand") was a youth organization in the ghetto. Members volunteered to visit the elderly and infirm, read aloud to them in their quarters, and help them with other tasks.

62 Hebrew for "meeting" or "discussion."

63 The categorical imperative is the central philosophical concept in the moral philosophy of Immanuel Kant, introduced in his *Groundwork for the Metaphysics of Morals* (1785). It is best known in its first formulation: "Act only according to that maxim whereby you can at the same time will that it should become a universal law."

64 A saying derived from Hebrew, German and Yiddish: "Don't talk that way in front of the child!" See Bondy, *Mezi námi řeceno*, pp. 84–5.

65 According to Jewish tradition, the age of adulthood is 13 for boys and 12 for girls. It is unclear as to why a 16-year-old would be regarded as a *jeletl*.

E. *Chaverim*, we've forgotten, we haven't learned our usual five vocabulary words of the day yet, and you know how important it is for us to be able to name all aspects of our daily lives in *ivrith*.[66]

B. Speaking of *ivrith*: I completely forgot, there's an *ivrith* seminar today, I have to run or I'll be late. Please excuse me, Aaron, but I have to leave a bit early—I'll stay longer tomorrow— *shalom*, *chaverim*.

A. *Shalom*. So, what are the five vocabulary words for today?

E. I've prepared them:

Bet simcha al galgalim = the *polička*[67]

Gan Eden = the Provisions Department

Gehinom = the *Jugendfürsorge*, that is a *nifal*.[68]

A. How do you know that?

E. Because it is passive.[69]

Im tirzu ehn zoth agadah[70] = When you have connections, there are no fairy tales.

---

66 According to survivor Lisa Gidron-Wurzel, a council for Jewish education in the ghetto invented Hebrew neologisms to describe life in Terezín/Theresienstadt. See Makarova et al., *University over the Abyss*, p. 148.

67 A complex trilingual joke. *Bet simcha al galgalim* (Hebrew for "a happy house on wheels") is an ironic translation of the Czech expression *bordel na kolečkách*, literally "a bordello on wheels," slang for "a mess." *Polička* (Czech for "small shelf") refers to the small shelves mounted on the bunk beds in the youth homes. They were often the only private space the young prisoners possessed, but the leaders of the youth homes sometimes threatened to remove them because they were not kept clean. For the importance of these shelves for the young prisoners, see Křížková et al., *We are Children Just the Same*, p. 51.

68 *Gan Eden*: Hebrew for "the Garden of Eden." **Gehinom**: Hebrew for "hell." **Jugendfürsorge**: see glossary. The young Zionists might have associated the *Jugendfürsorge* with hell because it organized labor assignments for all youth older than 14. **Nifal**: Hebrew for "passive," as in a passive verb form.

69 The meaning of this joke is unclear. All sources indicate that the *Jugendfürsorge* workers were anything but passive in their efforts to help the youth in the ghetto survive and to prepare them for life after the war.

70 Hebrew for "If you wish it, it is no fairy tale." This legend at the beginning of Theodor Herzl's utopian novel *Old-New Land* (1900) became a well-known motto of the Zionist movement. E's variation means that, in the ghetto, anything is possible if one has the right connections.

And the last one: *Totzereth Haarez*[71] = the *bonke*.

But now I have to hurry. There's a seminar today. It's not enough simply to do work all day; one must also educate oneself about work. Please excuse me, I have to go now.

A. Then I'm here all by myself . . . *shalom* . . . I should actually go to a *Freizeitgestaltung*[72] sometime too; otherwise I'll lose touch with my *chaverim*.

Voices are heard offstage, growing louder and coming nearer: "That's impossible," "That's wonderful," *etc.*

HERR FRÖHLICH. If I say it, you can believe it!

Enter chaverim B, C, D, and E. Instead of shovels they hold large posters. A is completely astounded.

D. Well, Aaron, you're still here and with a shovel in your hand? You're going to miss *aliyah*.[73] Hey, come with us—take the blade off that shovel and put something useful on it!

A takes the blade off the shovel and replaces it with a poster without words, only dots.[74]

Exit all, singing "Aha alinjnu."[75]

---

71 Hebrew for "Made in Israel." In this case, probably intended to mean "made in Terezín/Theresienstadt": a *bonke* (see glossary) was a rumor "manufactured" in the ghetto.

72 The *Freizeitgestaltung*, in addition to administering other types of cultural events, organized series of lectures on many topics, including Zionism. For information on the lectures given by Zionist leader Dr. Franz Kahn, see Makarova et al., *University over the Abyss*, p. 58.

73 Hebrew for "emigration to Israel."

74 Perhaps a further reference to *niqqud*.

75 A Hebrew song that was sung by Zionist youth. In the songbook *Shire Erets-Yisrael*, the lyrics are written *arzah alinu* (*arzah* meaning "to the land," that is, of Israel, and *alinu* meaning "we have gone up"). The *Aha alinjnu* in the original script may be a typing error, or a joke along the lines of the Huha Horra at the beginning of the *Purimspiel*. See Schönberg, *Shire Erets-Yisrael*, p. 8.

The Director crawls out of the box and calls others back.

The Director, A, B, C, D, E, the Zofeh.

DIRECTOR. Players, please don't take offense
    But you won't please the audience
    By criticizing in your play
    All the errors of their ways.
    Although it's quite hilarious,
    It simply can't go on like this!
    All the players laugh: ha ha ha ha!!!

A. Look how our director worries

B. But today we'll choose the story

C. Tomorrow, Shylock,

D. The wise old Nate,

E. *Die Fledermaus,*

A. Will be back on stage.

ZOFEH. But who likes that old *Purimspiel,*

B. A story that's not even real,

C. It ends the same way every year

D. That's really what they want to hear?

ZOFEH. A tale as ancient as the Bible,

A. A boring, old and dusty trifle.

DIRECTOR. Don't underestimate old rhymes;
    The public loves them every time.
    If you give them something new,
    The first thing that they ask of you
    Is: "I haven't heard anything about this, has it been in the
        newspapers?"
    And if "no, not yet" is what you say,
    Their interest evaporates.
    My friends, a hint:
    Unless it has appeared in print
    The truly novel, lastest thing

They don't find very interesting.
The moral of my story's clear:
Give them what they expect to hear.

A. Well, if that's the way you feel . . .
It's true that last year's *Purimspiel*
Pleased everyone, without exception
And truly fit the celebration.
We could put it on again.

DIRECTOR. Oh, yes, the scene where they all sing,

HAMAN. At dinner, as the queen requests,

DIRECTOR. Haman and the king are both her guests
For reasons they cannot begin to know.
Any objections to this show?
Then come, let's lose no time at all:
We take you to the banquet hall.

ACT VII

The King enters, singing.[76]

King, Haman, Esther, Mordechai.

KING. I don't know why I've been invited[77]
To come to dinner tonight
Perhaps the queen is angry
And wants to start a fight.

HAMAN. I don't know why I've been invited
To come to dinner tonight
Maybe the king cannot stand it
To be alone with his wife.

---

76 In this act the characters sing their lines to melodies from operas, operettas, and films. See sheet music on pp. 320–31 of this volume, IMAGES 10.6–17.

77 The King and Haman sing a parody of a verse from Heinrich Heine's *Buch der Lieder* (1827) known as "Die Lorelei." The poem has been set to music multiple times. The best-known version was composed by Friedrich Silcher in 1838.

KING. Tonight, what will it be?[78]

Perhaps you'll tell me

If your love belongs to me

Have you invited me here to tell me

I'm the only one that you hold dear?

HAMAN. Striking up a friendship with you[79]

Would be advantageous

Striking up a friendship with me,

Would that be so outrageous?

KING (*noticing Haman*). You too, she's invited you here[80]

You too, you too

How could she be so insincere

You too . . .

Beat it, Haman, beat it![81]

ESTHER. Gentlemen[82]

Welcome here to dinner, welcome here to dinner, welcome here to dinner . . .

KING. Lovely and sweet little queen[83]

Do you know what fidelity means?

Why is he here for dinner and drinking?

What were you thinking?

My little queen.

---

78 The song "Heute Nacht oder nie" is from the film *Lied einer Nacht* (1932). Music by Misha Spoliansky, lyrics by M. Schiffer. This song made Spoliansky famous, but in 1933 the Nazis banned his works because of his Jewish origins.

79 The song "Eine kleine Freundschaft mit Dir" is from the film *Liebeskommando* (1931). Music by Robert Stolz, lyrics by Robert Gilbert.

80 The song "Auch Du wirst mich einmal betrügen" is from the operetta *Zwei Herzen im Dreivierteltakt* (1933). Music by Robert Stolz, lyrics by W. Reisch.

81 The motif *Weiche, Wotan, weiche* from Richard Wagner's opera *Das Rheingold* (1869).

82 The song "Grüßt euch Gott, alle mit einander" is from the operetta *Der Vogelhändler* (1891). Music by Carl Zeller, libretto by Moritz West (Moritz Nitzelberger) and Ludwig Held.

83 The song "Kleine entzückende Frau" is from the film *Früchtchen* (1934). Music by Nicholas Brodszky, lyrics by Konrad Drey.

HAMAN. Who knew a woman's heart[84]
 Held such deception
 Bringing us both here
 To toy with our affections

KING. I've had enough of this,
 Enough of this business
 Deceitful to the core,
 That's just how she is

ALL. That's just how she is,
 That's just how she is,
 That's just how she is,
 That's how she is.

HAMAN. Now something wonderful's in store[85]
 What will we have for dinner?

KING. It's probably mostly made of pork

HAMAN. Horsemeat would be a winner

ESTHER. Keep guessing . . . what has cloven feet?
 The steak could be of camel meat[86]
 Oh, but the dumplings, the dumplings, the dumplings are
  made of wheat.[87]

 (*All three sit down.*)

HAMAN and KING. Drink, drink, Esther mine, drink[88]

---

84 The aria "La donna e mobile" is from the first act of Giuseppe Verdi's opera *Rigoletto* (1851).

85 The song "Es muß was Wunderbares sein, von Dir geliebt zu werden" is from the operetta *Im Weißen Rößl* (1930). Music by Ralph Benatzky, libretto by Benatzky, Hans Müller-Einigen, and Erik Charell, lyrics by Robert Gilbert. The work was banned in Nazi Germany because of the Jewish origins of its co-authors.

86 Camel meat, like pork, is not kosher.

87 Many dishes in the ghetto were prepared from some type of substitute. Lentil soup was made of synthetic lentil powder, and meat usually meant a few shreds of horsemeat boiled in a soup. The dumplings, however, which were actually made of wheat, represented a welcome exception. Jiří Shmuel Bloch, interview with Lisa Peschel, February 10, 2008.

88 The song "Trink, Brüderlein, trink" is often attributed to Wilhelm Lindemann but the music was actually written by Paul Bendix and the lyrics by T. P. Henning

Leave all your *daiges*[89] behind
Drink, drink, Esther mine drink

ESTHER. Drink, drink, darling king, drink
Leave all your *daiges* behind
Drink, drink, drink, Haman, drink
You'll both be *schicker*[90] tonight.

HAMAN and KING. Drink, drink, Esther mine, drink
Can't you get rid of this guy?
Drink, drink, Esther mine, drink,
My blood pressure's starting to rise.

KING. Yes, he's a minister, but lazy as hell.

HAMAN. I could be king very well.

KING. What do you see in him? you know that it's true:

HAMAN and KING. I am the right man for you.

KING. My love for you, his love for you[91]
Are not equal things
He is just a minister
But I, I am the king.
Now I hope you'll tell us both
Exactly why we're here.

ESTHER. Don't ask me why, don't ask me why
I thought you'd know, my dear.

HAMAN. Don't ask me any questions.[92]

ESTHER. Now it's time for your confession.

---

in 1927. Bendix (1870–1944) was deported from Berlin to Terezín/Theresien-stadt on May 29, 1943, where he perished.

89 Yiddish for "worries," from Hebrew *da'agot*. See Bondy, *Mezi námi řečeno*, p. 41.

90 Yiddish for "drunk," from Hebrew *shikor*. Ibid., p. 135.

91 "Meine Liebe, deine Liebe" is from the operetta *Das Land des Lächelns* (1929). Music by Franz Lehár and libretto, lyrics by Ludwig Herzer and Fritz Löhner-Beda.

92 The aria "Nie sollst du mich befragen" is sung by the title character in Richard Wagner's opera *Lohengrin* (1850).

KING. Oh won't you stop with this game[93]
> Don't try making me jealous.

HAMAN. What should I do about the fact that I'm so handsome?[94]
> What should I do about it, that they all love me?
> What should I do here at this most peculiar party
> That our queen Esther's thrown just for the king and me?

ESTHER. Don't ask, don't ask[95]
> Just look deeply into my eyes
> And you will see all you need to know.
>
> *Mordechai enters.*

MORDECHAI. Forgive me, my dear Esther[96]
> That *schifles*[97] I must give you
> I look around
> And clearly something's missing
> Why don't you serve
> *Scholet*, *ritschert*, and *bejlek*?[98]
> Here all I see is
> Only *chazir*![99]

ESTHER. How cold your hands are, uncle
> To warm them I will try

MORDECHAI. I have no *hentschkes*[100]
> A *nebbish* and dirt-poor am I!

---

93 The original German version begins with a direct quote "Santuzza, reize mich nicht" from the German translation of the duet between Santuzza and Turiddu in the opera *Cavalleria rusticana* (1890) by Pietro Mascagni (libretto by Giovanni Targioni-Tozetti and Guido Menasci).

94 The song "Was kann der Sigismund dafür, daß er so schön ist?" is from the operetta *Im Weißen Rößl*. Music by Ralph Benatzky, libretto by Benatzky, Hans Müller-Einigen, and Erik Charell, and lyrics by Robert Gilbert.

95 The song "Frag nicht" is from the film *Ein Lied geht um die Welt* (1933). Music by Hans May, lyrics by Erst Neubach.

96 The aria "Che gelida manina" is from Giaccomo Puccini's opera *La bohème* (1896).

97 Yiddish for "criticism."

98 All traditional Jewish dishes. See *scholet* (glossary).

99 Hebrew for "pig." Probably intended to insult Esther's guests as well.

100 Yiddish for "gloves."

HAMAN. I am, from head to toe . . . [101]

MORDECHAI. *Gamal gamali* . . . [102]

HAMAN. . . . so ready for your love.

KING. It was never love[103]
>   Just a flirtation insincere
>   Esther is my wife
>   You can be sure!

HAMAN. Come to me tonight, my dear[104]
>   All is ready, never fear
>   Come to me at ten
>   He won't see you then
>   For the lights go out at nine[105]
>   In the dark you will be mine.

KING. Into the fight, I can't believe my eyes [106]
>   You dare to try
>   Annoying my wife

(The manuscript ends here.)

---

101 The song "Ich bin von Kopf bis Fuß auf Liebe eingestellt" is from the film *The Blue Angel* (1930). Music and lyrics by Friedrich Holländer.

102 Hebrew for "camel." Mordechai again insults Haman by calling him by the name of a non-kosher animal. *Gamal, gamali* was a well-known Hebrew song. See Schönberg, *Shire Erets-Yisrael*, p. 87.

103 The song "Liebe war es nie" (1927) was a popular tango. Music by Fred Markesch, lyrics by Fritz Rotter.

104 The song "Hab' ein blaues Himmelbett" is from the operetta *Frasquita* (1922). Music by Franz Lehár, book and lyrics by A. M. Willner and H. Reichert.

105 Lights in the prisoners' housing in the ghetto had to be turned off by a certain time in the evening. The time varied according to the season of the year. See Adler, *Theresienstadt*, p. 92.

106 The aria "Votre toast, je peux vous le rendre," popularly known as "March of the Toreadors," is from Georges Bizet's opera *Carmen* (1875).

WALTER FREUD

IMAGES 10.6–17 **The medley from Act VII of the *Purimspiel*. Reconstructed and arranged by Winfried Radeke, graphics by Andreas Jocksch.**

22
mich liebst o - der nie. Bin ge - la - den
love be - longs to me. Have you in - vi - ted me
27
ich, um dir zu sa - gen: Schatz, ich lie - be dich.
here to tell me I'm the on - ly one that you hold dear?
32
Haman
Ei - ne klei - ne Freundschaft mit dir kä - me mir ge - le - gen; ei - ne klei - ne
Stri-king up a friend-ship with you would be ad-van - ta - geous. Striking up a
37
King
Freundschaft mit dir, du hättest nichts da-ge - gen? Auch du bist bei
friend-ship with me, would that be so out - ra - geous? You too, she's in-

WALTER FREUD

ein dir zum Es - sen noch ei - nen, was wird man mei - nen, du klei - ne Frau?
he here for din - ner and drin - king? What were you thin - king, my li - ttle queen?

Haman
O wie be - trü - ge - risch sind Wei - ber - her - zen, la - det sich zwei ein, mit ih - nen zu scher - zen.
Who knew a woman's heart held such de - cep - tion? Bring - ing us both here to toy with our af - fec - tions.

King
Hat man schon so - was je - mals ge - se - hen? Das sind die Frau - en, doch jetzt ist's ge - sche - hen,
I've had e - nough of this, e - nough of this busi - ness. De - ceit - ful to the core, that's just how she is.

All
ist's ge - sche - hen, ist's ge - sche - hen, ist's ge - scheh'n, doch jetzt ist's ge - scheh'n.
That's just how she is, that's just how she is, that's just how she is, that's how she is.

WALTER FREUD
88
Haman
King
(9) Es muss was Wun-der-ba-res sein,______ was wir jetzt es-sen wer-den. Das meis-te
Now some-thing won-der-ful's in store;______ what will we have for din-ner? It's prob-a-bly
(Tango)
93
Haman
Esther
ist wahrscheinlich Schwein,______ doch auch et-was von Pfer-den. Ihr bei-de ra-tet nicht so fehl,
most-ly made of pork.______ Horse-meat would be a win-ner. Keep gues-sing: what has cloven feet?
98
das Fleisch kann sein auch vom Ka-mel, a-ber die Knö-del, die Knö-del, die Knö-del, die sind aus
The steak could be of ca-mel meat, oh, but the dumplings, the dumplings, the dumplings are made of
103
King & Haman
Mehl.______ (10) Trink, trink, Es-ther mein, trink, las-se die
wheat______ Drink, drink, Es-ther mine drink, leave all your

Esther

dai-ges zu Haus;______ trink, trink, Es-ther mein, trink. Trink,
dai-ges be - hind.______ Drink, drink, Es-ther mine drink. Drink,

trink, Kö-nig mein, trink, las-se die dai-ges zu Haus,______ trink, trink,
drink, darl-ing king, drink, leave all your dai-ges be - hind.______ Drink, drink,

King & Haman

Ha-man mein, trink, schi-cker kommt ihr heut nach Haus.______ Trink, trink,
drink, Ha-man, drink, you'll both be schi-cker to - night.______ Drink, drink,

Es-ther mein, trink, schick doch die an-dern nach Haus;______ trink, trink,
Es-ther mine, drink, can't you get rid of this guy?______ Drink, drink,

WALTER FREUD
143
King
Es-ther mein, trink, die Gall' geht vor ihm mir her - aus. Er ist zwar Mi - nis - ter, doch faul wie ein
Es-ther mine, drink, my blood pressure's start-ing to rise. Yes, he's a minister, but la - zy as
152
Haman
King
Schwein. Fast Kö - nig könnt' ich hier sein. Was hast du von ihm, wo er doch nichts kann.
hell. I could be king ve - ry well. What do you see in him? You know that it's true:
161
King & Haman
King
Ich bin der rich - ti - ge Mann. Mei - ne Lie - be, sei - ne Lie - be, die sind gar nicht
I am the right man for you. My love for you, his love for you, are not e - qual
11
168
gleich; er ist nur Mi - nis - ter, doch ich hab ein Kö - nig - reich. Und ich möch - te ger - ne wis - sen,
things. He is just a min - is - ter; but I, I am the king. Now I hope you'll tell us both ex -

Esther
was du von mir willst. O frag mich nicht, o frag mich nicht, ich dach - te, dass du's fühlst.
act - ly why we're here. Don't ask me why, don't ask me why; I thought you'd know, my dear.

Haman
Esther to Haman
Nie sollst du mich be - fra - gen. Dir will ich es nur sa - gen.
Don't ask me a - ny ques - tions! Now it's time for your con - fes - sion!

King
San - tuz - za, rei - ze mich nicht, mach mich nicht ei - fer - süch - tig.
Oh, won't you stop with this game? Don't try mak - ing me jea - lous.

Haman
Was kann der Ha - man denn da - für, dass er so schön ist,_______ was kann der
What should I do a - bout the fact that I'm so hand - some?_______ What should I

193
Ha - man denn da - für, dass man ihn liebt. Was soll der Ha - man denn heut
do a - bout it, that they all love me? What should I do here at this
198
bei dem Fes - te ma - chen, das un - s're Kö - ni - gin ihm und dem Kö - nig
most pe - cul - iar par - ty that our queen Es - ther's thrown just for the king and
203
Esther
gibt. Fragt nicht, fragt nicht, schaut nur tief in mei - ne
me? Don't ask, don't ask, just look deep-ly in - to
15
208
Au - gen, und ihr könnt al - les wis - sen von mir.
my eyes, and you will see all you need to know.
16
sfz

Mordechai
Er - lau - be mir, mei - ne Es - ther, dass ich dir jetzt Schif - les ge - be. Was ich hier su - ch(e), doch
For - give me, my dear Es - ther that schif - les I must give you. I look a - round and
nir - gends a - ber se - he.
clear - ly some - thing's mis - sing.
Nun, ich su - che Scho - let, Rit - schert und Bej - lek, und was ich fin - d(e), ist
Why don't you serve scho - let, rit - schert and bej - lek? Here all I see is
rit.
affrettando rit. Esther a tempo
lau - ter Cha - ser. Wie eis - kalt ist dies Händ - chen, kommt, ich ma - che es Euch
on - ly cha - zir! How cold your hands are, un - cle, to warm them I will
affrettando rit. a tempo

237
Mordechai
rit.
affrettando
warm. Hab doch ka Hentsch - kes, ich bin doch neb - bich
try. I have no hentsch - kes; a neb - bish, and dirt-poor, am
rit.
affrettando
243
Haman
arm.
I.
18 Ich bin von
I am, from
248
Mordechai
Haman
Kopf bis Füß Ga - mal, ga - ma - li auf Lie - be ein - ge - stellt.
head to toe Ga - mal ga - ma - li ...so rea - dy for your love.
(18 a)
(18 b)
251
King
19 Lie - be war es nie, nur ei - ne klei - ne Lie - be - lei. Es-ther ist mein Weib,
It was ne - ver love, just a flir - ta - tion in - sin - cere. Es-ther is my wife;
(Tango)

Haman
256
___ es bleibt da - bei. Schatz, ich bitt' dich, komm heut Nacht, al - les ist be - reit ge -
___ you can be sure. Come to me to - night, my dear; all is rea - dy, ne - ver
260
macht, ___ komm erst ge - gen zehn, niemand wird ___ dich sehn,
fear. ___ Come to me at ten; he won't see ___ you then.
265
denn man löscht das Licht Punkt neun und im Finstern war - tet dein....
For the lights go out at nine; in the dark you will be mine.
King
269
Auf, in den Kampf, so geht's ___ nicht ___ an, dass der Ha - man be - läs - ti - gen kann.
In - to the fight, I can't be - lieve my eyes. You dare to try an - noy - ing my wife!

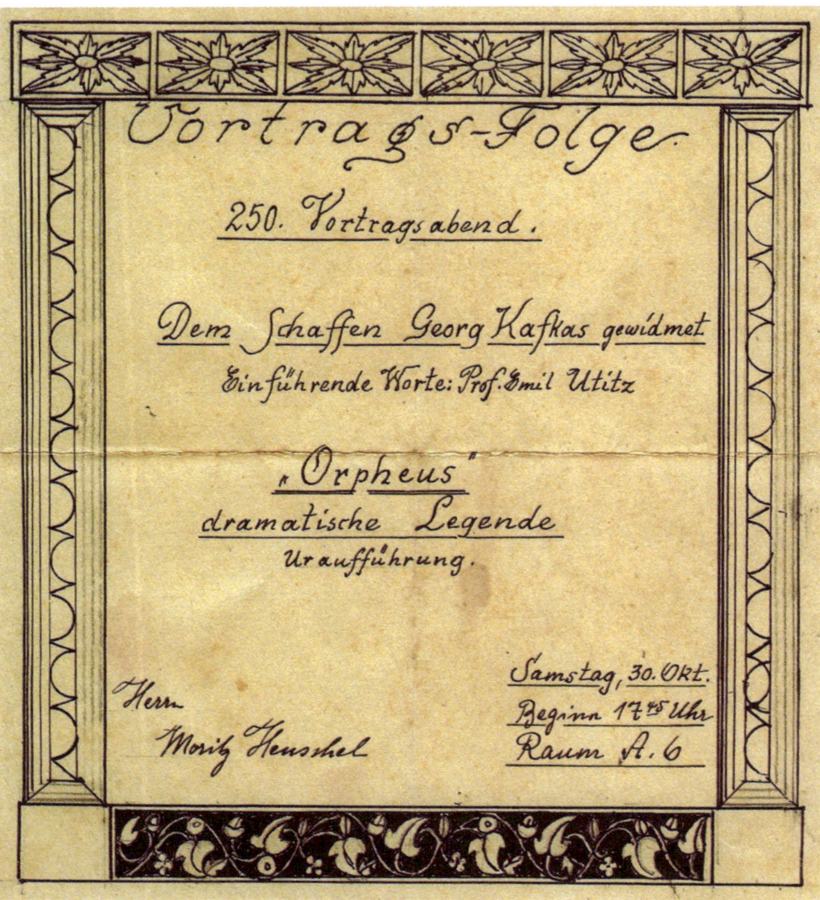

GEORG KAFKA

THE DEATH OF ORPHEUS

The work of young poet Georg Kafka, a distant relative of Franz Kafka, was highly regarded by older writers and scholars in the ghetto. Emil Utitz, professor of philosophy, psychology, and aesthetics at Prague's German University, asked Philipp Manes[1] to support Georg Kafka's work and spoke at the premiere of *The Death of Orpheus*.[2] Manes himself descri-bed Kafka as "a true poetic talent" and compared him with the young Hugo von Hofmannsthal.[3] Two of Georg Kafka's poems, "Death Prayer" (*Todesgebet*) and "Blessing of the Night" (*Segen der Nacht*), were pub-lished in 1960.[4] A third, untitled poem was published in the Terezín/Theresienstadt diary of Philipp Manes.[5] His dramatic poem *The Death of Orpheus* was found in the archives of the Jewish Museum in Prague.[6]

THE AUTHOR

Georg Kafka was born in Teplice-Šanov/Teplitz-Schönau on February 15, 1921. He began his secondary education there but graduated in 1939

IMAGE 11.1 *(facing page)* **Souvenir poster for the performance of Georg Kafka's Orpheus.**
Courtesy of the United States Holocaust Memorial Museum.

---

1 Philipp Manes was head of the Manes Group, which organized many German-language lectures and dramatic readings in the ghetto. For a list of the Manes Group's activities see the Terezín Memorial, inv. no. PT 3981.

2 There is no title on the original script. H. G. Adler called it *The Death of Orpheus* (*Der Tod des Orpheus*) and Manes called it simply *Orpheus*, which is also the title that appears on the preserved poster. See Adler, *Theresienstadt*, p. 759; Manes, *Als ob's ein Leben wär*, pp. 148, 245; and the United States Holocaust Memorial Museum, Morris and Hildegard Henschel Collection, inv. no. RG–24.021.

3 Manes, *Als ob's ein Leben wär*, p. 148.

4 Manfred Schlösser (ed.), *An den Wind geschrieben. Lyrik der Freiheit. Gedichte der Jahre 1933–1945* (Darmstadt: Agora 1960), pp. 211, 220.

5 Manes, *Als ob's ein Leben wär*, p. 351.

6 Shoah History Archive, Terezín Collection (T), inv. no. 326.

from the German-language *Gymnasium* on Štepanská street in Prague. He attended a teacher-training course organized by the Jewish community in Prague and taught for two years until he was deported with his parents from Prague to Terezín/Theresienstadt on July 23, 1942.[7]

In the ghetto, Georg Kafka wrote fairy tales, poems, and dramatic texts, and translated contemporary Czech writers into German. In his diary Manes describes how Kafka's employment provided him with rare access to writing materials:

> During the day he worked with the files of the central archives of the ghetto [. . .] and at night, when his duties allowed (when outgoing transport lists were being prepared, sometimes the typists worked all night, for several nights in a row), he sat at the typewriter, transcribing his creations.[8]

Kafka's first work written for the stage, the prose drama *Alexander in Jerusalem*, was not selected for presentation by the Manes Group. However, Manes considered the young author's next submission, *The Death of Orpheus*, to be "a lyrically mature work revealing great facility with language and full mastery of form."[9] In the fall of 1943 the Manes Group celebrated their two-hundred-and-fiftieth meeting by premiering the work as a staged reading. In the list of the Manes Group's activities only one actor is named: Friedrich Lerner.[10] As Manes wrote in his diary, Lerner read the poem alone "after a reading with the roles distributed did not result in the necessary unity of style. It was a great success for the young poet and for the performer."[11]

In the spring of 1944 Kafka wrote what was to be his last work for the stage: a puppet play titled *The Golem*.[12] His father died in March

---

7 Jürgen Serke, *Böhmische Dörfer: Wanderungen durch eine verlassene literarische Landschaft* (Vienna: Zsolnay, 1987), p. 450.

8 Manes, *Als ob's ein Leben wär*, p. 149.

9 Ibid.

10 Terezín Memorial, inv. no. PT 3981.

11 Manes, *Als ob's ein Leben wär*, p. 150.

12 Ibid., p. 269. The text *The Golem* (*Der Golem*) has not been found, but a review is preserved in the Theresienstadt Collection in the archives of Yad Vashem in Jerusalem, file 0.64/078.

1944, and when his mother was included in the transport scheduled to depart on May 15, 1944, he joined her voluntarily. Even after his deportation he remained a poetic presence in the ghetto: one of his works was awarded first prize in a poetry contest held in August 1944.[13] Kafka did not live to accept this recognition. His mother perished, probably murdered in the gas chambers of Auschwitz immediately upon arrival, and Kafka died months later in Schwarzheide.[14]

THE SCRIPT

H. G. Adler noted that *The Death of Orpheus* was "without reference to Theresienstadt or the period."[15] It is true that in his poem Kafka does not engage with the day-to-day details of the ghetto. However, the work does appear to reflect certain aspects of his own life; for example, it includes an emotionally wrenching scene between Orpheus and his mother, who rarely appears in treatments of the legend. But Kafka goes far beyond the autobiographical. In his lyrical rhymed text—which I have translated as blank verse, following the rhythm of the original as closely as possible—he addresses the most profound questions that confronted his fellow prisoners: How much is one prepared to sacrifice for a loved one? What is the nature of artists' responsibility toward those who rely on them? Can one make peace with death by embracing it? Although Orpheus inevitably perishes, Kafka's work does not end in despair. His friends and companions adopt his verses as their own, perpetuating his work even after his death.

---

13 Manes, *Als ob's ein Leben wär*, p. 391.

14 Adler, *Theresienstadt*, p. 619.

15 Adler, *Theresienstadt*, p. 759. According to Adler the reading was repeated often and with great success. The Manes Group's own records list four performances in 1943 and none in 1944. See ibid., p. 602; and the Terezín Memorial, inv. no. PT 3981.

THE AUTHOR

GEORG (in Czech, Jiří) **KAFKA** was born on February 15, 1921. He was deported from Prague to Terezín/Theresienstadt on July 23, 1942 and voluntarily joined a transport to accompany his mother, which departed for Auschwitz on May 15, 1944. He perished in Schwarzheide.

THE ACTOR

FRIEDRICH (BEDŘICH) LERNER, born on April 14, 1906, was deported from Tábor to Terezín/Theresienstadt on November 16, 1942, and to Auschwitz on September 28, 1944. He perished.

PROLOGUE

Alkaios, rustically dressed and holding a shepherd's staff, stands before the closed curtain.

ALKAIOS. Alkaios is my name, just a shepherd boy, the same
As all my friends, my brothers and companions.
My home is here, among these verdant canyons,
The quiet valleys, dark with dusk and peaceful.
The poet in our midst, though, loves me most
And sometimes he regards me dreamily,
When he, a simple shepherd, like us,
Joins us by our fire at night and then
He takes his lute out of its bandolier
Or plays upon the melancholy pipes.
Sometimes in harmony, we quietly join in
And sing along in gentle reverie.

What is it that the poet sees in me?
Why does he look at me with eyes so lustrous,
Strangely bright, as he begins to play?
Mature beyond my years, a boy no longer
Seventeen years old I'll be in springtime
But, much more I've experienced, believe me,
I've been in love before, as you have been,
But both of us were still so painfully shy,
We hardly dared exchange a longing glance.
How should I understand Orpheus's secret?
What is it that the poet sees in me?

Perhaps *you* could look deep into his heart
By listening to the rhythm of his verse.
Play out your life the way that we perform this play,
Present it earnestly, but oh, never forget:
It's just a play. Regard our tale,

So quickly here then gone,
As a model for your own life, if it pleases you:
Love your poet well, the way that we love ours,
Be like the legends, the tales that we have told you,
Still and sonorous, and with emotion deep.
Live with the poet his autumn melancholy
And celebrate with him when comes the spring.
Then will he love you as he loves his shepherds,
And when our brief scenes end, the curtain falls again,
You'll leave as much behind, as we leave of our world.

Gentle music, that through the evening drifts
And if it pleases the Unseen Ones well
Will ring forever as a quiet song . . .

The curtain rises. It is dark.

ORPHEUS (*voice*). Oh autumn of the earth, oh, deepest stillness,
The restless darkness of my solitude.
Whom can I offer these, my tired verses?
Flute melody, a sound slowly receding,
Oh autumn of the earth, deep solitude . . .

EURYDICE (*voice from afar*). My love, do you still gaze upon the water,
A mirror that reflects your gentle mourning?
Where are you, Orpheus? My longing's wings
Are heavy from the flight to your dreams' realm.

ORPHEUS (*voice*). Now in the evening light the earth resembles
My sleepy, languishing Eurydice.
My song, it ripened in our love's warm sunlight,
Two verses, oh, were we, within a poem of dreams.
Who played, back then, upon the soft and gentle
Strings of the lyre, glowing in the moonlight?
Oh autumn of the earth, oh deepest stillness . . .

*Slowly daylight breaks. Shepherds bring offerings of fruit and
wreaths of autumn flowers to the altar of Persephone.*

FIRST SHEPHERD. Through empty fields there blows a cold, dark wind.

SECOND SHEPHERD. Pan no more frightens nymphs out in the meadows.

THIRD SHEPHERD. I feel now like I did when I, a dreaming child,
     Was left alone, abandoned by my playmates.

OLD SHEPHERD. And without joy this year were our poor harvests,
     The autumn spent itself in stifling ground,
     The vineyard grapes that usually glow dark crimson,
     Like tongues of flame entwined, have not grown plump
          with nectar . . .

FIRST SHEPHERD. The gods are long departed from our valley
     And far away they play their merry games . . .

SECOND SHEPHERD. The peasant reaches, empty-handed, skyward,
     Up toward a God so infinitely far . . .

ORPHEUS (*voice from afar*). Oh autumn of the Earth, deep solitude . . .

THIRD SHEPHERD. Fog rises on the river banks already
     And muffles cries of fawns lost in the mist . . .

ORPHEUS (*voice from afar*). Where fades away my song, my
          happiness? My woe?

OLD SHEPHERD. We walk, slowly descending the staircase of our hours
     While sun and flowers alternate with snow . . .
     Death is a mystery . . .

FOURTH SHEPHERD. The fruit becomes the seed; however, its sweet
          juice
     A blessing granted by the generous gods.

FIRST SHEPHERD. Our autumn had no radiance, no vigor . . .

SECOND SHEPHERD. To know of spring and autumn, how each
          completes the other,
     (*Pointing to Persephone's altar*) Ask this maiden, who holds in
          slender hands
     The secrets of the earth and all its blessings . . .

CHORUS OF SHEPHERDS (*Strophe*). Persephoneia, oh![16] Lovely one
          who deep in Pluto's chambers

---

16 As in the original script, the chorus uses the Homeric form of the name
Persephoneia; elsewhere the form Persephone is used.

Sets blooming flowers ablaze, over the tables of stone
You, consecrated to death, your gestures of longing entangled
Caught in the folds of your dress, in folds that descend restlessly
And in your longing's footfalls, in reaches of Earth's endless
    vastness,
Which you, with strict-measured steps, encircle, a wandering
    shadow.

(*Antiphon*) Persephoneia, comforter among the shadows,
Maidenly, gentle, glowing with warm loving light,
You who will always return, you, consecrated to life
Leaving the twilight-filled house, you carry the earthenware
    jug
Filled to the rim with the dark, with poppies, and bearing
    the weight
The burden of suffering and might, from Pluto's terrible house,
Hold it tight, girl, in your arms, mourning your fate and
    yourself
Into eternity, into the spring and beyond.

CHORUS. Persephoneia, oh, you who the ominous path
    Cheerfully walk and the sorrow
    Of falling night you preserve, held in your sweet smiling
        features,
    You set blooming flowers ablaze, over the tables of stone
    You, the one in whose face, as if in the most precious vessel
    Life and death meet and make a heavenly wine.
    Grant to our earth renewed fertility . . .

ORPHEUS (*voice from afar*). Oh melody of deepest loneliness!
ALKAIOS. Leave her in peace; your chorus of petitions
    Is like a forest where she'll lose her way.
    Persephone, so gentle, lost herself
    In silence, standing just before the gate
    To the garden of your grievances that only baffle her.
    Just one has found her heart, as if young earth
    Has yielded herself humbly to the plow:
    He offered up his songs upon her altar fair

And to his sweet tones she inclined her ear.
Just one, just Orpheus, was by this girl beloved . . .

OLD SHEPHERD. The poets, they are like old wells, in ruins,
From which the waters never cease to run,
Young maidens come to cool their warm, flushed faces
In fresh water, before night begins . . .

ALKAIOS. Orpheus bound the day in clasps of bronze
And shattered the clay vessel of midnight
He brought to her, before the night had ended,
The glowing jewels, as light as birds in flight:
The shy rhymes that he had for her invented.

FIRST SHEPHERD. She kept him with her in her girlish night
Returned again, again, yet never had her fill
Of her singer and his merry dances.

SECOND SHEPHERD. And now on all the paths deep silence reigns . . .

ALKAIOS. She loved the figures traced out in his songs
And danced them all with feet as light as spring,

OLD SHEPHERD. And cheerful were the pastures in our valley
Full of fruit and glowing, lustrous, sweet . . .

ALKAIOS. All thanks to Orpheus; it was to him we owed
The greatness of the year and harvests rich.
An ecstasy seized beasts and trees and stones when
He played upon the lyre; they swayed, intoxicated
In his emotions' evening-quiet bay.
He simply smiled and he remained alone
And only played full of sweet drunkenness
Until, his passion spent, his great heart finally still
And lost in contemplation of the gods,
He stopped and set the golden lyre aside . . .

FIRST SHEPHERD. The earth was heavy with fertility.

SECOND SHEPHERD. His song was celebrated in all the fields' furrows
The juice pressed from the grape, the sweet tone of his harp
His love matured in slowly ripening fruit
On ancient trees deep in the olive groves.

THIRD SHEPHERD. Where is he now? Has he left us alone?

FOURTH SHEPHERD. The song of Orpheus, it penetrates the earth . . .

FIRST SHEPHERD. He sings no more? Does he not know his homeland?

ALKAIOS. Although the landscape lives in all his features,
    He's silent now. He has not taken up
    The lyre, he plays no more, since his beloved left . . .

FOURTH SHEPHERD. Call Orpheus! Call him, ask him for a song . . .

OLD SHEPHERD. Yes, call Orpheus, invoke the memories.

ORPHEUS (*voice from afar*). Farewell—oh, a word composed of
        dusk . . .

ALKAIOS. Our hands are as if bound and strangely heavy,
    He was the mediator of all our quiet wishes
    And was the ferryman of our poor hours
    Into which, like a boat, our dreams we gently loaded,
    Then rowed away, in yet-unknown directions
    Toward fulfillment on night's quiet shores . . .

OLD SHEPHERD (*Strophe*). Orpheus, oh where do you wander, on
        wild and overgrown pathways
    You who have left us now, deep in the moon absorbed.
    Are you the guest of Narcissus? Of Apollo? Of dancing
        Oreades?[17]
    Or do you dream alone
    Of the lost happiness of blissful twosomeness?

ORPHEUS (*voice, closer*). I am the lute that carries all your sadness . . .

OLD SHEPHERD (*Antiphon*). Hear, Orpheus, for you,
    The fast-wilting meadows cry out,
    The longing of perishing flowers, closing their petals forever,
    Weeping and calling, abandoned are we too . . .

ALKAIOS. We are a drink that spoils without you . . .

ORPHEUS (*voice, quite close*). The lyre, it falls silent when love dies.

---

17 In Greek mythology, an Oread or Orestiad was a type of nymph who lived in
mountains, valleys, and ravines.

CHORUS. Orpheus, you fall like the snow from distant skies, and veil
Us in a blanket of words, oh, wrap us up in your poem
Come to us, veil and star, feeling the pulse of the earth,
Who gives herself freely to none, surrenders to you and is yours,
When you her harvest-weary, her dusty brow you soothe.

Be an island in the breaking waves,
A towering column in the sanctuary,
Bright-colored flowers in the days of grayness
Be an answer to our darkest questions
And sound, like the sea, eternal beauty's fame!

ALKAIOS. Behold our hands, imploringly we raise them!

Orpheus, dressed all in black, appears on the rock.

ORPHEUS. Alone
Upon this peak
I know neither death nor life
Only the clouds, that distant winds are weaving,
Travel with me as companions now.
This peak, drenched always in the morning's glow
This mountain, my home
The blooming meadows are my countenance
The skylark's song, it is my handiwork
Eternal, like God's heaven, never ceasing,
Only wandering clouds my dream companions
And now my home, it is this peak
Alone.

You, however, only weakly mirror
The eternal flame.
You, who will never know God,
Nothing is yours.
You pile your ruins higher, longing to approach him
You dream of marble towers, of spirit fixed in stone
But you will never know the longed-for union.
Alone, upon this peak, I know I know neither death nor life . . .

ALKAIOS. This Orpheus was not the man, the master
The loving friend who bade us fond farewell.

The singer of the songs that wove their spell
To teach his friends humility, surrender . . .

ORPHEUS. Alkaios, 'tis you, who of friendship speaks?
I love you more than all the other shepherds
And from your face, your feminine features pale,
I read the echo of soft melodies,
That swarmed like bees from lute-strings resonating
And sometimes, glowing like the light of stars,
Come drifting through the silence of my nights.

ALKAIOS. Oh Orpheus, Orpheus, why are you silent now?
Oh vessel brimming over with song intoxicating . . .

ORPHEUS. What other choice remains to me, my friend?
What do you know, child, of the land of poppies
What do you know of longing just to rest,
Your heart still pure, like whitest alabaster . . .

ALKAIOS. Pure are you too, pure like me, as if from the sea arisen . . .

ORPHEUS. Already etched into my ageing features
Are sweet and guilty pleasures, vice of the lyre's strings
For boys like you, eyes dreamy, heavy-lidded,
The more mature squander themselves away
And crowns that would incite no king to envy,
They place, so tenderly, with tender fingers
Upon a boy's long and play-tangled hair . . .

OLD SHEPHERD. You've not yet reached the fullness of your years
Illuminated by an early glow
Your words are now of one who sees his end
And from the lively doings of his fellows
Turns his tired faced away, in silence dark.

ORPHEUS. Time is the only thing that brings us wisdom.
Your autumn of maturity you reach
In a flash of sudden understanding
When after years of wandering, you pause briefly
To bless your bread and wine at silent hearths.

CHORUS. For us, oh Orpheus, reach again for your lute,
Sing of your life's sweet fullness and abandon,

That we may enjoy the gods' secrets, revealed by you and
>your music,
Enjoy them at cheerfully laden banquet tables.

ORPHEUS. The lute, my friends, expect no more to hear it.
>Just melodies that echo in the winds.
>These verses, oh, that you so deeply craved,
>And all the songs of mine that so beguile you,
>Reverberations, that with me now fade . . .

OLD SHEPHERD. The gods' violin are you. Don't you feel the hand
>That holds you fast and plays upon your strings?

ORPHEUS. Oh, happy was I too, 'til in the shadowland,
>To which a narrow path winds down among the shades,
>Eurydice, beloved, too soon bade me farewell

ALKAIOS. Show us the lute, whose tone we all so long for,
>Please, Orpheus, if only from afar . . .

CHORUS. Brave is the heart of the man who looks upon eternal beauty
>He swings himself into the path of melodious, circling stars
>Lift up the holiest harp, held in the evening aloft
>Orpheus, show us the holy and shimmering lyre
>Show us the strings that Apollo has chosen to play,
>Like a torch gleaming at Bacchus's nightly feasts . . .

ORPHEUS. It lies submerged, sunk deep in blackest water.
>I broke it on the cliff that stands along the banks,
>Then let it slip into the watery darkness.
>It seemed to me the strings I'd torn and broken
>Sang quietly, sang on from darkest depths . . .

CHORUS. Alas, the lute, now submerged,
>No more song under the starlight
>Deep-flowing currents sound within its strings
>And in the depths even the Tritons weep.

DRYAD. Alas, no more song under the starlight.

CHORUS. Just as with Icarus's powerful wingstrokes
>Hope is what carried us up, hope was a gift from your lyre,
>Burned by the heat of the sun, a sun wrapped in black
>>mourning veils

We plummet now into the sea, singed by the heat of the flames
Falling and falling, down, deep in the house of the demons.

DRYAD. Alas, no more song under the starlight!

CHORUS. And in the depths even the Tritons weep.

ORPHEUS. It was your fate, to live in troubled times.

CHORUS. Oh, all the light fades away!
Cheerful wellsprings dry up,
Poisonous fog starts to rise,
Poet, your song dissipates . . .

DRYAD. Oh, all the light fades away!

CHORUS. Shepherd, your flock scatters wide!

ALKAIOS. And evenings, standing as if before locked coffers
The maidens listen in the dreamy distance,
The girls who loved the clear sound of your voice,
They wait for hours for a little song
Stay wakeful long before they finally rest . . .

DRYAD (*from afar*). Alas, no more song under the starlight . . .

ORPHEUS. Oh, if my lute were not already buried,
The girlish thing, I'd give it now to you.
For just above your head, my slim young shepherd boy,
I hear the wings of my destiny beating . . .
A note unknown is ringing through my halls
The earth, it sinks beneath my every step
It seemed to me today that I heard voices,
That called me home from my accustomed path.
Today I watched the leaves, so slowly, strangely falling,
As if they bore no more the weight of wishes . . .

You are still too young, all these things to fathom,
The autumn lies so lightly on your shoulders,
But one like me, with feet weary from wandering
Through lengthy melodies, he loves the word "perhaps."

Perhaps this is the day of which we've never spoken,
The hour made for us since the beginning,

Will finally take us up, like a tiny boat
That rocks until the children fall asleep . . .

ALKAIOS. Why do you, Orpheus, long so much for death?

ORPHEUS. I've seen our first creations fall to ruins
What we've of late acquired, it slips away . . .

OLD SHEPHERD. Yes, downward leads the staircase of our hours . . .

ALKAIOS. But one like you who moves through the fast-ebbing
And grayish days in mourning, a Titan,
He gives the shoreless streams of featureless endeavor
New meaning and direction for his friends.
To all the pain of life his heart lies open,
Vanished nations rise and live again in him.
His dream no more a thing, from which he late awakes,
For deep within his eyes, the very stars are born
And our God rests in him, as in brocaded night . . .

ORPHEUS. So you, a child, explain my little lifetime.
Oh hours, the hours that I have spent this way . . .

OLD SHEPHERD. One moment of fulfillment has more meaning
Than a hundred years of waiting before a portal closed.

ORPHEUS. Love was the only thing that freed my spirit.

CHORUS. May he who, like you, has lost Eurydice
Put on the black robes of mourning, as if for eternity.
Wander long roads in his solitude
Silent long, like one lost in a trance.[18]
But he shall one day reach for new robes of white,
Shall stride with vigor, as if born anew
To rejoin the choir of his companions.

ORPHEUS. Give back to me, ye gods, one single day
to savor from the springtime of my youth
To spend it at my lover's feet
And play upon the lute.

---

[18] In the original, "Schweige lang, entrückt wie ein Stylit" (Silent long, transported like a Stylite). Stylites, or pillar-saints, were Christian ascetics who in the early days of the Byzantine Empire stood on pillars, preaching, fasting, and praying.

And only one more thing would I then tell her.
I am with you
And even death I'll face with you, together,
But death would find no open door

Into our quiet dwelling, warm with sunset.
He'd turn away, majestically and still
Yet smiling gently, lost in memories
From our threshold he'd slowly walk away.

CHORUS. Sing, oh Orpheus, your departed beloved,
    To the cliffs and to the stones, to roots, to trees and forests
    Soon you will be with her, whom leave-taking no longer
        plagues,
    Mystically joined in the song, rhythmically dancing the
        dance . . .

ORPHEUS. He who, like me, has lost Eurydice,
    No longer knows the word that you've created.
    He listens only to the passing hours[19]
    In silence waits until the voices call . . .

HERMES (*voice from afar*). Orpheus!

DRYAD (*closer*). Orpheus!

HERMES (*voice, very close*). Orpheus!

ALKAIOS (*fearfully*). A stranger comes in search of Orpheus . . .

    Hermes appears at the altar of Persephone. Under his right arm
    he carries an object wrapped in black cloth.

HERMES. I seek the singer Orpheus. Will I find him here with you?

FIRST SHEPHERD. The singer Orpheus—my friend, we seek him too . . .

HERMES. And who stands there, still, as if made of stone,
    In deepest sorrow high upon the cliff?

ALKAIOS (*trying to divert his attention*). Oh, one of our priests, who
        speaks a thankful prayer . . .

---

19 In the original, "Lauscht nur den vielzuträgen Horen" (Listens only to the overburdened Horae). The Horae, or Hours, were three goddesses controlling orderly life. In one of their aspects they represented the three seasons the Greeks recognized: spring, summer, and autumn.

ORPHEUS. He does indeed; for he who now approaches
    Appears to be a messenger of the gods.

HERMES. Orpheus, I have also recognized you.
    The poet knows the envoy of his god
    To him, who in his homeland's oft a stranger,
    Sometimes the heavens extend a brotherly hand . . .

ORPHEUS. And so you found the way. Who has sent you here?
    Was it Grace? Of that I need no more.
    Or Hate? Oh, everything I owned, it has been taken
    And my hands are bare, as empty as my halls
    The shining world is hazy, without color.
    What is it that the gods could give to me?
    Oh, everything I owned, it has been taken
    Alone, upon this peak, I know neither death nor life.

HERMES. But some still think of you, though from afar
    Following your dreams and wakefulness.
    No one who lives for beauty lives alone . . .

ORPHEUS. Oh autumn of the Earth, deep solitude . . .

HERMES. And there is one, who over all your days
    Hovers like a cloud, one ever longing
    That just one smile will reconcile your world.
    Oh Orpheus, what should I tell that maiden?

ORPHEUS (*as if speaking to Eurydice*). Is this not more than what I
       meant to you,
  Together then,
  When over my distressed nature
  You often wept . . .?

  Of all the words that we gave one another
  Some stayed with me,
  Refrain beloved, sweet in my dark lifetime.
  "I am with you."

  I am with you, when through the leafless hedges
  The fall wind blows
  And in the fountains' bowls of whitest marble
  The nymph laments . . .

HERMES. Your greeting will I take into that darkest house
    Set gently there before her on the table
    Of metal cold, like flowers in a vase
    That one finds, unexpected, inside an empty room.

ALKAIOS. But you were likely sent by Apollo here to us
    To give Orpheus all of that god's beauty . . .

ORPHEUS. And what is beauty? Just an apparition
    Existing in our gaze, not in the thing itself
    That with its form sinks down into the grave.

ALKAIOS. Oh source of nameless pain, to hear these words from
       you . . .

ORPHEUS. The essence of these things I know too well
    To doubt that they will end in disappointment.

ALKAIOS. The wisdom of Athena guides your words.

ORPHEUS. And what is wisdom? A cloak of resignation,
    We wrap around our shuddering shoulders, standing
    Before eternity, in silent courts of judgment
    Where we attempt to justify our lives
    And bear the final coldness of their sentence . . .

HERMES. I bring you none of that. I bring you only love . . .

ORPHEUS. And what is love . . .

ALKAIOS. Master, hush now, hush,
    And leave to us this last unanswered question!
    Ask what is life, and why I must endure it,
    What are the gods, to whom I bow in prayer,
    Of all else, master, ask your mournful questions,
    Like sharpened blades they penetrate my heart,
    But what is love . . . Master, hush, oh Orpheus, hush . . .

ORPHEUS. Do you know what love is? It is this very silence.
    Concealing from the ones we love the knowledge
    Of all the horror meant for us alone.

HERMES. But now I have grown weary of this burden.

    Hermes puts down the covered gift, leaning it against a column
    of Persephone's temple.

ORPHEUS. Who was it, Hermes? Who has sent you to us?

HERMES. A name that rings for you with tender echoes.
    Eurydice . . .

ORPHEUS. The sweet smell of decay arises from such gifts
    That, from the depths, the dead to us deliver.
    As if, with their pale, outstretched hands, they tempt us
    To join them on the paths that lead down to their
        stronghold . . .

ALKAIOS. What lies concealed within these wrappings, Hermes?

HERMES. I do not know. This often is our mission,
    Delivering to lovers gifts unknown,
    Because the meaning shared between the two of them
    Is damaged if the uninitiated
    Presume to shed some light on the nature of their bond,
    The secret intimacy of the pair . . .

ORPHEUS. So let me free this dark, mysterious gift
    From the layers of black cloth that now conceal it . . .

HERMES. Now I will set out quickly on my journey
    And I, who carried through the night this darkness,
    Will bring bright words to her, that quiet girl
    And I will be your love's true messenger . . . (*Exits quickly.*)

ORPHEUS. I beg you all, please, leave me now as well . . .

*The shepherds exit. Alkaios hesitates until he, the last, joins the
others.*

ORPHEUS. Only you, Alkaios, you could almost stay here.
    Only almost. Go, child, how lovely, look,
    The fluttering leaves drift gently into evening . . .

*He slowly climbs down from the rock and approaches Eurydice's
gift. He stops in the center of the stage.*

    I was, beloved, ivy on the pathways
    That gently bordered and enclosed your steps.
    And often lay, when trapped in anxious nightmares,
    My head upon your lap.

And like a young wind tenderly I played
Within the dusky, soft folds of your dress
And sometimes I regarded your slim hands clasped together
Like young girls, weary but suffused with joy.

Oh, these soft hands, beds planted with white flowers
You were a springtime garden, in which I finally bloomed
A lullaby that wove its way around me
Your smile was, for my deeds, a rich reward.

I was a current that toward far shores flowed
But you, the water vessel fair of form
In which a maiden gently raised me from the void
And carried to her garden like a lamp
To pour me out upon the darkish blooms . . .

I was at prayer and you, you were the Word
While I was formless, you a perfect whole
I was so young, but you remained unsullied
An empty space was I, but you the site

Of the Garden of the World, God's hiding place
You covered me, in nights of expectation
With wilting leaves, composed of fairy tales.
When I awoke, you were no longer by me

And I found not a trace left by your gentle footsteps.
Where now is all that bliss? Where all that we have suffered?
Only your silent kiss I feel upon my cheek . . .

*While uttering the last few words, Orpheus has come gradually
closer to the covered gift. Now he stands immediately before it.*

Now here lies the secret you had brought to me
I often scattered violets in your hair
But I recall the gift that pleased you most:
When I made up a little song for you.
What present for me, child, have you wrapped in black?
Were you afraid that I'd laugh at your gift?
Is it so poor? Had you found nothing more

In Hades' empty hallways, than a brightly colored stone,
And sent it, hesitating, in deepest secrecy,
To me it would be rare and ever-precious . . .

*He reaches out to remove the covers. Algea suddenly steps out
from the background and speaks to him. He lets his hands fall
and turns around.*

ALGEA. Oh Orpheus, touch no gift that death has sent you,
Touch not this thing. Just once more be my child
The way you were before. Look, I am old, my son
And whimsical, as such old women are.
For years now I have asked nothing of you
Soon you shall hear my voice, my son, no more.
Look, your mother's hair, that once was golden
Flows now in snow-white waves back from her brow.
The time draws near when I shall ask no more.
Just one last thing you must still do for me
Do not accept this thing, delivered from the dead,
Do not touch it. Just once more, be my child,
Remember all the pain I bore for you . . .

ORPHEUS. My Mother, oh, so long I have not seen you
You followed your own path, almost like one of them,
The dead, who you now claim are strange to you.
Where were you, Mother? What so burdens you?

ALGEA. Orpheus, I've been weeping all this time . . .

ORPHEUS. I too have lived a long time without cheer . . .

ALGEA. Why, my Orpheus, have I only wept,
Have kept my distance, seeing you from afar?
Only because I knew you were in mourning
And sorrow found me when my path crossed yours . . .

ORPHEUS. It is no fault of mine, that I no longer laugh . . .

ALGEA. You are no more my child. Who took you, son, from me?

ORPHEUS. Oh Mother, life has done all this to us . . .

ALGEA. When still a boy, you dreamed and laughed just like the
others . . .

ORPHEUS. A boy, he dreams of charging right into the fray
    Hair flying, steers his chariot through the battle
    On my head a helmet, reddish gold
    And tongues of flame streak through the darkened sky,
    Meanwhile the pounding of the sea
    Circulates, pulsing, through my veins . . .

ALGEA. Such horrors, Orpheus, have come to pass,
    That I, your mother, almost have to wish
    A quick and painless death had found you then.
    Instead I see you growing ever paler,
    And watch as you stare long into dark river depths
    Haunted by incurable despair.

ORPHEUS. It's often women, suffering and patient
    Who bear the burden of the poet's curse
    As if his passion meant the guilt of secret vices
    And who, driven as he, through dark years headlong rushing
    Stops short upon the goal: eternity.
    His mother is the one who weaves a mantel
    Of loving words to wrap around her son,
    His lover bears it, humbly and in silence
    When he, in his delirium, cries out . . .

ALGEA. If you had only never known the lyre . . .

ORPHEUS. The fire would have consumed me nonetheless.

ALGEA. Happy is he who, never touched by God
    Knows not of fame, knows not the stringed lyre
    Who follows cheerfully his even path
    His eyes reflect no shine, but also see no horrors,
    His evenings without stars, but comfortable and cool
    And saying the word "life," describes a richness vast . . .

ORPHEUS. But I, I was possessed by a rare sorrow
    So early on, and never has it eased.
    My passion was for beauty, that lent its permanence
    To melodies of my beloved flute.

ALGEA. If only you had never met that maiden
    You would be happy, as all shepherds are
    And revel in the beauty of the earth . . .

ORPHEUS. In these long nights I listen to the falling
   Of raindrops, drenching fields now gray and bare
   And my heart was as glad to hear the autumn wind
   As others are to hear a dancing song . . .

ALGEA. Melancholy, sadness? You are not well, my child!

ORPHEUS. And now my home is with the evening wind
   At quiet hearths I love to sit and watch
   The way twilight spins slowly 'round the flames
   A ring of longing, as around young women

   I often kneel at dusk before the deep blue
   Of violets shy, embedded in soft grass
   And wish to be for them a vase so slender
   And sometimes kneel 'til skies glow grey with dawn.

ALGEA. You're no more used to life among the living
   Be as you are, and follow your own pathways
   And laugh sometimes, laugh, Orpheus, and summon
   Your grey-haired mother when you're filled with cheer
   And let a flicker brighten her dark nights.
   And this dark thing now give me as a gift.
   So long I've had no gift from you. You lock yourself
   In your own dreams and you need nothing more.
   But this thing, oh, I often shall admire it
   And kiss it sometimes. This is from my son!
   In my dark nights, now desolate and sleepless
   It will be with me, precious as your voice . . .

   *She tries to take Eurydice's gift, to carry it away. Orpheus blocks
   her way to the column.*

ORPHEUS. This is not for you; Eurydice's love
   Sent from afar the enigmatic messenger.

ALGEA. Do not accept this gift that death has sent you
   Your mother begs you, child . . .

ORPHEUS. No, Mother, this is mine,
   And meant for me and chosen just for me.

ALGEA. But give it to me. Give me this thing.
   Nothing there. Just a stone

And you were always good. You always listened to me.
You'll surely grant me this. I shall be happy then,
Through Orpheus's kindness happy. To you it only means . . .

ORPHEUS. The essence sweet of a life too early taken.
Not yours, oh Mother! This gift, it is mine
More than any fruit that my own labors won.
It is the longing for a total union
With my beloved, oh, who died so young.

ALGEA. Strong are the dead, much stronger than the living,
In yielding to her will, you have forsaken me.
Mighty are those who forgive easily
A God, raising his hands in consolation,
Lifts up the mother who now only weeps . . .

*She leaves slowly, in a posture of deep mourning. Orpheus reaches
for the dark object. Slowly he removes the cover.*

ORPHEUS. Just like a child who finally is allowed
A treasure, long concealed, to unwrap,
That now stands tall, a castle, in all his fantasies
So now am I. The landscape of my dreams
Lies spread before me now, its rolling hillsides
Caressed by a strange, flower-scented breeze . . .

*He has removed the last black cloth and holds the gift in his
hands: a golden harp, entwined in black laurel. In the setting
sun the lyre glows dark red and strange.*

Oh evening of my lifetime! Symbol of fulfillment
My lyre, it has now returned to me
I am no longer mute. Even the sunset sings
The tired world, once more awake and young
It dances now the dance it once taught me. (*Begins to play.*)

Wine
Intoxicating, filled with sweetness, drawn from the sun of
    warm southern slopes
Oh wine!
You, the wild-raving daughters of Bacchus!
Oh, you Bacchantes!

Wild-wanton daughters of worlds now in flames
Light all the torches and sing you my name
The world is mine!

*Bacchantes enter from all sides. They surround Orpheus and
begin with raving dances, pulling the singer with them.*

Oh, you Bacchantes!
I welcome you all to a feast for your master,
Swing now your skirts! Sing to your god and his warm
    southern lands,
Weave 'round my brow the immortal beguiling, with gods
    reconciling,
Blood-red and shining rose-woven bands!

BACCHANTES. With us, Orpheus, your playing, it calls us to you!

ORPHEUS. Whirlpools spin faster and plunge to the depths, you
    who despise a life lived passionless
See me, the one who has overcome all! Me! I will be free!
    I am free!

DRYAD. Free!

ORPHEUS. All of the burdens the gods placed upon me,
    Passion and song and the sheer weight of living
    I rend them in two with a stroke of the strings!

BACCHANTES. With us!

ORPHEUS. Melding in me all of nature's creatures, plants and the
    trees, even stones now are joyful
    Long kept in shackles, finally awakened, powerful cry.
Finally the death-inspired, terrible nightmare of an eternity,
    over at last!

DRYAD. At last!

ORPHEUS. Transparent ether!
    Trace of the spirits, rent by the storms of fierce-driving stars,
    You are the victor! Bridged by dreams, cosmic forces' eternal
    defender
    Look how the darkness flees! Life has claimed victory!
    Oh, you Bacchantes! Everywhere light!

DRYAD. Light!

ORPHEUS. Light have our burdens become!
> Dark tongues of flame start to rise! Judgment has come!

BACCHANTES. Light! Mystical trance!

ORPHEUS. Those who triumph, like me, join in the dance!
> Mine is the prize! All of my promise is used, all is fulfilled
> Raving and wild, dancing shoes winged by flame
> All of you, join in the dance!

BACCHANTES. Dance!

ORPHEUS. Faster!
> Spin the earth round till it starts to burn, flames leaping
>> higher with every turn
> Brighter and brighter!
> Tear, oh Bacchantes, the clouds from the sky, pale tattered
>> shrouds that conceal the gods' death!
> Remember the secret, to you I gave! And now, on top of the
>> gods' sinking grave
> Dance like a fire that consumes all the earth!

BACCHANTES. Tear down the clouds from the sky!

ORPHEUS. Light have our burdens become!
> The end of eternity!
> Everywhere, light!
> Everywhere happiness, gone is all loneliness!
> Finally the end is in sight, open the door into light!
> Tear all things stable apart, spirit in verse!

BACCHANTES. Tear all things stable apart, oh, his clothes tear to shreds,
> Spirit in verse, oh, and the flesh is free,
> Tear off the wreath from his brow, the wreath that from
> Bacchus he stole,
> Oh, break open his skull,
> Finally from spirit released,
> Feed on his brain!

*Orpheus is thrown to the ground, in the midst of the crowd of the
raving dancers.*

ORPHEUS. Alas, my death! Fading and falling star!

The Bacchantes leave him and, dancing in highest ecstasy, quickly vanish. Alkaios and the shepherds arrive. As they see Orpheus lying as if lifeless, they surround him, supporting his head . . .

ALKAIOS. Orpheus—dying!

OLD SHEPHERD. How could this come to pass
He's leaving us, who loved us once so well?

ALKAIOS. The poet's love is always a leave-taking
From all the thousand silent, earthly things
That echo with his words like shepherds' flutes

FIRST SHEPHERD. The poet's love is always a leave-taking . . .

ALKAIOS. Like birds in autumn, drawn to southern seas
He heeds the call of vague and distant dreams
You gather up his early-orphaned verses
String them together, like a chain of pearls,
On quiet evenings, pensive and alone,
You let them slowly glide between your fingers . . .

SECOND SHEPHERD. I am with you, when through the leafless hedges
The fall wind blows
And in the fountains' bowls of whitest marble
The nymph laments . . .

THIRD SHEPHERD. I often kneel at dusk before the deep blue
Of violets shy, embedded in soft grass
And wish to be for them a vase so slender
And sometimes kneel 'til skies glow grey with dawn . . .

FOURTH SHEPHERD. Oh autumn of the earth, oh, deepest stillness,
The restless darkness of my solitude.
Whom can I offer these, my tired verses?
Flute melody, a sound slowly receding,
Oh autumn of the earth, deep solitude . . .

EURYDICE (*voice*). Where are you, Orpheus? Let me no longer wait
In vain for the dear touch of my sweet husband!

ORPHEUS (*awakening from his unconsciousness*). And what is love?
The longing of two shadows
To seem like something real in the light . . .

EURYDICE (*voice*). Two verses, oh, are we, within a poem of
dreams . . .

ALKAIOS. You are the song that God sings to himself.

ORPHEUS (*dying*). And tell my mother she should weep no more . . .

*The shepherds lay him softly on the grass. It is very dark. Now
Alkaios lifts the dead one's harp high, so that they can see it.*

ALKAIOS. Hush, listen, friends, the sound of Orpheus's harp . . .

*The lyre glows and illuminates the scene. While the curtain slowly
falls, soft muted string music emerges from the lyre.*

THE INSULT—BUT UNINTENDED;
or, THE MAN WITH THE DEFECTIVE MEMORY
A Theresienstadt Courtroom Scene

INTRODUCTION

The following sketch was preserved in the archives of the Terezín Memorial in the Czech Republic.[1] The text unfortunately does not include the names of the author(s) or the performers, and none of the cabaret posters preserved in the collection mentions the sketch. Considering the frequent references to Vienna and the use of words more common in Austria than in Germany, it is likely that the author or authors were among the many Austrian cabaret artists in the ghetto.[2]

The author humorously portrays one of the lesser-known institutions in the ghetto: its court system.[3] The system included a criminal court that mostly addressed cases of theft, a labor court that resolved issues of work discipline, and a civil court that dealt with private conflicts among ghetto residents. Survivor Ruth Bondy wrote of the civil court:

> Most of the plaintiffs were older people, mainly from Germany, who were more sensitive about their dignity [. . .]. But perhaps what these people sought most of all was the reassurance that there was still justice, and a judge, in the world.[4]

In the sketch the conflict is resolved in a humorous way that not only disarms the plaintiff and charms the judge but entertains the courtroom—as well as the Terezín/Theresienstadt audience.

---

1 Terezín Memorial, inv. no. PT 4005.

2 Such words include *frozzeln* (to tease or make fun of someone) and *Zwetschge* (plum, probably derived from the Czech *švestka*).

3 For details on the court system see Bondy, *"Elder of the Jews,"* pp. 306–9; and Adler, *Theresienstadt*, pp. 453–92.

4 Bondy, *"Elder of the Jews,"* p. 308.

THE INSULT—BUT UNINTENDED; *or*, THE MAN WITH THE DEFECTIVE MEMORY

A Theresienstadt Courtroom Scene

CHARACTERS

> Judge
> Defendant
> Plaintiff
> Witness for the Defense

JUDGE (*to Plaintiff*). So, Mr. Neuschul,[5] tell the court what happened.

PLAINTIFF. I was standing at the entrance gate to the Leipzig barracks, Your Honor, right in the middle, to direct traffic, as is my responsibility as an officer of the *Ordnungsdienst*.[6] My duty, as you probably well know, is to prevent those who want to use the left lane when entering and exiting the barracks from doing so, and . . .

JUDGE. . . . to send them the right way.[7]

PLAINTIFF (*not understanding the subtle legal play on words*). Well, more precisely, to get them to use the right lane.[8] I interrupted my

---

5 The name "Neuschul" evokes medieval and early modern names for synagogues, such as the Altneuschul (in Czech, Staronová synagoga, the Old-New Synagogue) in Prague.

6 In the original, O.D.-Mann. See *Ordnungsdienst* (glossary).

7 In the original, the judge uses the word *Rechtsweg*, which means both "legal process" and "path to the right."

8 The joke is based on the daily reality of the prisoners: in the overcrowded ghetto, members of the *Ordnungsdienst* enforced the rule that pedestrians must

official duties for a moment to respond to Mr. Zahlmann's[9] question about where he should report for his hydrophilic labor assignment.[10] My answer was "Room number 336." Mr. Zahlmann responded, and I quote: "Three hundred thirty six? Three, three, six . . ." and, after thinking for a moment, added: "You idiot!" And with that he smiled pleasantly, which I could only interpret as an expression of contempt. When I asked his name, he identified himself without hesitation as Joseph Zahlmann. However, he was not able to tell me his transport number or his address from memory; instead, he read both to me from his notebook. While reading, he assured me again and again that he had not intended to offend me.

JUDGE. Mr. Zahlmann, do you admit to having addressed officer Karel Neuschul with the words "You idiot!"?

DEFENDANT. I admit that I spoke those words, but I did not address them to Mr. Neuschul; I surely had no reason to insult him!

JUDGE. Well, did you perhaps mean, by calling him "idiot," to express your gratitude or your high esteem for him?

DEFENDANT. Your Honor, I can explain everything. But you must allow me to begin from the beginning.

JUDGE. My time is limited.

DEFENDANT. I will be brief, Your Honor. Should I digress, please interrupt me immediately, because a stitch in time saves . . . Excuse me, Your Honor, how many stitches are in fact saved by a stitch in . . . ?

JUDGE. Are you trying to make fun of me?

DEFENDANT. Not at all, Your Honor, but I really and truly cannot remember how many stitches one saves with a stitch in time.

---

walk on the right side of the street. See Hyndráková et al., *Acta Theresiania*, p. 217.

9 The name "Zahlmann" means literally "Count-man" or "Number-man."

10 In the original, *hydrophile Arbeitseinsatz*, probably an elevated name for *Wasserdienst* (literally, "water service"). Monitors were assigned to washrooms to ensure that their fellow prisoners used the inadequate water supply sparingly.

JUDGE (*taken aback*). Well, nine, of course.

DEFENDANT. Thank you, Your Honor. So as soon as I start to digress, please stop me right away. (*Pause*) I see from your astonishment that you perhaps consider me mentally deficient. This is not true, Your Honor. I have half my wits about me.

JUDGE. All would be preferable.

DEFENDANT. Please excuse me; of course I meant all. Perhaps you have already noticed, Your Honor, that I have an unusually poor memory for numbers.

JUDGE. Indeed.

DEFENDANT. With any other kind of memory, I am at your service. Memory for places, memory for names, memory for faces . . . but for numbers—

JUDGE (*interrupts him*). What was your profession before the war?

DEFENDANT. After failing my secondary school exams, I became head waiter at the Ringkaffee in Vienna.[11] But not for long. I would always forget how many rolls each guest had eaten, and the guests would always forget to pay for those rolls. I was glad when, after World War I, the cafe was converted into a bank. So I stayed on as a bank clerk.

JUDGE. A bank clerk with no memory for numbers?

DEFENDANT. An unusual case, is it not? But it worked! If someone asked me about prices on the stock market—Siemens, Alpine, Daimler-Benz—of course, I wanted to appear well informed; so, I gave them some arbitrary figure.

JUDGE (*interested*). And what happened?

DEFENDANT. Well . . . some of our clients went broke, others became fabulously rich. When the bank collapsed, one of those who had become rich found a position for me as conductor of the Municipal Symphony Orchestra of Grammat-Neusiedel.[12]

---

11 A traditional and prestigious cafe in central Vienna.

12 Small town (now called Gramatneusiedl) about 30 km southeast of Vienna. In Austria it is a synonym for "provinciality."

I am actually a reasonably talented musician. For a while, things worked out wonderfully. But once, when I was supposed to conduct an important concert, I arrived a bit late. The orchestra was already assembled and the audience was getting restless. So I strode to the podium, took the baton, and conducted and conducted, and suddenly the orchestra stopped playing and the audience was in an uproar. At that moment the first violinist tugged at my sleeve and asked: "Maestro, which symphony are you conducting?" I said, "The Third, of course." "Really?" asked the violinist, "because this whole time we've been playing the Ninth!" And while we were debating the matter the owner of the hall jumped up, an enormous pentagonally built fellow—

JUDGE. You mean "squarely built"?

DEFENDANT. Excuse me, squarely built—he grabbed me by the arm and roared: "Pack up all your odds and evens and get out of here!"

JUDGE. He probably said "your odds and ends!"

DEFENDANT. That may be, Your Honor . . . in any case, speaking of "ends" . . . that is what my musical career had suddenly come to.

JUDGE. And what do you do here in Theresienstadt?

DEFENDANT. I work in the food service. My assignment: to remember the number of dumplings and rolls[13] distributed.

JUDGE. The right man for the right job![14] But now, at last, to the matter at hand! I'm still waiting for you to explain why, with the expression "You idiot!" you did not intend to insult Mr. Neuschul.

DEFENDANT. I should have explained that, Your Honor, when I mentioned my failed school exams. To try to pass my exam in

---

13 In the original, *Buchteln* (probably derived from the Czech *buchty*), a pastry made of soft yeast dough with a sweet filling.

14 Irregularities in the distribution of prisoners' rations were a great source of tension in the ghetto. The phenomenon is mentioned in several other texts in this collection.

history, with so many dates to remember, I had to resort to mnemonics. I presume you know what that is, Your Honor?

JUDGE. Why don't you refresh my memory?

DEFENDANT. It is the science of devising memory aids. One replaces the numbers with letters. For example, A for 5, J for 3, M for 4, and from the letters one forms code words and phrases. Do you know, for example, what *kvetsch* means?[15]

JUDGE. It's Yiddish for "complain."

DEFENDANT. Yes, but as a mnemonic device it stands for the discovery of America—1492. And what is *"mazeltov"*?

JUDGE. "Congratulations."

DEFENDANT. Yes, but also the end of the Thirty Years War—1648.

JUDGE. Very interesting! Go on.

DEFENDANT. Well, during the exam I was asked, among other things, in which year Charles VII of France concluded the peace of Arras. The mnemonic letters are L for 1, M for 4, I for 3, and A for 5. 1435—LMIA. From that I constructed, as a code phrase, the famous quote from Goethe's play, *Götz of Berlichingen*.[16]

JUDGE. Well, and did you pass the exam with honors?

DEFENDANT. Unfortunately not, because in my excitement I answered the professor with the code phrase instead of the date, and consequently was expelled from all institutions of higher learning. And you see, Your Honor, that explains the embarrassing incident with Mr. Neuschul. He answered my question about the hydrophilic labor assignment with the number 336. With lightning speed I substituted: I for 3, I for 3, O for 6, I-I-O, and in my haste I could think of nothing but the words "You idiot!" which I meant to say only to myself.

JUDGE. You have called a witness for the defense. Is he present?

---

15 In the original the word was *Gewure*, Yiddish for "strength."

16 The quote is "Leck mich im Arsch" (loosely translated, "kiss my ass").

WITNESS (*coming forward*). Yes, Your Honor. My name is Rüdiger Cohn,[17] Cohn spelled with C; transport number II/2–222; born 9/19/1909; address: Q555;[18] occupation: H.D. of the G.W.[19]

JUDGE. Thank you! What do you have to say in favor of the defendant?

WITNESS. Several days ago I was on duty at the intersection of L1 and Q3, and Mr. Zahlmann approached me and asked how to get to L609, as a certain lady he knows supposedly lived there. "Very simple," I said. "First go straight to L110, then turn on to Q4, follow the street until you get to 412, turn left and cross L3 at number 319. From L320, if you know the way, you can cut diagonally across the courtyard toward L425, and then follow Q8 directly to L609."[20] To that Mr. Zahlmann replied, "Please say the numbers again, only the numbers." So I did. The whole time, Mr. Zahlmann appeared to be concentrating intently. When I finished, he said: "If you don't arrive in Theresienstadt already *meshugge*, this town will make you *meshugge*."[21] "Well I never!" I said, "What do you mean by that?" And Mr. Zahlmann said, "That's the mnemonic code phrase for my way to L609."

DEFENDANT. I would like to add, Your Honor, that I did not find the lady, although I arrived correctly at the destination. A charming blonde, by the way. Your Honor, how would you normally rank a woman's appeal?

JUDGE (*indulgently*). Hmmm . . . on a scale from one to ten, maybe six.[22]

---

17 This comic name may be a joke at the expense of the German Jews in the ghetto (transports beginning with II were from Munich) and their own belief in their full assimilation into the German nation. It improbably combines an old Germanic first name with a clearly Jewish surname.

18 See L, Q (glossary).

19 H.D. and G.W.: See *Hilfsdienst* and *Ghettowache* (glossary).

20 As maps of the ghetto reveal, these directions are accurate.

21 Yiddish for "crazy."

22 In the original script the judge says "Sex," which is acoustically equivalent to the German number six (*Sechs*).

DEFENDANT. Then she deserves at least a twelve. Several weeks ago I made her acquaintance at a program of the *Freizeitgestaltung* . . .

JUDGE. None of this has anything to do with your case.

DEFENDANT. Please, one moment, Your Honor! When we parted I asked her if I could see her again and she replied: L609. I committed that number to memory with the code phrase "you sweetheart!"

JUDGE. Peculiar how you manage to adjust the code phrase to the situation.

DEFENDANT. Purely by chance, Your Honor! By the way, as I said, she did not live at L609, but somewhere else entirely. When we later met by coincidence, I chided her about that and she said: "But L609 is not my address, it's my transport number!" "And your residence?" I asked. "You can only get my address from the central registry, because they move me every three days."[23]

JUDGE. Get to the point!

DEFENDANT. Certainly, Your Honor. I only wanted to say that my poor memory for numbers is to blame for the fact that the lady and I have parted ways. The last time we were together, I gave her two kisses and said with the second: "There . . . all good things come in twos." "No," she said, "in threes." "No," said I, "only two." She insisted on three; I stood my ground at two. Who is right, Your Honor; all good things come in— how many?

JUDGE. Normally in threes, but in Theresienstadt we must make do with less and hence your economy is perfectly justified. But now finally to the point! Mr. Neuschul, after all that you have heard, do you declare yourself satisfied with the explanation provided by Mr. Zahlmann?

PLAINTIFF. After this clarification, it seems I have no other choice but to withdraw my libel suit. However, I would like to ask the

---

23 See *Zentralevidenz* (glossary). Prisoners were often required to move from one address to another on very short notice.

defendant, in the future, to use mnemonics with somewhat greater care.

DEFENDANT. Oh, a hundred thanks, Mr. Neuschul, a hundred thanks!

JUDGE. You may in good conscience multiply the number of thanks by ten, and in the future take into account that mnemonics, as Mr. Neuschul has suggested, is a very questionable science.

DEFENDANT. This I admit, Your Honor, but I think the end justifies the means.

JUDGE. Well, in your case, perhaps driving us around the bend justifies the means! The case, gentlemen, is closed.

In the courtroom there is general shaking of hands and shaking of heads.

Curtain.

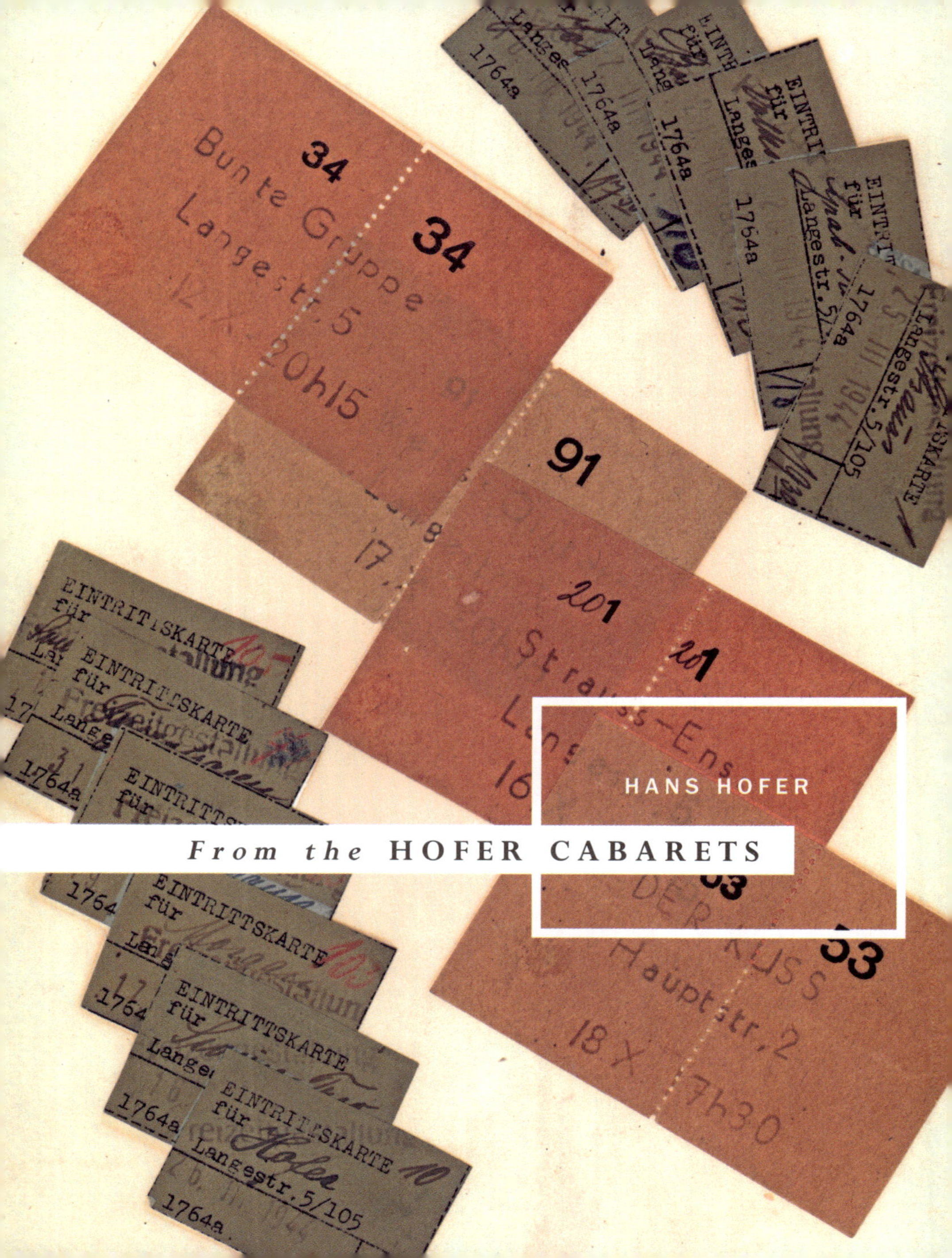
HANS HOFER
From the HOFER CABARETS

Several posters for performances with titles like *Everything with Music* (*Alles mit Musik*) and *Laugh Yourself Well* (*Lach Dich gesund*) testify to Hans Hofer's wide-ranging involvement in the cultural life of the ghetto. Only one of his songs, "The Theater Ticket" ("Die Theaterkarte"), has previously been published.[1] The works published here were found in the archives of the Jewish Museum in Prague and offer a fuller picture of Hofer's work in Terezín/Theresienstadt.[2]

THE AUTHOR

Much is known about the life of Hans Hofer, thanks to family documents and photographs preserved by Margaret Warden, the niece of Hofer's wife, Lisl. Hofer (real name Hans or Hanuš Schulhof), the son of actor Siegfried Schulhof, who also used the stage name Hofer, was born in Prague in 1907. In 1924 he moved to Vienna and performed in theaters there for several years. On April 8, 1938, shortly before Austria was annexed to Nazi Germany, he married Lisl (Elisabeth) Steinitz, a singer and dancer from Vienna. The newlyweds returned to Prague, where Hofer performed in a Jewish cabaret until 1941.

On July 27, 1942, Hans and Lisl were deported together to Terezín/ Theresienstadt, where both immediately immersed themselves in the German-language theatrical life of the ghetto.[3] They performed in their own cabarets, read roles in staged readings organized by Phillip

IMAGE 13.1 (*facing page*) **Tickets for various performances, including Hofer's cabaret and the Strauss Ensemble.**
Courtesy of the Terezín Memorial.

1 See the Terezín Memorial, inv. nos. PT 4072–6 and PT 4194–5. The text has been published in German in two anthologies: Migdal, *Und die Musik spielt dazu*; and Golden et al., *Chansons und Satiren aus Theresienstadt*. It has been included here as a valuable source of information on the administration of the cultural life of the ghetto.

2 See the Shoah History Archive, Terezín Collection (T), inv. no. 318f.

3 Hofer's cabaret began performing in August, 1942. See Weiner, *"Freizeit-gestaltung* in Theresienstadt," p. 220.

IMAGE 13.2 (*left*) **Lisl Steinitz in the 1930s.**
IMAGE 13.3 (*below*) **Lisl and Hans Hofer in the late 1930s.**
Both images courtesy of Margaret Warden.

Manes,[4] and performed in plays such as Theodor Herzl's *The Refugee*[5] and George Bernard Shaw's *The Man of Destiny*.[6] Hans Hofer also directed the operetta *Die Fledermaus*,[7] where Lisl appeared as Prince Orlovsky and he played the role of Frosch.[8] Although Hofer was bilingual, there is no record of his participation in any of the Czech-language cultural activities.

In the summer of 1944 Hofer assisted famous German-Jewish actor and director Kurt Gerron[9] during the shooting of the notorious Nazi propaganda film *Theresienstadt: A Documentary Film from the Jewish Settlement Area*.[10] His description of the filming provides a rare insider perspective on the Nazis' attempt to portray the ghetto as an independent Jewish city.[11]

In the mass transports of fall 1944, Hans was deported to Auschwitz. Lisl followed him just a few days later. They were both sent to further camps for forced labor. Remarkably, both survived. Hofer was liberated in Kaufering-Allach, a satellite camp of Dachau. A preserved registration document lists his profession as "actor."[12] Lisl was sent to the labor camp Flossenbürg and was liberated in Mauthausen.

---

4 For a list of the Manes Group's activities see the Terezín Memorial, inv. no. PT 3981.

5 Theodor Herzl, the founder of the Zionist movement, wrote this play (*Der Flüchtling*) and several other works for the theater. See the Terezín Memorial, inv. no. PT 3850.

6 The German title is *Der Schlachtenlenker*. See the Terezín Memorial, inv. no. PT 3911.

7 The operetta *Die Fledermaus* by Johann Strauss premiered in 1874.

8 See the Terezín Memorial, inv. no. 4045.

9 Kurt Gerron was one of the most prominent figures in European inter-war theater and cinema. See Barbara Felsmann and Karl Prümm, *Kurt Gerron—gefeiert und gejagt, Das Schicksal eines deutschen Unterhaltungskünstlers: Berlin, Amsterdam, Theresienstadt, Auschwitz* (Berlin: Hentrich, 1992).

10 The film is better known under the incorrect title, *Hitler Gives a City to the Jews*. See Margry, "Das Konzentrationslager als Idylle."

11 See Hans Hofer, "The Film about Terezín: A Belated Reportage," in František Ehrmann, Ota Heitlinger, and Rudolf Iltis (eds.), *Terezín* (Prague: Council of Jewish Communities in the Czech Lands, 1965), pp. 180–84.

12 "Dachau Fragebogen: Hans Hofer," October 10, 1944, in *Individual Documents Dachau: Häftlings-Personalbogen*, International Tracing Service collection, United States Holocaust Memorial Museum, 1.1.6.2, document no. 10094444.

Hans and Lisl returned to Prague in July 1945. After working briefly for the Jewish Religious Community in Prague, Hans Hofer again began to work as an actor for various theaters. In the 1950s he was engaged with the German-language traveling troupe of the Czechoslovak Rural Theater.[13] Perhaps his last Czech-speaking role was in the play *Lumpazivagabundus*[14] performed in June 1960 in Liberec, directed by fellow Terezín/Theresienstadt survivor Jan Fischer.[15]

---

13 The Rural Theater (Vesnické divadlo), later known as the State Traveling Theater (Státní zájezdové divadlo), was founded in October 1945 and brought theatrical performances to rural areas of Czechoslovakia. In 1954 a troupe performing in German was added to the 10 Czech-language troupes. See Jaroslav Pucherna (ed.), *Přijelo divadlo: patnáct let putování za divákem* (Prague: Státní zájezdové divadlo, 1961).

14 The full name of this play by Johann Nepomuk Eduard Ambrosius Nestroy is *Der böse Geist Lumpazivagabundus oder Das liederliche Kleeblatt* (premiere 1833).

15 Jan Fischer, interview with Lisa Peschel, February 2, 2008.

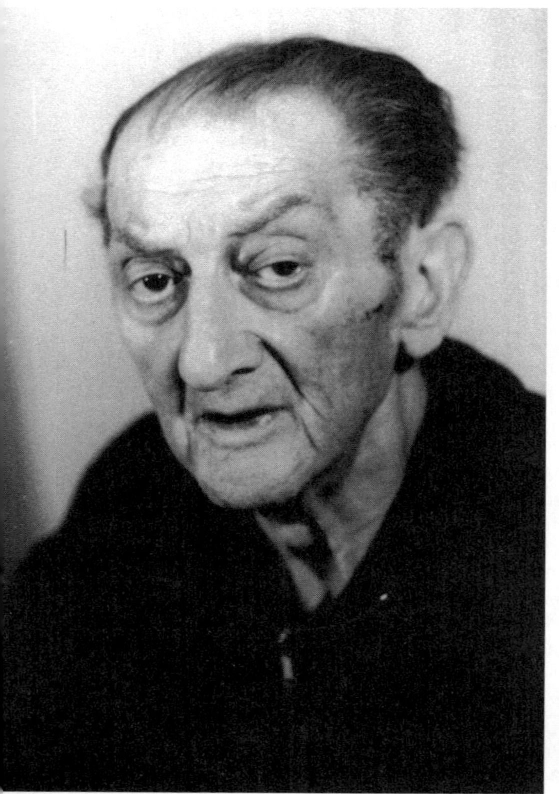

IMAGE 13.4 (*facing page, left*) **Hans Hofer immediately after his return from the concentration camps, 1945.**

IMAGE 13.5 (*facing page, right*) **Hans Hofer in a post-war theatrical role.**

IMAGE 13.6 (*above*) **Hans and Lisl Hofer in the 1950s.**

All images courtesy of Margaret Warden.

In 1960 he moved to the German Democratic Republic and joined the troupe of the Rostock Volkstheater. He played various comic roles, even reprising a role from the ghetto that, according to Lisl, was his favorite: Frosch in *Die Fledermaus*.[16] He retired in 1973 and died on April 12 of the same year. After Lisl completed her training as a lighting technician in Prague she followed him to Rostock and worked with the Volkstheater until she retired. In 1989 she returned to the ghetto for an interview with Volker Kühn, describing Terezín/Theresienstadt theater for his documentary film *Death Dance: Cabaret behind Barbed Wire* (*Totentanz: Kabarett hinter Stacheldraht*, 1990). She died in 1992, shortly after the film was shown on German television.

THE SCRIPT

Many of Hofer's texts, although ironically exaggerated, provide fairly accurately descriptions of how certain ghetto institutions actually functioned. He also does not shy away from addressing issues such as corruption and favoritism. He sets his tales of the peculiarities of ghetto life within familiar melodies, mostly from his beloved Vienna. His comic style may have provided German-speaking Jews with a few moments of pleasant nostalgia for the cultural forms of their pre-war lives, and his humorous look at navigating the bureaucracy of the ghetto may even have afforded them some temporary psychological relief regarding the frustrations of daily life in Terezín/Theresienstadt.

---

16 Kühn, *Kabarett im KZ*, p. 38.

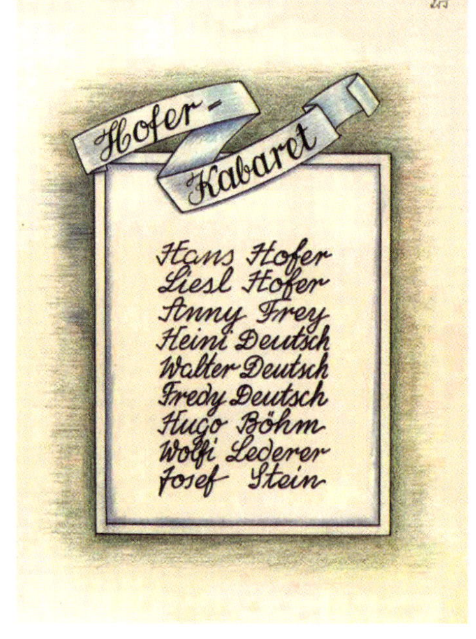

IMAGE 13.7 (*top left*) **A souvenir poster for Hans Hofer's revue *Laugh Yourself Well*.**

IMAGE 13.8 (*top right*) **A souvenir poster for Hans Hofer's revue *Everything with Music*.**

IMAGE 13.9 (*right*) **A souvenir poster for Hans Hofer's cabaret.**

All images courtesy of the Terezín Memorial.

Hans Hofer worked with many other artists in the ghetto. The following list includes only the actors and singers whose names appear on the posters for his own cabarets and revues.

THE AUTHOR

HANS HOFER (also known as Schulhof; in Czech, Hanuš) was born on April 12, 1907, and was deported from Prague to Terezín/Theresienstadt on July 27, 1942. On September 28, 1944 he was deported to Auschwitz. He was liberated in Kauffering-Allach.

THE ACTORS AND THE OTHER PARTICIPANTS

LISL HOFER (also know as **ELISABETH SCHULHOF** and, in Czech, **ALŽBĚTA SCHULHOFOVÁ**) was born on December 16, 1912 and was deported from Prague to Terezín/Theresienstadt on July 27, 1942. She was deported to Auschwitz on October 4, 1944. She was liberated in Mauthausen.

ANNA FREY (also written as **ANNIE** and **ANIE**) was born on November 23, 1868 and was deported from Plzeň/Pilsen to Terezín/Theresienstadt on January 18, 1942. She was liberated in the ghetto.

HEINI DEUTSCH is probably a nickname for **HEINRICH DEUTSCH**. Unfortunately it is not possible to identify him more closely; there are three individuals by that name in the database of the Institute of the Terezín Initiative.

WALTER DEUTSCH's full name was **PAUL WALTER DEUTSCH**. He was born on July 30, 1914. On August 4, 1943 he was deported from Berlin to Terezín/Theresienstadt and on September 28, 1944 to Auschwitz. He perished.

FREDY DEUTSCH, probably a nickname for **FRIEDRICH DEUTSCH**, does not appear in the database of the Institute of the Terezín Initiative.

The name **HUGO BÖHM** appears four times in the database of the Institute of the Terezín Initiative; unfortunately it is not possible to identify him more closely.

The name **JOSEF STEIN** appears 51 times in the database of the Institute of the Terezín Initiative.

FRITZ BENSCHER (also written **BENTSCHER**) was born on November 13, 1904. On June 25, 1943 he was deported from Hamburg to Terezín/ Theresienstadt and on September 28, 1944 to Auschwitz. He perished.

HANNELORE COHN (also written **HANELORE** and **KOHN**) was born on May 2, 1921. On June 30, 1943 she was deported from Berlin to Terezín/ Theresienstadt and on October 4, 1944 to Auschwitz. She survived.

HERMANN FEINER does not appear in the database of the Institute of the Terezín Initiative.

ALFRED KLEPPNER was born on December 9, 1903. On November 11, 1943 he was deported from Vienna to Terezín/Theresienstadt and on October 19, 1944 to Auschwitz. He perished.

FRIEDA (also **FRIEDL** or **FRIEDERIKE**) **HABER** was born on July 25, 1923. On October 15, 1943 she was deported from Berlin to Terezín/ Theresienstadt and on October 12, 1944 to Auschwitz. She perished.

ANNA (ANNIE) STEINER was born on January 15, 1891. On May 25, 1943 she was deported from Leipzig to Terezín/Theresienstadt. She survived until the liberation in the ghetto.

OTTO BEER (also written **TH[EODOR]. OTTO BEER** and **OTTO TH. BEER**) was born on August 14, 1900. On July 8, 1942 he was deported from Olomouc/ Olmütz to Terezín/Theresienstadt and on October 1, 1944 to Auschwitz. He perished.

F. SCHÖNFELD is probably **FRIEDRICH SCHÖNFELD**. He was born on August 5, 1895. On March 18, 1943 he was deported from Berlin to Terezín/ Theresienstadt and on September 29, 1944 to Auschwitz. He perished.

Rosalinde:	Eisenschimmel
Eisenstein:	Weiss
Adele:	Anny Frey
Dr. Falke:	H. Deutsch
Dir. Frank:	Fritz Benscher
Alfred, ein Tenor	Hary Hambo
Prinz Orlovsky:	Lisl Hofer
Dr. Blind:	Jos. Stein
Jda:	Sylvia Chaitman
Jvan:	Walter Deutsch
Frosch:	Hans Hofer

THE THERMOS

Music: "The Overcoat"[17]

Have you ever heard the story of the thermos, red and blue,
It belonged to Sara Lewinsohn and every word is true.
She arrived here from the Ostmark with a transport out of Wien[18]
And she brought a lot of luggage with her here to Terezín.
To her property she clings, so she carried her own things;
A suitcase and a basket and the thermos in a sack.
The top is blue, bottom red, "it's the fashion," as she said
In the middle, truth be told, a lovely band of harvest gold.[19]
Oh this thermos, red, blue, gold, was a wonder to behold.

Well she tried to drag her luggage from the station on her own
And she worked up quite a sweat; the summer sun was beating down
Suddenly appeared a young and strong and gallant gentleman
"I can see you're very tired; I'd like to help you if I can."
So she gave him the sack, sure that he would give it back,
When she turned 'round again, oh my word, away he'd run.
She looked there and she looked here, the young man had
    disappeared
She looked up and she looked down, but the gentleman was gone.
Vanished through and through, with her thermos red, gold, blue.

IMAGE 13.10 *(facing page)* **A souvenir poster for *Die Fledermaus*, directed by Hans Hofer and featuring Lisl Hofer as Prince Orlovsky.**
Courtesy of the Terezín Memorial.

17 These lyrics are sung to the melody of the song "The Overcoat" ("Der Überzieher"). Music and lyrics by Otto Reutter (1925).

18 Ostmark was the name of Austria when it was part of Nazi Germany, and Wien is the German-language name for Vienna.

19 In the original the color is described in a much earthier manner: *kakerlgelber Bakelit* (roughly translated, "child-shit-yellow Bakelite").

But the *Kripo*[20] caught the gentleman and brought the booty back
The suitcase and the basket and the maybe-empty sack
Oh, the first thing that she did was to search the sack right through
Hoping against hope to find the thermos red and blue.
There was joy in the air when she saw that it was there.
The top was red, bottom blue, she was happy through and
    through.
Bottom blue, top was red, with relief she was half dead.
And still there, so I'm told, was the band of harvest gold.
About the rest she didn't care; at least the thermos still was there.

When she came into the *Schleuse* she was searched immediately
And the first thing confiscated? Oh, her thermos, it was seized.
She saw it as an act of God; she let out not a peep
She just sat down in the corner, silently began to weep.
"Will I ever obtain such a gorgeous thing again?
Top was red, bottom blue, oh, whatever shall I do?
Bottom blue, top is red, it will surely be my end,
Never more will I hold it by the band of harvest gold."
They took all the food she brought, and the thermos came to naught.

When they gave her her points she ran to the hardware store[21]
And what she there discovered couldn't have surprised her more
Standing there in all its glory in the middle of the shelf
Was her own twice-stolen[22] thermos; Sara was beside herself.
She called, "Sir, by your leave, oh give me the thermos please
The top is red, bottom blue, I cannot believe it's true
Bottom blue, top is red, true to me until my death.
Please cut off forty points, I will gladly pay the price
I will spend no points on snacks if I can get my thermos back."
And she took it home and put it in the middle of her bed

---

20 See *Kripo: Kriminalpolizei* (glossary).

21 See *Bezugsschein* and *Verschleißstellen* (glossary).

22 Some of the goods in the ghetto stores were objects that had been confiscated from the prisoners themselves. See Adler, *Theresienstadt*, p. 125.

But the barracks had some visitors, the kind that we all dread.
The gendarme with three ladies,[23] well they soon had left the
    room,
But unfortunately with them left the thermos red, gold, blue.
So she ran to B V,[24] and she got a brand new *Schein*,[25]
Then ran back to the shop, there she almost blew her top
Because immediately she learned that her thermos had returned.
A man walked in the shop; he said, "Lady, listen up,
See that thermos on the shelf? I will buy it for myself."

She said "No, that can't be, this thermos belongs to me,
It came with me from Wien, all the way to Terezín."
So she screams and he yells, and they pull the flask pell-mell,
Pull it forth, pull it back, they are both on the attack,
Pull it fro, pull it to, lovely thermos red, gold, blue
The O.D., the O.W.,[26] and the fire brigade they came,
Suddenly, an uproar, people run into the store
And the thermos, whole no more, lies in pieces on the floor.
The top was red, bottom blue, what's Ms. Lewinsohn to do?
Bottom blue, top was red, now it really is the end.
But still whole, so I'm told, was the band of harvest gold.
All that's left is this song; for the thermos now is gone.

---

23 The SS employed ethnic German women who, accompanied by a gendarme, searched the prisoners' quarters for contraband and confiscated items at will.

24 B V indicates the Magdeburg barracks, where many administrative offices of the ghetto were located.

25 See *Schein: Bezugsschein* (glossary).

26 O.W.: *Ordnerwache* (Order Guard) was the name used from May to October 1942 for what was later called the *Ghettowache* (glossary).

SPA *BLOCKHAUS*[27]

Music: Wolfi Lederer[28]

Oh, lest I forget it, my address was requested
By a young man who's here with us tonight
If you'd also like to know it, upon you I'll bestow it
I'll tell you now just where I am to find:

(*Refrain*) I live in a *Blockhaus*
An old, miserable *Blockhaus*
Which stands right there, where streets L and Q meet.[29]
In all of the *Brockhaus*[30]
There's not a word about the *Blockhaus*
Although I searched under the letter B.
The windows, they are dusty,
The stairs are damp and slick
We all have diarrhea
But the toilets are never fixed
One day we of the *Blockhaus*
We all will move en bloc out
And our *Hausältester*[31] will dance with glee.

I sent to Prague a message, that I'd really like a package[32]
Because the portions here are much too small

---

27 *Blockhaus*: one of the former civilian houses, as opposed to the large barracks buildings.

28 Wolfi (Peter Wolfgang) Lederer, born on September 30, 1918, was deported from Prague to Terezín/Theresienstadt on December 4, 1941 and to Auschwitz on September 28, 1944. He survived. Many posters in the Terezín Memorial testify to his active involvement in the musical life of the ghetto. Unfortunately his original music for this song has not been preserved.

29 See L, Q (glossary).

30 The German encyclopedia *Der große Brockhaus*.

31 *Hausältester*: the head of a *Blockhaus* (as opposed to a *Gebäudeältester*, the head of a barracks building).

32 The prisoners were allowed to receive packages according to rules that fluctuated during the course of the war. See Beneš and Tošnerová, *Mail Service in the Ghetto Terezín*.

And I've written in my own hand my address for the postman
So that he will be able to recall

(*Refrain*)

THE COW

Music: "What People Live From"[33]

When I regard what our lives have become,
I ask myself, now, what are we living from?
The portions we get are so modestly sized,
That it's easier here to expire than to thrive.

Although fairly often we now have ground beef,
I must view the portion with some disbelief,
And I ask myself, with a tear in my eye,
For this tiny serving, an ox had to die?

Recently, during a long, sleepless night
I gave some deep thought to the state of our plight
My brilliant results I will share with you now:
That every small portion of beef is a cow.
And how I have come to this brilliant conclusion
I will now clarify and dispel your confusion.

Somewhere lives a farmer and he has a cow.
The cow does not eat; that disturbs him and how.
The farmer thinks, selling her before she dies
Will certainly bring me a much better price.
To the stockyards he drives her with skill and finesse
And says he must slaughter her under duress

---

33 These lyrics are sung to the melody of the song "What People Live From"
("Von was leben die Leut"). Music by A. M. Werau, lyrics by Oskar Kanitz, and
concept by A. Kaps (1931).

Once at the slaughterhouse he pays the fees
And they slaughter the cow there immediately.
There in the slaughterhouse, everyone's thrilled
The following people know they'll eat their fill:

The slaughterer who ends the cow's earthly days
The skinner who works in the most artful ways
The tanner who'll cure the cowhide to perfection
The veterinarian does the inspection
Each of them cuts off a piece for himself
And the rest is destined for the butcher's shelf.
The butcher, he buys what is left of the beast
In his own butcher shop he'll prepare for a feast.
And along with the butcher, everyone's thrilled
The following people know they'll eat their fill:

First the driver who brings to the butcher the meat
Takes a bit to his wife and his child for a treat.
The butcher, he cuts off a piece of his own
To prepare it for supper he sends it on home.
And the journeymen workers; they should get their share,
Don't forget the apprentices, just to be fair.
And whatever is left is now packed up and brought
To the butcher's group here in Theresienstadt.
And in this butcher's group, everyone's thrilled
The following people know they'll eat their fill:

First comes the driver, the meat's transport
Then the gendarme, who's the drivers' escort.
The man from the *Kripo* with his watchful eye
The Zelenka group[34] and *Wirtschaftspolizei*[35]

---

34 The Zelenka group was a detective group in the Economic Department (see *Selbstverwaltung* [glossary]) that investigated cases of theft in the food storehouses, the kitchens, etc. See Adler, *Theresienstadt*, pp. 353–4.

35 *Wirtschaftspolizei*: security division of the Economic Department.

The chief of the butchers and his secretary,
All of the workers and the veterinary.
Whatever is left is transported from there
By the *Wagenkolonne* to the Frigidaire.
In the *Wagenkolonne*, everyone's thrilled
The following people know they'll eat their fill:

The workers who load it, whether Kraus or Kohn,
Each as a souvenir takes a piece home.
The men who, like horses, drag the cart through the town,
Have certainly earned a small piece of their own.
The overseer who takes them to the freezer,
Greasing his palm makes the journey much easier.
They bring the fresh meat to where it will be stored,
And the salted meat right to the kitchen's back door.
And now in this kitchen, everyone's thrilled
The following people know they'll eat their fill:

The head of the kitchen, his wife and his son,
The *Menage* commission,[36] the cooks, each last one,
The stoker of the fire, the carrier of the coal
They all come to get their own piece of the whole
Then come the men from provisions, post-haste,
The *Wirtschaftsabteilung*,[37] they just want a taste.
And what's left of the cow? It's beyond belief:
One sixty-gram portion of tender ground beef.

Terezín, October 1943[38]

---

36 *Menagekommission*: a three-member body supervising the use of provisions
and distribution of food in each kitchen.

37 *Wirtschaftsabteilung*: Economic Department.

38 This is the only work by Hofer that was dated.

THE THEATER TICKET

Music: "The Conscientious Mason"[39]

1.

My very good friend, a certain Herr Schön[40]
Decided he'd go to the theater for a change.
And when he asked "Where are the tickets to buy?"
They said room 27 in building B V.
Herr Schön turns around and heads straight to B V,
"Now I'll get the tickets for me and my wife."
Herr Schön thinks, "Fine, I'll give B V a try."

2.

To the *Freizeitgestaltung* in B V he comes
And they tell him something that strikes Herr Schön dumb.
They explain to him there, they don't hand out the tickets
"Here at the *Freizeit*[41] they're only printed."
He asks them politely, "Then where do I get one?"
"For that you go upstairs to the *Arbeitsbetreuung*."[42]
Herr Schön thinks, "Fine, I'll go upstairs and try."

3.

And he comes to the office of *Betreuung*[43] B V
There he hears a strange buzzing, like a giant beehive.
An enormous crowd of almost 500 wait
Herr Schön joins the line; "I have time; it's okay."
"Don't stand around waiting," shouts a man at the door

---

39 These lyrics are sung to the melody of the song "The Conscientious Mason" ("Der gewissenhafte Maurer"). Music and lyrics by Otto Reutter (1920).

40 I have retained the German "Herr" instead of using "Mr." to preserve the rhythm of the original lyrics.

41 A common nickname for the *Freizeitgestaltung* (see glossary).

42 *Arbeitsbetreuung*: office responsible for the welfare of workers in the ghetto.

43 *Betreuung*: a nickname for the *Arbeitsbetreuung* (see glossary).

"You pick up the tickets in the *Einsatz*[44] B IV."
Herr Schön thinks "Fine, I'll give B IV a try."

4.

He asks for the tickets when he comes to B IV
The gentleman says, "You must wait six weeks more.
The folks on the list, they don't make a fuss
Some of them have been waiting for seventeen months.
And why must you go to *Tosca* direct?
Maybe with *Figaro* you'd be content."
Herr Schön thinks "Fine, I'll give *Figaro* a try."

5.

So after eight weeks of a frustrating wait,
B IV sends him tickets to *Figaro*—great!
As he comes to B V, "No Performance Today"
Is stamped on the poster—oh no—what a shame.
He timidly asks, "Will there be a reprise?"
"They'll play it again in, oh, two or three weeks."
Herr Schön thinks "Fine, two weeks later I'll try."

6.

He comes back in two weeks, but unfortunately late,
Far away from the entrance he stands and he waits.
When they open the show he presses to the fore
But the room's soon packed full and they shut the door.
They write on his ticket that he couldn't get in
So his ticket's still valid; he can come back again.
Herr Schön thinks "Fine, I'll try it next time."

7.

He comes back again, but no *Figaro* that night
There's another power shortage and they've turned out the lights.

---

44 *Einsatz*: short for *Arbeitseinsatz* (labor assignment [see glossary]).

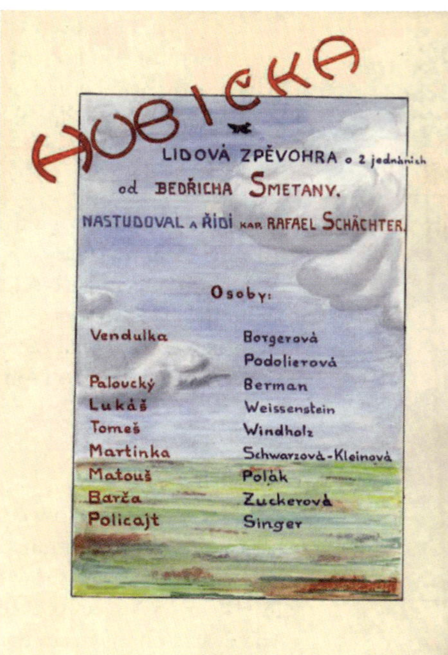

IMAGE 13.11 (*left*) **A souvenir poster for Puccini's opera** *Tosca*, **mentioned in Hofer's song "The Theater Ticket."**

IMAGE 13.12 (*right*) **A souvenir poster for Bedřich Smetana's opera** *The Kiss* (*Hubička*), **mentioned in Hofer's song "The Theater Ticket."**

Both images courtesy of the Terezín Memorial.

The next time they tell him, "We're not playing this;
Today there's no *Figaro*, today is *The Kiss*."[45]
"But I don't speak Czech, and even if I could . . ."
"Well, try again next time; your ticket's still good."
Herr Schön thinks "Fine, I'll try it next time."

8.

Schön asks the O. D. man, "When's my ticket good?"
The man answers as stiffly as a big block of wood.
"The tickets from Tuesday are valid on Sunday,
The tickets from Friday are valid on Monday.
The tickets from the first are good on the eighth.
The tickets from the eighth are for Christmas Day."
Herr Schön thinks "Fine, at Christmas I'll try."

9.

Then disgust overwhelms him, "This is no longer funny
I give up on these tickets; I just want my money."
He finds out in the office in building B IV
That B V received it a long time before.
In B V he hears from the *Kartenverwaltung*[46]
"Your money's downstairs
With the *Freizeitgestaltung*."
Herr Schön thinks "Fine, I'll go downstairs and try."

10.

But he just can't go on, he sits down on the floor
He can't make heads or tails of the shows anymore.
The tickets for *The Kiss*, they're good on the eighth,
And *Figaro*'s not playing until Christmas Day.
The tickets from B IV they're valid on Monday,

---

45 The opera *The Kiss* (*Hubička*) by Bedřich Smetana was performed in the original Czech in the ghetto. See the Terezín Memorial, inv. no. PT 3926.

46 Ticket adminstration.

Those from Wednesday on Friday,
From Saturday on Sunday.
Herr Schön thinks "Fine, now the *Zwockhaus*[47] I'll try."

VERSES TO "IN THE MORNING"[48]

A cook comes to the kitchen in the morning bright
He slowly gets to working in the afternoon all right
Then he *schleusses* a few dumplings in the evening with delight
Then the *Kripo* comes to get him in the middle of the night.

A commission is arriving in the morning bright
The kids play on the slide in the afternoon all right
They let them slide there, oh how cruel, 'til evening with delight
Their little butts are sore in the middle of the night.[49]

Mr. Kohn comes to the *Schleuse* in the morning bright
He's still waiting for the transport in the afternoon all right,
We still see him on the platform in the evening with delight
And he comes back to the barracks in the middle of the night.[50]

I dream the war is ending soon in the morning bright
And my hope increases in the afternoon all right
I'd hear about it even in the evening with delight
With news of freedom you can wake me in the middle of the night.

---

47 Insane asylum. See *Zwock* (glossary).

48 The source of the melody "In the Morning" ("Am Vormittag") is unknown.

49 According to a fellow prisoner, Hofer incorporated this verse into the song the same day the International Red Cross Commission visited the ghetto. See Taussig, "O terezínských kabaretech," p. 313.

50 Perhaps Mr. Kohn was on the reserve list for the transport. Prisoners on the reserve list were deported only if prisoners on the transport list did not appear or were removed from the list at the last minute.

VERSES TO "I DON'T THINK I AM QUITE NORMAL"[51]

Oh, I have traveled here to join you
In the Ghetto Terezín,
Because in Prague I heard a rumor
That here you eat like kings and queens.
Each day at noon I am delighted
I like the lunches most of all
And supper's plenty satisfying
I don't think I'm quite normal.

FROM VARIOUS QUODLIBETS[52]

THE MAIL

Music: "Hurrah, the Mail is Here"[53]

Oh the ghetto post's so fine
And it doesn't cost a dime
You can write a letter every day
It won't reach your loved ones anyway
When a package comes for you
By the time you get the news
And run to the office, they let you know
It was stolen days ago.

---

51 These lyrics are sung to the melody of the song "I Don't Think I Am Quite Normal" ("Ich glaub' ich bin nicht ganz normal"). Music by Armin Berg, lyrics by Louis Taufstein (1931).

52 A quodlibet is a piece of music combining different melodies, usually popular tunes, in a humorous manner. The term is Latin, meaning "whatever" or literally, "what pleases."

53 These lyrics are sung to the melody of the song "Hurrah, the Mail is Here" ("Trara, die Post ist da"). Music and lyrics by R. Löwenstein (1846).

THE BATH

Music: "Softly, So Softly"[54]

Lice, only lice seem to get a bath there,
If you have none, you'll find no place to spare.[55]
You're under the water with man and with louse
And with many more lice you'll come back to your house.

THE FOOD

Music: *Die Fledermaus*[56]

Happy there, who's unaware; what's in his food he doesn't care.[57]

THE WAGERLKOLONNE[58]

Music: "The Coach Song"[59]

I drove two gruff old Jews
They were harnessed to my wagon.

---

54 These lyrics are sung to the melody of the song "Softly, So Softly" ("Leise, ganz leise") from the operetta *A Waltz Dream* (*Ein Walzertraum*) by Oscar Straus. The libretto is by Felix Dörmann and Leopold Jacobsen (1907). Oscar Straus was the father of Leo Strauss, one of the authors in this volume.

55 That is, if you do not already have lice, you will not be admitted to the bath.

56 The melody appears near the end of Act I of *Die Fledermaus*. The original German lyrics are "Glücklich ist, wer vergisst, was nicht mehr zu ändern ist" ("Happy is he who forgets what can no longer be changed").

57 In the original manuscript, this song was followed by a one-line quodlibet titled "The Ghetto." It was sung to the melody "Es ist bestimmt in Gottes Rat," approximately translated as "It is written in God's law." Hofer's version of the lyrics was simply "Es ist bestimmt in Ghettos Rat" ("It is written in the ghetto's law"). The original text, written in 1825 by Ernst von Feuchtersleben, has been set to music by several composers, including Felix Mendelssohn (1839), Richard Wagner (1858), and Ferruccio Busoni (1879).

58 *Wagenkolonne* (see glossary), written in Viennese dialect.

59 These lyrics are sung to the melody of "The Coach Song" ("Das Fiakerlied"). Music and lyrics by Hofrat Gustav Pick (1885).

IMAGE 13.13 **A *Wagenkolonne* of Jewish laborers pulling elderly prisoners in a traditional funeral wagon. By F. Bloch.**
Courtesy of the Terezín Memorial.

IMAGE 13.14 **The main square of the ghetto before the *Stadtverschönerung*. By L. Haas.**

Courtesy of the Terezín Memorial.

THE MAIN SQUARE[60]

Music: "Mein Herr Marquis" from *Die Fledermaus*

There was once a square
No one set foot there
Barbed wire blocked everyone's way
Then they hauled in sand
The barbed wire was banned
New flower beds brightened our day

---

60 The square was renovated as part of the *Stadtverschönerung* in preparation for the visit of the International Red Cross Commission in June 1944.

IMAGE 13.15 **The main square of the ghetto after the *Stadtverschönerung*. By J. Spier.**

Courtesy of the Terezín Memorial.

They built in a hurry a pa-vi-lon
And rushed in the fiddles and sax-o-fones
And a forty-piece band,
Was suddenly there on hand . . .
Now concerts echo through the ghetto gloriously
And when I hear the music, it occurs to me:
So amusing, ha ha ha, their little project, ha ha ha
Seems so harmless, ha ha ha, who could object? Ha ha ha . . .
So amusing, ha ha ha, their little project, ha ha ha . . .
So very very very funny . . . are *they*.

Epilogue:

NEW YEAR'S EVE IN THE
OEDERAN SLAVE-LABOR CAMP

LISA ZECKENDORF-KUTZINSKI

INTRODUCTION

Lisa Zeckendorf was born in 1925 and grew up in Brno/Brünn. She was 16 years old when she was deported from Prague to the Terezín/Theresienstadt ghetto. In the ghetto she participated in the plays written by the author of the *Purimspiel* in this volume, Walter Freud. She was deported to Auschwitz on October 23, 1944, but was almost immediately selected for slave labor and sent to Oederan, a subcamp of the Flossenbürg concentration camp.

Late in December 1944, she and some other female prisoners asked their female guards if they could put on a cabaret for New Year's Eve. Their reply: "Yes, but it must be in German and we will be in the audience." She recalls that about 350 prisoners and twelve to fifteen of their guards attended the cabaret, which included sketches, songs and dance.

Now living in Israel, Lisa Zeckendorf-Kutzinski described this sketch to me during a visit to Prague in July 2009.[1] Her memory of it was so clear and her retelling so vivid that I asked her if she would write it down. Reproduced here is the translation of the German-language text she sent me just a few weeks later, complete with stage directions.

IMAGE 14.1 *(facing page)* **A performance in the ghetto. By P. Kien.**
Courtesy of the Terezín Memorial.

---

1 I am indebted to Lisa Zeckendorf-Kutzinski's cousin, Peter Brod, for introducing us.

NEW YEAR'S EVE IN THE OEDERAN SLAVE-LABOR CAMP

Dear guests of the holiday camp Oederan: for the New Year we would like to entertain you with the themes of fashion, hairstyle, and figure. But you must be open to all innovations, because what we will show you is the absolute latest thing in these areas. Let's start with fashion.

The most important change is to eliminate the division between summer and winter fashion—from now on, one wears only summer fashion, to glide lightly through life. We don't need to trouble ourselves anymore with bothersome underwear—one wears one's little dress on one's bare body, no brassiere, no panties, everything is pleasant and cool, especially, like now, in the winter. So, away with mass-produced outfits, heavy English fabrics, double-breasted blazers. Look at yourselves—you look like your grandmothers—the new fashion is young, with openings in strategic places. Our model Edith will now show you a dress to die for.[2]

(Edith strides with her hips swaying, turning and making her way across the stage. She wears a completely threadbare dress full of holes. Laughter and applause.)

Now for a new hairstyle—there's a revolution underway. The shape of one's head and skull are in demand. No more curlers, no permanent wave, no crimping iron—everything is airy and sexy—

IMAGE 14.2 *(facing page)* **A souvenir poster for the performance *What Was Mordechai Like?* This original work, written and directed in the ghetto by Walter Freud, featured Lisa (Liese) Zeckendorf as one of the actors.**
Courtesy of the Terezín Memorial.

---

2 In the original German, *todchic*, literally "deathly chic."

(deutsch)

Revue für Erwachsene
von Walter Freud.

REGIE: WALTER FREUD

AUSSTATTUNG: ALBIN GLASER

Mitwirkende:

Kurt Wolf,
Dov. Revesz,
Pata Fischl,
Liese Zeckendorf,
Hanne Taskier,
Erich Huppert,
Hans Epstein,
Karl Fleischer,
Jugendliche d. Heime: Q 710, L 410

AM KLAVIER: RAFAEL WIDDER

5 Wiederholungen — 8 V — 24 1 =

so, off with that hair! A smooth-shaven feminine skull is one of the most attractive features of the new woman. Please have courage; it looks exquisitely young and provocative.

(*Anna strides across the stage, smiling and stroking her smoothly shaven head. All three members of the cabaret do the same.*)

And now about your figure—girls, don't take this hard, but the new shape is *über*-slim; one wears one's bones in view, not with little cushions of fat in the right places. You are all much too fat—so, off with that cumbersome fat; slim and bony is sexy. European scientists have developed a new diet.[3] We will reveal the secret to you. In the morning, black chicory coffee, refusing milk and sugar, of course, and with it one piece of dry bread—by no means more. At midday, a thin soup, made with turnips that are actually intended for cattle, but that contribute greatly to weight loss. In the evening, black coffee again, this time with two pieces of dry bread. Weight loss is guaranteed, and with long-term maintenance of this diet, success is dead certain. The highest acceptable weight is eighty pounds, but she who can bring her weight down to seventy pounds is a queen.[4]

(*Lisa strides across the stage wearing a dress full of holes, stroking her bare skull, a walking skeleton. She believes herself to be a queen.*)

And now we wish you all a healthy and happy New Year.

---

3 Since guards were in attendance, Zeckendorf-Kutzinski recalls, "I changed the sentence about the scientists at the last minute. I actually wanted to say that this diet was one of the greatest achievements of *German* scientists, but my survival instinct warned me that this could be dangerous; so I said '*European* scientists.' Those idiot SS-women laughed themselves silly at the whole performance." Lisa Zeckendorf-Kutzinski, e-mail to Lisa Peschel, August 22, 2009.

4 This was Zeckendorf-Kutzinski's weight at the time of the performance.

AK, AK I, AK II. See *Aufbaukommando*.

Ältestenrat (Council of Elders). The advisory board to the head of the Jewish self-government (see *Judenältester*, *Selbstverwaltung*).

-ältester (elder). The suffix that denoted Jewish functionaries in the ghetto, from a *Zimmerältester* (room elder, head of an individual room in the prisoners' quarters) to the *Judenältester* himself. The Nazis considered other designations of status, such as "director," to be inappropriate for Jews. In the prisoners' quarters, for example, the *Blockältester* (block elder) was the head of a block of civilian houses; the *Gebäudeältester* (building elder) was the head of a barracks building. They were responsible for relaying the daily orders to the prisoners, for keeping records of deaths and illnesses, etc.

Arbeiterbetreuung or **Arbeitsbetreuung.** The office responsible for the welfare of workers in the ghetto.

Arbeitseinsatz. Labor assignment.

Aufbaukommando (building commando). The first two groups of young Jewish laborers deported from Prague to the ghetto. Transport AK I arrived on November 24, 1941, and transport J, also known as AK II, arrived on December 4, 1941. Most members of AK I and AK II were protected from outgoing transports until the autumn of 1944.

Bahnbau (railroad building). At the end of 1941, plans to build a railroad spur directly into the ghetto from the neighboring town of Bohušovice/Bauschowitz were prepared. Construction began on August 24, 1942, and the first train arrived in the ghetto on June 1, 1943.

Betreuung. See *Arbeiterbetreuung*.

Bezugsschein. A coupon worth a certain number of points that could be traded for items in the ghetto shops. See *Verschleißstellen*.

Blockhaus. A civilian house in the ghetto, as opposed to the large barracks.

Blockveranstaltung. Performances that took place in the prisoners' quarters, the hospitals and clinics, and the homes for the aged. In the summer they were staged outdoors.

bonke. A rumor, especially on optimistic topics such as German defeats and the end of the war.

cvok. A colloquial Czech term for an insane person.

Einsatz. See *Arbeitseinsatz*.

Entwesung. Disinfestation. Insects, especially fleas, lice, and bedbugs, were a constant problem in the ghetto. Prisoners were sometimes temporarily moved out of their quarters for the buildings to be disinfested.

Freizeitgestaltung. Literally, "Office for the Administration of Leisure Time." A division of the Jewish self-government (see *Selbstverwaltung*) that administered the cultural activities taking place in the ghetto. The word also became a nickname for any cultural program. The Freizeitgestaltung was first established in February, 1942, and existed in a quasi-legal state until it was officially approved by the camp commandant in August–September, 1942. By late 1942 it had become an independent subdivision of the Department of Internal Administration.

G.W. See *Ghettowache*.

gendarmes. Former members of the Czechoslovak army who carried out guard duties involving direct contact with the prisoners. According to survivor testimonies, most treated the prisoners fairly.

Gesundheitswesen. The Department of Health Services. See *Selbstverwaltung*.

Ghettowache (Ghetto Guard). An internal police force staffed by the prisoners.

Hilfsdienst (Assistance Service). Originally called the *Orientierungsdients* (Orientation Service), a division of the *Ghettowache* that provided information and assistance.

Judenältester (Jewish Elder). The head of the Jewish self-government (see *Selbstverwaltung*). There were three over the course of the ghetto's existence: Jakob Edelstein, Paul Epstein, and Benjamin Murmelstein. See the introduction to this volume.

Jugendfürsorge. The Department of Youth Care.

Kaffeehaus (coffeehouse). On December 8, 1942, a coffeehouse opened in building Q418 on the main square, where prisoners could order a cup of ersatz coffee and listen to music performed by their fellow prisoners. Entrance tickets valid for two hours were distributed to the prisoners on a rotating basis.

Kripo. See *Kriminalpolizei*.

Kriminalpolizei (Criminal Investigation Department). A division of the *Ghettowache* that investigated crimes such as theft. It was later renamed the *Detektivabteilung* (Detective Division).

L, Q. From July, 1942, until July, 1943, streets in the ghetto were indicated by the letters L (from German *lang*, long streets) and Q (from German *quer*, cross streets). When preparations began for the June 1944 visit of the International Red Cross commission, the streets received more attractive names.

Läden (shops). See *Verschleißstellen*.

Menage. The distribution of cooked meals (a pre-war Austrian military term). Prisoners stood in line at the various kitchens located around the ghetto, where members of the *Menagedienst* (food service) marked their meal tickets and gave them their rations.

O.D. See *Ordnungsdienst*.

Ordnungsdienst (Order Service). Until the summer of 1942, prisoners who were members of the *Ordnungsdienst* (O.D.) kept order inside the barracks. Later they were assigned to other security-related duties.

Orientierungsdienst. See *Hilfsdienst*.

Prominenter. Certain prisoners were designated by the SS or by Jewish leaders as "prominent" and given preferential treatment, such as better housing and increased rations.

revue. A multi-act popular theatrical entertainment combining music, dance, and sketches, frequently satirizing contemporary figures, news, or literature.

Schleuse (sluice; in Czech *šlajs, šlojs, šlojska*). One of the key terms in Terezín/Theresienstadt. Originally it referred to the building in the ghetto where arriving and departing prisoners were "processed." The location changed over the course of the ghetto's history. Once the railroad spur was built into the ghetto (see *Bahnbau*), the *Schleuse* was located in the Hamburg barracks. Since luggage was inspected in the *Schleuse* and items were often confiscated, *schleusen* (in Czech, *šlojsnout*) soon came to mean "to steal." (A similar term used in Auschwitz, "to organize," was unknown in Terezín/Theresienstadt). A whole range of related terms evolved that referred to inspections, theft, and stolen items.

scholet, ritschert and **bejlek**. Traditional Jewish dishes. *Scholet* (also known as *chulent, shalit,* etc.) is a Sabbath meal made from barley or rice, peas or beans, beef or goose, and spices. *Ritschert* is made of beans, barley, potatoes, beef, and spices. *Bejlek* is goose breast.

Selbstverwaltung (self-government). This is a relative term, since ultimate power remained in the hands of the Nazis. However, the Jewish leaders had a large degree of control over the daily operations of the ghetto. The structure of the *Selbstverwaltung* changed over time. In 1943 there were five departments, each with various divisions: Internal Administration (central registry and records, space management, the court system, postal services, the *Freizeitgestaltung*, etc.), the Economic Department (labor assignments, receiving and storage of materials and provisions, distribution of food, etc.), the Finance Department (central bookkeeping and statistics), the Technical Department (railroad building, electricity, waste management, street cleaning, fire department, etc.), and the Health and Social Services Department (all medical services, the homes for youth and the aged, etc.)

šmé, šmelina. fraud, dishonest business.

Sokol (Falcon). The Czech gymnastics and fitness association Sokol was established in the nineteenth century during the Czech National Revival period. The first Sokol rally was held in 1882; members of various chapters, including those founded by Czech émigrés in other countries, gathered to perform mass displays of choreographed exercises. The 1938 rally, the last held before the Second World War, was attended by 350,000 members. The organization was banned during the Nazi occupation and many Sokol leaders were arrested.

Stadtverschönerung. The "city beautification" that took place in preparation for the June 1944 visit of the International Red Cross commission.

Sudetenland. The Sudeten regions were the border areas of Czechoslovakia, mostly populated by ethnic Germans.

Verschleißstellen. The ghetto "shops." They replaced the *Verteilungsstellen* (distribution centers) where essential goods such as clothing were rationed out to the prisoners. The opening of the shops and the complicated system of points for the purchase of goods were announced in the daily orders of September 13, 1942. The first shops included a grocery store, a shop for clothes and shoes, and a drugstore. The shops were often stocked with goods stolen from the prisoners' luggage.

Voskovec and Werich. Jiří Voskovec and Jan Werich were two of the most beloved Czech performers of the 1920s–30s. In the late 1930s, they, with composer Jaroslav Ježek, staged several extremely popular anti-fascist revues at their Liberated Theater (Osvobozené divadlo) in Prague. For a brief description of their work in context see the introduction to this volume.

Wagenkolonne (wagon convoy). Traditional horse-drawn funeral wagons from the former Jewish communities of Bohemia and Moravia were used as vehicles in the ghetto for transporting everything from bread to corpses. They were loaded and pulled by a team of Jewish laborers called a *Wagenkolonne*.

Zentralevidenz (central registry). The *Selbstverwaltung* maintained card files (a central registry and smaller registries in the individual houses and barracks) of information on all the prisoners (current address and occupation in the ghetto, marital and family status, etc.).

Zwock. The German version of the Czech term *cvok*.

BIBLIOGRAPHY

ANTHOLOGIES OF THEATRICAL WORKS FROM THE TEREZÍN/THERESIENSTADT GHETTO

GOLDEN, Tania, Alexander Wächter, and Sergei Dreznin (eds.). *Chansons und Satiren aus Theresienstadt* (Songs and Satire from Theresiendstadt). Vienna: Rabenhof, 1992.

MIGDAL, Ulrike (ed.). *Und die Musik spielt dazu*: *Chansons und Satiren aus dem KZ Theresienstadt* (And the Music Plays Along: Songs and Satire from Theresienstadt). Munich: Piper, 1986.

PESCHEL, Lisa (ed.). *Divadelní texty z terezínského ghetta / Theatertexte aus dem Ghetto Theresienstadt, 1941–1945* (Theatrical Texts from the Terezín/Theresienstadt Ghetto, 1941–45) (Dalibor Dobiáš and Michael Wögerbauer trans.). Prague: Akropolis, 2008.

PUBLICATIONS THAT INCLUDE THEATRICAL TEXTS WRITTEN IN THE TEREZÍN/THERESIENSTADT GHETTO

LINDENBAUM, Walter. *Von Sehnsucht wird man hier nicht fett*: *Texte aus einen jüdischen Leben* (You Won't Get Fat from Yearning Here: Texts from a Jewish Life) (Herbert Exenberger and Eckart Früh eds.). Vienna: Mandelbaum, 1998.

MAKAROVA, Elena. *Long Live Life*! *or Dance around the Skeleton*. Jerusalem: Verba, 2001.

ŠORMOVÁ, Eva. *Divadlo v Terezíně 1941–45* (Theater in Terezín: 1941–45). Ústí nad Labem: Severočeské nakladatelství, 1973.

VRKOČOVÁ, Ludmila, *Rekviem sami sobě* (Requiem for Themselves). Prague: Arkýř, 1993.

ADLER, H. G. *Theresienstadt*: *das Antlitz einer Zwangsgemeinschaft* (Theresienstadt: The Face of an Involuntary Community). Göttingen: Wallstein, 2005.

BAR-GAL, Yoram. *Propaganda and Zionist Education*: *The Jewish National Fund, 1924–1947*. Rochester, NY: University of Rochester Press, 2003.

BEČVOVÁ, Romana. "'Beteiligt euch—es geht um eure Erde.' Erika Manns politisch-satirisches Kabarett 'Die Pfeffermühle' in der Tschechoslowakei" ("Participate—It's about Your World": Erika Mann's Political-Satirical Cabaret *The Peppermill* in Czechoslovakia). *Brücken*: *Germanistisches Jahrbuch Tschechien–Slowakei* 16 (2008): 229–50.

BELLER, Steven. *Vienna and the Jews, 1867–1938*. New York: Cambridge University Press, 1989.

BENEŠ, František and Patricia Tošnerová (eds.). *Pošta v ghettu Terezín / Die Post im GhettoTheresienstadt / Mail Service in the Ghetto Terezín* (Petr Liebl and Dagmar Lieblová trans.). Prague: Profil, 1996.

BERBEN, Paul. *Dachau, 1933–1945*: *The Official History*. London: Norfolk Press, 1975.

BLODIG, Vojtěch. "Poslední fáze ve vývoji terezínského ghetta" (The Last Phase in the Development of the Terezín Ghetto), in Vojtěch Blodig and Miroslav Karný (eds.), *Terezín v konečném řešení židovské otázky* (Terezín in the Final Solution to the Jewish Question), pp. 182–90. Prague: Logos, 1992.

BONDY, Ruth. *"Elder of the Jews"*: *Jakob Edelstein of Theresienstadt*. New York: Grove Press, 1989.

——. *Mezi námi řečeno*: *Jak mluvili Židé v Čechách a na Moravě* (Between Us: The Language of Jews in Bohemia and Moravia). Prague: Nakladatelství Franze Kafky, 2003.

BOTZ, Gerhard, "The Dynamics of Persecution in Austria, 1938–45," in Robert S. Wistrich (ed.), *Austrians and Jews in the Twentieth Century*: *From Franz Joseph to Waldheim*, pp. 199–219. New York: St. Martin's Press, 1992.

BURIAN, Jarka. *Modern Czech Theatre: Reflector and Conscience of a Nation*. Iowa City: University of Iowa Press, 2000.

ČAPKOVÁ, Kateřina. *Češi, Němci, Židé? Národní identita Židů v Čechách, 1918–1938* (Czechs, Germans, Jews?: National Identity and the Jews of Bohemia, 1918–38). Prague: Paseka, 2005.

——. "Tschechisch, Deutsch, Jüdisch—wo ist der Unterschied? Zur Komplexität von nationalen Identitäten der böhmischen Juden 1918–1938" (Czech, German, Jewish—What Is the Difference? On the Complexity of National Identities of the Bohemian Jews, 1918–38), in Marek Nekula and Walter Koschmal (eds.), *Juden zwischen Deutschen und Tschechen: sprachliche und kulturelle Identitäten in Böhmen 1800–1945* (Jews between Germans and Czechs: Linguistic and Cultural Identity in Bohemia, 1800–1945), pp. 73–84. Munich: Oldenbourg Wissenschaftsverlag, 2006.

CHLÁDKOVÁ, Ludmila. "Karel Poláček v Terezíně" (Karel Poláček in Terezín). *Terezínské Listy* XXVI (1996): 55–70.

——. *The Terezín Ghetto*. Prague: Naše vojsko, 1991.

COHEN, Gary B. *The Politics of Ethnic Survival: Germans in Prague, 1861–1914*. Princeton: Princeton University Press, 1981.

DALINGER, Brigitte. "Jiddisches Theater—Ein Grenzgänger zwischen den Sprachen und Kulturen" (Yiddish Theater—Crossing the Borders between Languages and Cultures). *Maske und Kothurn* 47(3–4) (2002): 89–100.

——. "*Verloschene Sterne*": *Geschichte des jüdischen Theaters in Wien*. ("Extinguished Stars": The History of Jewish Theater in Vienna). Vienna: Picus, 1998.

DOLL, Jürgen. *Theater im roten Wien. Vom sozialdemokratischen Agitprop zum dialektischen Theater Jura Soyfers* (Theater in Red Vienna: From Social-Democratic Agitprop to the Dialectical Theater of Jura Soyfer). Vienna, Cologne, and Weimar: Böhlau, 1997.

EHRLICH-FANTLOVÁ, Zdenka. "The Czech Theater in Terezín," in Rebecca Rovit and Alvin Goldfarb (eds.), *Theatrical*

Performance during the Holocaust, pp. 231–49. Baltimore: Johns Hopkins University Press, 1999.

ELIÁŠ, Věra. *On My Good Days I Feel That I am a Cupboard*. Seattle: Peanut Butter Publishing, 1992.

ENGLÄNDER, Otakar. *Geschichten aus der Geschichte meines Lebens* (Stories from the Story of My Life). Mainz: Selbstverlag, 1971.

FEDER, Richard. *Židovská tragedie: Dějství poslední* (A Jewish Tragedy: The Final Act). Kolín: Lusk, 1947.

FEDOROVIČ, Tomáš. "Neue Erkenntnisse über die SSAngehörigen im Ghetto Theresienstadt" (New Findings on Members of the SS in the Ghetto Theresienstadt), in Jaroslava Milotová, Michael Wögerbauer, and Anna Hájková (eds.), *Theresienstädter Studien und Dokumente 2006* (Theresienstadt Studies and Documents, 2006), pp. 234–50. Prague: Sefer, 2007.

FELSMANN, Barbara and Karl Prümm. *Kurt Gerron—gefeiert und gejagt, Das Schicksal eines deutschen Unterhaltungskünstlers: Berlin, Amsterdam, Theresienstadt, Auschwitz* (Kurt Gerron—Celebrated and Persecuted, the Fate of a German Entertainer: Berlin, Amsterdam, Theresienstadt, Auschwitz). Berlin: Hentrich, 1992.

FRANKL, Michal. *Emancipace od Židů, český antisemitismus na konci 19. století* (Emancipation from the Jews: Czech Anti-Semitism at the End of the Nineteenth Century). Prague: Paseka, 2007.

FRÝD, Norbert. *Lahvová pošta aneb konec posledních sto let* (Message in a Bottle; or, The End of the Last Hundred Years). Prague: Československý spisovatel, 1971.

GOLDEN, Tania, Alexander Wächter, and Sergei Dreznin (eds.). *Chansons und Satiren aus Theresienstadt* (Songs and Satire from Theresiendstadt). Vienna: Rabenhof, 1992.

GUTHRIE, William P. *The Later Thirty Years' War: From the Battle of Wittstock to the Treaty of Westphalia*. Westport, CT: Greenwood Publishing, 2003.

HAAS, Leo. "The Affair of the Painters of Terezín," in František Ehrmann, Ota Heitlinger, and Rudolf Iltis (eds.), *Terezín*, pp. 157–61. Prague: Council of Jewish Communities in the Czech Lands, 1965.

HÄBERER, Bruno. "Illegale Empfänger im Ghetto von Theresienstadt" (Illegal Radio Receivers in the Ghetto of Theresienstadt). *Radio Fernsehen Elektronik* 24(9) (1975): 282–4.

HAFTER, Andreas and Wolfgang Hafter. *Hugo Meisl, oder die Erfindung des modernen Fußballs: Eine Biographie* (Hugo Meisl, or the Invention of Modern Soccer: A Biography). Göttingen: Die Werkstatt, 2007.

HERMAN, Judith. *Trauma and Recovery: The Aftermath of Violence from Domestic Abuse to Political Terror*. New York, NY: Basic Books, 1992.

HOFER, Hans. "The Film about Terezín: A Belated Reportage," in František Ehrmann, Ota Heitlinger, and Rudolf Iltis (eds.), *Terezín*, pp. 180–4. Prague: Council of Jewish Communities in the Czech Lands, 1965.

HOLÝ, Ladislav. *The Little Czech and the Great Czech Nation: National Identity and the Post-Communist Transformation of Society*. New York, NY: Cambridge University Press, 1996.

HYNDRÁKOVÁ, Anna, Raisa Machatková, and Jaroslava Milotová (eds.). *Acta Theresiania, sv. 1: Denní rozkazy Rady starších a Sdělení židovské samosprávy, Terezín 1941–1945* (Acta Theresiana, Volume 1: Daily Orders of the Council of Elders and Announcements from the Jewish Self-Government, Terezín, 1941–45). Prague: Sefer, 2003.

JARKA, Horst. Introduction to Horst Jarka (ed.), *Jura Soyfer: Das Gesamtwerk* (Jura Soyfer: Collected Works), pp. 13–27. Vienna, München, Zürich: Europaverlag, 1980.

JELAVICH, Peter. "Cabaret in Concentration Camps," in Michael Balfour (ed.), *Theatre and War, 1933–1945: Performance in Extremis*, pp. 137–64. Oxford: Berghahn, 2001.

KARAS, Joža. *Music in Terezín: 1941–45*. Stuyvesant, NY: Pendragon, 1990.

KÁŠ, Svatopluk. *Kocourkovští učitelé, jejich historie a tvorba* (The Teachers' Choir of Kocourkov: Their History and Works). Prague: Dokořán, 2008.

KIEVAL, Hillel J. "Jews, Czechs and Germans in Bohemia before 1914," in Robert S. Wistrich (ed.), *Austrians and Jews in the Twentieth Century: From Franz Joseph to Waldheim*, pp. 19–37. New York: St. Martin's Press, 1992.

——. *The Making of Czech Jewry: National Conflict and Jewish Society in Bohemia, 1870–1918*. New York and Oxford: Oxford University Press, 1988.

KRAUS, F. R. *A přiveď zpět naše roztroušené* (And Bring Back Our Scattered Ones). Prague: Neumann, 1946.

KŘÍŽKOVÁ, Marie Rút, Kurt Jiří Koutouč, and Zdeněk Ornest (eds.). *We are Children Just the Same: "Vedem," the Secret Magazine by the Boys of Terezín*. Philadelphia: Jewish Publication Society, 1995.

—— and Kurt Jiří Kotouč. "Czech Literary Work," in *Art Against Death: Permanent Exhibitions of the Terezín Memorial in the Former Magdeburg Barracks*, pp. 177–204. Prague: Oswald, 2002.

KÜHN, Volker. *Kabarett im KZ* (Cabaret in Concentration Camps), booklet to the CD/DVD set *Totentanz: Kabarett im KZ* (Dance of Death: Cabaret in Concentration Camps). Neckargemünd: Edition Mnemosyne, 2000.

LAGUS, Karel and Josef Polák. *Město za mřížemi* (City Behind Bars). Prague: Naše vojsko, 1964.

LB. "Svědectví 'posledního cyklisty'" (The Testimony of "The Last Cyclist"), *Hlas revoluce*, June 22, 1961.

LICHTENSTEIN, Tatjana. "Making Jews at Home: Jewish Nationalism in the Bohemian Lands, 1918–1938." Ph.D. diss., University of Toronto, 2009.

LORENCOVÁ, Anna. "Židovský odboj podle vzpomínek pamětníků" (Jewish Resistance in Survivor Memory), in Zlatica Zudová-Lesková (ed.), *Židé v boji a odboji: Rezistence československých židů v letech druhé světové války* (Jews in

Struggle and Resistance: Resistance by Czechoslovak Jews during the Second World War), pp. 331–8. Prague: Historický ústav, 2007.

MAKAROVA, Elena. *Long Live Life! or Dance around the Skeleton*. Jerusalem: Verba, 2001.

——, Sergei Makarov, and Victor Kuperman (eds.). *University over the Abyss: The Story behind 520 Lecturers and 2,430 Lectures in KZ Theresienstadt, 1942–1944*. Jerusalem: Verba, 2004.

MANES, Philipp. *Als ob's ein Leben wär: Tatsachenbericht Theresienstadt 1942–1944* (As If It Were Life: A Factual Report from Theresienstadt, 1942–44) (Ben Barkow and Klaus Leist eds.). Berlin: Ullstein, 2005.

MARGRY, Karel. "Das Konzentrationslager als Idylle: Theresienstadt: Ein Dokumentar-Film aus dem Jüdischen Siedlungsgebiet" (The Concentration Camp as Idylle: Theresienstadt: A Documentary Film from the Jewish Settlement Area), in Fritz Bauer Institut (ed.), *Auschwitz. Geschichte, Rezeption und Wirkung: Jahrbuch 1996 Zur Geschichte und Wirkung des Holocaust* (Auschwitz. History, Reception and Impact: Yearbook, 1996, on the History and Impact of the Holocaust), pp. 319–52. Frankfurt and New York: Campus, 1996.

——. "The First Theresienstadt Film (1942)". *Historical Journal of Film, Radio and Television* 19(3) (1999): 309–37.

MENDELSOHN, Ezra. *The Jews of East Central Europe*. Bloomington: Indiana University Press, 1983.

MIGDAL, Ulrike (ed.). *Und die Musik spielt dazu: Chansons und Satiren aus dem KZ Theresienstadt* (And the Music Plays Along: Songs and Satire from Theresienstadt). Munich: Piper, 1986.

MIKLÍK, Josef. *Vzpomínky z Terezína* (Memories of Terezín). Prague: C.A.T., 1945.

NEUMANN, Stanislav K. *Československá cesta: Deník cesty kolem republiky od 28. dubna do 28. října 1933. Část druhá:*

Karpatské léto (Czechoslovak Journey: A Diary of Trips around the Republic from April 28 to October 28, 1933; Part 2, Carpathian Summer). Prague: Fr. Borový, 1935.

NIKLAS, Martin. "*. . . die schönste Stadt der Welt.*" *Österreichische Jüdinnen und Juden in Theresienstadt* (". . . The Most Beautiful City in the World": Austrian Jews in Theresienstadt). Vienna: DÖW, 2009.

PESCHEL, Lisa (ed.). *Divadelní texty z terezínského ghetta / Theatertexte aus dem Ghetto Theresienstadt, 1941–1945* (Theatrical Texts from the Terezín/Theresienstadt Ghetto, 1941–45) (Dalibor Dobiáš and Michael Wögerbauer trans.). Prague: Akropolis, 2008.

——. "The Prosthetic Life: Theatrical Performance, Survivor Testimony and the Terezín Ghetto, 1941–1963." Ph.D. diss., University of Minnesota, Minneapolis and St. Paul, 2008.

POLLAK, Michael. "Cultural Innovation and Social Identity in *fin-de-siècle* Vienna," in Ivar Oxaal, Michael Pollak, and Gerhard Botz (eds.), *Jews, Antisemitism, and Culture in Vienna*, pp. 59–74. New York: Routledge and Kegan Paul, 1987.

PUCHERNA, Jaroslav (ed.). *Přijelo divadlo*: *patnáct let putování za divákem* (The Theater Arrived: Fifteen Years of Traveling to Spectators). Prague: Státní zájezdové divadlo, 1961.

RASPANTI, Celeste Rita. *I Never Saw Another Butterfly*: *A Play*. Woodstock, IL: Dramatic Publishing, 1971.

ŘEPOVÁ, Daniela. "Emil Utitz a Terezín" (Emil Utitz and Terezín), in Jaroslava Milotová and Anna Lorencová (eds.), *Terezínské studie a dokumenty 2003* (Terezín Studies and Documents, 2003), pp. 169–212. Prague: Sefer, 2003.

ROTHKIRCHEN, Livia. "The Jews of Bohemia and Moravia: 1938–1945," in Avigdor Dagan, Gertrude Hirschler, and Lewis Weiner (eds.), *The Jews of Czechoslovakia*: *Historical Studies and Surveys*, VOL. 3, pp. 3–74. Philadelphia: Jewish Publication Society of America, 1984.

——. *The Jews of Bohemia and Moravia*: *Facing the Holocaust*. Lincoln: University of Nebraska Press; Jerusalem: Yad Vashem, 2005.

ROVIT, Rebecca. "A Carousel of Theatrical Performance at Theresienstadt," in Anne D. Dutlinger (ed.). *Art, Music and Education as Strategies of Survival*: *Theresienstadt, 1941–45*, pp. 122–43. New York: Herodias, 2001.

—— and Alvin Goldfarb (eds.). *Theatrical Performance during the Holocaust*: *Texts, Documents, Memoirs*. Baltimore: Johns Hopkins University Press, 1999.

ROZENBLIT, Marsha L. "Jewish Ethnicity in a New Nation-State: The Crisis of Identity in the Austrian Republic," in Michael Brenner and Derek Jonathan Penslar (eds.), *In Search of Jewish Community*: *Jewish Identities in Germany and Austria, 1918–1933*, pp. 134–53. Bloomington: Indiana University Press, 1998.

——. "The Jews of Germany and Austria: A Comparative Perspective," in Robert S. Wistrich (ed.), *Austrians and Jews in the Twentieth Century*: *From Franz Joseph to Waldheim*, pp. 1–18. New York: St. Martin's Press, 1992.

——. *Reconstructing a National Identity*: *The Jews of Habsburg Austria during World War I*. Oxford and New York: Oxford University Press, 2001.

——. "Sustaining Austrian 'National' Identity in Crisis: The Dilemma of the Jews in Habsburg Austria, 1914–1919," in Pieter M. Judson and Marsha L. Rozenblit (eds.), *Constructing Nationalities in East Central Europe*, pp. 178–91. Oxford: Berghahn, 2005.

SALLY-PRKNO, Emanuel. *Táborák ještě nezhasíná, Ascalona a dvacet jedna dalších nejhezčích písní Emana Sallyho-Prkna* (The Campfire Still Burns: Ascalona and 21 More of the Most Beautiful Songs by Eman Sally-Prkno). Prague: Ivanka Luftová / Miroslav Anger, 1994.

SAYER, Derek. *The Coasts of Bohemia*: *A Czech History*. Princeton: Princeton University Press, 1998.

418

SCHLÖSSER, Manfred (ed.). *An den Wind geschrieben*; *Lyrik der Freiheit, Gedichte der Jahre 1933–1945* (Written on the Wind: Lyrics of Freedom; Poems from the Years 1933–45). Darmstadt: Agora, 1960.

SCHÖNBERG, Jakob (ed.). *Shire Erets-Yisrael* (Songs of the Land of Israel). Jerusalem: Hozsaah Ivrith, 1947.

ŠEDOVÁ, Jana. Program notes to *Poslední cyklista* ("The Last Cyclist"). Prague: Divadlo Rokoko, 1961.

SERKE, Jürgen. *Böhmische Dörfer: Wanderungen durch eine verlassene literarische Landschaft*. (Bohemian Villages: Walks through an Abandoned Literary Landscape). Vienna: Zsolnay, 1987.

SHORE, Marci. "Engineering in the Age of Innocence". *East European Politics and Societies* 12(3) (1998): 397–443.

SKOCHOVÁ, Jarmila. "Literarisches Schaffen erwachsener Häftlinge im Konzentrationslager Theresienstadt" (Literary Creation by Adult Prisoners in the Concentration Camp Theresienstadt). *Judaica Bohemiae* 21(1) (1985): 29–31.

ŠORMOVÁ, Eva. *Divadlo v Terezíně 1941–45* (Theater in Terezín: 1941–45). Ústí nad Labem: Severočeské nakladatelství, 1973.

SPECTOR, Scott. *Prague Territories: National Conflict and Cultural Innovation in Franz Kafka's Fin De Siècle*. Berkeley: University of California Press, 2000.

SRBA, Bořivoj. "Divadlo za mřížemi: Projevy české divadelní tvořivosti v pracovních, internačních a koncentračních táborech a věznicích nacistické Třetí říše" (Theater Behind Bars: Czech Theatrical Creativity in Labor, Internment and Concentration Camps, and Prisons of the Nazi Third Reich). *Divadelní revue* 6(1) (1995): 9–27.

STAMBERG, Ursula. "Das Theaterleben der Jüdischen Bevölkerung Brünns" (The Theatrical Life of the Jews of Brünn). *Maske und Kothurn* 47(3–4) (2002): 67–81.

STEINER, František. *Fotbal pod žlutou hvězdou* (Soccer under the Yellow Star). Prague: Olympia, 2009.

STRÁNSKÝ, Pavel. *As Messengers for the Victims: From Theresienstadt to Theresienstadt, with a stop in Auschwitz-Birkenau and Schwarzheide* (Benjamin M. Block trans.). Prague: Rekan, 2000.

TAUSSIG, Josef. "O terezínských kabaretech" (On Terezín Cabarets), in Miroslav Kárný, Jaroslova Milotová, and Eva Lorencová (eds.), *Terezínské studie a dokumenty 2001* (Terezín Studies and Documents, 2001), pp. 310–46. Prague: Academia, 2001.

TŮMA, Mirko. "Memories of Theresienstadt," in Rebecca Rovit and Alvin Goldfarb (eds.), *Theatrical Performance during the Holocaust: Texts, Documents, Memoirs*, pp. 265–73. Baltimore: Johns Hopkins University Press, 1999.

UTITZ, Emil. *Psychologie života v terezínském koncentračním táboře* (Psychology of Life in the Terezín Concentration Camp). Prague: Dělnické nakladatelství, 1947.

VIETOR-ENGLÄNDER, Deborah. "'Festung meiner Jugend'. Bisher unbekannte Mädchentagebücher aus Theresienstadt und ihre Umsetzung im Unterricht der Mittelstufe" ("Fortress of My Youth": Previously Unknown Girls' Diaries from Theresienstadt and Their Implementation in Middle-School Teaching), in Barbara Bauer and Waltraud Strickhausen (eds.), *"Für ein Kind war das anders." Traumatische Erfahrungen jüdischer Kinder und Jugendlicher im nationalsozialistischen Deutschland* ("For a Child it was Different": Traumatic Experiences of Jewish Children and Youth in National Socialist Germany), pp. 408–20. Berlin: Metropol, 1999.

VRKOČOVÁ, Ludmila. *Rekviem sami sobě* (Requiem for Themselves). Prague: Arkýř, 1993.

WEINER, Erich. "*Freizeitgestaltung* in Theresienstadt," in Rebecca Rovit and Alvin Goldfarb (eds.), *Theatrical Performance during the Holocaust: Texts, Documents, Memoirs*, pp. 209–30. Baltimore: Johns Hopkins University Press, 1999.

WISTRICH, Robert S. *The Jews of Vienna in the Age of Franz Joseph*. New York: Oxford University Press, 1989.

ZEMANOVÁ, Pavla. "Die Theresienstädter Außenkommandos" (The Theresienstadt Labor Commandos) (Blanka Papešová trans.), in Miroslav Kárný, Jaroslava Milotová, and Michael Wögerbauer (eds.), *Theresienstädter Studien und Dokumente 2001* (Theresienstadt Studies and Documents, 2001), pp. 75–105. Prague: Academia, 2001.

DEUTSCHE GEBÄUDE

GESUNDHEITSWESEN

JUGENDFÜRSORGE

PROMINENTE

KAFFEEHAUS, BANK,

LÄDEN

PRODUKTION

LANDWIRTSCHAFT

KASERNEN

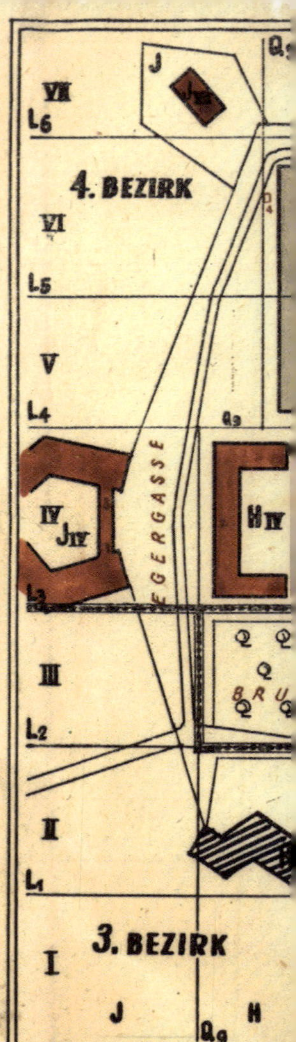